The Sch

GW01459416

Reader

ALSO AVAILABLE FROM BLOOMSBURY

The German Idealism Reader
edited by Marina F. Bykova
The Philosophy and Common Sense Reader
edited by Markar Melkonian
The Sublime Reader
edited by Robert C. Clewis
Introduction to Existentialism
by Robert L. Wicks
Medieval Philosophy
edited by Bruce Foltz

The Schelling Reader

Edited by
Benjamin Berger and
Daniel Whistler

BLOOMSBURY ACADEMIC
LONDON • NEW YORK • OXFORD • NEW DELHI • SYDNEY

BLOOMSBURY ACADEMIC
Bloomsbury Publishing Plc
50 Bedford Square, London, WC1B 3DP, UK
1385 Broadway, New York, NY 10018, USA
29 Earlsfort Terrace, Dublin 2, Ireland

BLOOMSBURY, BLOOMSBURY ACADEMIC and the Diana logo
are trademarks of Bloomsbury Publishing Plc

First published in Great Britain 2021
Reprinted 2021 (twice), 2022, 2023

Copyright © Benjamin Berger and Daniel Whistler, 2021

Benjamin Berger and Daniel Whistler have asserted their right under the Copyright,
Designs and Patents Act, 1988, to be identified as Editors of this work.

For legal purposes the Acknowledgements on pp. ix–xiv constitute
an extension of this copyright page.

Cover design by Charlotte Daniels
Cover image: Friedrich W.J. von Schelling (1775–1854)
(© Granger Historical Picture Archive / Alamy)

All rights reserved. No part of this publication may be reproduced or transmitted in
any form or by any means, electronic or mechanical, including photocopying,
recording, or any information storage or retrieval system, without prior
permission in writing from the publishers.

Bloomsbury Publishing Plc does not have any control over, or responsibility for,
any third-party websites referred to or in this book. All internet addresses given
in this book were correct at the time of going to press. The author and publisher
regret any inconvenience caused if addresses have changed or sites have
ceased to exist, but can accept no responsibility for any such changes.

A catalogue record for this book is available from the British Library.

A catalog record for this book is available from the Library of Congress
Library of Congress Control Number: 2020941214

ISBN: HB: 978-1-3500-5332-8
         PB: 978-1-3500-5333-5
         ePDF: 978-1-3500-5334-2
         eBook: 978-1-3500-5335-9

Typeset by Integra Software Services Pvt. Ltd.
Printed and bound in Great Britain

To find out more about our authors and books visit www.bloomsbury.com
and sign up for our newsletters.

Contents

7 System 225

8 History of philosophy 257

Part III The ideal world 285

9 Freedom 287

Preface and acknowledgements

F.W.J. Schelling (1775–1854) stands between J.G. Fichte and G.W.F. Hegel in the sequence of great German thinkers that follow in the wake of Immanuel Kant's Copernican revolution in philosophy. Anyone who takes the history of philosophy seriously will find it impossible to gainsay his enormous contribution, not only to what has recently been called 'the twenty-five years of philosophy'[1] (running from the *Critique of Pure Reason* of 1781 to the *Phenomenology of Spirit* in 1807), but, beyond that, to post-Hegelian currents and debates in the 1830s and 1840s. And yet, Schelling is also much more than an important figure within the German Idealist tradition: according to Martin Heidegger, Schelling 'shattered' idealism;[2] for Paul Tillich, he is to be listed alongside 'the other rebelling existentialists of the nineteenth century (Kierkegaard, the younger Marx, Nietzsche)';[3] and his philosophies of nature inspired later scientific advances in dynamics, electromagnetic field theory and theories of evolution.[4] Indeed, for Schellingians from Coleridge to Žižek, he represents, in Karl Jaspers's words, 'a prototype of modern possibilities;'[5] or, as Gabriel Marcel puts it: 'For thought that regards philosophy as a heroic adventure entailing risks and skirting abysses, he will always remain an exhilarating companion.'[6]

The Schelling Reader is the first comprehensive, English-language anthology of Schelling's writings, designed to introduce students to their range and diversity – those very features which have given rise to such a multifaceted reception history. It functions as a textbook to give students access to a large selection of readings from his philosophy in one volume. Hence, it includes many of the most important passages[7] from all of Schelling's major works, as well as lesser-known yet illuminating lectures, essays, dialogues and poems. The hope is thereby to help encourage, through this anthology, a new generation of readers excited by the experience of thinking alongside Schelling.

In order to make the *Reader* as accessible and helpful as possible to those approaching Schelling for the first time, the following principles have been employed in our editing:

1 Unlike any other volume on Schelling, chapters are here arranged thematically, and, within each chapter, there are extracts spanning the whole of his career from the mid-1790s to 1850. In this way, every period of Schelling's philosophical trajectory is fully represented, but, at the same time, extracts on the same theme – no matter how far apart chronologically – are placed next to one another. Such a structure, we hope, will allow readers to judge for themselves whether Schelling approaches these themes in the same way throughout his life or whether he changes his mind. That is, it addresses the Hegelian accusations of Schelling as a 'Proteus of philosophy' who 'carried out his philosophical education in public'.[8] Is Schelling simply an inconsistent philosopher who changes his mind and his system from one year to the next? And is this the case for each element of his thinking? Or are there ways in which Schelling's thought develops in a continuous fashion, building and elaborating upon his earlier ideas? This *Reader* is structured so that students can decide for themselves – when it comes to the absolute, to nature or to freedom – what continuities and discontinuities determine the path of Schellingian philosophy.

2 *The Schelling Reader* includes both expected and unexpected extracts from Schelling's corpus. For example, alongside the venerated passages on art from the conclusion to the *System of Transcendental Idealism* and on the copula from the *Philosophical Investigations into the Essence of Human Freedom*, we have included lesser-known texts, such as the poem *Heinz Widerporst's Epicurean Confession of Faith* and the mystic novel-cum-dialogue *Clara*. We have also been able to include, alongside previously translated works, a host of new translations of key Schellingian writings. Translated for the first time into English in this volume are the early programmatic *Is a Philosophy of History Possible?*; sections on life, freedom and the state from the 1804 *Würzburger System*; an obituary for Immanuel Kant; a lecture on the historical significance of Michael Faraday; passages from the lectures on philosophical empiricism from the 1830s; sections from Schelling's first lectures in Berlin (those at which Kierkegaard, Bakunin and Engels were present); the *Alternative Deduction of the Principles of Positive Philosophy*; and three sustained extracts from the *Presentation of the Purely Rational Philosophy* on topics as diverse as the unconditioned in negative philosophy, the spatial orientation of the organism and the nature and purpose of the state. What is more, the following also includes new translations of central passages from the *Philosophical*

Letters on Dogmatism and Criticism, the *Treatises Explaining the Idealism of the Science of Knowledge* and *On the Relationship of the Plastic Arts to Nature*. The reason behind the inclusion of such a range of sources is to highlight the many different methods, styles and genres Schelling adopted over the course of his life; it is – in other words – to stress the ever-experimental nature of Schellingian philosophizing, the impulse to try out new forms, new vocabularies and new concepts in order to articulate what matters for thinking.

3   The thematic arrangement of the chapters means, furthermore, that readers can dive into this anthology at any point without needing to follow a linear or cumulative sequence. We have nominally followed Frederick Beiser's and Iain Hamilton Grant's influential interpretations of Schelling by beginning with metaphysical topics, rather than methodological or epistemological ones. Nevertheless, any reader who wishes to begin by getting to grips with the concept of intellectual intuition or human freedom need not be constrained by the ordering of the chapters. There is, indeed, necessarily an element of arbitrariness in separating, for example, Schelling's description of the absolute from his methodological accounts of intuition or, similarly, his discussions of mythology from those of religion. Throughout, we have selected material that students dipping in and out of the volume will be able to engage without a previous understanding of Schelling's philosophy. And yet, this evidently does not mean – and cannot mean – that all of the chapters are easy reads: Schelling is an extraordinarily difficult philosopher, writing difficult prose and dealing with difficult concepts; there is no getting around that. While some of his texts are more accessible on first read, others are simply daunting. And this means that he should be read – as all philosophers should – with patience and intellectual charity. From the very beginning of the anthology, therefore, students will be faced with the high level of philosophical sophistication to which Schelling forever aspired. We have in no way attempted to bowdlerize or simplify Schelling's writings: the aim of *The Schelling Reader* is to provide a genuine experience of reading his works, with all its joys and frustrations.

4   Schelling's philosophy has often presented formidable challenges to teachers, and this has not been helped by the lack of a one-volume anthology or textbook in English. *The Schelling Reader* is intended to fill this gap not only by including a range of readings from every period of Schelling's output and by showcasing the vast array of

his interests and concerns (metaphysics, epistemology, philosophy of nature, ethics, aesthetics, political philosophy and philosophy of religion and mythology), but also by providing further reading suggestions and contextual introductions, directing the reader to the main themes, arguments and questions at stake in each chapter. This editorial guidance will, we hope, make the book useful for teachers, students and researchers alike; an accessible starting-point for all those beginning their journey with Schelling 'as an exhilarating companion'; indeed, a primary resource for all those turning, or returning, to Schelling.

*

First and foremost, we wish to thank the tireless efforts of all the translators – Lydia Azadpour, Kyla Bruff, G. Anthony Bruno, Joseph Carew, Iain Grant, Chelsea Harry, Tyler Tritten, Michael Vater, Graham Wetherall and Jason Wirth – who contributed so much to this volume, as well as Joseph Lawrence who made his translation of the 1811 *Ages of the World* available to us before publication. We are also immensely grateful to the community of Anglophone Schelling scholars who advised us in designing what follows, especially to Phoebe Page who provided helpful comments on a number of draft chapters. Liza Thompson and Lucy Russell backed the project throughout. Most of all, this volume would not exist without the support of Carmen De Schryver and Grace Whistler.

We are also very grateful for the permissions that have been granted to reproduce extracts from the following previously published translations:

F.W.J. Schelling, Andrew Bowie (translator), *On the History of Modern Philosophy*, 1994 © Cambridge University Press 1994, reproduced with permission.

F.W.J. Schelling, Bruce Matthews (translator), *The Grounding of Positive Philosophy: The Berlin Lectures*, 2007 © State University of New York Press 2007, reproduced with permission.

F.W.J. Schelling, Dale Snow (translator), *On the Relation of the Real and the Ideal in Nature*, in *International Philosophical Quarterly*, vol. 55.2, 2015 © Philosophy Documentation Center 2015, reproduced with permission.

F.W.J. Schelling, Douglas W. Stott (translator), *The Philosophy of Art*, 1989 © University of Minnesota Press 1989, reproduced with permission.

F.W.J. Schelling, E.A. Beach (translator), *On the Source of the Eternal Truths*, in *The Owl of Minerva*, vol. 22.1, 1990 © Hegel Society of America 1990, reproduced with permission.

F.W.J. Schelling, Fiona Steinkamp (translator), *Clara: Or, on Nature's Connection to the Spirit World*, 2002 © State University of New York Press 2002, reproduced with permission.

F.W.J. Schelling, Frederick de Wolfe Bolman, Jr. (translator), *The Ages of the World*, 1942 © Columbia University Press 1942, reproduced with permission.

F.W.J. Schelling, Fritz Marti (editor and translator), *The Unconditioned in Human Knowledge: Four Early Essays*, 1980 © Bucknell University Press 1980, reproduced with permission.

F.W.J. Schelling, Joseph P. Lawrence (translator), *The Ages of the World (1811)*, 2019 © State University of New York Press 2019, reproduced with permission.

F.W.J. Schelling, Keith R. Peterson (translator), *First Outline of a System of Philosophy of Nature*, 2004 © State University of New York Press 2004, reproduced with permission.

F.W.J. Schelling, Klaus Ottmann (translator), *Philosophy and Religion*, 2009 © Spring Publishers 2009, reproduced with permission.

F.W.J. Schelling, Mason Richey and Markus Zisselsberger (translators), *Historical-Critical Introduction to the Philosophy of Mythology*, 2007 © State University of New York Press 2007, reproduced with permission.

F.W.J. Schelling, Michael G. Vater (translator), *Bruno, or On the Natural and the Divine Principle of Things*, 1984 © State University of New York Press 1984, reproduced with permission.

F.W.J. Schelling, Rudiger Bubner (editor and translator), *German Idealist Philosophy*, 1997 © Reklam 1997, reproduced with permission.

F.W.J. Schelling, Thomas Pfau (editor and translator), *Idealism and the Endgame of Theory: Three Essays*, 1994 © State University of New York Press 1994, reproduced with permission.

F.W.J. Schelling, A. Arola and P. Warnek (translators), *Timaeus*, in *Epoche*, vol. 12.2, 2008 © Philosophy Documentation Center 2008, reproduced with permission.

F.W.J. Schelling, Andrew A. Davis and Alexi I.Kukuljevic (translators), *On Construction in Philosophy*, in *Epoche*, vol. 12.2, 2008 © Philosophy Documentation Center 2008, reproduced with permission.

F.W.J. Schelling, Errol E. Harris and Peter Heath (translators), *Ideas for a Philosophy of Nature*, 1988 © Cambridge University Press 1988, reproduced with permission.

F.W.J. Schelling, Judith Kahl and Daniel Whistler (translators), *Two Poems*, in *Clio*, vol. 43.2, 2014 © Indiana University Press 2014, reproduced with permission.

F.W.J. Schelling, J.G. Fichte, Michael G. Vater and David W. Wood (editors and translators), *The Philosophical Rupture between Schelling and Fichte*, 2012 © State University of New York Press 2012, reproduced with permission.

All efforts have been made to trace copyright holders. In the event of errors or omissions, please notify the publisher in writing of any corrections that will need to be incorporated in future editions of this book.

Notes

1   Eckhart Förster, *The Twenty-Five Years of Philosophy: A Systematic Reconstruction*, trans. Brady Bowman (Cambridge, MA: Harvard University Press, 2012).

2   Martin Heidegger, *Schelling's Treatise on the Essence of Human Freedom*, trans. Joan Stambaugh (Athens, OH: Ohio University Press, 1985), p. 97.

3   Paul Tillich, 'Schelling und die Anfänge des Existentialistischen Protestes,' in *Hauptwerke*, vol. 1, ed. Gunther Wenz et al. (Berlin: De Gruyter, 1987), p. 395.

4   See Gilles Châtelet, *Figuring Space: Philosophy, Mathematics and Physics*, trans. Robert Shore and Muriel Zagha (Dordrecht: Kluwer, 2000); Iain Hamilton Grant, *Philosophies of Nature after Schelling* (London: Continuum, 2006); and Marie-Luise Heuser, *Die Produktivität der Natur: Schellings Naturphilosophie und das neue Paradigma der Selbstorganisation in den Naturwissenschaften* (Berlin: Duncker & Humblot, 1986) and 'Space Philosophy: Schelling and Mathematicians of the 19th Century' *Angelaki* 21.4 (2016), pp. 43–57.

5   Karl Jaspers, *Schelling: Größe und Verhängnis* (Munich: Piper, 1955), p. 332.

6   Gabriel Marcel, 'Schelling fut-il un précurseur de la philosophie de l'existence?' *Revue de Metaphysique et de Morale* 62.1 (1957), p. 87.

7   It should be emphasized that the following are *extracts* and in no case do they completely reproduce the respective texts in their entirety, often missing out digressional sections and, particularly, Schelling's footnotes and use of Latin and Greek. In some cases, and with the aim of emphasizing the key themes of his thought, we have risked compromising the integrity of his texts by splitting them into various parts, presenting different extracts from the same text in multiple chapters. For those readers who wish to take the next step towards greater familiarity with Schellingian philosophy, there are many good scholarly and complete editions of his texts, a number of which are cited in this Preface and the 'Further Reading' sections at the end of each chapter.

8   G.W.F. Hegel, *Lectures on the History of Philosophy*, vol. 3, trans. E.S. Haldane and F. H. Simson (London: Routledge, 1896), p. 513.

Introduction to the *Reader*: The life and thought of F.W.J. Schelling

I

On 27 January 1775, Friedrich Wilhelm Joseph was born to Gottliebin Marie (Cleß) and Joseph Friedrich Schelling in Leonberg, a village fifteen kilometers west of Stuttgart. In 1777, his family moved south to Bebenhausen, near Tübingen, so that his father – deacon in Leonberg – could take up a teaching position in Semitic philology at the Bebenhausen cloister. Members of both sides of Schelling's family were Lutheran clergymen, and his father had a special esteem for the Swabian pietism of F.C. Oetinger and J.A. Bengel. From an early age, Schelling demonstrated an exceptional facility with language and philosophy: he learned Greek, Hebrew, Latin and Arabic, and, by the time he was fourteen, had undertaken a serious study of Plato and Leibniz.

In 1790, at the age of fifteen, Schelling began his studies at the Tübingen theological seminary, which he briefly attended with Friedrich Hölderlin and G.W.F. Hegel, both five years Schelling's senior; for a short while, they even shared a room. Although their formal training at the seminary was conservative, Schelling, Hölderlin and Hegel were united in their enthusiasm for what appeared to be the contemporary rejuvenation of both political life and philosophical science in line with the French Revolution and a radical reinterpretation of Kant's critical turn. In a jubilant expression of their shared commitment to the ideals of the French Revolution, they planted a 'freedom tree' in the seminary cloister; Schelling is sometimes credited as the first German translator of the *Marseillaise*.[1]

While in Tübingen, Schelling encountered the thought of J.G. Fichte, who briefly visited in June 1793 and May 1794 (and may or may not have met Schelling at this time[2]). Fichte's conception of the self-positing 'I' was profoundly important for Schelling, as was the second major influence upon his thought during this period: Spinoza, whose philosophy was undergoing something of a renaissance in Germany at the end of the eighteenth century. In April 1795, Schelling writes to his former roommate, Hegel: 'I have become a Spinozist!'[3] He began publishing his own philosophical work in 1794, and these texts of the mid-1790s – such as *Of the I as Principle of Philosophy* – bear the mark of both his Fichtean and Spinozist sympathies.

In the spring of 1796, Schelling moved to Leipzig where he worked as a private tutor and began his own intensive study of physics, chemistry and physiology. It was here that he wrote his *Ideas for a Philosophy of Nature*, which drew upon recent empirical discoveries in order to transform Kant's critical project of providing a metaphysical grounding for the natural sciences. In the autumn of 1798, after publishing a second major work on the philosophy of nature – *On the World-Soul* – Schelling moved again, this time to Jena, at the express invitation of Goethe, who Schelling had met and worked with on a previous visit to Jena and Weimar.

Schelling's years in Jena comprise an intense period of his career and personal life. In addition to publishing a number of important works, he was a (somewhat peripheral) member of the romantic circle. He became particularly close with Caroline Schlegel, the wife of August Wilhelm Schlegel, and the two ultimately began an affair, which negatively impacted Schelling's relationship with some of the other members of the group (particularly Friedrich Schlegel). In June 1800, Caroline's daughter, Auguste Böhmer, died of dysentery while in Bad Bocklet with Caroline and Schelling. Word soon began to spread that Schelling had intervened in Auguste's medical treatment and that he was responsible for her death; indeed, widely circulated pamphlets suggested that his idealist philosophy of nature and the medical practices connected therewith were ultimately to blame.

Although it came under serious attack, Schelling's philosophy of nature also continued to gain devotees during these years. His *Journal of Speculative Physics*, founded in January of 1800, made a significant impact on the philosophy and sciences of the day, thanks in no small part to the fact that it included his most important writings of the period. Schelling's increasingly apparent view that, within the whole system of philosophy, the philosophy of nature is more fundamental than transcendental idealism led to tensions in his intellectual friendship with Fichte. Although the latter had, by this point, left for Berlin on account of his 'atheism controversy', the two were in frequent contact and had even planned to edit a philosophical journal together. It gradually became evident, however, that the two held fundamentally irreconcilable positions regarding the nature of 'first philosophy'; by January 1802, they ceased communication.

One philosopher who sided with Schelling in the dispute over the future of idealism and the status of the philosophy of nature was Hegel, whose first publication was the 1801 *Difference Between Fichte's and Schelling's Systems of Philosophy*. Schelling had invited Hegel to Jena as a means of helping him advance an academic career. As one of their contemporaries anonymously writes, 'Schelling fetched a stout warrior to Jena from his fatherland Württemberg, through which he now gives notice to the astonished public, that even Fichte stands far below his own viewpoint.'[4] While teaching at the University of Jena, Hegel joined Schelling in editing the *Critical Journal of Philosophy*, which the latter had originally intended to edit with Fichte.

On 26 June 1803, Schelling and Caroline married, just five weeks after her official divorce from A.W. Schlegel. In the fall, Schelling took up a position in Würzburg, where he was made full professor of philosophy. Schelling and Caroline remained in Würzburg until April 1806, when, for political reasons, they were forced to move to Munich. While in Munich, Schelling became a member of the Bavarian Academy of Sciences and the General Secretary of the Academy of Fine Art. It was also during this period that Schelling fell out with Hegel. Although their final exchange of letters in 1807 is cordial and does not explicitly confront the nature of their disagreement, its source is clear: In the Preface to his *Phenomenology of Spirit*, Hegel criticizes a particular form of the philosophy of nature that was practised by certain followers of Schelling, if not by Schelling himself. Schelling could not help but take these remarks personally, and Hegel did little to mend the friendship.

A far more devastating event in Schelling's life occurred two years later, when Caroline died of dysentery on 7 September 1809 with Schelling by her side. During the summer of 1810, while still mourning Caroline's death, Schelling temporarily lived in Stuttgart where he presented a series of private lectures. He returned to Munich in the autumn and began his project on the *Ages of the World* – a project that he frequently announced but never published, and of which only fragments remain. In 1812, he published his last major piece of original philosophy during his lifetime: a critical response to Jacobi's charge that Schellingian philosophy leads to atheism.

Schelling also remarried in 1812. With his new wife, Pauline Gotter – the daughter of Caroline's friend, Luise – he had six children over the next twelve years: Paul Heinrich Joseph, Karl Friedrich August, Marie Louise Caroline, Clara, Julie Friederike Wilhelmine and Ludwig Hermann.[5] In December 1820, the Schelling family moved to Erlangen, where Schelling lectured on the *Ages of the World* and his system of philosophy more generally until 1827. During this period, Schelling's later philosophical view began to take form, and, upon returning once again to Munich, Schelling delivered lectures in which the late system further crystallized. Central to this new phase of his thought is the distinction between the 'negative' philosophy of reason and the 'positive' philosophy of historical existence; the latter is required to supplement the former in order to generate a complete philosophical account of reality that includes the history of mythological consciousness and Christian revelation.

There was one final institutional change to be made in Schelling's life. In 1841, he was called to Berlin by Wilhelm IV, the new King of Prussia, in order to take up the Chair of Philosophy which had been held by Hegel until his death in 1831. In Berlin, Schelling continued to lecture on the systems of negative and positive philosophy, and these late lectures were attended by many important philosophers, political theorists, historians and theologians, including some of the more significant thinkers of the next generation, such as Mikhail Bakunin, Jakob Burckhardt, Friedrich Engels and Søren Kierkegaard. Schelling's discussion of the limits of rational philosophy; his insistence on developing a metaphysical empiricism attentive to the free acts that constitute the history of the world; his argument for a philosophical system that focuses on historical existence as opposed to atemporal essence – all of this signalled to the philosophical community in Germany that the age of idealism was coming to a close. Indeed, although the next generation of philosophers did not follow Schelling with respect to either the details of his proposed 'philosophical religion' or his more general engagement with Christian orthodoxy, they understood the moment to herald the end of an era and a transition to something new.

Schelling became ill in his old age and, at seventy-nine, passed away on 20 August 1854 in the health spa, Bad Ragaz, Switzerland. He was one of the last of the great philosophers of his generation to die.

II

What kind of philosopher was Schelling? First and foremost, he was an ambitious philosopher who sought to understand the nature of reality as a whole. If Wilfrid Sellars is right in claiming that 'the aim of philosophy ... is to understand how things in the broadest possible sense of the term hang together in the broadest possible sense of the term,'[6] Schelling is a philosopher *par excellence*, a thinker who aimed to unify every fundamental feature of physical, mental and social reality into one system. Indeed, in seeking to incorporate everything there is into a unified whole, his thought can veer towards such abstraction that it becomes extraordinarily difficult to comprehend without spending a great deal of time and patience with his texts.

Schelling's insistence on understanding the most general sense in which everything that *is* 'hangs together' is not the only thing about his thought that makes it challenging to comprehend. He also seems to insist upon experimenting with a multitude of conceptions of reality and ways of presenting his findings to his audience. Schelling was not, then, the kind of philosopher who simply refines the details of a single system; on the contrary, his experimentations in thinking about the natural and the spiritual world were so central to his philosophical style that it led Hegel to declare that Schelling was a Proteus-figure, as mentioned in the Preface above, who never could settle into one position.[7] Yet Hegel's analysis is not the only possible way of interpreting this feature of Schelling's thought. Others have seen in his philosophical character something less passive and more persistent; they see a resolve precisely to refuse any final system. As Schelling's friend and protégé Henrik Steffens remarks, while Schelling did seem to develop his ideas in view of the public, he also sought to perpetually reinvent his system *for the sake of the system*, i.e. to resist its becoming a kind of dead thing.[8] In this way, the changes that appear to take place throughout Schelling's intellectual career might be seen as issuing from a deeper commitment to fundamental principles and a refusal to be boxed into one way of expressing philosophical ideas. In a letter from Caroline Schlegel to Friedrich Schlegel, we get a glimpse of this feature of Schelling's intellectual persona. She writes: '[Schelling] is a man who breaks through walls. Believe me, friend, he is a more interesting man than you give him credit for, a real primitive nature, something like mineral, real granite.'[9] It is perhaps worthwhile to keep this image of Schelling as 'granitic' in mind, if only to balance out the Hegelian interpretation of Schelling as 'protean'. For there is often an underlying consistency to Schelling's thought that is not always recognized on a superficial reading of the philosopher.

It would be naïve, however, to simply assert that Schelling's nearly sixty-year philosophical development did not involve substantial transformations; his thought cannot be reduced to a series of variations on one and the same theme. Although recent scholarship has called into question the strict periodization of Schelling's philosophy, it has traditionally been divided up into five major periods or stages corresponding to what have been interpreted as important shifts in how he frames the very task of philosophy itself:

(i)   *The Early Period (1794–1796).* The texts of the mid-1790s are often interpreted as belonging to a 'Fichtean' period that focuses on the absolute 'I' or subject as the ground of the system of knowledge and action.

(ii) *The Early Philosophy of Nature (1797–1800).* The work of this period focuses on the structure of the natural world. Although Schelling continues, during this period, the 'Fichtean' project of understanding how the mind comes to know nature (e.g. in the 1800 *System of Transcendental Idealism*), he now argues that philosophy must also demonstrate how nature comes to be aware of itself through the mind.

(iii) *The Philosophy of Identity (1801–1805).* With the publication of the *Presentation of My System of Philosophy*, Schelling announces his turn to the fundamental basis of both his transcendental idealism and his philosophy of nature. This period of Schelling's thought is often identified as the 'system of identity', since it is here that Schelling argues that mind and nature are, at the most basic level of reality, identical.

(iv) *The Middle Period (1809–1815).* In 1809, Schelling publishes his *Philosophical Investigations into the Essence of Human Freedom*, an essay that marks an important shift in his philosophical development. While Schelling continues to understand the absolute in terms of 'identity', he now emphasizes the developmental character of all that is – even interpreting 'identity' itself as processual. Traditionally, this period of thought is also interpreted as the beginning of Schelling's focus on freedom, contingency and that which is in some sense beyond the grasp of reason.

(v)   *The Late Period (1820–1850).* The last period of Schelling's thought is distinct from the earlier work in a number of important ways that all follow from the fact that Schelling now sets up a distinction between negative and positive philosophy: the former exhibits the rationally necessary features of reality and the latter attends to the historical fact of the actual existence of the world, a fact which cannot be grasped by sheer reason but requires empirical confirmation.

One of the aims of this book is to allow new readers of Schelling to come to their own conclusions about his philosophical development: by arranging the texts thematically and chronologically, we hope that it will be possible for new readers to discover both similarities and differences between the various periods of his thought. Our own view is that the apparent changes in Schelling's thought are often better understood *dynamically*: as one tendency in Schellingian thought comes to the fore, another tendency can lose its intensity, only to regain that intensity in subsequent years.

What, then, are some of the ideas that remain in play, in one way or another, throughout Schelling's intellectual development? The following six theses are often cited as key to Schelling's distinctive philosophical perspective:

(i) *Reality has an intelligible structure.* Precisely how one accesses the intelligible structure of reality is a difficult issue (and it is given detailed treatment in Chapters 5 and 6 of this volume); however, throughout the whole of his life, Schelling insists upon the rational character of being – even when he comes to argue that the ultimate *ground* of being is not immanent to reason. Indeed, on attending Schelling's lectures on the positive philosophy, Kierkegaard notes that, although 'the world is not a logical consequence of God's nature,'[10] for Schelling, 'the a priori content of the science of reason is … the whole of actuality.'[11]

(ii) *Modern thought must no longer ignore the philosophical significance of nature.* The intelligible structure of reality is not limited to the reality of the *mind* for Schelling, but extends to the natural world, as Chapter 3 below will show most clearly. For this reason, he is critical of what he sees as the unfounded priority given to the philosophy of mind in modernity. Philosophy must become, like it once was in ancient physics, attentive to the dynamic world of both organic and inorganic nature; it must become, or at least come to include, a non-reductionist, non-mechanical philosophy of nature.

(iii) *Consciousness is not all that exists; there is an unconscious dimension to reality.* Related to Schelling's interest in natural phenomena is his more general understanding of consciousness as being in some sense dependent upon non-conscious or unconscious processes. This ultimately leads him to the idea that the ultimate ground of being is not only unconscious but even arational.

(iv) *The basic elements of reality are parts of a whole.* Schelling is a thinker of unity, identity and totality, and he argues that the conscious and unconscious dimensions of reality can only be understood in terms of their place within a unified whole. Although his conception of this unity undergoes important changes from one period of thought to the next, he remains committed to some version of the slogan of his youth: *hen kai pan*, the one and all.

(v)   *Works of art exhibit the full truth of reality*. Although it is misleading to characterize Schelling as being interested in art over and above philosophy, Josiah Royce had good reason to describe him as the 'prince of the romanticists':[12] art is in no way deficient, for Schelling, but is a fully adequate way of presenting the structure of being.

(vi) *Reality is not, essentially, a 'substance' or 'thing', but a dynamic and productive process*. Indeed, one reason that art exhibits the full truth of reality is that it expresses the *unity* of all that is through a process of *creation*. Art is not, however, the only aspect of the world that Schelling understands in terms of a fundamental creativity. At different points in his career, he foregrounds the productive activity of nature, the generation of gods in mythological consciousness and God's free and creative activity in history.

By no means do these six theses exhaust the threads woven throughout Schelling's intellectual development; they are intended to simply guide the reader who is beginning to explore the fabric of Schelling's thought in what follows.

Notes

1   Xavier Tilliette, *Schelling: Biographie*, trans. Susanne Schaper (Stuttgart: Klett-Cotta, 2004), p. 18.
2   See Tilliette, *Schelling*, p. 27.
3   F.W.J. Schelling, *Historisch-Kritische Ausgabe*, Series Three, Volume One, ed. the Schelling Commission of the Bavarian Academy of Sciences (Stuttgart: Frommann-Holzboog, 2001), p. 22.
4   Karl August Böttinger, quoted in H.S. Harris, Introduction to G.W.F. Hegel, *The Difference Between Fichte's and Schelling's Systems of Philosophy* (Albany: SUNY Press, 1977), p. 67.
5   Tilliette, *Schelling*, p. 571.
6   Wilfrid Sellars, 'Philosophy and the Scientific Image of Man', *In the Space of Reasons: Selected Essays of Wilfrid Sellars* (Cambridge, MA: Harvard University Press, 2007), p. 369.
7   G.W.F. Hegel, *Lectures on the History of Philosophy*, vol. 3, trans. E.S. Haldane and Frances H. Simson (London: Kegan Paul, Trench, Trübner, 1895), p. 513.
8   Henrik Steffens, *Was ich erlebte: Aus der niedergeschrieben von Henrich Steffens*, vol. 5 (Breslau, Josef Mar und Komp., 1842), p. 73

9   Caroline Schlegel to Friedrich Schlegel, 14 October 1798; cited and translated in Robert J. Richards, *The Romantic Conception of Life: Science and Philosophy in the Age of Goethe* (Chicago: University of Chicago Press, 2002), p. 149.

10 Søren Kierkegaard, 'Notes on Schelling's Berlin Lectures', *The Concept of Irony*, ed. and trans. Howard V. and Edna H. Hong (Princeton: Princeton University Press,), p. 385.

11 Ibid., p. 341.

12 Josiah Royce, *The Spirit of Modern Philosophy: An Essay in the Form of Lectures* (Mineola, NY: Dover, 2015), p. 181.

Part I

Metaphysics

1

The unconditioned

Introduction

One reason Schelling – like Spinoza before him – is a difficult philosopher to begin reading is that, from the outset, many of his writings throw the reader straight into discussions of the fundamental structures of reality, immersing us in the subtlest of metaphysical questions without prologue or apology. Schelling, that is, reverses the modern priority given to epistemological and methodological concerns: he holds that metaphysics is first philosophy, which means studying him demands that we bracket any presupposition that metaphysical enquiry must be preceded by epistemological justification, such as the Cartesian method of doubt or the Hegelian phenomenology of consciousness. Therefore, although the first four chapters of this *Reader* - and the first chapter in particular - do include attention to some epistemological topics, they largely focus on Schelling's understanding of reality itself.

In many of his texts, Schelling is primarily concerned with identifying an 'absolute' or 'unconditioned' principle at the heart of his metaphysics – even if the meaning of this principle seems to change from one text to another. At different stages in Schelling's thought, the 'unconditioned' is understood as an 'I', a natural process, a divinity immanent to the world, and something 'beyond being'. But in each case, Schelling sees great importance in that which *is* unconditionally, i.e. that which conditions all things (*Dinge*) but is not itself conditioned (*bedingt*).

In fact, the metaphysical dualism between an *unbedingt* generative principle and that which it grounds – *bedingt* things in the empirical world – can be discerned in many of Schelling's philosophical writings from the earliest text excerpted below (*Of the I*) well into his middle period (represented below by *The Ages of the World*). In all of these texts, however, metaphysical dualism is tempered by an emphasis on strict metaphysical unity (whether it is a unity already realized or still incomplete). It is for this reason that Schelling is often read as a philosopher of 'the absolute', a philosopher who posits one single, unifying principle as the ground – and, in some cases, totality – of all that exists. This is part of his ongoing negotiation with the scandal of pantheism: he continually traverses a path between a Parmenidean metaphysics of all-encompassing unity that dissolves all real distinctions and a pluralistic metaphysics attentive to the differences between various domains of being.

The final two extracts in this chapter look beyond the so-called 'middle period' to the metaphysics of Schelling's late philosophy and, in particular, the ways in which the discourse of 'unconditioned', 'absolute' principles informs his interrelated projects of negative and positive philosophy. For instance, in his description of positive philosophy, the late Schelling radicalizes the search for a principle that is beyond the conditioned – beyond things, beyond products and beyond what is created – by setting up the task of philosophy as the quest for something so fully unconditioned that it is beyond thought itself. Metaphysics thereby becomes, in part, the attempt to think the unthinkable. (This means that, while Schelling is clearly involved in metaphysical speculation, he also finds himself working through methodological issues regarding the appropriate mode of access to the unconditioned, issues that will reappear in Chapter 6 of this volume.)

The following aims to guide the reader through five of the main ways that Schelling conceives the 'unconditioned': (i) as the absolute 'I' or self that grounds all knowledge (in the opening sections to the 1795 *Of the I*, Schelling's first substantial published work); (ii) as natural productivity (in the opening passage to the 1799 *First Outline of a System of the Philosophy of Nature*, which Schelling envisaged as a textbook overview for students taking his lectures in Jena); (iii) as the immanent development of the natural-divine cosmos (in the opening section on 'The Past', i.e. the archaic grounds of creation, of the third fragmentary version of Schelling's *The Ages of the World*, written in 1815); (iv) as that which conditions all conceivable determinations of being (from a lecture on the *Presentation of the Purely Rational Philosophy*, a course given in Berlin in approximately 1847); and (v) as the purely actual, transcendent creator of all that exists (in a late lecture entitled *Alternative Deduction of the Principles of Positive Philosophy* and delivered a couple of years earlier). A further way that Schelling conceives the unconditioned – namely, as the identity of self and nature, evident in texts from 1801 to 1806 – will be considered in Chapter 2.

Of the I as Principle of Philosophy (1795)*

§ 1

He who wants to know something, wants to know at the same time that what he knows is real. Knowledge without reality is not knowledge. What follows from that?

Either our knowledge has no reality at all and must be an eternal round of propositions, each dissolving in its opposite, a chaos in which no element can crystallize – or else there must be an ultimate point of reality on which everything depends, from which all firmness and all form of our knowledge springs, a point which sunders the elements, and which circumscribes for each of them the circle of its continuous effect in the universe of knowledge.

There must be something in which and through which everything that is reaches existence, everything that is being thought reaches reality, and thought itself reaches the form of unity and immutability. This something (as we can problematically call it for the time being) should be what completes all insights within the whole system of human knowledge, and it should reign – in the entire cosmos of our knowledge – as original ground of all reality.

If there is any genuine knowledge at all, there must be knowledge which I do not reach by way of some other knowledge, but through which alone all other knowledge is knowledge. In order to reach this last statement I do not have to presuppose some special kind of knowledge. If we know anything at all, we must be sure of at least one item of knowledge which we cannot reach through some other knowledge and which contains the real ground of all our knowledge.

This ultimate in human knowledge must therefore not search for its own real ground in something other. Not only is it itself independent of anything superior but, since our knowledge rises from any consequence to the reason thereof and in reverse descends from that reason to the consequence, that which is the ultimate and for us the principle of all knowledge cannot be *known* in turn through another principle. That is, the principle of its being and the principle of its being known must coincide, must be one, since it can be thought only because it itself is, not because there is something else.

---

*Translated by Fritz Marti from F.W.J. Schelling, *Sämmtliche Werke* (Stuttgart and Augsberg: Cotta, 1856–1861), Division One, Volume One.

Therefore it must be thought simply because it is, and it must be because it itself is being thought, not because something else is thought. Its assertion must be contained in its thought; it must create itself through its being thought. If we had to think something else in order to reach its thought, then that other entity would be superior to the ultimate, which is a contradiction. In order to reach the ultimate I need nothing but the ultimate itself. The absolute can be given only by the absolute.

Now the investigation is becoming more definite. Originally I posited nothing but an ultimate ground of any real knowledge. Now this criterion that it must be the last absolute ground of knowledge permits us at the same time to establish its existence. The last ground for all reality is something that is thinkable only through itself, that is, it is thinkable only through its being; it is thought only inasmuch as it is. In short, *the principle of being and thinking is one and the same.* The question can now be expressed quite clearly and the investigation has a clue which can never fail.

§ 2

Knowledge which I can reach only through other knowledge is *conditional.* The chain of our knowledge goes from one conditional [piece of] knowledge to another. Either the whole has no stability, or one must be able to believe that this can go on ad infinitum, or else that there must be some ultimate point on which the whole depends. The latter, however, in regard to the principle of its being, must be the direct opposite of all that falls in the sphere of the conditioned, that is, it must be not only unconditional but altogether *unconditionable.*

All possible theories of the unconditional must be determinable a priori, once the only correct one has been found. As long as it has not been established, one must follow the empirical progress of philosophy. Whether that progress contains all possible theories will be seen only at the end.

As soon as philosophy begins to be a science, it must at least *assume* an ultimate principle and, with it, something unconditional.

To look for the unconditional in an *object,* in a *thing,* cannot mean to look for it in the generic character of things, since it is evident that a genus cannot be something that is unconditional. Therefore it must mean to look for the unconditional in an *absolute* object which is neither genus nor species nor individual. (Principle of consummate *dogmatism.*)

Yet, whatever is a thing is at the same time an *object* of knowing, therefore a link in the chain of our knowledge. It falls into the sphere of the knowable.

Consequently it cannot contain the basis for the reality of all knowledge and knowing. In order to reach an object *as* object I must already have another object with which it can be contrasted, and if the principle of all knowledge were lying in an object I would in turn have to have a new principle in order to find that ostensibly ultimate principle.

Moreover, the unconditional (by § 1) should realize itself, create itself through its own thought; the principle of its being and its thinking should coincide. But no object ever realizes itself. In order to reach the existence of an object I must go beyond the mere concept of the object. Its existence is not a part of its reality. I can think its reality without positing it as existing. Suppose, for instance, that God, insofar as some define Him as an object, were the ground of the reality of our knowledge; then, insofar as He is an object, He would fall into the sphere of our knowledge; therefore He could not be for us the ultimate point on which the whole sphere depends. Also the question is not what God is for Himself, but what He is for us in regard to our knowledge. Even if we let God be the ground of the reality of His own knowledge, He is still not the ground of ours, because for us He is an object, which presupposes some reason in the chain of our knowledge that could determine His necessity for our knowledge.

The object as such never determines its own necessity, simply because and insofar as it is an object. For it is object only inasmuch as it is determined by something else. Indeed, inasmuch as it is an object it presupposes something in regard to which it is an object, that is, a subject.

For the time being, I call subject that which is determinable only by contrast with but also in relation to a previously posited object. Object is that which is determinable only in contrast with but also in relation to a subject. Thus, in the first place, the object as such cannot be the unconditional at all, because it necessarily presupposes a subject which determines the object's existence by going beyond the sphere of merely thinking the object. The next thought is to look for the unconditional in the object insofar as it is determined by the subject and is conceivable only in regard to the latter. Or, in the third place, since object necessarily presupposes subject, and subject object, the unconditional could be looked for in the subject, which is conditioned by the object and can be conceived only in relation to the object.

Still, this kind of endeavour to realize the unconditional carries a contradiction within itself, which is obvious at first glance. Since the subject is thinkable only in regard to an object, and the object only in regard to a subject, neither of them can contain the unconditional because both are conditioned reciprocally, both are equally unserviceable. Furthermore, in order to determine the relationship of the two, an ulterior reason for the determination must be presupposed, owing to which both are determined. For one cannot say that the subject alone determines the object because the subject is conceivable only in relationship to the object, and vice versa, and it would amount to the same if I were to treat as unconditional a subject determined by an object and an object determined by a subject. What is more, this kind of a subject as such is also determinable as an object, and for this reason the endeavour to turn the subject into an unconditional fails, as does the endeavour with an absolute object.

The question as to where the unconditional must be looked for becomes slowly clearer, owing to its inherent logic. At the outset I asked only in which specific object we could look for the unconditional, within the whole sphere of objects. Now it becomes clear that we must not look for it in the sphere of objects at all, nor even within the sphere of that subject which is also determinable as an object.

§ 3

The philosophically revealing formation of the languages, especially manifest in languages still well aware of their roots, is a veritable miracle worked by the mechanism of the human mind. Thus the word I have used casually thus far, the word *bedingen,* is an eminently striking term of which one can say that it contains almost the entire treasure of philosophical truth. *Bedingen* means the action by which anything becomes a *thing* (*Ding*). *Bedingt* (determined) is what has been turned into a thing. Thus it is clear at once that nothing can posit itself as a thing, and that an unconditional thing is a contradiction in terms. *Unbedingt* (unconditional) is what has not been turned into a thing, and what cannot at all become a thing.

The problem, therefore, which we must solve now changes into something more precise: *to find something that cannot be thought of as a thing at all.*

Consequently, the unconditional can lie neither in a thing as such, nor in anything that can become a thing, that is, not in the subject. It can lie only in that which cannot become a thing at all; that is, if there is an absolute *I,* it can lie only in the *absolute I.* Thus, for the time being, the absolute *I* is ascertained as *that which can never become an object at all.* For the moment no further determination is being made.

That there is an absolute I can never be proved objectively, that is, it cannot be proved with regard to that *I* which can exist as an object, because we are supposed to prove precisely that the absolute *I* can never become an object. The *I*, if it is to be unconditional, must be outside the sphere of objective proof. To *prove* objectively that the *I* is unconditional would mean to prove that it was conditional. In the case of the unconditional the principle of its being and the principle of its being thought must coincide. It is only *because* it is; it is thought only *because* it is thought. The absolute can be given only by the absolute; indeed, if it is to be absolute, it must precede all thinking and imagining. Therefore it must be realized through itself (§ 1), not through objective proofs, which go beyond the mere concept of the entity to be proved. If the *I* were not realized through itself, then the sentence which expresses its existence would be, 'if I am, then I am.' But in the case of the *I*, the condition 'if I am' already contains the conditioned 'then I'. The condition is not thinkable without the conditioned. I cannot think of myself as a merely conditional existence without knowing myself as already existing. Therefore, in that conditional sentence, the condition does not condition the conditioned but, vice versa, the conditioned conditions the condition, that is, *as* a conditional sentence it cancels itself and becomes unconditional: '*I am because I am.*' '*I am!*' is the unique form by which it announces itself with unconditional authority.

I am! My I contains a being which precedes all thinking and imagining. It *is* by being thought, and it is being thought because it *is*; and all for only one reason – that it *is* only and is being thought only inasmuch as its thinking is its *own*. Thus it *is* because it alone is what does the thinking, and it thinks only itself because it is. It produces itself by its own thinking – out of absolute *causality*.

'I am, because I am!' That takes possession of everyone instantaneously. Say to him: 'the I *is* because it is'; he will not grasp it quite so quickly because the I is only *by itself* and *unconditioned* inasmuch as it is at the same time *unconditionable,* that is, it can never become a thing, an object. An object receives its existence from something outside the sphere of its mere conceivability. In contrast, the I is not even conceivable unless it first exists as an I. If it does not so exist it is nothing at all. And it is *not at all thinkable except insofar as it thinks itself,* that is, *insofar as it is.* Therefore we must not even say: Everything that thinks is, because that kind of statement talks about the thinking as if it were an object. We can only say: *I think, I am.* Therefore it is clear that, as soon as we turn that which can never become an object into a *logical* object to be investigated, such investigations would labour under a peculiar *incomprehensibility.* We cannot at all confine it as an object, and we could not even talk about it nor understand each other with regard to it, if it were not for the assistance of the [intellectual] intuition [we have of our selves]. However, insofar as our knowledge is tied to an object, that intuition is as alien to us as the I which never can become an object.)

Thus the I is determined as unconditional only through itself.[1]

Yet, if it is determined at the same time as that which furnishes validity in the entire system of my knowledge, then a regress must be possible; that is, I must be able to *ascend* from the lowest conditioned proposition to the unconditional, just as I can *descend* from the unconditional principle to the lowest proposition in the conditional sequence.

You may therefore pick from any series of conditional propositions whichever one you want and, in the regress, it must lead back to the absolute I. Hence, to come back to a previous example, the concept of subject must lead to the absolute I. For if there were no absolute I, then the concept of subject, that is, the concept of the I which is conditioned by an object, would be the ultimate. But since the concept of an object contains an antithesis, the basic determination of this concept cannot stop at a mere contrast with a subject which in turn is conceivable only in relation to an object. The determination is possible only in contrast to something which flatly excludes the concept of an object as such. Therefore both the concept of an object and the concept of a subject which is conceivable only in contrast to some object must lead to an absolute which excludes every object and thus is in absolute contrast to any object. For if you suppose that the original position is that of an object which would not require the antecedent position of an absolute I as basis for all positing, then that original object cannot be determined *as* object, that is, as opposed to the I since, as long as the latter is not posited, nothing can be in opposition to it. Therefore any object posited as antecedent to any I would be *no* object at all; the very supposition cancels itself. Or again, suppose that there is an I, but only an I conceptually contrasted by the object, that is, an original subject; then this supposition likewise cancels itself for, where no absolute I is posited, none can be set aside by contrast. If there is no I antecedent to any object, neither can there be an object whose concept would set aside the I by contrast. (I have in mind a chain of knowledge that is conditioned throughout and attains stability only in one supreme, unconditional point. Now, whatever is conditional in that chain can be conceived only by presupposing the absolute condition, that is, the unconditional. Thus the conditional cannot be posited as conditional antecedent to the unconditional and unconditionable, but only owing to the latter by contrast to it. Therefore, whatever is posited as only a conditional thing is conceivable only through that [logically antecedent entity] which is no thing at all but is unconditional. The object itself then is originally determinable only in contrast to the absolute I, that is, only as the antithesis to the I or as non-I. Thus the very concepts of subject and object are guarantors of the absolute, unconditionable.)

§ 4

Once the I is determined as the unconditional in human knowledge, then the whole content of all knowledge must be determinable through the I itself and through its antithesis, and thus one must also be able to sketch a priori every possible theory regarding the unconditional.

Inasmuch as the I is the absolute I, that which is not = I can be determined only in contrast to the I and by presupposing the I. Any not-I posited absolutely, as if it were in no contrast to anything, is a contradiction in terms. If, on the other hand, the I is not presupposed as the absolute I, then the not-I can be posited either as antecedent to any I or as on a par with the I. A third alternative is not possible.

The two extremes are dogmatism and criticism. The principle of dogmatism is a not-I posited as antecedent to any I; the principle of criticism, an I posited as antecedent to all [that is] not-I and as exclusive of any not-I. Halfway *between* the two lies the principle of an I conditioned by a not-I or, what amounts to the same, of a not-I conditioned by an I.

(1) The principle of dogmatism contradicts itself (§ 2), because it presupposes an unconditional thing, that is, a thing that is not a thing. In dogmatism therefore, consistency (which is the first requirement for any true philosophy) attains nothing other than that which is not-I should become I, and that that which is I should become not-I, as is the case with Spinoza. But as yet no dogmatist has proved that *a* not-I could give itself reality and that it could have any meaning except that of standing in contrast to an absolute I. Even Spinoza has not proved anywhere that the unconditional could and should lie in the not-I. Rather, led only by his concept of the absolute, he straightway posits it in an absolute object, and he does so as if he presupposed that everybody who conceded him his concept of the unconditional would follow him automatically in believing that, of necessity, it had to be posited in a not-I. Once having assumed though not proved it, he fulfils the duty of consistency more strictly than any single one of his enemies. For it suddenly becomes clear that – as if against his own will – through the sheer force of his consistency, which did not shun any conclusion based on his supposition, he elevated the not-I to the I, and demeaned the I to a not-I. For him, the world is no longer world,

the absolute object no longer object. No sense perception, no concept reaches his One Substance whose nonfinitude is present only to the intellectual intuition. As everywhere, so also in this present investigation, his system can take the place of perfect dogmatism. No philosopher was so worthy as he to recognize his own great misunderstanding; to do so and to arrive at his goal would have been one and the same for him. No recrimination is more unbearable than the one made against him so often, that he arbitrarily presupposed the idea of absolute substance, or even that the idea sprang from an arbitrary explanation of words. To be sure, it seems easier to overthrow a whole system by means of a small grammatical remark, rather than to insist on the discovery of its final fundamentals which, no matter how erroneous, must be detectable somewhere in the human mind. The first one to see that Spinoza's error was not in the idea [of the unconditional] but in the fact that Spinoza posited it outside the I, had understood him and thus had found the way to [philosophy as a] 'science'.

§ 5

(2) Any system that takes its start from the subject, that is, from the I which is thinkable only in respect to an object, and that is supposed to be neither dogmatism nor criticism, is like dogmatism in that it contradicts itself in its own principle, insofar as the latter is supposed to be the supreme principle.

[...]

§ 6

The perfect system of [philosophical] science proceeds from the absolute I, excluding everything that stands in contrast to it. This, as the One Unconditionable, conditions the whole chain of knowledge, circumscribes the sphere of all that is thinkable and, as the absolute all-comprehending reality, rules the whole system of our knowledge. Only through an absolute I, only through the fact that it is posited absolutely does it become possible that a not-I appears in contrast to it, indeed that philosophy itself becomes possible. For the whole task of theoretical and practical philosophy is nothing else than the solution of the contradiction between the pure and the empirically conditioned I.[2] Theoretical philosophy, in order to solve the contradiction, proceeds from synthesis to synthesis, to the highest possible one in which I and not-I are identified, where, because theoretical reasoning ends in contradictions, practical reason enters in order to cut the knot by means of absolute demands.

If, therefore, the principle of all philosophy were to lie in the empirically conditioned I (about which dogmatism and the unfinished criticism basically agree), then all spontaneity of the I, theoretical as well as practical, would be quite unexplainable. For the theoretical I strives to posit the I and the not-I as identical and, therefore, to elevate the not-I itself to the form of the I; the practical strives for pure unity by exclusion of all that is not-I. Both of them can do what they do only inasmuch as the absolute I has absolute causality and pure identity. Thus the ultimate principle of philosophy cannot be anything that lies outside the absolute I; it can be neither a phenomenon nor a thing in itself.

The absolute I is not a phenomenon. Even the very concept of absoluteness forbids it. It is neither a phenomenon nor a thing in itself, because it is no thing at all, but simply and purely I, which excludes all that is not-I.

The last point on which all our knowledge and the entire series of the conditional depend, cannot be conditioned by anything ulterior at all. The entirety of our knowledge has no stability if it has nothing to stabilize it, if it does not rest on that which is carried by its own strength. And that is nothing else than that which is real through freedom. The beginning and the end of all philosophy is *freedom*!

Notes

1   Perhaps I can make this matter clearer if I return to the above-mentioned example. For me, God cannot be the ground of the reality of knowledge if He is determined as an object because, if so determined, He would fall into the sphere of conditional knowledge. However, if I should determine God not as an object at all but as = I, then indeed He would be the real ground of my knowledge. Still, that determination is impossible in the theoretical philosophy. Nevertheless, even in theoretical philosophy, which determines God as an object, a determination of God's essence as = I is necessary and then I must indeed assume that for Himself God is the absolute and real ground of His own knowledge, but not for me. For me, in theoretical philosophy, He is determined not only as I but also as object. Yet if He is an I, then, *for Himself*, he is not object at all but only I. Incidentally, it follows that one falsely depicts the ontological proof of God's existence as deceptive artifice; the deception is quite natural. For, whatever can say *I* to itself, also

says *I am*! The pity is that, in theoretical philosophy, God is not determined as identical with my I but, in relation to my I, is determined as an object, and an ontological proof for the existence of an object is a contradictory concept. [*Editors' Note*. This and the following note were published in the 1809 edition of *Of the I*.]

2   The word *empirical* is usually taken in a much too narrow *sense*. Empirical is everything that is in contrast to the pure I, everything essentially related to a not-I, even the original positing of any contrast as posited in some not-I, a positing which is an act that has its source in the I itself, the very act by which any contrasting becomes possible. *Pure is* what exists without relation to objects. *Experienced is what* is possible only through objects. *A priori is what* is possible only in relation to objects but not through them. *Empirical* is that which makes objects possible.

First Outline of a System of the Philosophy of Nature (1799)[*]

The Unconditioned in Nature

The subject which is to be the object of philosophy in a given instance must be viewed, in a word, as *unconditioned*. The question arises as to what extent *unconditionedness* might be ascribed to Nature.

1) First of all, we must try to secure the concept of the unconditioned. To this end, however, we are in need of a few principles that are assumed as well known from transcendental philosophy.

FIRST PRINCIPLE. *The unconditioned cannot be sought in any individual 'thing' nor in anything of which one can say that it 'is'. For what 'is' only partakes of being, and is only an individual form or kind of being. – Conversely, one can never say of the unconditioned that it 'is'. For it is* BEING ITSELF, *and as such, it does not exhibit itself entirely in any finite product, and every individual is, as it were, a particular expression of it.*

ELUCIDATION. What is asserted by this principle obtains universally overall and for the unconditioned in every science. For although only transcendental philosophy raises itself to the Absolute Unconditioned in

---

[*]Translated by Keith R. Peterson from F.W.J. Schelling, *Historisch-kritische Ausgabe*, ed. Wilhelm G. Jacobs und Paul Ziche (Stuttgart: Frommann-Holzboog, 2001), Series One, Volume Seven.

human knowledge, it must nevertheless demonstrate that every science that is *science* at all has its unconditioned. The above principle thus obtains also for the philosophy of nature: 'the unconditioned of Nature *as such* cannot be sought in any individual natural object'; rather a *principle* of being, that itself 'is' not, manifests itself in each natural object. – Now, since the unconditioned cannot be thought under the predicate of being, it obviously follows that as principle of all being, it can participate in no higher being. For if everything that 'is' is only, as it were, the colour of the unconditioned, then the unconditioned itself must everywhere become manifest through itself – like light that requires no higher light in order to be visible.

Now, what is this *being itself* for transcendental philosophy, of which every individual being is only a particular form? If, according to these very principles, everything that exists is a construction of the spirit, then *being itself* is nothing other than *the constructing itself*, or since construction is thinkable at all only as activity, *being itself* is nothing other than the *highest constructing activity*, which, although never itself an object, is the principle of everything objective.

Accordingly, transcendental philosophy knows of no originary being.[1] For if *being itself* is only *activity*, then the individual being can only be viewed as a determinate form or limitation of the originary activity. – Now *being* ought to be something just as little primary in the *philosophy of nature*; 'the concept of being as an originary substratum should be absolutely eliminated from the philosophy of nature, just as it has been from transcendental philosophy.' The above proposition says this and nothing else: 'Nature should be viewed as unconditioned.'[2]

Now Nature itself is, according to general consensus, nothing other than the *sum total of existence*;[3] it would therefore be impossible to view Nature as an unconditioned, if the concealed trace of freedom could not be discovered in the concept of being itself.[4] *Therefore* we assert: every individual (in Nature) is only a form of being itself; *being itself* however = absolute activity. For, if being itself is = to activity, then the individual being cannot be an absolute *negation* of activity. Nevertheless, we must think the natural product itself under the predicate of being. However, viewed from a higher standpoint, this being itself is nothing other than a *continually operative*[5] *natural activity* that is extinguished in its product. – Originally, no *individual being* at all (as an accomplished fact) is present for us in Nature, for otherwise our project is not philosophy, but empirical investigation. – We must observe what an *object* is in its *first origin*. First of all, everything that is in Nature, and Nature considered as sum total of *existence*, is not even present for us. To philosophize about Nature means *to create* Nature. Every activity perishes in its product, because it reaches only to this product. Thus we do not know *nature as product*. We know Nature only as *active* – for it is impossible to philosophize about any subject which cannot be engaged in activity. To philosophize about nature means to heave it out of the dead mechanism to which it seems predisposed, to quicken it with freedom and to set it into its own free development – to philosophize about nature means, in other words, to tear *yourself* away from the common view which discerns in nature only what 'happens' – and which, at most, views the act as a *factum, not the action itself* in its acting.[6]

2) We have answered the first question (how unconditionedness may be ascribed to Nature) through the assertion that Nature has to be viewed as *absolutely active*. This answer itself drives us to the new question: how can Nature be observed as absolutely active, or more clearly expressed: *in what light must the totality of Nature appear to us, if it is absolutely active?*[7]

The following principle must serve us in answering this question.

SECOND PRINCIPLE. *Absolute activity cannot be exhibited by a finite product, but only by an* INFINITE *one.*

ELUCIDATION. The Philosophy of Nature, so that it does not degrade into an empty play with concepts, must demonstrate a corresponding *intuition* for all of its concepts. Therefore, the question arises how an absolute activity (if there is such a thing in Nature) will present itself empirically, i.e. in the finite.

– Possibility of the exhibition of the infinite in the finite – is the highest problem of all systematic science. The subordinate sciences solve this problem in *particular cases*. Transcendental philosophy has to solve the problem in its greatest *universality*. – This solution will doubtless eventuate in the following result.

The illusion that surrounds the entire investigation concerning the infinite in all sciences issues from an amphiboly in this concept itself. – The *empirically infinite* is only the external intuition of an *absolute (intellectual) infinity* whose intuition is originally in us, but which could never come to consciousness without external, empirical exhibition. The proof of this is that this intuition comes to the fore precisely when the empirically infinite series lying before the imagination is obliterated ('I blot it out, and you lie fully before me'[8]). If, that is, the finite can be intuited only externally, then the infinite cannot even be presented in external intuition otherwise than through a *finitude* which is never complete, i.e. which is *itself infinite*.

In other words, it can only be presented by *infinite becoming*,[9] where the intuition of the infinite lies in no individual moment, but is only *to be produced* in an endless progression – in a progression, however, which no power of imagination can sustain. Therefore, reason determines either to obliterate the series,[10] or to assume an ideal limit to the series which is so far removed that in practical employment one can never be compelled to go beyond it (as the mathematician does when he assumes an infinitely large or small magnitude).

But now, how must one represent an infinite series if it is only the external exhibition of an *original* infinity? Are we to believe that the infinite is produced in the series through *aggregation*, or rather ought we to represent any such series in *continuity*, as one function running to infinity? – The fact that in mathematics, infinite series are composed of magnitudes, proves nothing on behalf of that assumption. The *originally infinite* series, of which every individual series in mathematics is an imitation, does not arise through *aggregation*, but through *evolution*, through evolution of a magnitude already *infinite in its point of origination* which runs through the entire series. The whole infinity is originally concentrated in this one magnitude. The succession in the series signifies only, as it were, the individual *inhibitions*[11] which continually set bounds to the expansion of that magnitude into an infinite series (an infinite space), and which moreover happens with an infinite velocity and would permit no real intuition.

The genuine concept of an *empirical infinity* is the concept of an *activity*[12] that *is infinitely inhibited*. But how could it be inhibited to infinity if it did not flow into infinity and if it did not deposit its whole infinity in every individual point of the line that it describes?

CONSEQUENCES FOR THE PHILOSOPHY OF NATURE
(which are at once to be seen as the response to our second question above).

FIRST CONSEQUENCE. *If Nature is absolute activity, then this activity must appear as inhibited ad infinitum.*[13] (*The original cause of this inhibition must again only be sought* IN ITSELF, *since Nature is* ABSOLUTELY *active.*)

SECOND CONSEQUENCE. *Nature* EXISTS *nowhere as product; all individual productions in Nature are merely apparent products, not the absolute product that always* BECOMES *and never* IS, *and in which the absolute activity exhausts itself.*[14]

According to the first principle, an *original duality* must simply be presupposed in Nature. For it permits of no further derivation, because it is the only condition under which an infinite is finitely presentable at all, i.e. the condition under which a Nature is at all possible. Through this original antithesis in itself, Nature will now be for the first time truly whole and complete in itself.[15]

Since Nature gives itself its sphere of activity, no foreign power can interfere with it; all of its laws are immanent, or *Nature is its own legislator* (autonomy of Nature).

Whatever happens in Nature must also be explained from the active and motive principles which lie in it, or *Nature suffices for itself* (autarchy of Nature).

They are both contained in the proposition: *Nature has unconditioned reality*,[16] a proposition which is precisely the principle of a philosophy of nature.

Notes

1   of no being in itself. [*Editors' Note.* This note and those that follow record Schelling's own later additions to the text.]
2   The philosopher of nature treats nature as the transcendental philosopher treats the self. Thus Nature itself is an unconditioned to him. This is not possible, however, if we proceed from objective being in Nature. In philosophy of nature objective being is as little something originary as in transcendental philosophy.
3   and to that extent Nature would be understood as *object*.
4   if the trace of a loftier concept, the concept of activity, did not lie in the concept of being itself.
5   uniformly operative.
6   In the usual view, the original productivity of nature disappears behind the product. For us the product must disappear behind the productivity.
7   productive.
8   *Translator's Note.* From Albrecht von Haller's 'Incomplete Poem on Eternity' (1762).
9   by *letting-become*.
10   When the series is obliterated, nothing remains except the feeling of an infinite tendency in ourselves –.
11   through reflection.
12   tendency.
13   otherwise no empirical presentation of it is possible.

14 Productivity is originally infinite; thus even when a product comes to be, this product is only an apparent product. Each product is a point of inhibition, but the infinite still 'is' in each point of inhibition.

15 and so it should be.

16 = Nature has its reality by virtue of itself – it is its own product – a whole, self-organizing and organized by itself.

The Ages of the World, 3rd version (1815)*

Even as the outcome of the future, God has taken pains to envelop in dark night the beginning of the past. It is not given to everyone to know the end, it is given to few to see the primordial beginnings of life, to fewer still to think through the totality of things from the first to the last. As by an inevitable fate, the senses of those are confused who pursue such an investigation not by reason of an inner impulse, but as imitation; for fortitude is necessary to hold fast the continuity of movement from beginning to end. But, where action alone is decisive, they would like to smooth over everything with pacific, general concepts, and to present a history where, in reality, scenes of war and peace, pain and pleasure, deliverance and peril, alternate as a mere sequence of thoughts.

A light in this darkness is that just as man, according to the old and nearly threadbare saying, is the world on a small scale, so the processes of human life from the utmost depths to its highest consummation must agree with the processes of universal life. It is certain that whoever could write the history of his own life from its very ground, would have thereby grasped in a brief conspectus the history of the universe. Most men turn from the obscurities of their own inner lives just as from the depths of that great life, and avoid a view into the abysses of that past which still is in man too much as present.

Because of this avoidance, and because I am conscious that I do not discuss something known or popular, or what is in agreement with what is accepted, it seems all the more necessary to me first to recall the nature of all that happens, how everything begins in darkness, since no one sees the goal, and the individual occurrence is never intelligible by itself, but only the entire event when it has completely transpired. We must also recall

---

*Translated by Frederick de Wolfe Bolman, Jr. from F.W.J. Schelling, *Sämmtliche Werke* (Stuttgart and Augsberg: Cotta, 1856–1861), Division One, Volume Eight.

that all history, not only in reality but also in narration, can only be relived; it cannot be communicated by a universal concept all at once, as it were. Whoever wishes knowledge of history must make the long journey, dwell upon each moment, submit himself to the gradualness of the development. The darkness of the spirit cannot be overcome suddenly, nor with a single blow. The world is not a riddle whose solution could be given in a single word; its history is too involved to be presented, as it were, in a few short, chopped-off sentences on a page of paper, as some seem to wish.

But to tell the truth, in true science as little as in history are there propositions properly speaking, that is, assertions which are valid in and by themselves or apart from the movement by which they are produced, or which have an unlimited and universal validity. What is essential in science is movement; deprived of this vital principle, its assertions die like fruit taken from the living tree. Propositions which are unconditioned, that is, valid once for all, are antagonistic to the nature of true science, which consists in progress. [...]

God is the oldest of beings. This judgement is said to be as ancient as Thales of Miletus. But the concept of God is of great, indeed, of the very greatest compass, and not thus to be expressed in one word. Freedom and necessity are in God. The latter is already acknowledged in that a necessary existence is ascribed to him. To speak naturally, necessity is in God before freedom, inasmuch as a being must first be in order to be able to act freely. Necessity lies at the basis of freedom and, as far as there can be such a distinction in God, is the first and oldest thing in God himself, which is only to be clarified by further consideration. Now, even though the God who is the necessary is also he who is the free, the two are not the same. What a being is by nature and what it is by freedom are two quite different things. If it were already everything by necessity, then it would be nothing by freedom. And yet, by common consent, God is the most spontaneous being.

Everyone recognizes that God created beings besides himself, not by virtue of a blind necessity of his nature, but by the highest spontaneity. Indeed, to be more exact, by virtue of God's mere necessity there would be no creature, since that necessity only refers to God's being as his own. Thus in creation God surmounts by freedom the necessity in his nature, and it is freedom which overcomes necessity, not necessity which overcomes freedom.

What is necessary in God we call God's nature. Its relation to freedom is similar to (not the same as) the relation which Scripture shows between the natural and the spiritual life of man, where, by the former, is understood not merely that which is commonly called physical, namely, corporeal; soul and spirit, if not born again, that is, raised to a different, higher life, as well as the body, also belong to the natural life. The abstract concept of nature is as little known to all antiquity as to Scripture.

But even this nature of God is living, is indeed the greatest vitality, and not to be expressed at once. Only by progress from the simple to the compound, by gradual generation, may we hope to attain the entire concept of this vitality.

All agree that the deity is a being of all beings, the purest love, infinite communicativeness and emanation. Yet they wish at the same time that it exist as such. By itself, however, love does not come to be. To be is se-ity [*Seinheit*], own-ness, seclusion. Love, however, is the nought of ownness; it does not seek what is its own, and therefore also by itself cannot have being. Hence a being of all beings is by itself without support and supported by nothing; it is in itself the antithesis of personality. Thus another power making for personality must first give it a ground. An equally eternal power of selfhood, of egoity, is demanded so that the being which is love may subsist as independent and be for itself.

There are thus two principles even in what is necessary in God: the outflowing, outspreading, self-giving essence, and an equally eternal power of selfhood, of return unto self, of being-in-self. Without his further deed, God is in himself both of these, that essence and this power.

It is not enough to see the antithesis; it must also be recognized that these contraries are equally essential and original. The power by which the essence confines itself, denies itself, is in its kind as real as the contrary principle; each has its own root, and neither is to be derived from the other. For if this were to be the case, then the antithesis would again immediately cease. But it is in itself impossible that exact opposites be derived from each other.

[...]

The true meaning of that unity which was originally asserted is therefore this: one and the same (= x) is the unity as well as the antithesis; or the two opposites, the eternally negating and eternally affirming potency, and the unity of the two, constitute the one, indivisible primordial essence.

And only now, after the complete development of that initial concept, are we able to view primal nature in its complete vitality. We see it in a sense broken down primitively into three powers. Each of these powers is able to be for itself, as unity is unity for itself, and each of the opposites is the whole, complete essence. Yet there cannot be one without the others, for only together do they fulfil the entire concept of the godhead, and only God must be. None of these powers is necessarily and by nature subordinated to the others. With respect to that indivisible primordial essence, the negating potency is as essential as the affirming one, and the unity, again, is not more essential than each of the opposites is by itself. Thus each has also precisely the same claims to be the essence, that which is [*das Seiende*]; none can by nature be satisfied merely to be, or not to be that which is.

The law of contradiction, which says that opposites cannot in one and the same case simultaneously be that which is, finds its application here at last. God, according to the necessity of his nature, is an eternal No, the highest being-in-self, an eternal retraction of his nature into himself, in which retraction no creature could live. But with a like necessity of his nature, although not as the same, but according to a completely dissimilar principle, one different from the first, God is the eternal Yes, an eternal outgoing, giving, communicating of his essence. Each of these principles is in just the same way the essence, that is, each has the same claim to be God or that which is. Yet they are mutually exclusive; if one is that which is, then the other can only be what is not [*das nicht Seiende*]. But God is just as eternally the third principle or unity of the Yes and the No. As the opposites exclude each other from being that which is [*seiend-Sein*], so the unity again excludes the antithesis, and thus each of the opposites; and again, the antithesis as such, or even each one of the two opposites, excludes the unity from being what is [*seiend-Sein*]. If the unity is that which is, then the antithesis, that is, each of the opposites, can only be what is not. And again, if one of the opposites and thus the antithesis is, then the unity can only retreat into what is not.

Now it is not as if all three could remain inactive and the contradiction itself thus remain hidden. For these three compose the necessary nature, the essence, which is not permitted not to be, which absolutely must be. But the essence can only be the inseparable union of these three; none by itself would fulfil the entire concept of the necessary nature (of the godhead), and each of these three has the same right to be the essence, i.e. that which is.

[...]

Contradiction alone brings life even into the first necessary nature, which we have considered merely conceptually until now. In primal nature there is thus necessarily a decision, even if one which happens only blindly, since each of the three principles, whose indissoluble concatenation constitutes this primal nature, is by its nature that which is; but if the one is such, then necessarily the others are not, and at the same time primal nature does not have the freedom to be or not to be. If the one is, then the other is not; yet each should and must equally be that which is. Thus there is nothing left but an alternate positing, since now the one is, the others not, and then again one of the latter two is and the others not. Yet, in order that this alternating positing may happen in that primordial impulse to be, it is necessary that one be the beginning or what is first [*das erste Seiende*], and that after this there be a second and a third, and from this again the movement returns to the first, and thus there is an eternally ending and eternally renewing life.

But just in order that one begin, that one be the first, a decision must ensue, which, to be sure, cannot happen consciously, by deliberation, but only in the pressure between the necessity and the impossibility of being, by a violence blindly breaking the unity. That alone in which a determinative ground for the priority of the one and the consequence of the other can be sought, however, is the particular nature of each one of the principles, a nature which is distinguished from their common nature, which consists in this, that each is equally original, equally independent, and each has the same claim to be that which is. Not that one of the principles would have to be absolutely the one which precedes or which follows, but only that, permitted by its special nature, the possibility is given to it to be the first, the second, or the third.

Presentation of the Purely Rational Philosophy (c. 1847)*

The science that is above all sciences – even before it exists for itself – is there for the other sciences, for none of these are justified on account of their object. If one would demand, for example, that physics should first prove the existence of matter, it would less likely focus on this than demand that the inquisitor search for the answer in another science. Likewise, every other science follows certain general and particular presuppositions without critically discussing their validity or pursuing them up to the final grounds. Consequently, these sciences univocally point to a science that explicitly concerns itself with the presuppositions that they, accordingly, posit not merely outside themselves but rather above themselves. The science, therefore, that is above all sciences also searches for the object that is above all objects. This cannot in turn be *a being* (for, whatever is some specific

---

*Translated by Tyler Tritten from Lecture 13 in F.W.J. Schelling, *Sämmtliche Werke* (Stuttgart and Augsberg: Cotta, 1856–1861), Division Two, Volume One.

being is already annexed by one of the other sciences), but one can only say that it is *that which is being*.[1]

This object can already be preferentially sought for its own sake; for, given that human nature is in general desirous of knowing, it will naturally and most readily desire that in which there is the most to be known. Moreover, if we, according to Aristotle, also love the types of knowledge that come to us through the mere senses not merely on behalf of our enjoyment or our needs but for their own sake, and amongst these we foremost desire those through which we know the most (already, an ancient book says: the eye never has enough of seeing nor the ear its fill of hearing[2]), then for us the knowledge of the object that is above all others and in which all others are conceived will be the one most worthy of desire for its own sake. This desiring may already merit the name 'philosophy'. For, even the pure knowledge of that object for itself and without any further consequence should already be called the highest possible *sophia* [wisdom] and if one sees that it must be acquired and that, in this sense, it must be learned, then it is the highest thing to be learned in itself, the *megiston mathema* [highest teaching], as Plato puts it.[3]

Admittedly, this object will be sought not only for its own sake, but for the sake of *science*, namely, with the intention that for us everything should be derived from the object. In this respect, it is also called the *principle*. Should this derivation be successful, then the science that arises through this means will be deductive *in the highest sense*. Under the *deductive* sciences in general belong even those which are particularly demonstrative (the mathematical sciences). These, however, posit certain limits for themselves which they do not transgress. Their points of departure are *definitions* also in the sense of borders (*horismoi*), which they give to themselves in order not to stray beyond that from which deduction is no longer possible. These sciences, therefore, also do not possess the unconditioned understanding of things, but only from these boundaries. For just this reason even that by virtue of which the subject matter develops does not proceed from the object itself but simply collapses into the subject and only produces a conditioned conviction. The highest science is indeed derivative from a higher principle, from the unconditioned principle.

How the highest science, however, is conducted in this derivation still lies far afield. The first question is how to reach the *principle*. This was shown in the previous lecture but by no means generally stated and explained. It is, for example, not stated whether that presentation is itself scientific and, if it is not science, what it would otherwise be. That even the path to the principle itself would again be a science appears evidently unthinkable. One can derive everything from the principle but the principle itself from nothing, since nothing is above it. Also, if every other science points of its own accord to a higher science that cannot in turn be a science like them but simply science *simpliciter, science itself,* which, for this reason, cannot also proceed from a principle but only from that which, against all else, is the principle as such, then it would be absurd to think that this science would itself again make recourse to science and so plunge the matter into the infinite. That science must therefore occur once which can never be preceded by science in an equivalent sense, namely, a science that is itself already derived from a principle.[4]

If not a science, then there must minimally be a *method* that leads to the principle. Aside from the deductive science, which moves from the principle as from the universal to the particular, there can only be *one* other science, that of the inverted path from the particular to the universal, thus that science generally termed inductive. But now how should inductive science be applicable here? From where should the particular come to us which is the path to the universal?

Let us remember the distinctions of being that we found in the prior lecture, although indeed only in the course of a historical development and not without proceeding from the concept given through Kant (of the totality of all possibilities[5]). The distinctions of being indicate that each of these is only that which is being in a *certain* sense, thus they are not that which is being *unconditionally*, but they *are* and *are not*; they are in one sense and are not in another, thus each is only conditionally, only hypothetically, i.e. each actually only *can be.* The distinctions of being show that it is first said of *that* which, all by itself, is all modes of being in itself that it *is* that which is being. Here the path accordingly proceeded from what is that which is being only in a particular way, and hence only what it *can be* in general, to that which it is universally, to that which it is as such. Now, would not such a path not also be termed induction? Certainly it would but, according to the concept which one customarily associates with this term, only on condition that the elements of this induction would be derived from experience.

Now, it would certainly not be unthinkable in general that science might indeed descend forth from the unconditioned principle in a continuous series unto that which is given in accord with experience and in this sense it would arise *a priori.* Yet the principle itself would only be reached through procession from experience and what is given *a posteriori.* It would be reached *in this manner* – namely, it would have to be expressed in general terms – because the question cannot be of how the individual might surmount to any science at all. In this respect, therefore, even the Aristotelian dictate that the first concepts must be known by us through induction is not applicable. For, apart from this nobody would imagine that the soul which is still entirely similar to a *tabula rasa* [blank slate] might be elevated to philosophy and not rather that first the one who has become acquainted with the whole breadth and depth of that to be conceived through experience is the one most called to philosophy. Even for the one who has been elevated to the highest standpoint and to the thought of the science originating there, indeed, even for this one, only a new school of experience will be disclosed. Individual experiences are communicated only in the form of confessions and I do not suppose I am in error in believing that some would appear more learned if they would have limited themselves to confessions instead of wanting to be philosophers by profession. The Arabic philosopher Ibn Yaqdhan, in the well-known story that Edward Pococke published under the title *Philosophus autodidactus*,[6] has sought to portray the inner advance of the individual from the first impressions to actual philosophy. Yet, what holds for the individual must also hold for the masses. At least we will become the ones who, just now, have shown across which steps contemporary philosophy, in order to fulfil the task that has been imparted to it by Christianity, has advanced up to the present moment. An equivalent advance, an equivalent testing of the possible positions between the earliest standpoint, for which that which is being was in objects of experience – air, fire etc. – took place up until Plato, who was the first to be elevated to a consciousness of that which is being as being [*dem seyend-Seyenden*], the *ontos on* [what is being-ly] as he called it, as something set apart from all matter. Certainly, at least we, who accept an actual *history* of philosophy, will contradict the following assertion: Philosophy is a science of experience in this subjective sense. The question, however, which is of concern, is rather the objective one of whether the elements of that induction, which, as is now settled for us, can be the solitary method that leads to the principle itself, are to be derived from experience.

[…]

Until now we have taken induction only in the particular sense that the elements of which it makes use are derived from experience. Taken alone, one wonders whether this restriction lies in the concept of the method itself, for which it rather seems to suffice that one runs through the particular to the universal irrespective of how this particular is given. That it is able to be given only through experience is for the time being still an unjustified assumption. The path upon which we embarked in the last lecture, admittedly in a manner that was more experimental than decisive, comprised a traversal through the different modes of being ($-A$, $+A$, $\pm A$[7] are for themselves *singulars* = the *kath' hekasta* [what is the case at any time];

they are not yet the universal itself). It was a traversal through that which is only possibly and determinately that which is being to that which is actually and universally that which is being. Should this traversal any less be called induction simply because its moments are not derived from experience (in the customary sense) but are found *in pure thinking* (even if we are only just now becoming aware of this) and for this reason alone are found in such a manner that we can be assured of completeness in such a way that is never true of the other type of induction?

In fact, if we recall how we arrived at the elements of that which is being, it thus appears that we are thereby determined *only through that which is possible and impossible in thinking*. For, if it is asked 'What is that which is being?' it is not at our discretion what we want to posit first and what we posit afterwards concerning what that which is being can be. In order to know what that which is being is we must attempt to think it (which nobody can be forced to do in the way one is compelled to represent that which his senses impose upon him). Yet, whoever attempts it will quite quickly become aware that the first claim to be that which is being is only something to which the pure subject of being is entitled. Thinking refuses to posit anything at all before this; the first cognizable (*primum cogitabile*) is *only* this. Another expression which has become a classic through Spinoza is, '*id, cujus conceptus non eget conceptu alterius rei*' [that whose concept does not need the concept of any other thing], which is likewise *only* true of that which is not in the objective sense (for everything objective [*alles Gegenständliche*] presupposes something against which it stands) but rather in the originary [*urständlichen*] sense. As we can also say, it is only that which is being *in itself.* Herein lies a privation (*stérēsis*) which does not let us rest but having posited *this* (what is being only in itself) we *must* also posit the other. For, being which is *only* objective and subjectless, thus (as we can equally state the matter), that which is being *outside itself*, likewise clearly appertains to complete and perfect being. Only we cannot express this all at once, such that we say that if we can posit being as this and as that, then we can posit it as this only at first and as that only afterwards so that we can now determine both also as *moments* of that which is being. Evidently, however, in this manner privation is posited in both and thus there is no standstill. What, meanwhile, was not immediately to be thought has become possible through just this, that both contraries go in advance. In this way that which is being – which in the first place was only able to be subject and in the second place only object – has both that against which it is as subject as well as that against which it is as object. It therefore has that through which it is both and yet can remain One in itself, whence the concept arises of that with power over itself, of being which is with itself (in being-with-itself lies both the in-itself and that which is being-outside-itself). This, therefore, is only the third possibility. That which is being, in this sense (as that which is being-with-itself), is only possible as the excluded third, if we again permit ourselves to use this expression in the affirmative sense where the discussion is merely of contrariety – which in relation to the contradictorily opposed is negative and the possibility of the third is denied – namely, in such a way that to exclude means *to posit* outside itself.

The spontaneous use of expressions that cause one to recall known logical axioms by itself indicates the region in which we find ourselves, namely, that region in which laws of thinking are laws of being. These laws do not determine, as Kant so generally believed, the mere form, but the content of knowledge in the preparatory region of *the* science that has as principle not another science but rather, according to Aristotle, *reason*. This is not *any* thinking at all but *thinking itself*, which has a domain for itself, a region that it *shares* with no other knowledge, that thinking of which the aforementioned Aristotle says (in the well-known argument of the second book of the *Posterior Analytics*) that it surpasses the *truth* and *perspicacity* of science. We just had a demonstration of this; since, for example, in thinking nothing can be *prior* to the subject, so it will not be known but felt, exceeding through this immediacy every mediated (at first disclosed or discovered through some new development) truth of evidence. Nothing could be more ill-advised than to want to seek the principles and the principle in the same manner as one new to science deigns to proceed. It will be better, however, to return to this later in the course of our conversation. Thinking, we said, has its own content. This content, which reason alone has from itself and not from anything else, is *that which is being* in general and in particular only those *moments* can be, of which each for itself only *can be* that which is being (namely, if the others accompany it). Each is thus only a possibility or potency of that which is being. *These* possibilities, however, cannot be thought simply like other possibilities but rather as how that which is being can in no way *not* be thought (since, if that which is being is taken away, so all thinking is also taken away). These possibilities, therefore, are those not just to be thought but those not at all not to be thought, thus those which are necessarily thought. Hence, in their way and in the domain of reason, they *are* just as much as the realities of experience are in *their* manner and in *their* domain. These possibilities are the first possibilities from which all others are derived, possibly becoming for us principles of all being.

[...]

Subject, object, subject-object: that is the stuff of origin of that which is being. What is wanted, however, is not that which is being but that which *is* that which is being, that is the objective. The aim is the *principle* that really is that which is being (the others are merely possible principles). For, that being *by virtue of which* it alone *is* that which is being is something independent from its being as that which is being. It is, therefore, that through which it is itself even independent from that which is being. It is the being that it has in *itself*, thus that it has independently of those presuppositions which proceed only in thinking and are only *logoi protera* [prior principles]. It is the being in virtue of which it is *protos on*, first in being, before which none other precedes and that, for this reason, is already something particular. It is the being in which thinking has its *aim*. When we approach it, thinking is consummated and has its full satisfaction. What is possible by virtue of thinking, what lets itself be thought, *is thought*, thus *above* this being no more is to be thought, thus not even more to doubt; it is *simply indubitable* being. This is that, therefore, from which one can begin, namely, if one first has it for itself.

This, which is in some sense being, is accordingly the *object* sought since Descartes but not found. This is the thing determined completely through the Idea, of which Kant speaks, which is thus also found in pure thinking prior still to all science, hence the thinking that cannot be mediated has its aim in this and science its presupposition. Reason strives after this not in order to rest there but at first rather, as will be shown, in order to reach everything else from it as something likewise determined through thinking. Reason strives after this in the great examination or hearing, from which reason has its name and towards which it intends to pull everything thinkable and actual – in order to speak nothing freely, i.e. to let be valid, what reason has not brought forth from the object in pure thinking – so that after the expulsion of everything foreign (heteronymous) the perfect transparency of knowledge is possible and the path is at least opened to that thoroughly autocratic or self-governing science.

Notes

1   After thinking has become free even with respect to its object and is directed solely towards itself, what can it then seek, what can it want? Evidently, it does not want that which is utterly non-being [*das ganz Nichtseyende*]; for, then it would have nothing, not even anything from that which is *a* being. Now, that which lies at the ground of every such something is that which is

being, not however in its purity but rather that which is being posited with a determination, which therefore also cannot be an object of *pure* thinking. Thus, it is only *that which is being* which pure thinking can want, which at the present, however, has no further determination for us than its difference from everything that is simply a being or non-being. (When one has found *that which is being* in pure thinking, then it can first be shown whether one can remain with pure thinking alone or not.)

2   *Translator's Note.* Ecclesiastes 1:8.

3   *Translator's Note. Republic* VI, 505a3.

4   The Aristotelian statement applies here: 'There is no demonstration of demonstration and, moreover, no science of science.' *Posterior Analytics* II, 19.

5   *Editors' Note.* This is the Kantian concept of 'complete determination' introduced in 'The Ideal of Pure Reason' section of the *Critique of Pure Reason* (A572-3/B600-1).

6   *Editors' Note.* Ibn Tufail's novel, later translated as *The Improvement of Human Reason: Exhibited in the Life of Hai Ebn Yokdhan*, and which became an important source for Defoe's *Robinson Crusoe*.

7   *Editors' Note.* These symbols signify the three potencies of being that thought uses to construct all possible determinations of what is, can be or must be. Schelling goes to on to discuss their status in what follows.

Alternative Deduction of the Principles of Positive Philosophy (c. 1845)*

Our point of departure is that which precedes all thinking, that which exists unconditionally. The task – in this alone which is given in advance, in unconditioned being or existing (for we actually see only this in the beginning, as the *quiddity* [whatness] in it is still hidden for us) – our task, is to find the actual *monas*, i.e. that which remains, that principle which stands above everything, even in that alone which is given in advance. For, if this is to be found already with that being which precedes all thinking, which we want to call unprethinkable being, thus if the *monas* is already to be found with unprethinkable being, this *is* the question. Perhaps this

---

*Translated by Tyler Tritten from F.W.J. Schelling, *Sämmtliche Werke* (Stuttgart and Augsberg: Cotta, 1856–1861), Division Two, Volume Four.

being is only the first in being, only the first manner of appearance of the actual *monas*. It is thus to be asked whether that unprethinkable being simply permits no opposition by which it is altered and in opposition to which it could hence comport itself as something contingent. We must get away from it, get free of unprethinkable being [*das unvordenkliche Seyn*], in order to arrive at the *Idea*. This would only be possible if, through one dialectic or another, unprethinkable being would itself be shown as contingent – not as what is *simply* contingent, but yet as what is only contingently that which is necessary. Now, we have indeed affirmed that, in that which unprethinkably exists, *actus* [act] precedes all potency. That which exists necessarily is not first possible and then actual, but it is actual at once; it begins with being. Thus, that still unknown quiddity, that X of unprethinkable being, is admittedly antecedently or a priori only that which is *being*. But nothing prohibits that just this, that which is a priori being, after the fact, *post actum*, (which is here rightly appropriate to say) may be that-which-can-be. We only say that nothing prohibits this. We do not yet say that it is actually so – this can first be proved by means of succession, a posteriori. A priori only the possibility is to be apprehended that just that which in a foregoing manner is pure being may be that-which-can-be after the fact. Just for this reason, because this potency did not precede unprethinkable being, it was not able to be *overcome* in the *actus* of this unprethinkable existing. By this means, however, a not-to-be-excluded contingency is posited in unprethinkable existing. [...] Even in pure *actus* as such there is something contingent, that which merely *actu* [actually] exists necessarily or, as we can for this reason also call it, that which exists blindly. [...] That which surpasses the mere *actus* of existing, that which can be beyond this, that which for this reason is now no longer that which merely *actu* exists necessarily but rather only still that which exists essentially, i.e. that which necessarily exists necessarily, can be the *natura necessaria* [necessary nature], and the *natura necessaria*, even independently from *actually* existing, from the *actus* of existing, is that which exists necessarily, namely, according to its nature or its essence.

This *natura necessaria* would thus be first and foremost (1) that which is being unprethinkably, (2) that which has the capacity to be something other, (3) that which sways freely between both as Spirit, freely because against the capacity to be it would comport itself as being and against being it would comport itself as capacity to be.

[...]

Reason, posited outside itself at the end of negative philosophy,[1] shocked, as it were, because it sees that it cannot possess in this philosophy its *true* content as an actual content, decides to proceed from being prior to all thinking. Reason is subjected to this being, however, only in order immediately again to be erected against the same with the question concerning *what* that which is being unprethinkably is; for, in this, reason has at once and immediately only unprethinkable existing itself, just as in the inference which, as Kant says, nobody can *hold at bay*: 'if something exists (the hypothetical part of the expression shows that the presupposed is here that which can just as likely be as not be, i.e. merely contingent being), so must there be *some such something* (*what* it thus is remains undetermined) which exists in a necessary manner.' If, in the beginning, we know nothing of that which exists necessarily except its necessary existing and now the question is raised concerning its *whatness*, then the only thing to be asked is whether that which is being unprethinkably is only that *actu* or whether it is that which exists necessarily according to its *nature* (instead of this question, one could more concisely ask whether it is itself that which exists necessarily). Now, this, whether that which *actu* exists necessarily, from which we make our advance, is itself that which exists necessarily, is not to be seen a priori. For, this which *actu* exists necessarily no longer has a *prius* itself from which we could reach for it; it is, as we assumed and presupposed, the absolute *prius* and, what we are further capable of recognizing from it, it can merely be something recognized a posteriori. Accordingly, we will therefore go to work again so that we assume from the following disjunctive proposition the second part as hypothesis: 'that which *actu* exists necessarily is either this merely or that which exists necessarily itself', in order to conclude that if it is in this way for it, if in that which *actu* exists necessarily that which exists necessarily itself is (if in *necessario existens* [existing by necessity] the *natura necessaria* is), then the following must be found: namely, this, the major premise, in its general form, which we have now also at first only brought to realization. The minor premise can then only be this, namely, that all of this, which we have demonstrated as a consequence of that hypothesis, is found as what is actual, whereby then even that hypothesis has ceased to be hypothetical. [...] That which is *natura sua* [by its own nature] existing necessarily must transcend, must surpass, merely *actu* necessarily existing. It must be *more* than this alone since it cannot, in this *more*, again be that which is being; for, it is already this in advance, thus it will only be able to be that-which-*can*-be, and indeed that which can be as *self*-surpassing, surpassing its unprethinkable being. It will not be *actus* in *potentia* (potency of an *actus*); for, it is this (*actus*) a priori, thus only *potentia potentiae* [the potency of a potency]. This is now surely sufficiently obvious. [...]

We distinguish that which is *actu* existing necessarily from that which is existing necessarily itself. This is, for now, merely an *Idea*, that which *we* presuppose in unprethinkable being, but *if* it is in this (this is just our hypothesis), then it too must be raised, by means of the appearance of the opposed potency, into its Idea, i.e. it must see itself as that which is existing necessarily no longer merely in accord with *existing* but in accord with its *nature*. This is first actually God; for, God is, as was elaborated earlier, not that which is simply necessary but he is the *necessarily* necessary essence, the *natura necessaria*, who, in order to be this, does not need existing itself, who remains that which is being necessarily even when necessary being or existing is suspended. [...] It remains valid here, from the concept of that which is merely and indeed *actu* being necessarily, from which Spinoza in particular is unable to break away, to reach for the concept of that which is *natura sua* being necessarily. The dialectical here consists in the acknowledgement of the contingent in *actu* necessary existing. If, in that which is merely *actu* being necessarily, that which is being necessarily *itself* is, so must that being, that *actus*, present itself to the latter as something contingent and accordingly as something able to be suspended, not as something able to be suspended immediately and through itself – this would be impossible – but, to be sure, as able to be suspended through a being that comes thereafter, through a being outside of it, which, accordingly, must show itself as possibility. *Through* the appearance of the potency of an *other* being, merely *actu* necessary existing, which precedes this potency itself, appears as something contingent, something able to be suspended, something also capable of *not* being. Even with this, however, that which exists gets free of its existing and appears in the necessity it has independently from *this*. At bottom, we were yet only able to *want* this from the beginning, that which is necessary according to its *nature*. What presented itself *immediately* and at the first, that which is *actu* being necessarily, we have only posited *because we were not able to do otherwise*, thus, as it were, only blindly. It is blind reason which posits nothing as *actu* being necessarily. What we have named that which is being unprethinkably was, as it now shows itself, actually only the *actus* of *actus purus* [the act of pure act] [...]. Now, however, insofar as the *actus* of *actus purus* is suspended, *actus purus* itself remains behind as essence and is posited as essence. The true concept of God is none other than *actus purus* itself, i.e. to be *actus purus* as essence.

Note

1   *Editors' Note.* For an account of Schelling's distinction between positive and negative philosophy, see Part Two, Chapter 6 of this book.

Further reading

While all of Schelling's writings make metaphysical claims that have pertinence to this chapter, the full versions of the texts excerpted in both this chapter and Chapter 2 are particularly important for understanding Schelling's account of the 'unconditioned' or 'absolute'. For further reading on Schelling's metaphysics, consult:

Frederick C. Beiser, *German Idealism: The Struggle against Subjectivism, 1781–1801* (Harvard University Press, 2008), Part IV.

Dalia Nassar, *The Romantic Absolute: Being and Knowing in Early German Romantic Philosophy, 1795–1804* (University of Chicago Press, 2014), Part III.

Dale E. Snow, *Schelling and the End of Idealism* (SUNY Press, 1996).

Tyler Tritten, *Beyond Presence: The Late F.W.J. Schelling's Criticism of Metaphysics* (De Gruyter, 2012).

Tyler Tritten, *The Contingency of Necessity: Reason and God as Matters of Fact* (Edinburgh University Press, 2017), Part II.

Eric Watkins, 'The Early Schelling on the Unconditioned.' In Lara Ostaric (ed.), *Interpreting Schelling: Critical Essays* (Cambridge University Press, 2014), 10–31.

Slavoj Žižek, *The Indivisible Remainder: On Schelling and Related Matters* (Verso, 2007).

2

Identity and difference

Introduction

In contrast to the broad, fifty-year sweep presented in most of the chapters of this *Reader*, the extracts in this chapter focus on one specific issue in Schelling's metaphysics as it developed over one decade: the issue of the relation between identity and difference.

One of the effects of the popularity of Fichte's *Wissenschaftslehre* in the mid-1790s was to draw early German Idealists towards the concept of identity like moths to a flame. Fichte's first proposition, I = I, was supposed to guarantee the validity of its more abstract correlate, A = A, as the grounding logical principle of all systematic construction; the system was to begin with an assertion of identity. This made sense to many philosophers of the period, because some identity between the subject of knowing and the object of knowledge seemed to be a condition of the possibility of knowledge itself and thus of the very practice of philosophizing. (Of course, the idea here does not first emerge with German Idealism but can be traced at least as far back as the Empedoclean principle, 'like is known by like', to which Schelling refers at the beginning of his *Freedom* essay.)

The question with which the early German Idealists struggled was how to describe such identity – and, more specifically, how to describe the relation between it and difference. That is, if a system is grounded in identity, then how is it to explain the manifold differences of the sensible world? Whence comes difference? And does the ineluctable irruption of differences within the system alter how the philosopher ought to understand the very concept of identity? These are some of the basic logical and metaphysical questions that occupy Schelling at the beginning of his philosophical career, and his answers to them inform many of his ideas about nature, freedom, art, religion and politics. As should become clear from the texts that follow, Schelling's descriptions of the concepts of identity and difference serve to ground – often directly – his understanding of all natural and social phenomena.

The extracts below, moreover, track a very significant development in Schelling's thought – and one that stands at the centre of any attempt to distinguish between earlier and later 'Schellings'. From the uncompromising identity philosophy presented in its founding document, the *Presentation of My System of Philosophy* of May 1801, in which only quantitative difference is admitted into absolute identity, Schelling proceeds to seemingly backtrack on this austerity by revising his concept of identity to include a more robust form of difference, a line of thought that is pursued in the dialogue, *Bruno*, written later the same year and published in 1802. The third text extracted below, *On the Relation of the Real and the Ideal in Nature* – a treatise on the philosophy of nature from 1806 which introduces the second edition of *On the World-Soul* – exhibits Schelling's growing concern with the precise ontological significance of the copula or the 'bond' between the two terms in any judgement, e.g. the 'is' in the judgement 'the grass is green'; in what ways is 'grass' identified with 'greenness' in such a judgement, and in what ways are they differentiated? This line of thinking comes to fruition in Schelling's seminal *Freedom* essay of 1809, with a famous passage on pantheism that reinterprets the copula as a grounding relation in order to avoid what he there sees as the sterile and lifeless, traditional understanding of identity as self-sameness. Finally, in the series of private lectures given in 1810 known as *The Stuttgart Private Lectures*, Schelling expands on what this life-giving reinterpretation of A = A means for his metaphysics as a whole, particularly his doctrines of God and creation.

Presentation of My System of Philosophy (1801)[*]

§ 1. DEFINITION. I call *reason* absolute reason, or reason insofar as it is conceived as the total indifference of the subjective and objective.

It is not the place here to justify this turn of speech, since its only function is to generally awaken the idea that I shall connect with this word. – Just a brief indication must be given, then, of how one comes to understand reason

---

*Translated by Michael G. Vater from F.W.J. Schelling, *Historisch-kritische Ausgabe*, ed. Manfred Durner (Stuttgart: Frommann-Holzboog, 2009), Series One, Volume Ten.

this way. One gets there by reflecting on what presents itself in philosophy [as occupying a position] between the subjective and the objective, which evidently must be an item standing indifferently over against both extremes. The thought of reason is foreign to everyone; to conceive it as absolute, and thus to come to the standpoint I require, one must abstract from what does the thinking. For the one who performs this abstraction reason immediately ceases to be something subjective, as most people imagine it; it can of course no longer be conceived as something objective either, since an objective something or a thought item becomes possible only in contrast to a thinking something, from which there is complete abstraction here; reason, therefore, becomes the true *in-itself* through this abstraction, which is located precisely in the indifference point of the subjective and the objective.

The standpoint of philosophy is the standpoint of reason, its kind of knowing is a knowing of things as they are in themselves, i.e. as they are in reason. It is the nature of philosophy to completely suspend all succession and externality, all difference of time and everything which mere imagination[1] mingles with thought, in a word, to see in things only that aspect by which they express absolute reason, not insofar as they are objects of reflection, which is subject to the laws of mechanism and has duration in time.

§ 2. *Outside reason is nothing, and in it is everything.* If reason is conceived as we have demanded in § 1, one immediately becomes aware that nothing could be outside it. For if one supposes that there *is* something outside it, then either it *is* for-itself outside of reason and is then the subjective, which is contrary to the assumption, or it *is* not for-itself outside reason and so stands to this something-outside-it as objective item to objective item, and is therefore objective, but this again is contrary to the assumption (§ 1). Therefore nothing is outside reason, and everything is in it.

Remark. There is no philosophy except from the standpoint of the absolute, throughout this presentation, no hesitation on this matter will be entertained: reason is the absolute to the extent that it is conceived just as we determined it (§ 1); the present proposition, accordingly, is valid only under this assumption.

Explanation. All objections to this view could only refer to the situation that one is accustomed to viewing things not as they are in reason, but only as they appear. Therefore, we do not tarry with their refutation, since in what follows we must prove that everything that *is,* is in essence equal to reason and is one with it. The proposition as formulated would need of no proof or even explanation but would instead rank as an axiom, if so many people were not entirely unaware that there could be nothing at all outside reason unless reason posited it outside itself, reason never does this, however, only a false employment of reason which is joined to an inability to make the abstraction demanded above and to forget the subjective element in itself.

§ 3. *Reason is simply one and simply self-identical.* Were this not so, the being of reason would require some additional ground other than reason itself: since reason itself contains only the ground that it is, not that some other reason would be; reason would not be absolute, which is contrary to the assumption. *Reason is therefore one in an absolute sense.* But if one supposes the reverse of the second clause, namely that reason is not self-identical, then that in virtue of which it is not identical to itself must still be posited in it, and, since *outside* it (*praeter ipsam*) there is nothing (§ 2), this other factor must therefore express the essence of reason, and since, moreover, everything is in-*itself* only in virtue of its capacity to express the essence of reason (§ 1), this other factor too, considered in itself or in reference to reason, would again be equal to reason, united with it. *Reason is therefore one* (not only *ad extra* [extrinsically], but also *ad intra* [intrinsically], or) in itself, i.e. it is simply self-identical.

§ 4. The ultimate law for the being of reason, and, since there is nothing outside reason (§ 2), for all being (because it is comprehended within reason) is the law of identity, which with respect to all being is expressed by A = A.

The proof follows immediately from § 3 and the propositions that precede it.

Corollary 1. By all other laws, accordingly, if there are such, nothing is determined as it is in reason or in itself, but only as it is for reflection or in appearance.

Cor. 2. The proposition A = A is the sole truth posited *in itself*, hence without any reference to time. I designate such a truth an eternal truth, not in an empirical but in an absolute sense.

§ 5. *Definition.* I call the A of the first position the subject, to differentiate it from that of the second, the predicate.

§ 6. The proposition A = A, conceived universally, says neither that A on its own *is*, nor that it is as subject *or* predicate. Instead, *the unique being posited through this proposition is that of identity itself, which accordingly is posited in complete independence from A as subject and from A as predicate.* *The proof* of the first assertion is furnished in the *Wissenschaftslehre* § 1; the second part of the proposition follows of itself from the first and is contained within it. Since abstraction is made from the being of A in its own right, and also from its status as subject and predicate, the sole thing remaining from which abstraction cannot be made, which is therefore really posited in this proposition, is absolute identity itself.[2]

§ 7. *The sole unconditioned cognition is that of absolute identity.* Since it alone expresses the *essence* of reason (§ 3), the proposition A = A is also the unique unconditionally certain proposition (§ 4, Corollary 2), but absolute identity is also posited through this proposition (§ 6). Therefore [its cognition] is etc.

Remark. The preceding series of statements was advanced merely to show the unconditioned character of this cognition. For this cognition *itself* is not really proven, precisely because it is unconditioned.

§ 8. *Absolute identity simply IS and is as certain as the proposition A = A is.* Proof. Because it is immediately posited along with this proposition (§ 6).

Corollary 1. Absolute identity cannot be conceived except through the proposition A = A, yet it is posited through this proposition as *standing in being.* Therefore it *is* by virtue of being thought, and *it belongs to the essence of absolute identity to be.*

Cor. 2. *The being of absolute identity is an eternal truth,* since the truth of its being is equivalent to the truth of the proposition A = A. But [the proposition A = A] is [the sole truth that is in itself] (§ 4, Cor. 2) etc.

§ 9. *Reason is one with absolute identity.* The proposition A = A is reason's law of being (§ 4). Now by means of this proposition absolute identity is also immediately posited as standing in being (§ 6), and since the being of absolute identity is identical with its essence (§ 8, Corollary 1), reason is also (§ 1) one with absolute identity itself, not only in being but in essence.

Cor. Therefore the being of reason (in the sense defined in § 1) *is just as unconditioned* as that of absolute identity, or: *BEING belongs equally to the essence of reason and to that of absolute identity.* The proof follows immediately from the preceding.

§ 10. *Absolute identity is simply infinite.* – For if it were finite, then the ground of its finitude would lie either in itself or not in itself, outside it; in the first case, it would be the cause of some determination in itself, hence something simultaneously causing and caused, and therefore not absolute identity; in the second case, the ground of its finitude would be outside it. But there is nothing outside it. For if there were something outside it by which it might be limited, it would have to be related to this outside something as objective item to objective item. But this is absurd (§ 1). Therefore just as surely as it *is,* is it infinite, i.e. it is simply infinite.

§ 11. *Absolute identity can never be abolished AS identity.* For it belongs to its essence to be, but it *is* only because it is absolute identity (§§ 6, 8, Cor. 1).

Therefore it can never be abolished as such, for otherwise being would necessarily cease to belong to its essence, i.e. something contradictory would be posited. Therefore, etc.

§ 12. *Everything that is, is absolute identity itself.* Since identity is infinite and can never be abolished as absolute identity (§§ 10, 11), everything that is must be absolute identity itself.

Cor. 1. *Everything that is, is in itself one.* This proposition is merely the inversion of the preceding one, and so follows immediately from it.

Cor. 2. Absolute identity is the unique item that absolutely is or is *in itself*; so everything is in itself only to the extent it is absolute identity itself, and to the extent that it is not absolute identity itself, it is simply not *in itself.*

§ 13. *With respect to being in itself, nothing has come into being.* For everything that subsists in itself is absolute identity itself (§ 12). This, however, has not entered into being, but simply is; therefore it is posited without any connection to time and outside all time, for its being is an eternal truth (§ 8, Cor. 2). Consequently, everything viewed as being in itself is absolutely eternal.

§ 14. *Nothing, considered intrinsically, is finite.* The proof is drawn from § 10 in the same way as that of the preceding proposition.

Cor. It follows that from the standpoint of reason (§ 1) there is no finitude, and that considering things as finite is precisely the same as not considering them as they are in themselves. – To the same extent, to consider things as differentiated or multiple means not to consider them *in themselves* or from the standpoint of reason.

Explanation. The most basic mistake of all philosophy is to assume that absolute identity has actually stepped outside itself and to attempt to make intelligible how this emergence occurs. Absolute identity has surely never ceased being identity, and everything that is, is considered in itself – not just the appearance of absolute identity, but *identity itself*, and since, further, it is the nature of philosophy to consider things as they are in themselves (§ 1), i.e. insofar as they are infinite and are absolute identity itself (§§ 14, 12), true philosophy consists in the demonstration that absolute identity (the infinite) has not stepped outside itself and that everything that is, insofar as it is, is infinity itself – a proposition that Spinoza alone of all previous philosophers acknowledged, even if he did not fully carry out its demonstration, nor express it clearly enough to avoid being misunderstood ever after.

[...]

§ 23. *Between subject and predicate,[3] none other than quantitative difference is possible.[4]* For 1) any qualitative difference between the two is unthinkable. – *Proof.* Absolute identity *is,* independent of A as subject and object (§ 6), and it *is* equally unconditioned in both. Now since it is the same equal absolute identity that is posited as subject and object, there is no qualitative difference. Consequently, there remains 2) since there is no possible difference between the two in terms of being itself (because they are equally unconditioned as s.[ubject] and o.[bject], thus the same in essence), there remains only a quantitative difference, i.e. one that obtains with respect to the *magnitude* of being, such that the same identity is posited [as subject and object], but with a predominance of subjectivity or objectivity.

Explanation. We ask the reader to follow us in this proof with at least the provisional trust that it will become perfectly intelligible after one simply forgets previously obtained ideas, especially those of the customary concepts *subjective* and *objective,* and thinks in each proposition exactly and only what we wish thought, a suggestion which we make here, once and for all. This much at least is clear to everyone at the start, that we admit no opposition between subject and object (since what is posited in the one position and in the other is the very same identity; subject and object are thus in essence one), but perchance just some sort of difference between subjectivity and objectivity, which since they pertain to the form of being of absolute identity, belong to the form of every being, perhaps not in an identical way, but subsisting together in such a way that they can be alternately posited as predominant – all of which we do not yet assert here, but only advance as a possible conception. For the sake of greater clarity, we add the following remark. Since the same A is posited in the predicate and in the subject position in the proposition A = A, doubtless there is posited between the two utterly no difference at all, but an absolute indifference of the two, and difference, and consequently discriminability of two, would become possible only if either predominant subjectivity or predominant objectivity were posited, in which case A = A would have changed into A = B (B is adopted as a designation for objectivity); now either this factor or its opposite might be the predominant one, but in either case, difference commences.[5] If we express this predominance of subjectivity or objectivity by the exponent of the subjective factor, it follows that if A = B is posited, there is also conceived a positive or negative power of A, so that $A^0 = B$ must be the case just as much as A = A itself, i.e. it must be the expression of absolute indifference. Difference is simply not to be understood in any other way than this.

[...]

§ 25. *With respect to absolute identity NO quantitative difference is conceivable.*

Since this identity is identical (§ 9) to the absolute indifference of the subjective and the objective (§ 1), neither the one nor the other can be discriminated within it.

Cor. Quantitative difference is possible only *outside of* absolute identity. This proposition is just the inversion of the preceding one; it is certain, even if there is nothing except absolute identity.

§ 26. *Absolute identity is absolute totality.* – Because it is itself everything that is, or, it cannot be conceived as separated from everything that is (§ 12). It *is*, therefore, only as everything, i.e. it is absolute totality.

Definition. I call absolute totality the universe.

Cor. Quantitative difference is possible only outside absolute totality. This proposition follows directly from § 26 and § 25, Cor. 1.

§ 27. *Definition. What exists outside totality I designate in this context an INDIVIDUAL being or thing.*

§ 28. *There is no individual being or individual thing in ITSELF.* For the unique *in-itself* is absolute identity (§ 8). But this is only as totality (§ 26).

Remark. There *is* also nothing in itself outside totality, and if something is viewed outside the totality, this happens only by an arbitrary separation of the individual from the whole which is effected by reflection. But in itself this separation simply does not happen, since everything that is, is one (§ 12 Cor. 1) and is absolute identity itself inside the totality (§ 26).

[...]

§ 32. *Absolute identity is not cause of the universe, but the universe itself.* For everything that *is*, is absolute identity itself (§ 12). But the universe is everything that is, etc.

Remark. The long and profound ignorance about this principle will perhaps excuse our dwelling a while longer on this proof that absolute identity is the universe itself and that it cannot be under any other form than that of the universe. This may be especially necessary for those who stand so firm and hardened, as it were, in common sense beliefs that they cannot be torn away from them by philosophical argument (the taste for which they lack). I am nonetheless convinced that everyone will be persuaded of this proposition when he reads over the following propositions attentively and sees that they have been irrefutably proven, to wit: 1) that absolute identity is only under the form of the proposition $A = A$, and that, since it is, so too is this form; 2) that this form is *primordial*, therefore linked with the absolute identity of subject and object; 3) that identity cannot be *actual* (*actu*) under this form – it is assumed it is, since absolute identity is *actu* merely because it is *potential* – unless the indifference expressed in the proposition A = A is quantitative; 4) that this quantitative indifference can *be* only under the form of absolute totality, thus, of the universe, that accordingly absolute identity, insofar as it is (*exists*) must be the universe itself.

[...]

§ 37. *Quantitative difference of the subjective and the objective is the ground of all finitude, and conversely, the quantitative indifference of the two is infinitude.*

[...]

§ 45. *Neither A nor B can be posited in itself, but only one and the same [identity] with predominant subjectivity as well as objectivity and the quantitative indifference of the two.*

Proof. There is nothing in itself outside absolute identity (§ 8), but the latter is posited unto infinity under the form of s.[ubjectivity] and o.[bjectivity] (§ 21 ff.), therefore, unto infinity (e.g. in some single part) neither subjectivity nor objectivity can be posited for itself, so when quantitative difference (A = B) is posited, it is only under the form of the predominance of one factor over the other, and this occurs equally in the whole and in the part (§ 39). But there is no reason that one should be posited as predominant over the other. Therefore both must be posited as predominant simultaneously, and this again is inconceivable without the two reducing their opposition to quantitative indifference. Therefore neither A nor B can be posited in itself, but only the identical with predominant s.[ubjectivity] and o.[bjectivity] at the same time, and the quantitative indifference of the two.

§ 46. *Subjectivity and objectivity can be posited as predominant only in opposite tendencies or directions.* [...]

Cor. Absolute identity's form of being can thus be universally conceived through the image of a *line*

$$\frac{{}^{+}A = B \qquad\qquad A = B^{+}}{A = A^{0}}$$

wherein the very same identity is posited in each direction, with predominant A or B in the opposite directions, while A = A itself falls at the point of equilibrium. (We signify the predominance of one factor over the other with the + sign.)

Explanation. For further consideration we attach some general reflections about this line.

A) The same identity is posited throughout the line, and even at $A = B^+$ is posited not B *in itself,* but only [that factor as] predominant. Exactly the same holds for A at $A^+= B$.

B) What holds for the line as a whole, holds too for each individual section of it unto infinity. – *Proof.* This is because absolute identity is posited endlessly or unto infinity, and is posited endlessly under the same form (§ 39). Therefore what holds of the whole line, holds too for each part of it unto infinity.

C) Accordingly, the constructed line is divisible unto infinity, and its construction is the ground of infinite divisibility.

Remark. From this it is evident too why absolute identity is never divided (§ 34, Cor.). That is, in every section [of the line divided] there are still three points, i.e. the entire absolute identity which *is* only under this form. – But just this fact, that absolute identity is never divided, makes possible the infinite divisibility of that which is not absolute identity, which is therefore (§ 27) an individual thing.

D) I designate $A^+= B$ and $A = B^+$ the poles [of the constructed line], but $A = A$ the indifference-point. So each point of the line, depending on how it is viewed, is the indifference-point and pole or its opposite [one of the end-poles]. – For since the line is infinitely divisible (C), and division is unconstrained in every direction, since the same [identity] *is* in every direction (A), then every point can also serve as indifference-point relative to some other, or become now one, now the other of the two opposed end-poles, depending on how I divide [the line].

Cor. From this it is clear: a) how the line, abstracted from the fact that I divide it (*idealiter* [ideally]) is, when viewed *realiter* [in reality] or in itself, absolute identity in which there is simply nothing to divide; b) how with this line, since it is the fundamental form of our entire system, we never *in abstracto* [abstractly] step outside the indifference-point.

E) The two poles may be considered as infinitely close to one another or as infinitely remote from each other. – This follows directly from the preceding propositions.

F) An infinite lengthening of this line could never produce more than these three points. – This proposition is the mere inversion of one part of the above.

§ 47. *The constructed line* (§ 46, Corollary) *is the form of being of absolute identity in the part as in the whole.*

Notes

1   *Marginal Note*. For imagination is related to reason, as phantasy is to understanding. The former is productive, the latter reproductive.
2   *Marginal Note*. The principle A = A *needs* no demonstration. It is the ground of all demonstration. What is posited by it is only unconditioned being-posited. But where this unconditioned being-posited manifests itself is completely a matter of indifference for the principle. – This A in the subject position and the other in the predicate position is not what is really posited; what is posited is only the identity between the two.
3   *Editors' Note*. That is, between the first 'A' in A = A and the second 'A' in A = A.
4   *Marginal Note*. What is derived from this same form is therefore equally eternal with absolute identity.
5   *Marginal Note*. Whether this difference is actual is completely undecided here.

Bruno, or On the Natural and the Divine Principle of Things (1802)*

BRUNO.[1] We can all agree on this fundamental notion: the idea [of the absolute], wherein all opposites are not just united. but are simply identical, wherein all opposites are not just cancelled, but are entirely undivided from one another.

So I begin by praising this principle as first and prior to all else, for if we do not adopt this identity of opposites as our principle, only two other cases are possible. Either we posit as our first principle the kind of identity that is opposed to opposition, or we shall have to suppose that opposites themselves constitute the first principle. In the first case the principle would be posited along with some opposite, [but this is impossible, since our principle would not be primary]. The second case is impossible as well, for every pair of opposites is really and truly an opposition only insofar as its members must be posited in one and the same thing.

LUCIAN. I shall obey your command to question you, and remind you of it early on. Good sir, take care not to entangle yourself in contradiction right at the start! For identity is necessarily opposed to opposition, since it

---

*Translated by Michal G. Vater from F.W.J. Schelling, *Sämmtliche Werke* (Stuttgart and Augsberg: Cotta, 1856-1861), Division One, Volume Four.

is impossible to conceptualize identity without contrasting it to opposition, or to think of opposition apart from its contrast to identity. It must therefore be impossible to posit the reality of identity without positing some real opposite along with it.

BRUNO. There is just one thing you seem to have overlooked, my worthy fellow, namely this: since we make the identity of all opposites our first principle, 'identity' itself along with 'opposition' will form the highest pair of opposites. To make identity the supreme principle, we must think of it as comprehending even this highest pair of opposites, and the identity that is its opposite as well, and we must define this supreme identity as the identity of identity and opposition, or the identity of the self-identical and the nonidentical.

LUCIAN. Quite clever, the way you jump over the trap and postulate an identity which itself connects identity and opposition! But how can you acknowledge the reality of opposition in the latter context [viz. the contrast of identity and opposition] and not be forced, for that very reason, to posit it within the former context too [or within identity itself]? Thus it seems there is no way you can reach a pure identity, no way you can attain the sort of identity that is not distorted by difference.

BRUNO. It certainly seems, my friend, that you are claiming that opposition distorts identity in both senses of the term, the identity that is opposed to opposition and the supreme identity as well, the one wherein identity itself is identical to difference. Whichever of the two you meant to assert, I intend to talk you into the opposite point of view. [Let us consider the latter case first.] If you maintain that identity and difference are opposites with respect to the supreme identity, and that the supreme identity is thus distorted by some opposition, I deny it; specifically, I deny your premise, that in the context of the supreme identity, identity and difference are opposed to one another. Hence you would be able to predicate being distorted by difference only of the kind of identity that is opposed to difference, the one that is 'identity' only insofar as it is the opposite of 'difference'. But you could not ascribe being affected by difference to that identity which transcends the opposition of identity and difference and in whose sight this opposition itself simply does not exist. Or am I wrong?

LUCIAN. I will agree for now, at least in the case of the supreme identity.

BRUNO. So you still maintain that the inferior kind of identity is affected by its opposition to difference? [This was the first sense of your objection].

LUCIAN. Of course.

BRUNO. But how are identity and difference opposed, absolutely or relatively?

LUCIAN. What do you mean by 'absolute opposition' and 'relative opposition'?

BRUNO. I say that things are relatively opposed if they can cease being opposites and can be united in some third thing. Such an identification is unthinkable for absolute opposites, though. You will have an example of relative opposition if you think of two chemical substances with opposite properties, for they can be combined and so produce a third substance. You will have an example of the other sort of opposition if you think of an object and the mirror image of that object. For can you conceive of any third thing that would allow mirror image to pass over into object or permit the object to be transformed into an image? Aren't they precisely so related that one is object, and the other image, absolutely, necessarily, and eternally distinct from one another?

LUCIAN. Certainly.

BRUNO. So what sort of opposition do you think we have to posit between identity and difference?

LUCIAN. Necessarily an absolute opposition, at least on your understanding of the situation, for you will allow their unification [not in some third, mixed thing, but] only in some higher identity.

BRUNO. Excellent! Except for the fact that you have presumed that this higher identity is cancelled and inoperative! For was it not true that you thought that identity was only distorted or diminished to the extent that it was opposed to difference?

LUCIAN. That is what I said.

BRUNO. But only if you think the higher identity is cancelled and inoperative, will identity and difference be opposed. Therefore the correct way to think of the pair is as merely relatively opposed.

LUCIAN. Certainly.

BRUNO. And since they are merely relatively opposed, so too they can be united only in a relative manner, just like the two chemical substances we discussed earlier, and [if that is the case, each will remain what it is, but] they will reciprocally restrict or limit one another.

LUCIAN. Necessarily.

BRUNO. And only to the extent that they mutually restrict and limit one another will identity be distorted, by which you mean exactly this, that identity comes to participate in difference.

LUCIAN. Quite right!

BRUNO. So when you assume that identity is beclouded by difference, you necessarily posit a relation of cause and effect between the two. It is similar to the practice of armchair philosophers who posit unity here, multiplicity there, unity exerting causal influence upon multiplicity and multiplicity acting upon unity. Yet they concede that the two mutually fit into one another, like bevelled joints of wood.

LUCIAN. God forbid I should seriously maintain such a doctrine of quantity!

BRUNO. Then you cannot seriously maintain [the first sense of your objection] either, that we must suppose that the identity whose opposite is opposition is distorted or diminished by difference.

LUCIAN. Certainly not. But one thing does not follow from your views on relative opposition and relative identity; they imply that only in the unique case of absolute opposition can opposites be absolutely identified, and vice versa! How is this so?

BRUNO. Indeed it follows! Think back for a moment to our previous example. Tell me, can you imagine a perfect identity between an object and its image, granted that it is totally impossible that the two coexist in some third substance? So you will have to suppose that they are identified in some higher sort of entity wherein that which makes an image an image, namely light, is identical with that which makes an object an object, namely body. Now if you posit the kind of world order or constellation of things where, generally speaking, if an object exists, so does an image, and if an image exists, so does an object, then necessarily, for this very reason, image and object would be together everywhere since they nowhere coincide. For things that are absolutely and infinitely opposed can only be united infinitely. And what is infinitely united can never split itself up in any way; therefore what is absolutely self-identical and absolutely indivisible must, for this very reason, be absolutely opposed to itself.

[But let us apply this to your contention that difference beclouds relative identity.] If you wanted to have identity really distorted by difference, you would have to abstract identity from the identity of identity and opposition, then suppose its independent reality; then you would have to contrast difference to it as its relative opposite. But all this is impossible, for this relative identity you have produced by abstraction is nothing outside of absolute identity, and only within the latter is it anything at all. And whatever you assert about this relative identity can be truly predicated of it only in the context of absolute identity. But in the context of absolute identity, we cannot imagine that relative identity is distorted or diminished by difference, for in the absolute perspective identity is simply not opposed to difference at all. In the absolute there is nothing but transparency, pure light. This you understand, for you have already admitted that there are no shadows of obscurity or confusion in the domain of absolute identity, inasmuch as the absolute encompasses the finite as well as the infinite, and not just as united [after the fact], but as indivisibly one.

LUCIAN. But you are certain that you have surpassed all oppositions in the entity you call the identity of identity and opposition? How do other pairs of opposites, any such as you would care to make in working out your philosophy, fit into this absolute identity?

BRUNO. On the first point, why should I not be certain? One of two cases will necessarily be true: All the typical pairs of categories we could fashion must either fall under the principle we call 'opposition' or they must fall under the heading 'identity and opposition'.

Note

1   *Editors' Note.* In this text, Schelling imagines a dialogue between four interlocuters: Bruno, Lucian, Alexander and Anselm. Bruno is, by and large, Schelling's mouthpiece, as Socrates is for Plato.

On the Relation of the Ideal and the Real in Nature (1806)*

The most obscure thing of all, yes, obscurity itself according to some, is matter. However, it is precisely this unknown root out of which arises all the forms and living appearances of nature. Without knowledge of it, physics is without a scientific basis, and science itself loses the bond by means of which the idea is connected to reality. I take matter neither to be something independent of the absolute unity, which might underlie it as a kind of stuff, nor do I regard it as mere nothingness; but rather I agree with Spinoza's statement in one of his letters, who when asked

---

*Translated by Dale Snow from F.W.J. Schelling, *Sämmtliche Werke* (Stuttgart and Augsberg: Cotta, 1856–1861), Division One, Volume Two.

if the multiplicity of corporeal things could be derived a priori out of the mere concept of extension (in the Cartesian sense), answered: I take matter instead for an attribute in which the infinite and eternal essence expresses itself.[1] Since in this case every piece of matter in itself must be an expression of the whole universe, it can hardly be an attribute that reflects the infinite essence, but rather must be regarded as the epitome of all attributes. The ancients already partly knew and partly suspected that matter had an opposition, a duality, at its foundation. That this is overcome through a third element and that it in itself presents a closed and identical triplicity is everywhere acknowledged since the new challenge posed by these investigations. Still the profundity of this subject retains an irresistible attraction for the observer, and pulls him in again and again, at least so long as he cannot convince himself that he has fully grasped it, as it appears to me to thus far be the case. For this reason I believe I have accomplished something neither unnecessary nor undesirable to the learned, when I communicate in a simple presentation the summarized results of my investigations, concerning the principles, the final results of which are matter, in the fullest sense of the word. The same principles are necessarily those of nature as a whole and finally those of the cosmos itself, and by following them we might be able to develop a symbolic picture, based on matter itself, from which the inner workings of the universe and the highest principles of philosophy could be developed. We hope that this development does not appear as a foreign addition to a work,[2] which has no worth other than the true one, to be grounded in intuition and reveal via a series of justified intimations, the all-encompassing meaning of that law of dualism which we encounter just as definitely in the most individual appearances as in the whole of the world. Already the first look at nature teaches us what the last one does; because matter expresses no other or lesser bond than that which is in reason, the eternal identity of the infinite with the finite. We recognize in things first of all the pure essentiality itself, that cannot be further explained, but rather explains itself. We see this essentiality, however, never in itself, but rather always and everywhere in a wondrous union with that which could not subsist by itself and is only illuminated by being, without ever being able to become anything essential in its own right. We call this the finite or the form.

The infinite cannot be added to the finite; for it must then be able to in itself arise out of the finite, that is, it must not be infinite. But it is just as unthinkable that the finite be added to the infinite; for it cannot exist at all prior to it, and only first becomes something in the identification with the infinite.

Both must therefore be united through a certain original and absolute necessity, if they are to appear bound together at all.

We call this necessity, at least until we find another expression, the absolute bond, or the copula.[3]

And in fact it is clear that this bond, in the infinite itself, is the true and real infinite. It would in no way be unconditioned, were the finite or nothingness to be opposed to it. It is absolute only as the absolute negation of nothingness, as absolute affirmation of itself in all forms, thus only as that which we have called the infinite copula.

It is also just as clear that reason does not recognize the true and in every relation unconditioned, when it only conceives of the infinite as the opposite of the finite.

If it is essential for each to affirm itself in the form of the finite, then it is at the same time this form, and since it exists only through the bond, then it must appear to itself as an expression of the same unity of the infinite and the finite.

Just as necessary and eternal as these two are also together as bond and bound, indeed the identity and the particularity of these is itself only the real and at the same time higher expression of this first identity. Should the bond be posited in the first place, then it must abolish itself as bond, if it is not to posit the infinite reality in the finite, that is, if it does not at the same time posit that which is bound.

The bond and that which is bound do not constitute a doubled and differing reality; but rather that which is in the one is also in the other; that in terms of which the bound is in no respect like the bond is necessarily nullified, since the essentiality consists precisely in the absolute identity of the infinite and the finite, therefore also in that of the bond and what is bound.

We can acknowledge between these two no other difference than that which we can find in the law of identity (through which the relationship of the predicating and the predicated is expressed as eternal), according to whether we reflect upon the absolute sameness, the copula itself, or upon the subject and predicate as equated, and how the former and the latter are above all inseparable, just as it also is with the bound and the bond.

The bond expresses in the bound at the same time its own essence as identity. This can therefore to that extent be regarded as its expression. If I were to remove from the expression what it received from that of which it is the expression, nothing would remain save inessential characteristics, for instance those that it has by virtue of being a mere expression, and an empty schema; thus the bond itself and the expression are not two different things, but rather either one and the same thing viewed from different perspectives, or the one is indeed an essence and the other inessential.

It is the same distinction that some have made between the *esse substantiae* [substantial being] and the *esse formae* [formal being], from which it is equally easy to see that it is not a real, but merely an ideal difference.

We can express the bond in its essence as the infinite love of itself (which is the highest in all things), as the infinite desire to reveal itself, except that the essence of the Absolute cannot be thought of as distinct from this desire, but rather just as this willing-of-itself.

It is precisely this affirming-of-itself, regardless of the form, that is in itself infinite, which is why it can never in any respect become finite.

The Absolute is, however, not only a willing of itself, but rather a willing in infinite ways, that is in all forms, grades and potencies of reality.

The expression of the eternal and infinite willing-of-itself is the world.

If we look at this expression for that which it has received from the bond, and with respect to which it resembles it, the positive in it, and not the inessential characteristics: then it is not different from the absolute itself, but rather is only the complete copula, displayed in its progressive development.

We stand here at precisely the first and most important point of its unfolding.

Notes

1   *Editors' Note.* Letter 83 to Ehrenfried Walther von Tschirnhaus. See Baruch Spinoza, *The Letters*, trans. Samuel Shirley (Indianapolis/Cambridge: Hackett, 1995), p. 355.

2   *Editors' Note.* This essay was published as an appendix to the second edition of Schelling's treatise *On the World-Soul*, first published in 1798.

3   *Editors' Note.* The concept of the copula, which plays a crucial role in this chapter and, indeed, in Schelling's philosophy as a whole, has its roots in classical logic and designates the term that links the subject to its complement in a statement of identity, e.g. the word 'is' in the sentence 'the grass is green'.

Philosophical Investigations into the Essence of Human Freedom and Related Matters (1809)*

Another interpretation of pantheism is, to be sure, one which is generally considered to be more to the point, namely that it constitutes a total identification of God with all things, a confusion of creature and creator, from which a mass of still more difficult and insupportable assertions are then deduced.[1] However a more complete differentiation of things and God can hardly be conceived than is made in the teaching of Spinoza which is said to be the classic instance of that identification. God is that which is in itself and is conceived solely through itself, whereas the finite necessarily exists in another being and can only be conceived with reference to it.[2] Manifestly, in consequence of this distinction, things are not different from God merely in degree or because of their limitations, as a superficial view of the doctrine of modes might indeed seem to imply, but they differ from God *toto genere* [in kind]. Thus whatever their relation to God may be, they are absolutely differentiated from God through the fact that they can exist only in and dependent upon another being (namely himself), and that their concept is a derivative one which would not even be possible without the concept of God. By contrast, the concept of God alone is independent and primary and self-affirming, all else being related to it only as what is affirmed, or as the consequence to the antecedent.[3] Only on this assumption are other attributes of things valid, their eternality for instance. God is by nature eternal; things are so only through him and as a consequence of his existence – that is, in a derivative manner. Just because of this difference, the sum of all individual things cannot constitute God, as is usually set forth, since no kind of combination can transform that which is of nature derived into that which is by nature original, just as little as all the points in a circumference taken together can constitute the whole, since the latter by its very definition necessarily precedes them. Still more preposterous is the inference that in Spinoza each individual being must be identified with God. For even if the daring expression that each object is a modified God

---

*Translated by James Guttmann from F.W.J. Schelling, *Sämmtliche Werke* (Stuttgart and Augsberg: Cotta, 1856–1861), Division One, Volume Seven.

were found in his work, the elements of this concept are so contradictory that it falls apart in the very act of being assembled. A modified God, that is to say a derived God, is not God in the real, distinctive sense; this one addition puts things back in their place which everlastingly distinguishes them from God. The reason for such misinterpretations which other systems have also experienced in full measure, is found in the general misunderstanding of that law of identity or of the meaning of the copula in judgement. It can readily be made comprehensible to a child that in no possible proposition, which is generally mistaken to declare the identity of subject and predicate, the equivalence of the two or even their immediate connection is affirmed. Thus, for example, the proposition, 'This body is blue', does not mean that the body in and of reason of its being a body is also a blue body, but only that the object designated as this body is also blue though not in the same sense. Nevertheless, this mistake which indicates complete ignorance as to the nature of the copula, has repeatedly been made in our time with respect to the higher application of the law of identity. If, for example, the proposition is advanced that the perfect is the imperfect, it signifies: the imperfect exists not by means of those attributes in and through which it is imperfect, but by means of the perfection which it contains. But for our contemporaries it has this significance: perfection and imperfection are equivalent, everything is one and the same, the worst and the best, folly and wisdom. Or take the proposition: the good is the evil – by which is meant: Evil has no power to exist in itself; that which is real in it, considered in itself, is good. This statement is held to mean: the eternal difference between right and wrong, between virtue and sin, is being denied, and from the point of view of logic they are the same. Or if, in another connection, it is explained that necessity and freedom are one, meaning that in the last instance the essence of the moral world is also the essence of the world of nature, it is taken to mean: Freedom is nothing but a force of nature, a mainspring which like all others is subordinate to mechanism. The same thing occurs with the proposition that the soul and body are one, which is made to mean: The soul is material, a gas, ether, nerve current and the like. For the opposite, that body is soul, or, in the preceding statement, that apparent necessity can itself be a case of freedom, though this could quite as well be deduced from the proposition, is shrewdly put to one side. Such misunderstandings, if they are not intentional, imply a degree of dialectical immaturity which Greek philosophy transcended almost in its first beginnings and make the recommendation of a thorough course in logic an urgent duty. The profound logic of the ancients distinguished subject and predicate as the antecedent and the consequent *(antecedens et consequens)* and thus expressed the real meaning of the law of identity. Even a tautological statement, if it is not to be altogether meaningless, retains this relationship. Thus if one says: A body is body; he is assuredly thinking something different in the subject of the sentence than in its predicate. In the former, that is, he refers to the unity, in the latter to the individual qualities contained in the concept, body, which are related to the unity as the *antecedens* to the *consequens*. Just this is the meaning of another older explanation, according to which subject and predicate are discriminated as being the unexpressed and the expressed *(implicitum et explicitum)*.

Nonetheless, the defenders of the foregoing assertion will now say, we are not at all concerned in pantheism with the fact that God is all (which cannot well be avoided in view of the usual conception of his attributes) but we are concerned with the circumstance that things are as naught, that this system does away with all individuality. To be sure this new characterization seems to be in contradiction to the preceding one, for if all things are naught, how is it possible to confuse God with them? For in this case there would be nothing at all except pure, unclouded divinity. Or, if there is nothing beside God (not only *extra Deum* but also *praeter Deum* [not only outside God but beside God]) how then can he be 'all things' except in name; so that the entire conception seems to dissolve and evaporate into nothing. In any case it seems questionable whether much is gained by resurrecting such general labels, for though they may occupy places of honour in the history of heresy, they seem to be much too clumsy as handles for the products of the spirit in connection with which, as in the most delicate phenomena of nature, subtle modifications cause fundamental changes. It might moreover be doubted whether the last mentioned characterization is applicable even to Spinoza. For if he recognizes nothing beside *(praeter)* Substance, except its mere modes, with which he identifies things, then this conception is indeed an altogether negative one, which expresses nothing essential or positive. It serves at first, in fact, merely to define the relation of things to God, not what they may be, considered in themselves. But the inadequacy of this definition does not imply that things contain nothing at all which is positive, even though they be of a derivative nature. The most drastic expression in

Spinoza is probably the statement: The individual being is Substance itself viewed in one of its modes, that is, in one of its consequences. If we let infinite Substance = A, and infinite Substance regarded in one of its consequences = A/a; then that which is positive in A/a is, indeed, A. But it does not follow on this account that A/a = A, *i.e.* that infinite Substance regarded in its consequences is to be considered exactly the same as infinite Substance as such. Or, in other words, it does not follow that A/a is not a distinctive and particular substance, even though it be a consequence of A. To be sure, this is not set forth in Spinoza. However we are, in the first place, speaking of pantheism in general; so that the only question is, whether the view expressed is inherently incompatible with Spinozism. This can scarcely be asserted, since it has been admitted that Leibniz's monads, which are precisely the same as what is expressed in the above A/a, are not a decisive measure against Spinozism. Without an interpretative amendment of this sort some of Spinoza's utterances remain puzzling, for instance the statement that the essence of the human soul is a vital idea of God's which is declared to be eternal and not transitory. Thus, even if Substance were but temporarily present in its other modes, A/b, A/c, it would be eternally present in that one mode, the human soul, = a. And in this way as A/a, it would everlastingly and in an eternal way be divorced from itself as A.

To proceed, if the denial of freedom, not of individuality, should now be declared to be the essential characteristic of pantheism, then a multitude of Systems would come under this heading which are otherwise essentially differentiated from it. For the true conception of freedom was lacking in all modern Systems, that of Leibniz as well as that of Spinoza, until the discovery of Idealism. And the sort of freedom which many among us have conceived, even those boasting of the liveliest sense thereof, a freedom, namely, consisting of the mere mastery of intelligence over senses and passions, could be deduced from Spinoza himself without difficulty, indeed quite easily and with superior decisiveness. Thus it seems that the denial or affirmation of freedom in general is based on something quite other than the acceptance or non-acceptance of pantheism, the immanence of things in God. For if, at the first glance, it seems that freedom, unable to maintain itself in opposition to God, is here submerged in identity, it may be said that this apparent result is merely the consequence of an imperfect and empty conception of the law of identity. This principle does not express a unity which, revolving in the indifferent circle of sameness, would get us nowhere and remain meaningless and lifeless. The unity of this law is of an intrinsically creative kind. In the relation of subject to predicate itself, we have already pointed out the relation of ground and consequence; and the law of sufficient reason is therefore just as ultimate as the law of identity. The Eternal, as such, must, on this account, also be this ground, without mediation. That for which the Eternal is by its nature the ground, is, to this extent, dependent and, from the point of view of immanence, is also conceived in the Eternal. But dependence does not exclude autonomy or even freedom. Dependence does not determine the nature of the dependent, and merely declares that the dependent entity, whatever else it may be, can only be as a consequence of that upon which it is dependent; it does not declare what this dependent entity is or is not. Every organic individual, insofar as it has come into being, is dependent upon another organism with respect to its genesis but not at all with regard to its essential being. It is not incongruous, says Leibniz, that he who is God could at the same time be begotten, or contrariwise; it is no more contradictory than for one who is son of a man himself to be a man. On the contrary, it would indeed be contradictory if that which is dependent or consequent were not autonomous. There would be dependence without something being dependent, a result without a resultant (consequentia absque consequente), and therefore no true result; that is, the whole conception would vitiate itself. The same thing is true of concepts being implied in others. A single organ, like the eye, is possible only in the organism as a whole; nevertheless it has a life of its own, indeed a kind of freedom, as is manifestly proven through those diseases to which it is subject. If that which is conceived in another could not have its own life, there would be a concept without a conception: that is, nothing would be conceived. We attain a much loftier point of view by regarding the divine Being itself, the very idea of which would be completely incompatible with a result which was not a living creation, – that is, the positing of something autonomous. God is not a God of the dead but of the living. It is incomprehensible that an all-perfect Being could rejoice in even the most perfect mechanism possible. No matter how one pictures to oneself the procession of creatures from God, it can never be a mechanical production, no mere construction or setting up, in which the construct is naught in itself. Just as certainly, it cannot be an emanation in which that which has flowed forth remains the same as its source, thus lacking individuality and independence. The procession of things from God is God's self-revelation. But God can only reveal himself in creatures who resemble him, in free, self-activating beings for whose existence there is no reason save God, but who are as God is. He speaks, and they are there. Though all the world's creatures were but the thoughts of the divine mind, they would on this very account necessarily have life. Thus thoughts are doubtless born in the soul; but a thought once born is an independent power which works on in its own way, and which indeed grows so great in the human soul that it masters its own mother and prevails over her. However, divine imagination, which is the cause of the differentiation of the world's beings, is unlike human imagination and never gives to its creations a merely ideal reality. The products of divine imagination must be independent beings, for wherein does the limitation of our imagination consist than precisely in our seeing things as dependent. God beholds all things in themselves. Only the Eternal exists in itself, as Self-secured, Will, Freedom. The concept of a derivative absoluteness or divinity is so little a contradiction that it is actually the central concept of all philosophy. This sort of divinity characterizes nature. Immanence in God is so little a contradiction of freedom that freedom alone, and insofar as it is free, exists in God, whereas all that lacks freedom, and insofar as it lacks freedom, is necessarily outside God.

Notes

1   *Editors' Note.* This passage occurs as part of Schelling's response to the 'pantheism controversy', which had rumbled on in German philosophy over the previous two decades. Pantheism had been defined by F.H. Jacobi and Friedrich Schlegel as the system of pure reason, such that it was both the fulfilment of philosophy and also the condemnation of the philosopher as unable to avoid commitment to a system promoting fatalism and atheism. The idea that a rational philosophical system robs God of the property of transcendence is an essential part of this critique.

2   *Editors' Note.* These are references to Spinoza's definitions in Part I of the *Ethics*.

3   *Editors' Note.* The terms *antecedens* and *consequens* will play a pivotal role in the rest of this passage. They emerge from traditional logic where they signify, respectively, the premise and result of a syllogism; the antecedent is thus a condition or ground of the consequent.

Stuttgart Private Lectures (1810)*

What is the principle of my system?

This principle has been expressed in a variety of ways:

(a) as the principle of absolute [and] unconditional identity, to be well distinguished from an absolute indifference; the identity that we refer to here is an *organic* unity of all things. Every organism possesses unity without, however, enabling us to conceive of its parts as being one and the same. Thus, in the case of the human body all difference among organs and the functions dissolves into one indivisible life whose sensation as an indivisible and harmonious one equals the sensation of wellbeing; yet the parts and functions that constitute this organic whole are not, therefore, the same; the stomach, for example, obviously does not have the function of the brain, etc.

(b) This principle, then, found its more specific expression as the absolute identity of the *Real* and the *Ideal*. This is not to say that the Real and the Ideal are numerically or logically the same but, instead, designates an *essential* unity; it is the same aspect that is posited in both forms, though it is proper in each of these forms and not one essence. If, for example, Jacob was also called Israel, he was always the same individual and thus was not being individualized differently by his different names. Such is not the case, however, with the identity of the Real and the Ideal. If we posit

$$\frac{A}{B = C}$$

then B and C are identical because they are in essence A, whereas they differ from one another as forms, i.e. each considered in and of themselves; B can never become C, and C can never become B, [and] likewise A inheres also in B and in C equally as a unique essence. Precisely because it is the same essence that inheres in each one, there exists among them an *essential* (i.e. not merely formal, logical, or nominal) unity, which is simultaneously accompanied by an authentic opposition or dualism, because none of these can be sublated into the other. For by virtue of the fact that A individualizes itself in both B and C, the latter two are equally entitled to existence. Yet why has the first principle been determined as that of the identity of the Real and the Ideal? The determination was designated to indicate, first of all, that

---

*Translated by Thomas Pfau from F.W.J. Schelling, *Sämmtliche Werke* (Stuttgart and Augsberg: Cotta, 1856–1861), Division One, Volume Seven.

neither the Real nor the Ideal as such could ever be the absolute, but that both of these are only subordinate forms of the proper *primordial Being*. Furthermore, this [formula] is to express positively that *the same* essence inheres in both of these. My principle might be most easily explained by recalling Fichte's philosophy. Fichte reaches the conclusion [that there is] no existence other than what is *for itself*. Only the self [is] for itself; what follows from this is self-evident. Yet I disagree with his premise because subject and object constitute the universal form in matter as well as in the self (and only later can we point up the differences that separate the two): thus the force that repels a body is the objective, whereas what attracts the body is a force that returns to this body, hence a subjective force. Fichte does not know of this dualism that inheres in identity.

(c) Alternatively, I expressed the principle of my philosophy in straightforward manner as the *absolute* or *God*. However, here the absolute is the principle of all of philosophy; philosophy is strictly a whole, living and creative in God, whereas the dogmatic systems of Leibniz, Wolff and even Kant only add God after the fact. The difference between my philosophy and philosophy in general, as well as theology, to which it bears an affinity, is that theology is more of an abstraction from philosophy; it takes God as a particular object, so to speak, whereas philosophy understands God simultaneously as the supreme reason for the explanation of all things, thereby opening up the idea of God also for all other objects. The following [remarks] are related to these considerations.

We are often asked how, if philosophy conceives of God as its ground, we can arrive at a knowledge of God or of the absolute. There is no answer to this question. The existence of what is unconditional cannot be proven like the existence of something finite. The unconditional is the element wherein any demonstration becomes possible. Where the geometrician, when setting about the demonstration of a given concept, does not begin by proving the existence of space but rather presupposes it, philosophy, too, does not demonstrate the existence of God but confesses that it could not even exist without the absolute or God. Everything can be presented only in the absolute; hence the unconditional does not precede the practice of philosophy, but philosophy in its entirety is occupied with the existence of the former, [and] all of philosophy is properly speaking the progressive demonstration of the absolute, which therefore cannot be demanded from the outset of philosophy. Hence, if the universe cannot be anything but the manifestation of the absolute, and if philosophy is nothing but the spiritual presentation of the universe, philosophy, in general is itself but the manifestation, i.e. the ongoing proof of God.

Let us now proceed to the following proposition: the primordial essence is necessarily and by its very nature the absolute identity of the Real and the Ideal. Not much is said with this proposition, however, except that it offers us the concept of the primordial Being, though not [this Being] as an *actual*, authentic one. Hence, if we say that the essence of man is an absolute identity of freedom and necessity, and that a free principle and a necessary principle are always already united in man, we thereby attain a concept of man, to be sure, yet we do not yet have the living, authentic human being; for to obtain the latter (i.e. an authentic human being) it is requisite that we consider man insofar as these principles are indeed in opposition and contest within him. Put differently, the primordial Being as the absolute identity of the Real and the Ideal is itself posited only in a subjective manner, whereas we also need to comprehend it objectively: the absolute identity of the Real and the Ideal must not only be *in and of itself* but also *outside itself*, [that is,] it must be actualized – it must also disclose itself in existence as that which, in its essence, is the absolute identity of the Real and the Ideal. However, everything can become manifest only through its opposite, i.e. identity through nonidentity, difference and distinguishable principles. How this might apply to God we shall leave open for the time being, and we merely wish to point out *that* a separation, a difference must be posited if we ever wish to make the transition from essence to existence.

This transition from identity to difference has often been understood as *a cancellation of identity;* yet that is not at all the case, as I intend to demonstrate without delay. Much rather it is a doubling of the essence, and thus an intensification of the unity, something that is once again aptly illustrated by means of an analogy with ourselves. Consciousness arises only with the separation of principles that existed implicitly in man beforehand, such as the rational and the irrational. Neither of the two is meant to be erased. It is precisely in this discord between the two, and in its eventual resolution, that our humanity must prove itself. If, then, we become conscious of ourselves – when light and darkness begin to separate within ourselves – we do not properly transcend *ourselves*, [for] the two principles remain within us as their unity. Nor are we deprived in any way of our essence but, instead, we attain ourselves in a twofold form, namely in unity and in separation. The same [hold true] for God.

If we posit A = A as the state of a self-rational Being, we must already take note of three aspects of this formula: (a) A as object, (b) A as subject, (c) the identity of the former two; yet all of this is [understood] as indistinguishable in a real sense. Meanwhile the difference of these principles is to be posited; that is, with A as subject and A as object being distinguishable, A = A is converted into A = B; yet because there nevertheless prevails the unity of essence the expression of difference is not

$$\frac{A}{A = A} \text{ but rather } \frac{A}{A = B}$$

that is, one and two; $A = B$ is the bifurcation, whereas A [designates] the unity, and the whole expression designates the living, actual and primordial Being. A possesses an object, a mirror in $A = B$. Hence the primordial essence is in and of itself always unity; namely, the *unity of the opposition and of the bifurcation*.

Only now can we ask, how is this division possible in God? Because the bond of principles in God is indissoluble, a division seems altogether *impossible*, and yet it is indispensable for any revelation. How, then, are we to resolve this contradiction?

If the primordial Being in A and B is once again the whole, A and B can exist separately without, thereby, cancelling the bond of principles. Thus we would have to assume that the primordial essence would remain whole in each of the separated entities and that it would be posited as the whole in them; thus B would be composed of B (i.e. the Real), of A (i.e. the spiritual), and of their unity. The same would also apply to A. And yet, would such a conception not already posit a *factual* distinctness? Far from it. The formula

$$\frac{A}{B = A}$$

asks us to understand the upper A as the essence itself. However, because precisely this identity also constitutes the copula in $A = A$ (the form), we may call this identity, to the extent that it inheres in a form, the essence within form. Hence we have (1) an essence in itself and (2) an essence in form. Still, as long as this form is $A = A$ (and the principles have not been differentiated), the essence in form is identical with, and not distinguishable from, the essence in itself. Now such capacity for differentiation is to be posited by way of conceiving of form in two subordinate and differential forms as follows:

$$\frac{A}{} = \text{essence in itself}$$

$$A = A = \text{essence in absolute form}$$

$$\frac{A}{B = C}$$

However, because each of these forms comprises once again the same bond also found in absolute form, each of them is once again dissolved into the *essence of the absolute form* and thus into essence *in itself*.

This brings us back full circle, except that *now, instead of the mere factors of A = B, we have the two unities*, i.e. we have only a more highly developed unity, though not any *difference*.

Nevertheless, this conversion of absolute form into two subordinate forms or, which is the same, this complete transfiguration of the *whole* primordial Being into the Real and Ideal opens the requisite path toward the finite and real differentiation.

Closer inspection reveals that between the two unities there subsists an actual difference, even though it is not *posited as actual*. The Real unity (the one under the exponent of B) presents itself as Being whereas the Ideal unity (that under the exponent of A) presents itself as the *position of Being*. Being, however, is also inherently positional: hence the position of Being [in A] is the *position of a position*, i.e. a position *of the second potency*.

It is here that we arrive at the concept of the *potencies*[1] so crucial for our entire investigation. Initially, we have something superior and something inferior, that is, an *axiological* difference. The Ideal ranks higher than the Real in respect to its dignity. We could present the matter in the following formula:

(a) Being cannot exist for itself. By virtue of the indissoluble bond, neither B nor A can exist for itself. The *Real* Being is therefore only A in B or under the exponent of B; this we can also express as $A = B = \text{first potency}$.

(b) A cannot exist independently either but, as a position of the first potency, it must contain the latter within itself in an ideal sense; hence, $A^2 = \text{second potency}$.

Both unities or potencies are once again comprised by the absolute unity, the latter, understood as the common position of the first and the second potency, thus being A^3; and the thoroughly developed expression of the initial [proposition] $A = A$ thus reads:

$$\frac{A}{B = C}$$

Yet this formula provides us with more than a merely axiological difference. The first potency must by its very nature precede the second one; that is, between the two potencies there exists a priority and a posteriority; the Real is by its very nature the first [*natura prius*], and the Ideal is the latter. The inferior [potency, i.e. B] thus is indeed posited *before* the superior one, though not in an axiological sense, which would be contradictory, but as regards its *existence*.

Meanwhile the priority that we have established for the first potency amounts to only an ideal or logical priority of the Real over the Ideal, not though to an actual one. We have demonstrated merely that a differentiation is *possible* and how. Yet how are we to arrive at the actuality of such a differentiation?

The ground for this actuality can indeed be found only in the primordial Being or God, for which we have already established the medium. Namely, as we have just seen, it is also in God that the first potency takes logical precedence over the second one, the former being by its very nature the first, and the latter coming second. Hence, if the primordial Being wants to effect a bifurcation of potencies, it must posit this priority of the first potency as an actual one (i.e. must convert the merely ideal or logical priority into an actual one); that is, it must restrict itself spontaneously *to the first [potency]*, and it must cancel the simultaneity of the principles as it originally inheres in the primordial Being itself. To thus cancel the simultaneity, however, neither affects the inner (essential) unity – for such [unity] does not depend on simultaneity – nor does it cancel the bond between the potencies; for once the first potency has been posited, we must immediately also posit the second and the third ones. When the priority of the first potency becomes an actuality, the identity of the potencies in the absolute is not being cancelled, [but] it is merely transmuted into a linkage or coherence of the latter ones. Prior to this step, the potencies inhere in the absolute in complete indifference and indistinguishability. Likewise, time in general, be it as unity or as eternity, exists implicitly in the absolute. By virtue of restricting Himself to the first potency – by being spontaneously only *One*, although capable of being *All* – God effects a beginning of time (*nota bene*:

not *in* time). By way of His retreat into to the first potency we initially come to conceive of a limitation in Him; yet because such a [notion] contradicts His essence, which is by its very nature *all powers*, there eventually occurs a progress from the first potency to the second and thereby a certain form of time. Thus the potencies are simultaneously posited as periods in the self-explication of God.

Related General Remarks

(1) A passive limitation is indeed a mere insufficiency or a relative lack of power; however, to limit oneself, to concentrate oneself in one point, yet also to hold on to the latter with all one's might and not to let go until it has been expanded into a world, such constitutes the greatest power and perfection. As Goethe says:

Whoever wills greatness must concentrate himself;
Only in self-restriction is the artist revealed.[2]

The capacity to concentrate one's own power is the key to originality properly speaking and the root of [our] strength. In $A = B$, B itself is the contracting moment, and when God restricts Himself to the first potency, this especially ought to be called a concentration. Concentration, then, marks the beginning of all reality. For this reason, it is the concentrating rather than the expanding nature that possesses a primordial and grounding force. Thus the beginning of creation amounts indeed to a *descent* of God; He properly descends into the Real, contracts Himself entirely into the Real. Yet such an act does not imply anything unworthy of God but, in fact, it is this descent that marks the greatest act for God and, indeed, for Christianity as well. By contrast, a metaphorically elevated God will benefit neither our minds nor our hearts.

(2) This act of restriction or descent on the part of God is spontaneous. Hence the explanation of the world has no other ground than the freedom of God. Only God Himself can break with the absolute identity of His essence and thereby can create the space for a revelation. To be sure, all genuine, that is, absolute, freedom is an absolute necessity. For it is impossible to adduce any further ground for an act of absolute freedom; such an act is because it occurs in such a given manner, that is, it is unconditional and thus it is necessary. Ordinarily, freedom is recognized only where a choice has been made and where a state of indecision has prevailed, followed by a decision. Yet he who knows what he wants acts without any decision, whereas he who chooses does not know what he wants and consequently does not really have a will. All choice is the consequence of an unilluminated will. If God

acts with good reason, His freedom is highly subordinate. That is, to have Him elect the best world from an infinite number of worlds is to grant Him the least degree of freedom. One such act, thoroughly absolute, is what founds our character. Character also originates in a form of concentration whereby we afford ourselves a form of determinacy; the more intensive this determinacy is, the more character we have. No one argues that man elects his character, which is to say that character is not the result of freedom in its ordinary sense; and yet it is imputable. Here, then, we have an instance of this identity of freedom and necessity.

(3) God's self-restriction implies a beginning *of* time, though not a beginning *in* time. God himself is not, therefore, being placed in time.

Time is posited in the Real, yet the Real is not God himself although it is indissolubly connected with Him. For the Real in God is *Being* or existence, whereas the Ideal [in God] is the *existing*, that wherein the Real and Ideal are one, that is, the actually existing, living God.

Time is posited in the Real (in the Being of God). Yet the [Real], considered in its *wholeness*, does not exist in time, but only the discrete and limited entity within the Real [is capable of] progression and development. 'Yet do we not posit such time *in* the Real *for* God, and would God not thereby be affected by time?' I answer: to the extent that *difference* is posited in the Real – and thereby time – God is once again the position of this difference $= A^2$, which contains simultaneously and eternally all of what, according to the proposition $A = B$, develops strictly in a temporary manner. Because God – conceived of in an absolute manner, i.e. God insofar as He is neither mere existence (the Real) nor merely the existing ([absolute] subject), but God as A^3 – contains $A = B$ in perpetual correlation, this $A = B$ once again dissolves in Him, seen as a subject (A^2), or in His consciousness into the eternity of His essence.

A^2 (God as subject) is the focal point or the unity of time.

God conceived of absolutely, A^3, is neither eternity nor time but the absolute identity of the two. Everything that exists in time is eternal in God as a subject, and everything that is thus eternal in Him, as a subject, is temporal in Him as an object.

Notes

1 *Editors' Note.* In the following, Schelling plays on the meaning of the German 'Potenz' as both potency and power.

2 *Editors' Note.* 'Nature and Art'. See J.W. Goethe, *Selected Poems*, trans. John Whaley (Evanston: Northwestern University Press, 1998), p. 83.

Further reading

Further discussions of identity and difference are to be found in many of Schelling's works from the first decade of the nineteenth century. It is worth examining his comments on identity and the copula in the 1804 *System of Philosophy in General* (partially translated in Pfau [ed.], *Idealism and the Endgame of Theory*) and the various drafts of the *The Ages of the World*. Michael Vater's extensive introductions and commentaries to his translations of Schelling's works, particularly *Bruno*, are invaluable – as are the following:

Benjamin Berger and Daniel Whistler, *The Schelling-Eschenmayer Controversy, 1801: Nature and Identity* (Edinburgh University Press, 2020), Chapter 3.

Andrew Bowie, *Schelling and Modern European Philosophy* (Routledge, 1993), Chapters 4 and 5.

Manfred Frank, '"Identity of Identity and Non-Identity": Schelling's Path to the "Absolute System of Identity"'. In Lara Ostaric (ed.), *Interpreting Schelling: Critical Essays* (Cambridge University Press, 2014), 120–44.

Sean J. McGrath, 'The Logic of Schelling's *Freedom Essay*.' Available online: http://www.metaphysicalsociety.org/2015/papers/McGrath.pdf.

Dalia Nassar, *The Romantic Absolute: Being and Knowing in Early German Romantic Philosophy, 1795–1804* (University of Chicago Press, 2014), Part III.

Mark J. Thomas, 'The Mediation of the Copula as a Fundamental Structure in Schelling's Philosophy.' *Schelling Studien* 2 (2014): 20–39.

Michael G. Vater, 'Schelling's Philosophy of Identity and Spinoza's *Ethica more geometrico*.' In E. Förster and Y. Melamed (eds), *Spinoza and German Idealism* (Cambridge University Press, 2012), 156–74.

Daniel Whistler, 'Identity Philosophy.' In Kyla Bruff and Sean J. McGrath (eds), *The Palgrave Schelling Handbook* (Palgrave, 2021), 74–92.

3

Nature

Introduction

For much of the twentieth century, only a brief stage of Schelling's philosophical development was identified as a 'philosophy of nature', namely, the texts of 1797–1800, which initiated Schelling's distinctive philosophical study of the natural world. Yet it is now widely acknowledged that Schelling continued to write about and lecture on the philosophy of nature throughout his life. The oft-quoted remark in the *Freedom* essay that 'the whole of modern European philosophy since its inception (through Descartes) has this common deficiency – that nature does not exist for it and that it lacks a living basis'[1] expresses a fundamental Schellingian insight that is repeated throughout the various systems he constructs. Indeed, for most of Schelling's career, he argues that everything to be found in the 'spiritual' or 'ideal world' of human existence depends in some sense upon nature, and any philosophy worthy of the name must attend to this natural basis or ground of the ideal world. Even in his late thought, when he comes to understand nature as the creation of a transcendent 'Lord of being', Schelling continues to insist upon the importance of a philosophical presentation of nature's structure.

Schelling takes nature to have three general 'levels' or 'stages'. The first level corresponds to the 'dynamic construction of matter', in which material bodies are understood to be constituted by the forces of repulsion and attraction. Beginning in 1799, Schelling follows Franz Baader in identifying gravity as a third force that unifies repulsion and attraction; thus, this first level of nature is often described as simply 'gravity' or 'matter'. At the second level, nature involves the 'universal categories of physics': magnetism, electricity and the chemical process. At this level, nature is not only spatially extended material but material that appears to have qualitative specificity. And just as Schelling often calls the entire first level of nature 'gravity', he often calls this second level 'light'. Finally, at the third level, nature proves to be alive in the activity of plants, animals and human organisms. According to Schelling, this third level of nature – life – is characterized by three moments or activities: sensibility, irritability and reproduction.

Central to Schelling's philosophy of nature is the idea that each level of nature is a 'higher' or more complex expression of a lower level. This is why he identifies the levels of nature with mathematical 'powers' or 'potencies' (*Potenzen*). For example, organic life is material nature 'raised to a higher power' (typically represented as A^3), and – at the more specific level of analysis – the organic moment of irritability is electricity raised to a higher power or potency.

This chapter contains some of the more important texts in which Schelling presents his understanding of nature's potencies and their connections. The passage from Schelling's first major work in the philosophy of nature – the first edition of the *Ideas for a Philosophy of Nature* (1797) – includes his early conception of the dynamic construction of matter, along with his related discussion of the solar system. The passage from the *Introduction to the Outline* (1799) investigates the connection between the second and third levels of nature, which amounts to a consideration of the relationship between inorganic and organic nature. Life is then given a more detailed treatment in the *System of Philosophy in General and the Philosophy of Nature in Particular* (1804), which includes Schelling's brief remarks about the human organism as the ultimate 'identity' of plant and animal forms of life.

This chapter also includes Schelling's discussion – in the dialogue, *Clara* (c. 1810) – of how the metaphysical 'links' between the different elements of nature raise important aesthetic, psychological, ethical and scientific questions. One thing Schelling points out here is that, by observing natural processes at work and experimenting with nature, a person can make discoveries about the structure of the natural world which she would not expect to be the case – an insight that Schelling takes up again in the *Lecture on Faraday's Most Recent Discovery* (1832). This lecture also returns to the topic of the universal categories of physics and demonstrates the continued importance of the philosophy of nature for the late Schelling – something that should not be lost sight of despite his focus, during this period, on the philosophies of mythology and revelation.

Note

1   *Philosophical Inquiries into the Essence of Human Nature*, trans. James Guttmann, p. 30.

Ideas for a Philosophy of Nature (1797)*

On Attraction and Repulsion in General, as Principles of a System of Nature

We assume, for the time being, that the laws of reciprocal attraction and repulsion are *universal* laws of nature, and ask what would necessarily have to follow from this assumption.

If both are *universal laws of nature*, they have to be conditions for the possibility of a nature as such. But we begin by considering them only in regard to *matter*, insofar as it is an object of our knowledge *in general*, and apart from any specific or qualitative diversity it may possess. So these laws must first be considered as conditions for the possibility of matter as such, and there must be no matter originally conceivable, without there being attraction and repulsion between it and some other.

This we presuppose. Whether and why it should have to be so will be investigated later on.

Matter, for us, has hitherto been no more than just something extended in three dimensions, which *occupies* space.

Let us now postulate attraction and repulsion between two *original* masses, for this is the least that we can presuppose; we can imagine these masses as large or small as we please, but with the restriction that we take them to be *equal* (for as yet we have no reason to suppose them unequal). We then get the following result: Their attractive and repulsive forces would have to *cancel* one another (reciprocally *exhaust* each other); their attractive and repulsive power is merely a *communal* one, and since it is only by means of these forces that they reveal their presence in space, the ground of difference between them also lapses, and they cannot be regarded as opposing masses, but only as a single mass.

But no matter is, or can be, anything but forces attracting and repelling through action and reaction; so unless, in addition to these two basic masses, A and B, we have a third mass, C, upon which they now exert their common effect, A and B will in fact = 0, since their forces mutually cancel, and now

---

*Translated by Errol E. Harris and Peter Heath from F.W.J. Schelling, *Sämmtliche Werke* (Stuttgart and Augsberg: Cotta, 1856–1861), Division One, Volume Two.

present only a single common force; for there is nothing for them to act upon, and nothing that could act upon them; but if we posit a third mass (still equal to the first two), what follows?

The latter, in virtue of its original powers of attraction and repulsion, will now compel A and B to direct their common force towards it; the power of each one acts jointly on the other two, and each one now prevents the other two from exhausting their original forces upon each other.

If, however, instead of the two *equal* masses, A and B, we suppose two *unequal* ones, then their forces on either side will not in fact be *reciprocal*, but the force of the one (say A) will entirely cancel that of the other (B), and thus we shall again have only one mass, having a surplus of force, which we cannot conceive of without at once giving it another object on which to use it.

So in both cases, in order to conceive the relationship between two basic masses, we are already obliged to append in thought a second relation, in which they both stand to a third mass, and this is as true of the smallest masses as it is of the largest.

If we consider the relationship between three original, equal masses, which all mutually attract and repel, then no one of them will exhaust its powers on the others, for each one perturbs at every moment the action of any one upon the rest. Thus according to the same law by which, for example, C perturbs the effect of B upon A, A in turn perturbs the effect of C upon B. But at this instant the effect of A upon C is perturbed by B, and so this interchange continues indefinitely, since it is forever reconstituting itself. Thus the action of each one upon the other two must constantly persist, indeed, since it is constantly reconstituted, but it has to be thought of at every single instant as infinitely small, since it is forever being perturbed; and since the original forces of matter can only act as *moving* forces, the motion which each one occasions in the other two will be conceived as infinitely small. So in a system of bodies which are all assumed to be *equal*, no motion occurs.

So if *motion* is to arise in a system, the masses have to be supposed *unequal*. And it follows already, from this very fact, that the most primal motion by means of dynamic forces cannot be rectilinear. This must also be the case, if a *system* of bodies is ever to be possible at all. For since the concept of *system* implies it to be a self-contained whole, the motion in the system must likewise be conceivable only as *relative*, without being connected with anything present outside the system. But this would be impossible if all the bodies in the system were moving in a straight line. A system, on the other hand, in which subordinate bodies describe orbits, approximating more or less to circles, about a common immovable centre, has no need of an empirical space existing outside it, even with respect to possible experience (so that its motion may be conceived as relative). For in fact (as has been shown by Newton already, and by Kant), the motion in such a system bears no relation to any empirical space existing outside it; yet it is not an absolute, but a relative, motion – relative, that is, with respect to the system itself, in which the bodies belonging to it constantly change their relationships to one another, but always with respect only to the space which they themselves enclose by their motions (around the common centre). With respect to any other possible system, the system presupposed is absolutely one.

So even if we supposed such a system to be subordinated to one still higher, that would not alter *among themselves* the relationships of the system, as a self-contained whole. All motion *in* this system occurs only with respect to the system itself. So any motion that might accrue to it with reference to another system would necessarily be a motion of the *whole* system (regarded as a unity). Such a motion of *the whole system* (in relation to a system outside it) would, with respect to the system itself, be *absolute*, i.e. no motion at all (and so it must be, if the system is to be a system). So wherever the whole moves in the universe, the system in itself remains the same, its bodies forever describe the same orbits, and the inner relationships which govern, for example, the change of seasons, of climate, etc., on the individual body, also accompany the system throughout a career for which millennia provide no measure.

Since, therefore, the subordinate system is equivalent to *one* body, in relation to the higher one, and since the attractive forces of the whole system can be thought of as united at the centre, the central body would have at the same time to belong to a higher system (as a planet, carrying the other bodies along with it as satellites), without this relationship having any influence on the internal relations of the subordinate system. For the force whereby the central body is drawn towards the midpoint of another system is at the same time also the force whereby it attracts the planets of *its own system*. Thus it is subject to the same laws as those governing the single system of the world, and in resolving the problem of how matter as such is *originally* possible, the problem of a possible universe has also been solved.

Having once pursued the principles of universal attraction up to their full height,[1] we can now descend again to individual bodies of the system. By the same law which keeps such a body in its orbit, everything upon it must tend towards the centre. This motion towards the centre of the larger body is called *dynamic*, because it occurs by means of dynamic forces. [...]

[I]n every body that is moving, I suppose *internal rest*, that is, an equilibrium of the inner forces; for it moves only insofar as it is matter *within specific boundaries*. But specific boundaries can be thought of only as the product of opposing forces that reciprocally limit each other.

But this equilibrium of forces, this rest in the parts of the body, I cannot envisage save by reference to the opposite – absence of equilibrium and motion of the parts. But in that the body is *moving*, this is *now* not supposed to occur, for it is taken to move as a body, i.e. as matter within specific confines (in a mass). So again I cannot think of this disturbed equilibrium (the movement of parts in the moving) body as *real*, though I must necessarily think of it as *possible*. But this possibility is not to be merely an *imagined* one; it has to be a *real* possibility, having its ground in the matter itself.

But matter is *inert*. Motion of matter without external causes is impossible. So even this motion *of the parts* cannot occur without external causes. But now, so far as we know at present, only a *moving* body can *communicate* motion to another. But the motion of the *parts* that we are talking of is supposed to be quite different from that produced by impact, by communication – it is meant, indeed, to be the opposite of this. Since it cannot, therefore, be a motion communicated to another by a *moving* body, then – as necessarily follows – it must be a motion which even the body at rest communicates to what is at rest. Now every motion produced by *impact* is called *mechanical*, but motion produced by the body *at rest* in *what is at rest* is called *chemical*; so we would have a hierarchy of motions, as follows:

All other motions are necessarily preceded by the original *dynamical* motion (that is possible only through forces of attraction and repulsion). For even *mechanical* motion, communicated, that is, by impact, cannot occur without action and reaction of attractive and repulsive forces in the body. No body can be struck without itself exerting *repulsive* force, and none can move *en masse*, without *attractive* forces operating within it. And still less can a *chemical* motion occur without a free play of the dynamical forces.

Chemical motion is just the opposite of *mechanical* motion. The latter is communicated to a body by *external forces*, the former occasioned in the body by *external causes*, indeed, but yet, so it seems, by internal *forces*. Mechanical motion presupposes *parts at rest* in the *moving body*; chemical motion, on the contrary, *motion of the parts* in a body that *does not move*.

[...]

Thus already in the chemical properties of matter there are actually lying the first seeds, albeit still quite undeveloped, of a future system of Nature, which in its most diversified forms and structures can evolve up to the point at which creative Nature seems to return back into herself. Thus the way is at once pointed out for further inquiries as to where in Nature the necessary and the contingent, the mechanical and the free, part company. Chemical phenomena constitute the middle term between the two.

It is this far, then, that the principles of attraction and repulsion actually lead us, as soon as we regard them as principles of a *universal system of Nature*. It is all the more important to look more deeply into the reason for these principles, and our right to the unrestricted use of them.

[...]

Basic Principles of Dynamics

Matter occupies a space, not through its mere *existence* (for to assume this is to cut off all further inquiry, once and for all), but through an inherently *moving force*, whereby the *mechanical* motion of matter first becomes possible.[2] Or rather, matter is itself nothing else but a moving force, and independently of this is at best something merely thinkable, and can no longer be anything real, the object of an intuition.

This inherently moving force is necessarily opposed to another force that is likewise inherently moving, and can be distinguished from the former only by its opposite direction. This is the force of attraction. For if matter possessed merely repulsive forces, it would disperse into the infinite, and a specific quantity of matter would nowhere be met with in any possible space. All spaces would therefore be empty, and there would simply be no matter there at all. Now since repulsive forces can be inherently limited neither by themselves (for they are entirely positive) nor by empty space (for although expansive force becomes weaker in inverse proportion to space, there is no degree of it that is actually the smallest possible – *quovis dabili minor*), nor by other matter (which we are not yet entitled to assume), we have therefore to postulate an inherent force of matter operating in a direction opposite to the repulsive, namely an attractive force, which attaches, not to any special kind of matter, but to matter generally and *as such*.[3]

It is now no longer a question as to why only these two basic forces of matter are necessary. The answer is, because a finite in general can only be the product of two opposing forces. [...]

[S]ince matter is nothing else but the product of an original synthesis (of opposite forces) in intuition, we thereby escape the sophisms concerning the infinite divisibility of matter, in that we no more need to maintain, with a self-misconceiving metaphysics, that matter is *made up* of infinitely many parts (which is absurd), than we require, with the atomists, to set limits to the freedom of the imagination in the act of division. [...]

That matter is *made up* of parts, is a mere judgement of the understanding. It consists of parts, *if* and *for so long as* I wish to divide it. But that in itself it originally consists of parts is false, for originally – in productive intuition – it arises as a *whole* from opposing forces, and only through this *whole in intuition* do parts become possible for the *understanding*. [...]

Now it is upon these dynamical principles that the very possibility of a mechanics reposes, for it is clear that the movable would have no power of moving *through its movement* (through impact), if it did not possess originally moving forces,[4] and thus the mechanical physics is undermined in its foundations. For the latter is clearly a quite topsy-turvy mode of philosophizing, since it presupposes what it attempts to explain, or rather, what it thinks it can itself overturn with the aid of this presupposition.

Notes

1   That a world-system is possible *at all* can have no reason other than the principles of attraction and repulsion. But that it should be *this particular* system can and must be explained solely by the laws of universal attraction; why? – more on the subject later.

2   *Editors' Note.* A reference to Kant's *Metaphysical Foundations of Natural Science*.

3   [...] It is clear, therefore, that each of these two forces, considered in its boundlessness, leads to absolute negation (the void). [*Editors' Note.* The above passage also paraphrases Kant's position in the *Metaphysical Foundations.*]

4   *Editors' Note.* Another reference to Kant's *Metaphysical Foundations*.

Introduction to the Outline of a System of the Philosophy of Nature (1799)[*]

The most universal problem of speculative physics may now be expressed thus: *to reduce the construction of organic and inorganic products to a common expression*. We can only provide the main principles of such a solution, and

[*]Translated by Keith R. Peterson from F.W.J. Schelling, *Historisch-kritische Ausgabe*, ed. Wilhelm G. Jacobs und Paul Ziche (Stuttgart: Frommann-Holzboog, 2001), Series One, Volume Seven.

of these, for the most part, only such as have not been completely educed in the *Outline* itself (third principal division).[1]

A

Here at the very beginning we lay down the principle that *since the organic product is the product in the second power, the* ORGANIC *construction of the product must be, at least, the sensuous image of the* ORIGINAL *construction of* EVERY *product*.

(a) In order that the productivity may be at all fixed at a point, *limits must be given*. Since *limits* are the condition *of the first phenomenon*, the *cause* through which limits are produced *cannot be a phenomenon*, it withdraws into the interior of Nature, or the interior of each respective product. In organic nature, this limitation of productivity is shown by what we call *sensibility*, which must be thought as the first condition of the construction of the organic product.

(b) The immediate effect of confined productivity is an *alternation of contraction and expansion* in the matter already given, and as we now know, constructed, as it were, for the second time.

(c) Where this alternation ceases, productivity passes over into product, and where it is again restored, product passes over into productivity. – For since the product must remain productive to infinity, *those three stages of productivity must be capable of being* DISTINGUISHED in the product; the absolute transition of the latter into product is the cancelling of product itself.

(d) Just as these three stages are distinguishable in the *individual*, they must be distinguishable *in organic nature as a whole*, and the graduated series of organizations is nothing more than a graduated scale of *productivity itself*. (Productivity exhausts itself to degree c in the product A, and can begin with the product B only at the point where it left off with A, that is, with degree d, and so on downward to the *vanishing* of all productivity. If we knew the absolute *degree* of productivity of the *earth* for example – which is determined by the earth's relation to the sun – the limit of organization upon it might be more accurately determined by this means than by incomplete experience – which must be incomplete for this reason, if for no other, that the catastrophes of Nature have, beyond doubt, swallowed the last links of the chain. – A true system of natural history, which has for its object not the *products* of Nature but *Nature itself*, follows the *one* productivity that battles, so to speak, against freedom, through all its windings and sinuosities, to the point at which it is at last compelled to perish in the product.)

It is upon this dynamical graduated scale in the individual, as well as in the whole of organic nature, that the construction of all organic phenomena rests.

B

These principles, stated universally, lead to the following fundamental principles of a universal theory of Nature.

(a) Productivity must be *primarily* limited. Since *outside* of limited productivity there is[2] *pure identity*, the limitation cannot be established by a difference already existing, and therefore must be furnished by *an opposition arising in productivity itself*, to the existence of which we here revert as a first postulate.[3]

(b) This difference thought *purely* is the first condition of all[4] activity, the productivity is attracted and repelled[5] between opposites (the primary limits); in this alternation of expansion and contraction there necessarily arises a common element, but one which exists only *in change*. – If it is to exist *outside* of change, then the *change itself* must become fixed. – The active factor in change is the productivity sundered within itself.

(c) It is asked: (α) By what means such alternation can be fixed at all. – It cannot be fixed by anything that is contained as a *member* in the alternation itself, and must therefore be fixed by a *tertium quid* [third thing].

(β) But this *tertium quid* must be able to *prehend* that original antithesis; however, *outside* of that antithesis nothing *exists*[6] – it[7] must therefore be originally contained in it, as something that is mediated by the antithesis, and by which in turn the antithesis is mediated; for otherwise there is no reason why it should be originally contained in that antithesis.

The antithesis is dissolution of identity. But Nature is *primarily* identity. – In that antithesis, therefore, there must again be a striving toward identity. This striving is immediately conditioned *through* the antithesis; for if there was no antithesis, there would be identity, absolute rest, and therefore no striving toward identity.[8] – If, on the other hand, there were not identity in the antithesis, the antithesis itself could not endure.

Identity produced from difference is indifference; that *tertium quid* is therefore a *striving toward indifference*, a striving which is conditioned by the difference itself, and by which it, on the other hand, is conditioned. [...]

Gravity is simple, but its *condition* is duplicity. – Indifference arises only out of difference. – The cancelled duality is matter, inasmuch as it is only *mass*. [...]

Now there will be exactly as many stages in the dynamical process as there are stages of transition from difference to indifference.[9]

(α) The first stage will be marked by objects *in which the reproduction and recancelling of the antithesis at every moment is still itself an object of perception.*

The whole product is reproduced anew at every moment.[10] That is, the antithesis which is cancelled in it springs up afresh every moment; but this reproduction of difference loses itself immediately in *universal* gravity.[11] This reproduction, therefore, can be perceived only in *individual* objects, which seem to gravitate *toward each other*; since, if to the one factor of an antithesis its opposite is offered (in another) *both factors* become *heavy with reference to each other*, in which case, therefore, the universal gravity is not cancelled, but a special one occurs *within* the universal. – An instance of such a mutual relation between two products is that of the earth and the magnetic needle, in which the continual recancelling of indifference in gravitation toward the poles is ascertained.[12] It is the continual sinking back into identity[13] in gravitation toward the universal point of indifference. – Here, therefore, it is not the *object*, but the *reproduction of the object itself* that becomes object.[14]

(β) At the first stage, the duplicity of the product again appears *in* the identity; at the second, the antithesis will divide up and distribute itself among different objects (A and B). From the fact that the one factor of the antithesis attained a *relative* preponderance in A, the other in B, there will arise, according to the same law as in (α), a gravitation of the factors *toward each other*, and so a new difference, which, when the relative equilibrium is restored in each, results in *repulsion*.[15] – (Alternation of attraction and repulsion, *second* stage in which matter is seen) – Electricity.

(γ) At the second stage the one factor of the product had only a *relative* preponderance.[16] At the third it will attain an *absolute* one – in the two bodies A and B, the original antithesis is again completely represented – matter will revert to the *first stage* of becoming.

At the *first stage* there is still PURE *difference*, without substrate;[17] at the second stage it is the *simple* factors of two PRODUCTS that are opposed to each other; at the third it is the PRODUCTS THEMSELVES that are opposed; here is difference in the *third* power.

If two *products* are absolutely opposed to each other,[18] then in each of them singly indifference *of gravity* (by which alone each *is*) must be *cancelled*, and they must gravitate *toward each other*.[19] (In the second stage there was only a mutual gravitating of the *factors* to each other – here there is a gravitating of the products.)[20] – This process, therefore, first assails the *indifferent element of the* PRODUCT, that is, the products themselves dissolve.

Where there is equal difference there is equal indifference; difference of *products*, therefore, can end only with *indifference* of *products*. – (All indifference deduced until now has been only indifference of substrateless, or at least simple, factors. – Now we come to speak of an indifference of products.) This striving will not cease until a joint product exists. The product, in forming itself, passes, from both sides, through all the intermediate links that lie between the two products,[21] until it finds the point at which it succumbs to indifference, and the product is fixed.

[...]

We must leave it to our readers themselves to make out the conclusions to which the principles here stated lead, and to consider the universal interdependence which is introduced by them into the phenomena of Nature. – Nevertheless, to give one instance: when in the chemical process the bond of gravity is loosed, the phenomenon of *light* which accompanies the chemical process in its greatest perfection (in the process of combustion) is a remarkable phenomenon which, when followed out further, confirms what is stated in the *Outline* [...]: 'The action of light must stand in secret interdependence with the action of gravity which the central bodies exercise.'[22] – For, is not the indifference dissolved at every step, since gravity, as ever active, presupposes a continual cancelling of indifference? – It is thus, therefore, that the sun, by the distribution exercised on the earth, causes a universal separation of matter into the primary antithesis (and hence gravity). This universal cancelling of indifference is what appears to us (who are endowed with life) as *light*; wherever, therefore, that indifference is dissolved (in the chemical process), there light *must* appear to us. – According to the foregoing, there is *one* antithesis which, beginning at magnetism and proceeding through electricity, finally dissipates in the chemical phenomena.[23] In the chemical process, that is, [319] *the whole product* becomes $+E$ or $-E$ (the *positively* electric body, in the case of absolutely *uncombusted* bodies, is always the *more combustible*.[24] Whereas the *absolutely incombustible* is the cause of every *negatively* electric condition). And if we may be allowed to invert the case, what else are bodies themselves but condensed (confined) electricity? – In the chemical process the whole body dissolves into $+E$ or $-E$. Light is everywhere the appearing of the *positive* factor in the primary antithesis; hence, wherever the antithesis is restored, *light* is there for us, because generally only the positive factor is beheld, and the negative one is only felt. – Is the connection of the diurnal and annual deviations of the magnetic needle with light now conceivable – and, if in every chemical process the antithesis is dissolved – is it conceivable that light is the cause and beginning of all chemical processes?[25]

[...] The first inception of original production is the limitation of productivity through the primitive antithesis, which, *as* antithesis (and as the condition of all construction), is distinguished only in *magnetism*; the second stage of production is the *alternation* of contraction and expansion, and *as* such becomes visible only in *electricity*; finally, the third stage is the transition of this change into indifference, a change which is recognized as such only in *chemical* phenomena.

MAGNETISM, ELECTRICITY AND CHEMICAL PROCESS are the *categories* of the original construction of Nature[26] – the latter escapes us and lies outside of intuition, the former are what of it remains behind, what stands firm, what is fixed – the general schemata for the construction of matter.

And (in order to close the circle at the point where it began), just as in organic nature, where in the graduated series of sensibility, irritability and formative drive the secret of the production of the *whole of organic nature* lies in each individual, so in the graduated series of magnetism, electricity and chemical process, so far as the series of powers can be distinguished in the individual body, is to be found the secret of the production *of Nature from itself*.[27, 28]

C

We have now approached nearer the solution of our problem, which was to reduce the construction of organic and inorganic nature to a common expression.

Inorganic nature is the product of the *first* power, organic nature of the second[29] (this was demonstrated above; it will soon appear that the latter is the product of a still higher power). – Hence the latter, in view of the former, appears contingent; the former, in view of the latter, necessary. Inorganic nature can take its origin from *simple* factors, organic nature only from *products*, which again become factors. Hence an inorganic nature generally will appear as having been from all eternity, organic nature as having *originated*.

In organic nature, indifference can never come to be in the same way in which it comes to exist in inorganic nature, because life consists in nothing more than a continual *prevention of the attainment of indifference*,[30] through which there manifestly comes about a condition which is only, so to speak, extorted from Nature.

By organization, matter, which has already been composed for the second time by the chemical process, is once more thrown back to the initial point of formation (the circle above described is again opened); it is no wonder that matter always thrown back again into formation at last returns as a perfect product.

The same stages through which the production of Nature originally passes, are also passed through by the production of the organic product; only that the latter, even *in the first stage*, at least begins with products of the *simple* power. – Organic production also begins with limitation, not of the *primary* productivity, but of the *productivity of a product*; organic formation also takes place through the alternation of expansion and contraction, just as primary formation does; but in this case it is a change taking place, not in the simple productivity, but in the compound.

But there is all of this, too, in the chemical process,[31] and yet in the chemical process indifference is attained. The vital process, therefore, must again be a higher power of the chemical; and if the schema that lies at the base of the latter is duplicity, the schema of the former will of necessity be *triplicity*.[32] But the schema of triplicity is[33] that[34] of the galvanic process [...]; therefore, the galvanic process (or the process of excitation) stands a power higher than the chemical, and the third element, which the latter lacks and the former has, prevents indifference from being arrived at in the organic product.[35]

As excitation does not allow indifference to be arrived at in the individual product, and since the antithesis is still there (for the primary antithesis still pursues us),[36] there remains for Nature no alternative but separation of the factors into *different* products.[37] – The formation of the individual product, for that very reason, cannot be a completed formation, and the product can never cease to be productive.[38] – The contradiction in Nature is that the product must be *productive*,[39] and that, notwithstanding, the product, *as* a product of the third power, must pass over into indifference.[40] This contradiction Nature tries to resolve by mediating *indifference* itself through *productivity*, but even this does not succeed, for the act of productivity is only the kindling spark of a new process of excitation; the product of productivity is a *new productivity*. The productivity of the *individual* now indeed passes over into this as its product; the individual, therefore, ceases to be productive more rapidly or slowly, and Nature reaches the point of indifference with it only after the latter has descended to a product of the second power.[41]

And now the result of all this? – The condition of the inorganic (as well as of the organic) product, is duality. In any case, however, the organic *productive product is so* only from the fact *that the difference* NEVER *becomes indifference.*

It is[42] therefore *impossible* to reduce the construction of organic and of inorganic product to a *common* expression, and the problem is incorrect, and therefore the solution impossible. The problem presupposes that organic product and inorganic product are mutually *opposed*, whereas the latter is only the *higher power* of the former, and is produced only by the higher power of the forces through which the latter also is produced. – Sensibility is only the higher power of magnetism; irritability only the higher power of electricity; formative drive only the higher power of the chemical process. – But sensibility, irritability and formative drive are all only included in that *one* process of excitation. (Galvanism affects them all.)[43] But if they are only the higher functions of magnetism, electricity, etc., there must again be a higher synthesis for these in Nature. And this, however, it is certain, can be sought for only in Nature, insofar as, viewed as a whole, it is absolutely organic.

And this, moreover, is also the result to which the genuine science of nature must lead, i.e. that the difference between organic and inorganic nature is only in Nature as object, and that Nature as originally productive soars above both.[44]

Notes

1   *Editors' Note.* Schelling is referring here to the third part of the *First Outline of a System of the Philosophy of Nature*, which precedes the *Introduction to the Outline.*

2   only [*Editors' Note.* This and the following notes record Schelling's own later additions to the text.]

3   The first postulate of natural science is an antithesis in the pure identity of Nature. This antithesis must be thought quite purely, and not with any other substrate besides that of activity; for it is the condition of all substrate. The person who cannot think activity or opposition without a substrate cannot philosophize at all. For all philosophizing only concerns the deduction of a substrate.

4   natural.

5   The phenomena of electricity show the scheme of nature oscillating between productivity and product. This condition of oscillation or change, attractive and repulsive force, is the real condition of formation.

6   For it is the only thing that is given us to derive all other things from.

7   that *tertium quid.*
8   That *tertium quid* (1) must be directly determined through the antithesis; (2) the antithesis must likewise be conditioned through that third factor. Now by what is the antithesis conditioned? It is antithesis only by virtue of that striving towards identity. For where there is no striving towards unity, there is no antithesis.
9   *Editors' Note.* That is, there will be three stages in the dynamical process.
10 Every body must be thought as reproduced at every step, and therefore also every total product.
11 The *universal*, however, is never perceived, for the simple reason that it is universal.
12 By which what was said above is confirmed, that falling towards the centre is a compound motion.
13 The reciprocal cancelling of opposite motions.
14 Or the object is seen in the first stage of becoming, or of transition from difference to indifference. The phenomena of magnetism even serve, so to speak, as an incentive to transport us to the standpoint beyond the product, which is necessary in order for the construction of the product.
15 The opposite effect will result – a negative attraction, i.e. repulsion. – Repulsion and attraction stand to each other as positive and negative magnitudes. Repulsion is only negative attraction, attraction only negative repulsion; as soon, therefore, as the maximum of attraction is reached, it passes over into its opposite, into repulsion.
16 If we designate the factors as + and – electricity, then, in the second stage, + electricity had a relative preponderance over – electricity.
17 for it was only out of it that a substrate arose
18 If the individual factors of the two products are no longer opposed, but the whole products themselves are absolutely opposed to each other.
19 For a product is something in which antithesis cancels itself, but it cancels itself only through indifference of gravity. When, therefore, two products are opposed to each other, the indifference in each *individually* must be absolutely cancelled, and the whole products must gravitate towards each other.
20 In the electric process, the *whole product is not* active, but only the one factor of the product, which has relative preponderance over the other. In the chemical process in which the *whole product* is active, it follows that the indifference of the whole product must be cancelled.
21 for example, through all the intermediate stages of specific gravity
22 *Editors' Note.* Second Division of the *First Outline*, p. 100.
23 The conclusions which may be deduced from this construction of dynamical phenomena are partly anticipated in the preceding. The following may serve for further explanation. The chemical process, for example, in its highest

perfection, is a process of combustion. Now I have already shown on another occasion that the condition of light in the body undergoing combustion is nothing else but the maximum of its positive electrical condition. For it is always the positively electrical condition that is also the combustible. Might not, then, this coexistence of the phenomenon of light with the chemical process in its highest perfection give us information about the ground of every phenomenon of light in Nature? What happens, then, in the chemical process? Two whole products gravitate towards each other. The *indifference* of the *individual* is therefore *absolutely* cancelled. This absolute cancelling of indifference puts the whole body into the condition of light, just as the partial cancelling in the electric process puts it into a partial condition of light. Therefore, the light too that seems to stream to us from the sun is nothing else but the phenomenon of indifference cancelled at every step. For as gravity never ceases to act, its condition – the antithesis – must be regarded as springing up again at every step. We should thus have in light a continual, visible phenomenon of gravitation, and it would be explained why, in the planetary system, it is exactly those bodies which are the principal seat of gravity that are also the principal source of light. We should then, also, have an explanation of the connection *in which* the action of light stands to that of gravitation.

The manifold effects of light on the deviations of the magnetic needle, on atmospheric electricity, and on organic nature, would be explained by the very fact that light is the phenomenon of indifference continually cancelled – therefore, the phenomenon of the dynamical process continually rekindled. There is, therefore, one antithesis that prevails in all dynamical phenomena – in those of magnetism, electricity and light; for example, the antithesis that is the condition of the electrical phenomena must already enter into the first construction of matter; for all bodies are certainly electrical.

24 Or rather, conversely, the more combustible is always also the positively electric; whence it is manifest that the body which burns has merely reached the maximum of + electricity.

25 And indeed it is so. What then is the absolutely incombustible? Doubtless, simply that by means of which everything else burns – oxygen. But it is precisely this absolutely incombustible oxygen that is the principle of negative electricity, and thus we have a confirmation of what I have already stated in the *Ideas for a Philosophy of Nature*, i.e. that oxygen is a principle of a negative kind, and therefore the representative, as it were, of the power of attraction; whereas phlogiston, or, what is the same thing, positive electricity, is the representative of the positive, or of the force of repulsion. There has long been a theory that the magnetic, electric, chemical and, finally, even the organic phenomena are interwoven into one great interdependent whole. This must be established. – It is certain that the connection of electricity

with the process of combustion may be shown by numerous experiments. One of the most recent of these that has come to my knowledge I will cite. It occurs in Scherer's *Journal of Chemistry*. If a Leyden jar is filled with iron filings, and repeatedly charged and discharged, and if after the lapse of some time this iron is taken out and placed upon an isolator-paper, for example, it begins to get hot, becomes incandescent, and changes into an oxide of iron. – This experiment deserves to be frequently repeated and more closely examined – it might readily lead to something new.

This great interdependence, which a scientific system of physics must establish, extends over the whole of Nature. It must, therefore, once established, shed a new light on the *history* of the whole of Nature. Thus, for example, it is certain that all geology must start from terrestrial magnetism. But terrestrial electricity must again be determined by magnetism. The connection of north and south with magnetism is shown even by the irregular movements of the magnetic needle. – But again, with universal electricity, which, no less than gravity and magnetism, has its indifference point – the universal process of combustion and all volcanic phenomena stand in connection.

Therefore, it is certain that there is one chain going from universal magnetism down to the volcanic phenomena. Still these are all only scattered experiments. In order to make this interdependence *fully* evident, we need the central phenomenon, or central experiment, of which Bacon speaks oracularly – I mean the experiment wherein all those functions of matter, magnetism, electricity, etc., so run together in one phenomenon that the *individual* function is distinguishable – proving that the one does not lose itself immediately in the other, but that each can be exhibited separately, an experiment which, when it is discovered, will stand in the same relation to the *whole* of Nature, as galvanism does to organic nature.

26 of matter.

27 of the whole of Nature.

28 Every individual is an expression of the whole of Nature. As the existence of the *single* organic individual rests on that graduated series, so does the whole of Nature. Organic nature maintains the whole wealth and variety of its products only by continually changing the relation of those three functions. – In like manner inorganic Nature brings forth the whole wealth of its products only by changing the relation of those three functions of matter to infinity; for magnetism, electricity and chemical process are the functions of matter generally, and on that ground alone are they categories for the construction of all matter. The fact that those three factors are not phenomena of special kinds of matter, but *functions of all matter universally*, gives its real, and its innermost sense to dynamical physics, which, by this circumstance alone, rises far above all other kinds of physics.

29 That is, the organic product can be thought only as subsisting under the hostile onslaught of an external nature.

30 in prevention of the absolute transition of productivity into product

31 The chemical process, too, does not have substrateless or simple factors; it has *products* for factors.

32 the former will be a process of the third power.

33 in reality.

34 the fundamental schema.

35 The same deduction is already furnished in the *Outline*, p. 118. – What the dynamical action is, which according to the *Outline* is also the cause of excitability, is now surely clear enough. It is the *universal action* which is everywhere conditioned by the cancellation of indifference, and which at last tends towards intussusception (indifference of products) when it is not continually prevented, as it is in the process of excitation. (Original note.)

36 The abyss of forces down into which we gaze here opens up with the single question: in the *first* construction of our earth, what can have been the ground of the fact that no genesis of new individuals is possible upon it, otherwise than under the condition of opposite powers? Compare an utterance of Kant on this subject, in his *Anthropology*. (Original note.)

37 The two factors can never be *one*, but must be separated into different *products* – in order that thus the difference may be permanent.

38 In the product, indifference of the first and second powers is arrived at (e.g. by excitation itself comes an origin of *mass* [i.e. indifference of the first order], and even chemical *products* [i.e. indifference of the second order] are reached), but indifference of the third power can never be reached, because it is a contradictory idea. (Original note, excluding bracketed additions.)

39 i.e. a product of the third power

40 The product is productive only from the fact of its being a product of the third power. But the idea of a productive product is itself a contradiction. What is productivity is not product, and what is product is not productivity. Therefore, a product of the third power is itself a contradictory idea. From this it is even manifest what an extremely artificial condition life is – wrenched, as it were, from Nature – subsisting against the will of Nature.

41 Nothing shows more clearly the contradictions out of which life arises, and the fact that it is altogether only a heightened condition of *ordinary* natural forces, than the contradiction of Nature in what it tries, but tries in vain, to reach through the *sexes*. – Nature *hates* sex, and where it does arise, it arises against the will of Nature. The separation into sexes is an inevitable fate, with which, after Nature is once organic, it must put up, and which it can never overcome. – By this very hatred of separation it finds itself involved in a contradiction, inasmuch as what is odious to Nature it is compelled to develop in the most careful manner, and to lead to the summit of existence,

as if it did so on purpose; whereas it is always striving only for a return into the identity of the genus, which, however, is enchained to the (never to be cancelled) duplicity of the sexes, as to an inevitable condition. – That Nature develops the individual only from compulsion, and for the sake of the genus, is manifest from this, that wherever in a genus it *seems* desirous of maintaining the individual longer (though this is never really the case), it finds the genus becoming more uncertain, because it must hold the sexes farther asunder and, as it were, make them flee from each other. In this region of Nature, the decay of the individual is not so visibly rapid as it is where the sexes are nearer to each other, as in the case of the rapidly withering flower, in which, from its very birth, they are enclosed in a calix as in a bridal bed, but in which for that very reason the *genus* is *better secured*.

Nature is the *laziest of animals* and curses separation because it imposes upon it the necessity of activity; Nature is active only in order to rid itself of this compulsion. The opposites must forever shun, in order forever to seek each other; and forever seek, in order never to find each other; it is only in *this* contradiction that the ground of all the activity of Nature lies. (Original note.)

42 insofar.

43 Its effect upon the power of reproduction (as well as the reaction of particular conditions of the latter power upon galvanic phenomena) is less studied still than might be needful and useful. See the *Outline*, p. 120. (Original note.)

44 That it is therefore the same Nature, which, by the same forces, produces organic phenomena, and the universal phenomena of Nature, and that these forces are in a heightened condition in organic nature.

System of Philosophy in General and the Philosophy of Nature in Particular (1804)*

§ 201 *The organism necessarily takes form in two different, opposed realms. Once again, relative to the organism, one of these realms belongs more to gravity, the other to light;*[1] *in the one, identity prevails, and in the other totality.*[2] – This opposition is expressed in nature as the opposition of the plant and animal realms. – It surely requires no proof that the plant, which

*Translated by Benjamin Berger and Graham Wetherall from F.W.J. Schelling, *Sämmtliche Werke* (Stuttgart and Augsberg: Cotta, 1856–1861), Division One, Volume Six.

is also in coherence with the earth, is the purest illustration of that higher process of cohesion in which matter becomes entangled when light enters into it. It is the actual earth-spirit, which in the anorganic realm of nature was rigidity incarnate, that now raises its head in the plant and greets the sun. Contained within the more developed body of the plant, it once again follows the law of a higher magnetism, namely, the magnetism between the earth and sun; that is, it strives to unify matter and light, once again solely under the form of identity. If the plant merely followed its drive, it would grow all the way up to the sun and establish this identity. – In the animal taken as a whole, it is for the most part totality which prevails (just as identity prevails in the plant). This is made clear, from one perspective, by the formation of the animal organism according to all dimensions [...] yet without subordination under a prevailing identity. This latter [identity] is first attained in the human being, who amounts to the complete resolution of the problem of the unity of identity and totality. As such, the form of the human being's outward appearance alone is enough to make apparent its place between the animal and the plant. [...]

§ 202 *The midpoint of the two worlds of prevailing identity and prevailing totality*, i.e. the common point beginning from which both take form in opposite directions, *is the world of pure disaggregation*, or of totality with the complete negation of identity (in the same way that the inorganic world is identity with the complete negation of totality). This point in nature is characterized by the realm of *infusoria*. In a world which even the assisted eye barely penetrates, this creature stirs – a creature which is not only unknown with respect to its boundaries but is also fully indeterminable. It seems to be constantly appended anew by nature and lies in the middle between the potential and actual organization of matter. I have long since regarded infusoria as the common midpoint between the animal and plant worlds, or, more precisely, as the turning point from which, in completely opposite directions, in flight from one another, the animal and plant worlds take form. This much is so obvious even at the level of experience that it is astonishing that it could have been overlooked for so long. It is at the point where the plant and animal are equally incomplete that they show most determinately their origin in this indeterminate world. [...] It will require more precise investigation to determine whether it can be demonstrated that the majority of cryptogamic plants, such as sponges, tremella, conifers, etc. also have their ground in infusoria, whether they are perhaps also merely the encasing of infusoria, just as on the other side, where animal nature too lingers at the level of mere germination, as in corals, which are simply the encasing and product of polyps. In the meantime, it is already clear from what is known definitively that the two opposed directions taken by nature in the plant and animal realms both suggest a common midpoint, which can only fall in the world of infusoria. If there were really no opposition between animal and plant so complete as that between opposed directions that nonetheless commence from a common starting point, the most developed plants would have to join up with the lowest animal genera. Yet the opposite is the case, which proves that each of these natural realms is a different world, where only the incomplete creations of each can coincide with those of the other, while the more perfect are furthest apart from one another. The class of *zoophytes* is found at the point where the plant and the animal are still equally incomplete; and so there is another common midpoint between the two worlds, where both appear in equally incomplete form and are one in this limited sense; it is only [in departing from] this midpoint in absolutely opposed directions that each most perfectly takes form in its singularity, so that the most fully developed animal and the most fully developed plant stand furthest from one another. (At this stage, the human being remains entirely out of play, given that what appears separately in the animal and plant realms is again seen as one in the human as complete allness.) Since the discovery of the world of infusoria, the most varied ideas about it have been given consideration; but surely the only genuine possibility among them is the one that was already suggested by Leibniz, namely, to recognize the actual infinity of the matter within it, which here appears merely deprived of its *position* or *identity* – the infinity owing to which, as Leibniz says, each part of matter is not only infinitely divisible, but is actually divided, and is like a garden full of plants or a body of water full of living creatures [...]

§ 204 *When light, infinite possibility, is incorporated into matter solely as the infinite possibility of itself, it is bound to matter only for the first dimension.* – The first dimension is everywhere that of selfhood, the continuation of the self (e.g. in magnetism). Thus, where infinite possibility is bound to matter solely as the infinite possibility of itself, it follows that light and matter are only united for the first dimension.

Addition. Reproduction in the general sense of the word corresponds to this dimension. For it is by virtue of reproduction that the organic being contains an infinite possibility, yet only as the infinite possibility of itself either as individual (in growth, etc.) or as genus (in procreation). In this respect, organic activity thus appears primarily as a higher process of cohesion – but the individual does not yet go beyond itself. As such, this dimension is primarily represented by plants.

§ 205 *When light, infinite possibility, is incorporated into matter as the infinite possibility of other things qua other, it is also wedded to matter for the second dimension.* For the second dimension is always the one whereby a thing is in other things, just as the first is the one whereby it is in itself. It is for this reason that the first dimension is the dimension of identity, while the second is the dimension of difference.

Addition. To this dimension corresponds living movement, or what is usually called the *irritability* of the organism. (I retain this term in spite of its clumsiness so as not to waste time improving names.) Through irritability or movement, the organism is imparted with an infinite possibility of other things, but without intussusception,[3] i.e. precisely as *other* things, to which it is first connected by *movement.*

Movement is thus here the expression of the difference between possibility and actuality. The possibility of things lies within the organism, while their actuality lies outside of it.

It is remarkable that in this regard, too, infusoria come down on the side of the second dimension. Although they have neither actual reproduction (since for most, their shape is not even fixed) nor senses, they are nonetheless capable of the fastest movement, sometimes through extremely resistant media, appearing as sparks of life that flare up here and there, as electrical orbs, bubbles, etc.

§ 206 *When light, the infinite possibility of things, is connected to matter as the possibility of other things whose actuality nonetheless at the same time falls in the circle of the organism, it is also wedded to matter for the third dimension.* – The third dimension is always the synthesis of the first two. In the first, the organism was productive, but only of itself, without going beyond itself. In the second, it took up the possibility of other things into itself, but as other things, i.e. with difference. The *synthesis* will be the following: that, as in the first dimension, the organism is productive, but productive of other things *qua* other, in such a way that these things, *qua* other, are nonetheless within the organism. As is easy to see, this synthesis is only achieved by the organic being becoming *intuitive*, perceptive. The organism does not go beyond itself in perception; intuition falls within the organism itself and yet is at the same time the intuition of other things, things external to the organism.

Addition. To this third dimension corresponds the *sensibility* or perceptivity of the organism. [...]

§ 208 *The moment of magnetism in the organic process is the moment of reproduction* – this follows already from § 204. – The magnet, too, has within it the possibility of propagating its form or polarity through infinitely many intermediaries, albeit in such a way that it is [merely] given substance [from without]. By contrast, in the organism, the activity which in the anorganic was mere form now becomes essential. [In the organism,] matter has no existence separable from its form; it is itself magnetism and exists only in the absolute identity of this form. Likewise, magnetism has here taken hold of substance itself, which appears in its present infinitude (albeit merely under the form of magnetism). – In organic reproduction, the form of magnetism is absolutely one with matter, not different as it is in the lower potency; this is the difference between organic propagation and the propagation that takes place in the inorganic natural realm. […]

§ 209 *In reproduction as such, all dimensions repeat themselves.* Either the organic essence contains the infinite possibility of itself under the form of merely relative identity (as in the case of the reproduction of the self qua individual), or it contains the infinite possibility of itself under the form of relative difference (as in the case of the reproduction of self qua genus). […]

§ 214. *The moment of electricity in the organic process can only express itself through an alternation of expansion and contraction in one and the same organ.*

Proof. With regard to organic phenomena, the opposition of the real and ideal principles can also be expressed as the opposition of expansion and contraction. Now although the two principles are posited identically in reproduction, they are posited under the form of the first dimension (§§ 204, 208), i.e. under the form of *succession*. In reproduction, where the schema of magnetism still prevails, the opposed moments could still fall outside of one another, appearing in separate points, as in magnets, where one pole = contraction and the other = expansion.[4] Yet in the moment under consideration, the ideal and the real, and thus also contraction and expansion, are not posited under the form of linear opposition; rather, they are posited identically under the form of the second dimension, i.e. under the form of simultaneity and side-by-sideness. As such, they can no longer fall outside of each other in *different* points (as they do in plants), but only in *one and the same* point. What is called for is that expansion and contraction should be entirely equal. Yet they are opposed to one another; contraction cancels expansion and expansion (so it would seem) cancels contraction. This contradiction can only be resolved by means of the concept of *alternation*, in which an entirely equal moment is attributed to both (expansion and contraction or, what is the same, length and width), and the preponderance given to the *width* in one moment is countered by an equal preponderance of length in the other moment, and vice versa.

[...] [T]here must be an organ for this moment in which an alternation of the two opposed states – limitation of length with the expansion of width and limitation of width with the expansion of length – coexist. Such an organ can only be the *muscle*, and the phenomenal expression of the whole moment is thus the alternation, from moment to moment, of contraction and expansion in terms of length and width – irritability. This concurs with § 205, where we found irritability – living movement – to be the expression of the unity of both principles of the second dimension.

[...]

§ 217 *The third moment of the organic, or that which corresponds to the chemical process, is the moment of sensibility.*

The determining characteristic of the third moment or the third dimension is always, including in the chemical process, that identity and difference themselves become one, are synthesized. Now with regards to the organism, the first moment (reproduction) was the moment of identity; the organism was limited to itself and thus persisted in equality with itself. In the second moment (that of irritability) the organism went beyond itself, taking the possibility of other things up within itself, such that identity was suspended. Now where both are synthesized, i.e. where the organism, without going beyond its identity, nonetheless posits the possibility of other things as actuality within itself, this must be the third moment of the organic process in general. This synthesis of identity and difference is posited *only* in sensibility; for only in sensibility is the infinite possibility of other things connected to the organism, without the organism (in order to posit its actuality) needing to go out beyond itself, out of its identity, as it does in movement. According to the account already given in § 206, in sensibility, the organism is productive, as in the first dimension, yet here it is productive *of other things* (in accordance with the second dimension). Thus, since it is only in sensibility that there is a genuine synthesis of the *first* two moments of the organic process, they also act as the third moment of the organic process in general.

[...]

§ 259 *The only particular [being] in which the essence of a celestial body, i.e. infinite substance, takes shape as absolute, potency-less identity, is the human organism.* – For (1) the organism, as explained in § 190, is the universal expression of the becoming-one of the two attributes, the objective and the subjective. Yet the particular organism in which the essence of the celestial body, i.e. the infinite substance itself, takes shape as potency-less identity (2) can be neither a mere animal nor mere plant organism; for in both series, nature under the universal exponents of identity nonetheless follows different directions; in the plant, it develops the relation of the celestial body to the centre [i.e. the sun] more extensively; in the animal, the relation of the centre to the celestial body. The particular organism that is required here can thus only be one that is neither a mere plant nor mere animal organism, and so one that stands equally opposed to both, and is not the synthesis of the two, but rather their absolute identity. That the human being is the only such organism would accordingly need to be demonstrated at all possible moments. This alone, along with the entire construction of the human organism (not *as organism* in general, as occurs in physiology, but as the *human organism*, as potency-less form [*Bild*] of potency-less identity), would be a matter for a science of its own, one that does not exist and that should take the name of *anthroposophy* – something entirely different from what has hitherto been known as anthropology. Here, then, are some things that can be stated briefly and without too much detail or proof.

The upright posture and formation of the human being, not present as concretely or decisively in any animal, are themselves a highly significant indication of the status of the human as the key to nature, as that which is neither merely animal nor merely plant, but rather their absolute identity. It is significant that the upright orientation of plants, which is merely the expression of their striving from the earth towards the sun, is turned into a horizontal orientation in the animal kingdom; in animal life, the organic sun has infiltrated the animal, but the animal looks only to the earth and is drawn to it through nourishment, desire and even the construction of the body. [...] The plant is but an organ of the earth, an organ through which it speaks to the sun (making it more noble than the animal); the animal is an organ of the sun, through which it speaks to the earth. By contrast, the human being is torn from the earth like the animal and erect like the plant. It is the organ of the earth, by means of which it apprehends not just the sun, but rather the entire heavenly sphere, according to the ancient aphorism concerning nature:

> *It gave to man a sublime countenance and commanded him to look up to the heavens and the stars with an exalted gaze.*[5]

[...]

The human is thus the paradigm of all living things, to which the harmony and unison of the universe are innate. It is the potency-less form of potency-less identity; it is not only in the centre, but is also at the same time the centre itself and is thereby in immediate communion and identity with all things, which becomes knowledge; all movements of nature large and small are concentrated within it, all forms of actuality, all qualities of the earth and the heavens. In a word, it is the world-system, the wealth of infinite substance in the small = the contracted, God become human.

Notes

1   *Editors' Note.* As the third potency of nature, the organism involves both the first potency (gravity) and the second (light) – albeit, in varying proportions, depending upon the form of life.
2   *Editors' Note.* 'Identity' and 'totality' are two key concepts in Schelling's 1804 *System*. Whereas identity is the immediate, affirmative expression of the absolute *as one*, totality is the expression of the absolute as *all that there is*, i.e. everything.
3   *Editors' Note.* That is, without relating to other things in the mode of self-nourishment.
4   *Translators' Note.* Reading *Expansion* for *Extension*.
5   *Translators' Note.* Ovid, *Metamorphoses* 1, 85–6.

Clara (c. 1810)*

The doctor[1] [...] spoke up here and said: You are right, only the most ordered minds should occupy themselves with the question of a life hereafter, only bright and joyful minds should approach these regions of eternal joy and peace. No one should devote themselves to this investigation until they have gained a firm and solid ground here, within nature, on which they can base their thoughts. Only those who understand our current life should speak about death and a hereafter. Any skimming over of our current condition, any knowledge that hasn't developed purely from what is present and real and that tries to anticipate something to which the spirit wouldn't naturally have led is reprehensible and leads to fanciful imagination and error.

In this way, said the clergyman, would you reject all knowledge about things in the hereafter, as I do; for who, indeed, could say that they have understood life?

I do not know, the doctor replied, whether anyone can say that; but I do know that I don't consider it to be absolutely impossible. We simply mustn't seek it too high up, we mustn't cut the root off right at the beginning, which

---

*Translated by Fiona Steinkamp from F.W.J. Schelling, *Sämmtliche Werke* (Stuttgart and Augsberg: Cotta, 1856–1861), Division One, Volume Nine.

draws strength, life and substance into itself from nature's soil and which can then, indeed, push its blooms right up to the heavens. And we must especially give up the thought of deriving life from something different and higher, as if we were simply wanting to grasp that. Not 'top down' but 'bottom up' is my motto. And, I believe, this motto is also quite appropriate to the humility that is so fitting for us in many respects. However, he added, I see that the sun is already setting behind the hills and I am concerned about our friend and the autumn evening air; so let us set off.

Clara quickly bade farewell with a glance toward the distant hills, and once my daughters had been picked up from town we rode back down again toward the mountain entrance and our valley. We sat together in silence and Clara was quiet and pensive. Finally, the doctor brought up a discussion about monastic life: Why do people usually think that monastic life is so pleasant and beautiful? Is it because everyone likes to think that behind the monk's habit there lies the ideal of a clear and peaceful person who has found his own equilibrium; an ideal that everyone wants to realize, but which they nevertheless don't know how to? For certainly only the mob can be influenced by external motivations, the life of luxury, the carefreeness of this state and similar such things.

Only the beautiful location of the cloisters could win me over, Theresa said, the hills on which they are so often built, the fertile valleys that surround them.

[…]

It surprises me, I said, that none of us has cited the beneficent effect that a carefree seclusion could have on the arts and sciences.

Could, answered the doctor, but that it hasn't had for some time now; and then we would only have learned works and the hard work of those who put together collections to cite as proof thereof.

Nevertheless, I answered, the arts and learning would suffer more than a little if all these rich cloisters with their magnificent buildings, their considerable collections of books, their churches with their many altar pieces, their murals and their artistic wood carvings were to disappear.

Yes, said Theresa, and the whole area would become dreary. Indeed, I don't know what sight is more beautiful than a magnificent building with towers and domes rising up in the middle of nature's riches, surrounded by rippling cornfields with water, woods and vineyards in the distance, where everywhere everything is alive with the hustle and bustle of people. The most beautiful town does not have this effect on me; it represses nature such that only at some distance from the city can nature come to be found once more.

But the simplicity of mixing the unbounded richness of a country district with what is magnificent and great, this alone is what is true and fitting.

But then, I said, my Theresa would have to include castles and the nobility's beautiful country seats, too.

Oh no, she answered, above all I love constancy, where I see things keeping or staying together. Even in our time goods pass from one hand to another, one family dies out, nobility moves into the city, and if they ever move out of the city it is only in order to offend the peace and quiet of these beautiful valleys with their contrasting way of life and their loud entertainment.

You are right, my child, I responded, but don't forget that your point of view on the subject can't be the one that is generally held, at least not in the wild times we are facing now. Of the significance that these institutions once held, they have perhaps kept only the picturesque. However, one will find it easier and more agreeable to close down the institutions altogether than to restore them in accordance with their original aim in a way that would be appropriate for our times. When I see such a quiet cloister down below in the valley, or go past one on a hill from which it looks down, I have often thought to myself: if one day the time should come for all these monuments of a bygone time, please let at least one of our princes think to preserve one or two of these sanctuaries, to keep the buildings and their goods together, and to endow them to the arts and sciences. However, only he who really lives within the spirit – the true academic and artist – is truly spiritual. Merely exercising piety as a way of life, without combining it with lively and active scientific research, leads to emptiness and eventually even to that mechanicalness devoid of heart and soul that would itself have belittled monastic life even in times such as ours. In those centuries when knowledge did not spread far, when monks were the only depositories of science and knowledge, they were also the true clergymen, the truly spiritual; since then the rest of the world has outstripped them so powerfully that they have increasingly ceased to be spiritual any more. The sciences have the same end as religion; their best times were and are those in which they are in accord with it. However, if there are countries in which the cloisters were reordered into schools when the change in faith came about, then that is not what I meant.

So what do you mean? the doctor asked.

What I meant was this: it is here on this hill that the next great German poem should be composed, it is here in this valley that a Platonic academy should gather, like that in Cosentina.[2] Men from all of the arts and sciences should live a truly spiritual life here, in harmony and free from worry: they shouldn't be locked up in towns, in the constrictive conditions of society and far from nature. For the German spirit loves solitude as it loves freedom; anything conventional oppresses it. Unlike the tame scholar or poet who puts on whatever appearance so-called society desires and takes its praise and applause, the fodder of vanity, from society's hands and lips as he also takes the fodder of his physical needs, the German spirit loves to roam through woods, hills and valleys, suckled only by nature's breast. The German spirit is not like a regular river that is dammed in and flows through only prescribed banks and countries; it is like the moistness in the earth whose secret pathways no one explores. This moistness nevertheless penetrates and stimulates everything wherever it goes; it gushes forth clear and free, unconcerned whether someone happens along this path and refreshes himself therein, but strengthens and refreshes him who does not shun the solitary mountain tracks, the cliffs and the remote valleys. It is a shame that after fully developing all of this in my head, I often have to tell myself that it will all remain only a pleasant dream, for the Germans seem to have been destined never to be treated in accordance with their own characteristics. The Germans have to have foreign standards forced on them, because those who could change this situation so seldom have the heart to be as they truly are – for what would the neighbors say if one wanted to treat the Germans as German!

So, the doctor said, let us congratulate ourselves anew on our fortunate situation in which we can spend our days in continual traffic with nature without thereby being cut off from the world. I have seen the most beautiful cloisters in the world. I have often been moved by a longing for the contemplative life that seems to pass so eternally and peacefully in places such as on Monte Cassino, in the woods of Camadoli and in the beautiful cloisters by the Main and the Rhine. But I always changed my mind when I noticed how far away from nature that whole way of life leads, how a tediousness and even disgust towards nature came about as a consequence of the self-torment that is imposed upon the committed as a strict law. Out of all possible orders there is only one I wish to be maintained, one that appears to me to fill a need in human society. It is the Carthusian Order. Under this order's statutes so many people have been able to continue lives that would otherwise have become quite unbearable. It is the only sanctuary for those who are truly unfortunate, for those who have a hasty deed or error to bewail to which the enthusiasm of youth or social circumstances drove them, and whose consequences are dreadful and can no longer be rectified. The world and its hustle and bustle that takes anyone in its grip who doesn't cut himself off from it, the very participation therein that awakens their fate would break their heart. Life itself would be a humiliation to them had they not already entered a place of peace and seclusion here, a place similar to the one to which we go after death, where the pain about what is irrevocable fades into melancholy and into a general recognition that there is no longer anything desirable in life for the person who has overcome it and a recognition that the fate of a mortal person is above all a sad one. Nowhere have I made more interesting acquaintances than in the Carthusian cloisters, particularly those in France; nowhere have I gained a more profound look into human life and its manifold intricacies. What refuge other than the grave would remain open to him who was so unfortunate as to have been blamed for a wrong he did not do, and thereby to have forfeited his happiness in life, if this charitable society didn't open its arms to him. Underneath its outward appearance of sheer austerity, this society nurtures the most benevolent intentions. It is where life, as it were, flows timelessly by and the quiet existence of the plants is the only existence in which the cloisters' members still take an active part, holding up to them a lasting picture of calmness and seclusion. I even learned a lot about my own craft from the members of this order, for by observing generally, and plants in particular, over a long period of time they have learned about the wonderful relationships plants have to people.

It is true, I said, I have often been surprised at how much you achieved with things that appeared to be minor and inconsequential and that appeared to bear absolutely no relation to the danger of the situation.

– and just because of that, he added, I couldn't have used them in a city where people are best acquainted with the most dangerous remedies and where they have no belief in those simple things.

Thus, Clara said, would you have thereby preferred a residence in a small country village to one in a city?

Not just as a consequence of that, he answered. The natural scientist belongs in the country. I have learned more about physics from the farmers than from the academics' lecture halls. Observation is still the best. How much there is to observe from early morning right up to the complete silence of nightfall outside, from living through one long summer's day, whose end one does not think one will live to see. Here I have observed things about the most universal effects of nature; I have observed things about light, sound, the role of water on the earth and in the clouds, the coming and going of natural forces; I have watched animal life, but in particular I have observed things about plants that no academic could have told me. Whosoever does not see natural life as a whole, who doesn't come to understand its language in its very details, also does not know the extent to which the human body is itself truly a smaller nature within a larger one, a smaller nature that has unbelievably many analogies and links to the larger – links that no one would think to exist had observation and application not taught us that it is so.

I am often terrified of these links, Clara said here, and of the thought that everything is related to man. Indeed, if another power within me didn't balance out this horror of nature, I would die from the thought of this eternal night and retreat of light, of this eternally struggling beingness that never actively is. Only the thought of God makes our inner being light and peaceful again.

At that very moment the lights of a nearby house not far from her home shone into the carriage that itself came to a stop just a few minutes later. Theresa went up with Clara and we others all went our own ways home.

Notes

1   *Editors' Note.* Besides a few minor characters (such as the clergyman and Theresa), there are three major figures in this dialogue: Clara, the priest and the doctor. The latter tends to give expression to Schelling's 'nature-philosophical' perspective.

2   *Editors' Note.* A scientific academy founded in the sixteenth century that, under the direction of Bernardino Telesio, focused on the investigation of nature.

On Faraday's Most Recent Discovery (1832)*

In scientific discoveries that are *first* in one way or another, and that open a succession of new enquiries, a certain amount of *luck* and *accident* always play a role. It is therefore inevitable that something of this origin should at first attach to them that only a later era will rid them of. This will require that the accidental element in its first appearance be removed in order to accentuate the hidden essence in its purity, and finally to bring it fully to light.

---

*Translated by Iain Hamilton Grant from F.W.J. Schelling, *Sämmtliche Werke* (Stuttgart and Augsberg: Cotta, 1856–1861), Division One, Volume Nine.

The contingent factor in Galvani's initial discovery, for instance, which became a fruitful mother of other, equally important discoveries, lay in the *animal organ* that was regarded as the proper object of the experiment. It was precisely here, however, in what had been considered the essential element, that Volta recognized the contingent factor in the experiment. He firstly asserted that in it, the animal muscle was not treated as such, but only as a semifluid body substituting for a wholly fluid body. With insatiable acuity and by experiments of the highest refinement and artistry, he sought the *universal*, namely, the electrical significance of the phenomenon until he got to the crux, which our famous and commendable countryman Alexander von Humboldt had expressed a few years earlier, albeit only in the form of the wish that he would like to find a similar increase in the galvanic reaction as took place through common electrical reactions in a Leiden jar.

With the invention of the Voltaic pile,[1] the phenomenon in which it was first thought we might at last disclose the secret of voluntary and involuntary movements of animals in an electricity properly inherent in animal organs, and thus a fact pertaining to the theory of organic nature, was decisively repositioned within the scope of the *general* theory of nature. Having taken this view, the phenomenon could no longer be confined only to the electrical process but had already intruded upon the chemical domain. The chemical effect of the galvanic chain had also been previously noted on a small scale, but from its first appearance, the pile cast some doubt over this connection through the observable electrolysis of water that always accompanied its actions.

Now, particularly as regards this issue, Davy, another extraordinary man, has equipped himself with this recently discovered device in order, by the electrolysis of alkalis, by reducing earths to their metallic cores, and especially by so-called electrical conduction experiments (*Überführungsversuche*),[2] to transform chemistry as a whole not only *materially*, but also and especially *physically*, and thus to initiate a system gradually emerging under the name of electrochemistry: given the aim of the present lecture, we cannot pursue this any further here.[3]

The influence of the Voltaic pile on general chemistry must be considered a great and powerful by-product of the original discovery; but concerning the phenomenon itself, the pile has fundamentally taught us nothing more than we learned from the first, simple experiment, where the two water-producing gases appeared at the battery's poles. Let me add a single remark. Anyone who has acquired knowledge of these so-called conduction-experiments (I recall with the vivid pleasure how, in the company of our unforgettable

Gehlen,[4] he was from the first extraordinarily dubious about them, [while] I was convinced of their truth) or who has seen how, by the actions of the Voltaic pile in all decompositions, the materials – not just gases for instance, but also acids, alkalis, earths, even metals – were carried from one pole to its opposite, and such that while in transit, they did not even stop for any intermediary in their way to which they would otherwise strive fiercely to bond; every other attraction as it were forgotten, and following only the upward promptings, as though dead and insensitive to any enticement, they passed through every medium in order to appear pure and free of all admixture at the appropriate pole of the pile; anyone who has seen this *truly* astonishing thing could doubt no longer that to the activity in the pile everything called 'ponderable' is but a plaything, and will be unable to resist its effect.

The galvanic process had now completely overstepped the limit within which it had at first seemed contingently sealed. It had extended its powerful dominance over the entire domain of chemistry. Are we to believe that it will confine itself here, or that the power here formed will not turn to other areas?

Physics knew three different phenomena in which inanimate matter seems to offer certain signs of having an inner life of its own. The most material, the most complex and most widespread of these phenomena were chemical. Confined within a narrow circle, the more fluid phenomena already manifested electricity. The narrowest circuit, however, is formed by the magnetic phenomena of attraction and repulsion, that are, as it were (due precisely to their narrower material extension, and because, being less fluid, they appear more intimately bound up with substance, the prejudice can be maintained that they are the original and the eldest) at the same time the first stirrings of a life still entirely bound to matter and incapable of its own transformation.

Now the first thing that strikes the eye of every observer in comparing these three phenomena was the similarity of the magnetic and electrical phenomena. That the two should be considered not as one but as related is already shown in the circumstance that in each, mutually antithetical and, as it were, weight-bearing potencies arise and seek their antitheses, while the same flees the same. To think the connection of the two with chemical phenomena seems a more remote prospect. Meanwhile, if we consider that an antithesis that is no less strong but only with a greater variety of dress, as it were, is manifest in the attractions and repulsions between chemical elements, and that here too, antitheses such as alkalis and acids strive zealously to bind and, just as with the two electricities and magnetisms, suspend their antithetical properties towards one another, then we are not far from thinking that the same antithesis is operative in chemical phenomena, only more materially and variously mediated, so to speak, as acts more freely and independently in electrical phenomena, while being more evidently bound to a specific substance in magnetic phenomena.

In fact a few Germans ventured to state, even before the discovery of the Voltaic pile, that magnetism, electricity and chemism were but three forms of one and the same process, which for that very reason could no longer be called separately magnetic, electrical or chemical, but should be addressed by the general name of the *dynamic process*; that these forms, as the *universal categories* of the process of nature, must actually be contained in the galvanic, and indeed, as uniting them all, even if not in immediately distinguishable ways.

Now the Voltaic pile did indeed furnish the indubitable fact of the continuity or indeed the unity of the electrical and chemical antithesis; and since the affinity of electrical and magnetic phenomena had always impressed itself on observers, so, in direct consequence of the axiom that two things that are the same as a third are also the same as each other, the conclusion was unavoidable that the same continuity must also be found between magnetic and chemical phenomena. This would be all the more natural following the discovery of the Voltaic pile, since especially in Germany, there were many who held the belief that this great phenomenon, upon which chemism had already become dependent, could not fail also to draw magnetism into its magic circle. Only those whose talent (less for combining than compiling) was more apt to pay more attention to the uncomprehendingly isolated manifold of appearances than those suffused with spirit, might venture pre-emptively to mock this expectation as wild enthusiasm.

After a long and wretched period, during which one might expect that spirit would have been completely worn down by endless, pointless detail that at best led to nothing conclusive and to no real results, there at last appeared Ørsted's discovery – the third great discovery in this sequence – which taught us that even the magnetic needle was subject to the actions of the Voltaic pile. While every intellectual engaged in the study of nature anticipated this discovery to a greater or a lesser degree, others at first all but begrudgingly accepted it or explained it away as merely a random finding.[5]

To understand the Ørstedian phenomenon we must distinguish two states of the Pile: that is, it is called *closed* when the opposing poles are connected by a conductor, and *open*, when the connection is removed. Until then, the phenomena observed in the pile were primarily electrical but, just like those in the convulsions produced in animal parts, they were evident only *at the moment of either the closing or opening* of the pile. As soon as the pile is closed, all outward signs of electrical tension cease. Amongst the effects of the pile manifest *while in a closed state*, we had until now observed only substantial chemical changes, such as those produced by humidified alkalis or salts in metallic solutions. But what change proceeds during the closed state in solid, electrically conducting bodies subjected to its actions was until then completely unknown. Ørsted's experiment shows that all bodies of this kind, and not only conducting bodies but also the elements of the pile, *even the pile itself,* become *magnets* when they are in a closed state or are put into magnetic tension.

The moment a body takes on magnetic properties, it becomes, not only over its whole surface but, by way of a more profoundly penetrating action, everywhere in its interior and throughout its entire volume, so to speak a double being [*Doppelwesen*], in which, *rather than excluding one another,* two (what shall we call them? we cannot say 'two bodies', but two *spirits* or, if it seems more rational,) *potencies,* their antithesis notwithstanding or indeed precisely because of it, support one another, like twins born at the same time and raised as brothers, in such a form that, when the one is manifestly dominant in one direction, the other, by some kind of silent compact, emerges as predominant in the opposite direction. This is the state into which a solid, electrically conducting body is set when placed within the closed pile; this state too is transitory and, when the pile is opened, disappears once more.

Hence the ever-expanding galvanic chain has also absorbed magnetism into itself and declares itself as that *central phenomenon* that already the astute Bacon sought and anticipated. Since it contains all three forms[6] within it, it can no longer be named after just one of them. Nothing more seems then to be wanting; the boldest hopes of scientific divination were not only fulfilled but, as is Nature's wont, surpassed.[7]

Yet the connection between magnetism and electricity was still one-sided, as the latter experiment has shown. It was revealed that a closed galvanic chain transfers a solid body into transitory magnetism. But the demands of the scientific spirit are endless. Surely it also demands to see the reverse, namely, a direct transition from mere magnetism into electrical phenomena. Indeed! On closer consideration, however, can this be promised, or even hoped for? According to what has already been shown, the magnet acts as a constantly closed chain, and genuine electrical effects (sparks, light bundles, the convulsion of animal parts) are evident only in the *moment* of either the closing or opening of the pile. And who could think it possible that the means were found to so determine the magnet as to produce a moment of closing or opening in it, and therefore the possibility of electrical effects?

Yet just this has recently happened via a discovery of which only preliminary and very general information has reached us, though it left the issue itself quite obscure and did not provide any detail regarding the means employed in the experiment. This experiment was reserved for the English scientist *Faraday*, who followed through on Ørsted's experiment with as much single-mindedness and spirit as his great predecessor *Davy* had once pursued the electrochemical aspect of Volta's discovery. In consequence of this discovery we are therefore now able, with the aid of magnetic convulsions in the connective tissue of dead animals alone, to produce sparks and other effects proper only to the electrical current.

After the foregoing developments it is unnecessary to point out that only with this experiment that the consequences of the great discoveries of Galvani, Volta and Ørsted are entirely confirmed and comprehensively drawn out.[8]

To my mind, however, nothing could provide a worthier introduction to today's anniversary celebration of the founding of our Academy,[9] than to announce such a discovery, which is a scientific triumph, in its annals, and furthermore, or so at least it seems to me, it is by far the most gratifying event to have occurred in the scientific field for a long time. For Ørsted's phenomenon has not even borne its true fruit yet because a predilection that is hard to overcome for everything that has mass and an aversion to all that is spirit still refuse to acknowledge what these phenomena so clearly and manifestly articulate. This latest discovery will succeed in surpassing even this final obstacle. The great phenomenon whose full development has been worked on these last forty years will, exalted again, emerge from the darkness and rise like the sun, casting light over everything in the field of natural science.[10]

Of course, this discovery belongs only to one special science, one might say. But the narrow-minded thinking that considers an expansion affecting one part of science as good fortune for that part alone may be assumed neither in a learned society whose arising is due precisely to the mutual draw of all the sciences, nor in this noble assembly that, by your very presence at this celebration, attests to the fact that what is common to and binds all the sciences is nothing alien to you and that, simply because it is what is *truly* universal, is worth articulating before men of universal culture.

Every science has, if I may say so, something *vital* in it (for the universal theory of nature in which it is found precisely that process whose formal variation and essential unity we have just sought to exhibit); and every organized spirit already has within it the feeling and the sense for precisely what is living in every science.

If at any time more intense cooperation ensues between the special sciences, it is a sign that each has attained a life of its own, i.e. that in itself, each is imbued with that vitality that, like a common sensorium, so to speak, cannot be grasped without a universal empathy, without awakening a corresponding movement in all the others. Should an inhibition or an obstacle be introduced into this properly living nexus in a science, the others suffer with it; if by contrast there is a release on the part of one science, the others simultaneously feel expansive and exalted.

Setting aside the resistance of those who find the diffuse and the piecemeal more agreeable, and who seem to fear that the sciences, whose shapeless mass is already barely manageable, will draw closer together, it is amongst the delightful observations occasioned by scientific progress in our time that, in spite of all such resistance, the sciences have nonetheless drawn closer together. Yet it cannot be denied, on the other hand, that in earlier times, interest in scientific discovery was more widespread. Many amongst us still remember the time when galvanism was first made known, and the vivid interest that this phenomenon aroused not only among naturalists, but also scholars and, indeed, all professions, who took it, as it were, as a universal good fortune and welcomed it as the precursor and an announcement of untold revelations of the most profound secrets of life.

We all know what has now supplanted this innocent joy in the advances of human knowledge. All the more, then, must all those who appear to find the present mood undesirable rejoice in every expansion of human knowledge, which manifests the hope that the sciences again acquire a more universal and profound attraction for those minds that have become estranged from it.

It can be said again of the Germans in general, whether intended as praise or blame, that their lack is always greater on the part of understanding and judgement than on that of willing and feeling. It may therefore be asserted that, at least as regards *Germany*, the true calamity of our time is to be sought not in a profound, moral perversity as we readily assume, than in a widespread fantasy that is sadly accepted by all, that contaminates everything, falsifies everything and, because it leaves nothing solid on which we might rely, necessarily spreads a feeling of general insecurity.

In such circumstances, men of great experience, of unshakable good sense and of a purity of will above all doubt, even by their mere existence act to strengthen and preserve. In such a time, not only German literature, but also Germany itself suffers every painful loss it can endure. We lack *that man* who towered like a mighty column over all inner and outer tumult like a Pharus[11] giving heart to many, lighting all the ways of the spirit and, as the natural enemy of all anarchy and lawlessness, always and only owed the dominance he exercised over the spirit to the truth and the proportion found in it. In the mind and, I might add, in the heart of this man Germany was certain to find a last judgement of fatherly wisdom, a conciliatory verdict about everything in art or science, in poetry or life, that roused it. Germany was not orphaned, she was not a pauper; however weak and whatever the inner turmoil, she was great, rich and powerful in spirit – for as long as *Goethe* lived.

Of course nobody doubts that, insight and experience aside, renewal lies only in genuine science. Hence those wiser rulers deserve all the more gratitude who, over measureless and limitless time, prudently restore the inner measure that protects more securely than any external barrier. Recognizing true evil, they consider it an especially sacred duty to their people, to the present and the future of the species, to promote serious, profound and robust science over empty fantasy. The more painfully such a general disturbance which, were it to continue, it would soon put an end to all higher striving of the human spirit is felt, the more heartfelt is the gratitude this Academy owes to its noble protector for the support and encouragement with which His Grace has, in the past year of its existence, furnished it. All the more justifiable are the confidence and hope with which, as regards the means necessary to fulfilling its duties *worthily* and *in a timely manner*, Royal favour is sought for its future.

Notes

1   *Translator's Note.* Alessandro Volta's 'wet' battery (1797) was premised on the idea that living matters, contrary to Galvani's assumptions, were unnecessary elements in electrical generation. It piled alternating discs of silver, salt-water soaked wadding or electrolyte, and copper, the whole then producing an electromotive force.
2   *Translator's Note.* Now called 'electron transfer' experiments.
3   What is crucial in this experiment is that the acid, for instance, transferred from the silver to the zinc pole, did not even turn the litmus paper red while

in transit, but did however when transferred from the zinc pole, and in such a manner as to turn increasingly red as it advanced towards the silver pole. Goethe once remarked that texts that contain an unwelcome counter to or correction of dominant opinion are *secreted*, i.e. removed as far as possible from general knowledge. We may also make the same remark regarding *experiments*, which have no place within the constraints of accepted theories. This is in particular what Davy's experiments have encountered. Up until a few years ago, I would come across many persons, well-informed in the natural sciences, to whom these experiments remained entirely unknown. It is also worth noting that, at least as far as I know, these experiments have until now not in the least undermined the standard conclusions from geognostic facts, although Davy himself already pointed this out.

Whether anyone has made any application of these electrochemical decompositions (metastases) for explaining organic (physiological) phenomena is equally unknown to me.

4   *Translator's Note.* Adolph Ferdinand Gehlen (chemist), editor of the *Neuen allgemeinen Journals der Chemie* (1803 6) and the *Journal für Chemie und Physik* (1806–10).

5   [Ludwig Wilhelm] Gilbert […] tells us that he regarded Ørsted's discovery with suspicion when he first heard of it, and only by [Adam Wilhelm] Hauch, [Ludwig Levin] Jacobson and others being named as witnesses was his mistrust overcome to the extent that he himself undertook the experiment. Hence the first report of the discovery would be introduced in the following terms. 'What strenuous research and effort was unwilling to provide, was provided by accident to Professor Ørsted of Copenhagen during his lectures on electricity and magnetism the previous winter. He and the *worthy* naturalist in whose company the finding was observed, have demonstrated completely, by their experiments, the important discovery that …' etc. What was for Ørsted a mere *finding* becomes, through collaborating with 'worthy naturalists' such as Hauch and Jacobson, a discovery, for which these gentlemen are due equal shares with the rationalist Ørsted. In Ørsted's first report, printed immediately after these words, nothing about an accident that, during a lecture, placed the finding in his hands, can be found; the 'accident' is entirely Gilbert's insertion. […]

6   *Translator's Note.* The galvanic, the electrical and the magnetic.

7   Astronomers have therefore hypothesized, as is well known, a single, as yet unknown planet between Mars and Jupiter. Instead of just one, Nature offered four quite remarkable little planets, gratifyingly disrupting the earlier uniformity of the solar system.

8   The main intention was of course (as also articulated in the immediately following sentence) to announce Faraday's recent discovery, which had just become known, at a solemn occasion. For those who, half out of duty or from

inclination, have followed the advances made since Galvani's first discovery, the preceding historical discussion will of course be unnecessary either to explain the most recent discovery to them or to provide them with some conception of its importance. It is easy to see, however, that lectures held due to the provisions of the Public Sitting of our Academy are not intended for professionals, but specifically to the public attending this sitting and find out a great deal from it. Amongst these, however, there are always persons of broad insight who participate eagerly in everything worth knowing, to whom it is not undesirable to obtain a comprehensible and explanatory account of the course and succession of scientific discoveries that have already attracted general attention due to their importance, although such an account may contain nothing new for the discipline's membership. Allow me to add that I belong to the eldest now living and eagerly followed the progress of Galvani's discovery, in which I earlier participated through my own experiments as well. Therefore, forgive me for taking the earliest opportunity to express my joy at this most recent and, to my mind, entirely decisive discovery here, in this Academy, which has always had as its motto not only to know things, but also their causes – *rerum cognoscere causas* [to know the causes of things].

It was furthermore not the intention of this lecture merely to enumerate these historical discoveries we are discussing, nor to present them as windfall from a mere sequence of happy accidents, but rather the opposite: the aim of this lecture was to show their necessary interconnectedness and therefore at the same time to explain how, after the first beginning, luck and accident certainly helped, the influence of this blind power increasingly diminished in the course of the discovery, because discoveries develop out of one another with a certain necessity and were more or less predicted by intelligent naturalists. In reviewing this remarkable sequence of discoveries, it is with a certain patriotic regret that we might remark that not a single German naturalist participated in any of the important discoveries. On the other hand we can be glad to see in this fact a great experience, surprisingly confirming that, although it cannot be denied that mere spirit and thought are unable *alone* to do anything in the empirical sciences (how could they do anything at all without the aid of experience?) nor can it be understood the other way round, as has been the case for some Germans who, over the last twenty years, were all but alone in the field of physics in adhering to the dictum that, conversely, true salvation was to be sought in disenchanted and thoughtless empiricism. The man who in his philosophy of chemistry articulated bold, universal axioms (for having done which a German in his Fatherland could expect only opposition and even scorn) and whose fascinating literary remains clearly attest to a deeply philosophical mind (Davy): this man decomposed the alkalis, discovered the transmission of ponderable material from one pole to the other and completely transformed chemistry. Conversely, those who see only accident in the sequence of great discoveries in the physics of recent times and, in the end, in natural phenomena themselves, and who have for three decades maligned and even piously persecuted every intention of grasping phenomena scientifically and interconnectedly; might we not ask them after so long a time, what if any notable contribution to scientific advance we owe to them?

9   *Editors' Note.* This lecture was giving at the Bavarian Academy of Science on 28 March 1832, the sixty-third anniversary of the founding of the Academy.

10   Ørsted's discovery has been scrutinized in such detail that, little by little, the line of thought was lost; new and widespread doubt has seemingly arisen regarding determinations already successfully established by Davy. Such doubt is completely laid to rest by Faraday's experiment, and just as in the domain of spirit a great, luminous thought renders a whole number of petty, wretched and overworked associations of ideas (much admired by the feeble-minded) redundant and buries them in deserved obscurity, so the discovery of electromagnetism will liberate science from a great mass of insignificant experiments that contribute nothing decisive. At the same time, if I am not wholly in error regarding the way in which the phenomenon is brought about, this experiment will also enable wholly new combinations, leading us part-way into a higher domain.

11   Pharus, according to Strabo (*Geography* 17.1.6), is an island with a many-storied tower of (reflective) white marble acting as one of the seven lighthouses at Alexandria surrounding the 'harbour of the happy return'.

Further reading

As the passages throughout this volume demonstrate, Schelling discusses the natural world in many of his writings. However, the best places to begin an in-depth study of the philosophy of nature in English translation are: the *Ideas for a Philosophy of Nature*, the *First Outline for a System of the Philosophy of Nature* and the *Presentation of My System of Philosophy*. In recent years, the philosophy of nature has received significant scholarly attention. The following should help the interested reader in making sense of this aspect of Schelling's thought:

Frederick C. Beiser, *German Idealism: The Struggle against Subjectivism, 1781–1801* (Harvard University Press, 2008), Part IV.

Benjamin Berger and Daniel Whistler, *The Schelling-Eschenmayer Controversy, 1801: Nature and Identity* (Edinburgh University Press, 2020).

Iain Hamilton Grant, *Philosophies of Nature after Schelling* (Continuum, 2006).

David Farrell Krell, *Contagion: Sexuality, Disease, and Death in German Idealism and Romanticism* (Indiana University Press, 1998), Part II.

Lara Ostaric, 'The Concept of Life in Early Schelling.' In Lara Ostaric (ed.), *Interpreting Schelling: Critical Essays* (Cambridge University Press, 2014), 48–70.

Dale Snow, *The End of Idealism* (SUNY Press, 1996), Chapter III.

Michael Vater, 'Bringing Nature to Light: Schelling's *Naturphilosophie* in the Early System of Identity.' *Analecta Hermeneutica* 5 (2013): 1–15.

Ben Woodard, *Schelling's Naturalism: Motion, Space and the Volition of Thought* (Edinburgh University Press, 2019).

4

Time, space and the categories

Introduction

In the *Critique of Pure Reason*, Kant famously argues that all objects of possible experience conform to our forms of intuition (i.e. space and time) and the categories of our understanding (i.e. categories of quantity, quality, relation and modality). From his earliest publications, Schelling – deeply influenced in this respect by Maimon and Fichte – may well have agreed with Kant that natural objects must conform to the categories, as well as space and time, if they are to be objects of possible experience; however, he was not so willing to accept the details of Kant's view. The passages excerpted below – traversing fifty years of Schelling's philosophical development – represent moments of his incessant scrutiny of this transcendental idealist heritage, as well as exemplifying the ways in which he felt compelled to move beyond it.

These interrogations of Kantian philosophy comprise the following:

1 First, there is Schelling's early insistence that the forms of synthetic judgement (summarized in the Table of Categories) must be understood as part of a larger story about the self-positing of the I and its self-differentiation. This claim is made in the first passage reproduced below from *Of the I*, in which he makes use of the resources of the post-Kantian turn to thetic and antithetic forms of judgement in order to rewrite the Table of Categories genetically.

2 Schelling soon began to insist that any description of the conditions of objective experience (i.e. experience of spatiotemporal objects) must be grounded in a more expansive philosophy of nature. In this regard, he became increasingly interested in the fact that the three dimensions

of space appear to be linked to certain qualitative features of the natural world, namely, magnetism, electricity and chemical processes, each of which expresses a distinct formulation of the relationship between identity and difference (see Chapters 2 and 3 above). In the 1803 additions to the *Ideas for a Philosophy of Nature* excerpted below, Schelling makes some very brief yet suggestive remarks about the way length, breadth and depth are defined not only by various formulations of the connection between identity and difference, but also by their correspondence to the categories.

3 The mature Schelling ultimately came to reject the subjectivist implications of Kant's critical philosophy and, with it, the need to ground discussions of space, time and the categories in the knowing subject. This 'cosmological turn' – central to the texts of the early 1800s – led to the elaborate (and extremely difficult) theory of time at the heart of his middle period. Its most explicit formulation is to be found in the 'Genealogy of Time' from the first draft of the *Ages of the World* (1811). Here, just as Schelling had already complicated the Kantian theory of space by attending to the qualitative specificity of the spatial dimensions, so too does he challenge the mechanistic conception of time by emphasizing the ontological difference between past, present and future.

4 Finally, the late Schelling turns to Aristotle to undo Kant. His reflections on space in his 1840 lectures on negative philosophy – found in the final section of the chapter below – are evidence both of his continued interest in the question of dimensionality and of a return to the notion of the subject as a means of explaining the significance of living in a spatially extended world. Yet rather than focusing on the transcendental subject of Kantian idealism, Schelling draws upon Aristotle's account of the animal body and its motion in order to further develop his philosophy of space.

Of the I as Principle of Philosophy (1795)[*]

All unconditionally posited propositions, that is, all those whose positing is conditioned only by the identity of the I, can be called *analytical*, because their being posited can be deduced from themselves. Therefore, better

---

*Translated by Fritz Marti from F.W.J. Schelling, *Sämmtliche Werke* (Stuttgart and Augsberg: Cotta, 1856–1861), Division One, Volume One.

yet, they can be called *thetic*. Thetic propositions are all those which are conditioned only by being posited in the I, that is, since everything is posited in the I, all those which are unconditionally posited.

[...]

Up to the present, the determination of the forms of modality has not yet been made quite clear. True, the original forms of being and not-being are basic to all other forms. They contain thesis and antithesis (the contrast between I and not-I), but in an entirely general *formal* way. If this contrast is to be mediated by a *synthesis*, then these general forms must express that synthesis in a likewise entirely general and *formal* manner. For that very reason, *material* (objective) possibility, reality and necessity do not belong among the original forms which precede all synthesis. For they express *materially* what the original forms express only *formally*, that is, they express it in relation to an *already accomplished* synthesis. Therefore these three forms are no categories at all, since categories really are the forms through which the synthesis of the I and the not-I is determined. But the three together are the *syllepsis* of *all* categories. Since they themselves express only positing, and since the [nine real] categories (of relation, of quantity and of quality) furnish the positability of the not-I in the I, the [other] three [of modality] themselves can no longer be *conditions* of this positability, they can only be the *result* of synthesis, or *sylleptic concepts of* all synthesis.

Originally, *pure being* is only in the I, and nothing can be posited in this form [of pure being] that is not posited as equal to the I. For that reason, pure being is expressed only in thetic propositions, because in them the posited is not expressed as something opposed to the I, as *object*, but is determined only as the reality of the I as such.

The characteristic formula for thetic propositions is 'A is', which means that it has an identical sphere of being of its own, into which everything can be posited that is conditioned only by the being of A, and by its being posited in the I. However, since A expresses being as such, there must be a general formula for the antithesis as well, which must be A ≠ −A. By virtue of that, since A is posited in the I, −A is necessarily posited outside the I, independent of the I, in the form of not-being. In the manner in which the first formula makes possible an original thesis, the second furnishes the possibility of an original antithesis.

Yet just this original thesis and antithesis is the problem of all synthesis in philosophy[1] and just as the pure forms of modality express the form of thesis and antithesis originally and universally, they also must contain the *form* of a possible synthesis, originally and *before* all synthesis. This form is the *determination of not-being* by being, and it is the original basis of determination of all possible synthesis.

Pure being is thinkable only in the I. The I is posited purely and simply. The not-I, however, is in contrast with the I, and therefore, according to its original form, it is *pure impossibility*, that is, it cannot be posited in the I at all. Still, it ought to be posited in the I, and the *synthesis* brings about this positing of the not-I in the I by means of identifying the form of the not-I itself with the form of the I, that is, it strives to determine the not-being of the not-I through the being of the I.

Since *pure being* is the original form of all positability in the I, and since the positability of the not-I in the I can be accomplished only by synthesis, the form of pure being, if transferable to the not-I, can be thought only in terms of *strict conformity with the synthesis as such*. (In Kant's language: *objective possibility*, i.e. possibility pertaining to an *object* as such, is contained only in conformity with a synthesis. And that means positability in the I.) For originally the not-I is a *logical* impossibility for the I. For the I there are only thetic propositions, but the not-I can never become the content of a thetic proposition and it directly contradicts the form of the I. Only inasmuch as the not-being of the not-I is determined by the being of the I, that is, inasmuch as there occurs a *synthesis* of being and not-being, the not-I becomes positable in the I. Therefore the possibility of so positing it can be thought only as conformity with synthesis as such. Consequently, the logical possibility of the not-I is conditioned by the objective, the formal by the material possibility.

It follows that *problematic* propositions are those whose logical possibility is conditioned by their objective possibility. In logic itself they stand under the pure form of being, which precedes all synthesis, and they cannot possibly count as a genus by itself. Since they are only an expression of a *logical* possibility dependent on objective possibility, and since logical possibility is the same everywhere, they belong to logic only with regard to that quality which makes them *problematic* propositions. I call the objective possibility, inasmuch as it furnishes the logical possibility (or is a schema of the logical) the *objective-logical* possibility. Propositions that express only *pure* being and *pure* possibility I call *problematic* propositions. These, therefore, occur in logic only insofar as they are at the same time essential propositions.

Existential propositions are determined by the original opposition of the not-I and receive their possibility only through synthesis. They are therefore conditioned by the objective-logical possibility, although they do not express mere possibility. The objective-logical possibility posits the not-I merely into synthesis *as such*, but an existential proposition posits it into some *particular* synthesis. Yet the not-I, in order to be elevated to the form of the I, needs to be posited only by means of the schema of *pure being*, by its mere possibility, that is, by synthesis *as such*, just as the I is posited by the thesis as such. (Where there is thesis there is I, and where there is I there is thesis.) But the original form of the object is conditionality. By virtue of that form, inasmuch as it can be represented by the schema of time, the objects attain *existence* only by reciprocally determining their *position* in time, that is, by their existence in some *particular* synthesis. Here, therefore, a new synthesis must occur, just as, originally, being and not-being could be brought together only owing to the determination of not-being by being. So the result of that synthesis, which is objective possibility, can be brought together with reality in the new synthesis, owing to the determination of the latter by the former. Now, objective-logical possibility means being posited in synthesis *as such*, and reality means being posited in a *particular* synthesis. Therefore the not-I can be posited in a particular synthesis only because it is simultaneously posited in synthesis as such. That means it is posited in *all* synthesis, because *all* synthesis is synthesis itself as well as particular synthesis.

I believe that the whole progression of this synthesis will become clearer to the reader by being presented in the following table.

Table of All Forms of Modality
I.

1.	2.
Thesis	*Antithesis*
Absolute *being absolute positability* originally determined only in *and by the I*.	Absolute *not-being*, absolute independence from the I, and *absolute nonpositablity* determinable only in contrast to the I.

3.

Synthesis

Conditional positability, by means of *absorption* into the I, i.e. *possibility* of the not-I.[2] (This possibility is called objective-logical possibility because the not-I becomes *object* only by absorption into the I, and because this absorption into the I becomes possible only by a preceding synthesis itself [through categories]; conformity with *synthesis as such* [with the categories]; temporal *existence* itself.)

II

1.	2.
Thesis	*Antithesis*
Conditioning through synthesis *as such*, i.e. through objective absorption in the I. *Objective-logical possibility; existence in time as such.*	*Objective* conditioning, not determined by the I *alone*; existence in a particular synthesis (in time), i.e. in reality .

3.
Synthesis

Conditioning of being-posited (determined by the *object*) in a *specific* synthesis, by being posited (determined by the I) in the synthesis *as such*; existence[3] in *all* synthesis. Determination of reality by the objective-logical possibility – *necessity*. (Therefore the whole progression of synthesis goes 1. from being and not-being to possibility, 2. from possibility and reality to necessity.)

Since time is the condition of all synthesis and, on that account, is produced by the transcendental power of imagination through and in the synthesis, one can present the whole issue in the following manner. The *schema* of the *pure* being (the latter being posited *outside of all time*) is temporal existence itself (owing to the action of synthesis itself). Therefore objective possibility means simply being posited in time. Since existence in time is subject to change, the object, though posited in time as such, is positable and yet also not positable. In order to *posit* an object, I must posit it in a *specific* time, which is possible only because some other object determines its position in time and, in turn, allows its own position to be determined by it. Yet the not-I is to be posited only by its own *possibility*, only by the schema of pure being.

But the schema of its own particular form resists such positing through mere possibility because this schema makes it conceivable only as posited in a *specific* time. Now, just as time *as such* is the schema of complete *timelessness*, *all* time (i.e. the actual, infinitely progressing synthesis) is in turn a presentation (image)[4] of time as such (i.e. of the action of synthesis as such) owing to which existence in time *as such* becomes existence in a *specific* time. *All* time therefore is nothing else than an image of time as such, yet it is also a specific time because *all* time is as specific as any single part of time. Thus, insofar as the not-I is posited in a specific time, it receives its *original* form (of change, multiplicity, negability) and insofar as it is posited in time as such it expresses the schematic original form of the I, substantiality, unity, reality. However, it is posited in a specific time only inasmuch as it is simultaneously set in time as such, and vice versa. Its substantiality can be conceived only in regard to change, its unity only in regard to multiplicity, its reality only in regard to negation (i.e. with negation – but in infinite progression).[5]

Notes

1 Among the categories of each individual form, the first one is always the expression of the original form of the I, the second is the original form of the not-I and the third and last one is the synthesis in which the two first ones are united and only now obtain sense and meaning in referring to the object. Note that the form of quality relates to the form of modality, the form of quantity to the form of relation; therefore, the *mathematical* categories are determined by the dynamic categories and not vice versa. [*Editors' Note.* This note and those that follow were published in the 1809 edition of *Of the I.*]

2 Owing to its original contraposition (antithesis), the not-I is an absolute impossibility. In the synthesis it receives *possibility*, but only *unconditional* possibility. Thus it exchanges conditional possibility for unconditional possibility.

3 Existence is the joint form under which possibility, reality and necessity stand. The difference between them lies only in the *determination of time* itself, not in the positing or not-positing in time as such. *Existence* as such is therefore the result of the first synthesis. In the second it is determined as possibility in the thesis, as reality in the antithesis and as necessity in the synthesis.

4 That which mediates the schema with the object is always an image. Schema is that which hovers in time as such, image is that which is posited in a specific time and yet positable for all time, whereas the object is posited for me only in a specific time.

5 The result of these deductions is that only the forms of being, of not-being and of not-being determined by being can belong to logic, since they precede all synthesis and are the basis of all synthesis, and since they contain the original form according to which alone any synthesis can be performed. It also follows that the schematized forms of possibility, reality and necessity, made possible only by an antecedent synthesis, belong to logic only because they themselves are determined by those original forms. Thus, for instance, problematical propositions do not belong to logic insofar as they express objective possibility but only inasmuch as they express objective-*logical* possibility; not insofar as they express a *being-posited in the synthesis* as

such, but only inasmuch as their *logical thinkability* has been transmitted at all through this synthesis. In short, the three forms of the problematical, assertoric and apodictic propositions belong to logic only inasmuch as they are simultaneously the sheerly formal forms of the original synthesis (which is the determination of the not-being by being; *existence as such*), and not insofar as they express the material form – the existence in the *synthesis as such*, in the specific synthesis and in *all* synthesis.

Ideas for a Philosophy of Nature (1803)*

No inquiry has been surrounded, for the philosophers of every age, by so much darkness as that concerning the nature of matter. And yet insight into this question is necessary for true philosophy, just as all false systems are shipwrecked from the very outset on this reef. Matter is the general seed-corn of the universe, in which is hidden everything that unfolds in the later developments. 'Give me an atom of matter,' the philosopher and physicist might say, 'and I will teach you from thence to apprehend the universe.' The great difficulty of this inquiry might also be inferred from the very fact that, from the inception of philosophy up to the present day, in very different forms, admittedly, but always recognizably enough, matter, in by far the majority of so-called systems, has been assumed as a mere given, or postulated as a manifold, which has to be subordinated to the supreme unity, as an existing stuff, in order to comprehend the formed universe in terms of the action of the one upon the other. As surely as all those systems which forsake that opposition on which the whole of philosophy turns, leaving it unresolved and absolute precisely in its utmost boundaries, have never even attained to the *Idea* or *task* of philosophy, so equally is it obvious, from the other side, that in all systems of philosophy hitherto, including those which express, more or less, the archetype of truth, the still-undeveloped and merely imperfectly grasped relationship of the absolute world to the world of appearance, of Ideas to things, has also made unrecognizable the seeds of true insight into the nature of matter that were contained in them. Matter, too, like everything that exists, streams out from the eternal essence,

---

*Translated by Errol E. Harris and Peter Heath from F.W.J. Schelling, *Sämmtliche Werke* (Stuttgart and Augsberg: Cotta, 1856–1861), Division One, Volume Two.

and represents in appearance an effect, albeit indirect and mediate only, of the eternal dichotomizing into subject and object, and of the fashioning of its infinite unity into finitude and multiplicity. But this fashioning in eternity contains nothing of the corporeality or materiality of the matter that appears; the latter is the *in-itself* of that eternal unity, but appearing through itself as merely *relative unity*, in which it takes on corporeal form. The in-itself appears to us through individual real things, insofar as we ourselves reside in this act of fashioning only as singularities or transit-points, on which the eternal stream deposits so much of that which in it is absolute identity, as is coupled with its particularity; for insofar as we also know the in-itself in the one direction only, that means that we do not know it as such, since it is simply the eternal act of knowledge, in its two undivided aspects, and as absolute identity.

Matter, absolutely considered, is therefore nothing else but the real aspect of absolute knowing, and as such is one with eternal Nature herself, wherein the mind of God, in eternal fashion, works infinitude into finitude; to that extent, as the whole begetting of unity in difference, matter again incorporates all forms, without itself being like or unlike anyone of them, and as the substrate of all potencies is not a potency itself. The absolute would truly divide itself, if it did not also, in the real unity with matter, portray at the same time the ideal unity, and that in which both are one, for only the latter is the true reflection of the absolute itself. So matter, too, can no more divide itself than the absolute divides itself into matter (the real aspect of the eternal producing), in that, just as the absolute is symbolized in matter, so matter now in turn symbolizes itself, as the in-itself, through the individual potencies within it, and thus, in whatever potency it may appear, still always and necessarily appears once more as the totality (of the three potencies).

Now the first potency within matter is the fashioning of unity into multiplicity, as relative unity, or into distinguishability, and as the latter, indeed, it is the potency of appearing matter purely as such. The in-itself, which implants itself into this form of relative unity, is again the absolute unity itself, save that in subordination under the potency whose dominant element is difference or non-identity (for what dominates in every potency is that which takes up the other), it transforms itself out of absolute unity into the mutually external as *depth*, and appears as the third dimension. And again the two other unities, the first that of the implanting of unity into difference, which defines the first dimension, and the other that of the converse formation of difference into unity, which defines the second, are the ideal forms of this reality of appearance, which in the complete production of the third dimension appear as undifferentiated.

The same potencies are also present in the corresponding potency of the ideal series, but there they exist as potencies of an act of knowledge, whereas *here* they appear displaced into an other, namely a being.

The first, which is transformation of the infinite into the finite, is in the ideal series *self-consciousness*, which is the living unity in multiplicity that appears deadened, as it were, in the real series, expressed in being as the *line*, or pure length.

The second, which is the opposite of the first, appears in the ideal as sensation; in the real it is sensation become objective, made rigid, as it were, the purely sensible, or quality.

The two first dimensions in physical things are related as quantity and quality; the first is their determination for reflection or the concept, the other for judgement. The third, which in the ideal is *intuition*, is the positor of relation; substance is the unity as unity itself; accident is the form of the two unities.

In both series the three potencies are one: The eternal act of knowledge leaves behind in the one only the purely real aspect, in the other the purely ideal, but precisely for that reason, in both it leaves the essence, albeit only in the form of appearance. Hence Nature is only intelligence congealed into a being, its qualities are sensations faded out into a being, while bodies, as it were, are its deadened intuitions. The highest life here conceals itself in death, and only through many barriers does it again break through to itself. Nature is the plastic aspect of the universe; even the pictorial art kills its Ideas, and transforms them into corpses.

It should be noted that the three potencies must be viewed, not as successive, but in their simultaneity. The third dimension is third, and real as such, only insofar as it is itself posited in subordination under the first (as a relative implanting of unity into multiplicity), and conversely, the first two can emerge as form-determinations only by reference to the third, which to that extent is again the first.

We still have to speak here of the relationship of matter and space. For just because in the former the whole is indeed embedded, but only in the *relative* unity of unity and multiplicity, and only the absolutely-real is also the absolutely-ideal, the latter [space] appears, for the present potency, as distinct from the real, as that *in which* this real exists; but precisely because this ideal, simply for its own part, is without reality, it also appears as *sheerly* ideal, as space.

From this it is evident that matter and space alike are pure abstractions, that one gives proof of the inessential nature of the other, and conversely, that in the identity or common root of both, precisely because they are what they are only as opposites, the one is not space, and the other not matter.

Ages of the World, 1st version (1811)*

As we have permitted ourselves to repeat any number of times, the fatherly or contracting force is posited more and more as something past and latent. We have thereby made our opinion clear that this does not happen all at once, as if the force of contraction were overcome with one stroke. [...] On our own supposition, being is not overcome in a flash or without meeting with resistance.

On this assumption, there arises a continuous struggle between the principle which posits being as past and the principle which posits it as present. Or, since the presence of being depends on the unity of the forces, whereas mere being becomes past only insofar as the one that is frees itself from it, there arises an ongoing struggle between the principle that posits being as a unity on the one hand and the principle that posits it as a duality on the other.

But in this struggle itself there is always a duality, with 'the one that is' being posited to some degree as present, while being is posited to some degree as past. Correspondingly, the completed duality (which would immediately go over into the highest unity) is correspondingly left to the future. In this way, and in every moment, time arises, and always as the *whole* of time, as time in which past, present and future are dynamically held apart from one another while precisely thereby being joined together.

But since this relation cannot remain stable, given that being is constantly being more and more overcome, each of the times posited in this manner is followed by another time, through which the first time is now posited as past. In other words, different *ages* arise.

An origin or beginning of time is unfathomable from any mechanical point of view, just as little as the beginning of life is thinkable without forceful differentiation and active polar opposition. If, as one might ordinarily think, time moves only in one direction, it would be necessary to think of it in

---

*Translated by Joseph P. Lawrence from F.W.J. Schelling, *Die Weltalter Fragmente: In den Urfassungen von 1811 und 1813*, ed. Manfred Schröter (Munich: Biederstein, 1946).

a contradictory way. It would have to have the capacity to precede itself, throwing itself ahead of itself even before it existed as time. It would have to precede itself, because all time that arises presupposes a time that came before it. But it would have to do so without itself having been time, for otherwise its beginning will not have been a true beginning. If it is true (and it is without any doubt) that every beginning of time presupposes a time that already was, then it would be necessary that a real beginning does not have to await the passing by of the time that precedes it, for on the contrary that time must already have been past from the beginning. A beginning of time is thus unthinkable unless an entire mass is already posited as past and another as future. For it is only within this polar holding apart that within each moment time breaks forth.

Such a beginning arises naturally from the point of view developed here. What now follows are the principal moments of the entire genealogy of time, as they have been prepared in what has been said up until now.

The essence or real force within time lies in the eternal. By this we do not mean the most original pristine essentiality, however, for this is less the eternal than eternity itself. Because it is quite simply beyond time, there is no predetermination of time to be found in it. Instead, what we refer to here as the eternal is to be understood as the first existing being. The unity which is in it is no longer the tranquil limpidity of pure eternity, but instead eternity become real and active. Within it, past, present and future are already secretly posited, in their unity. The past is posited through being, the present through the one that is. And lying enveloped and completely hidden away within it is the last and highest unity (the unity of unity and opposition).

But even the eternal, as observed already earlier, is itself only the beginning of the beginning. It is not yet the real beginning. It is like the seed of a plant which, though containing the possibility of beginning the plant, is by no means itself that beginning.

An actual beginning can only come from absolute freedom. In that original unity, which conceals everything within it, it is love that pushes toward separation and articulation. But love itself is still only a searching for the beginning, without being able to find it. All of the confusion, all of the chaos which we feel inwardly whenever we seek to learn something genuinely new, arises out of the search for a beginning that we cannot find. To find the beginning is to find the word that resolves all conflict. This holds also for that condition of self-contradiction and internal conflict into which the first existent is thrown by love. This is why it is said: in the *beginning* was the word.

To the degree that a condition of a peaceful but completely inner unity has to be thought of as preceding the condition of contradiction, it seems legitimate to ask how early or late the demand for revelation came to stir itself within that unity, so that, pushing toward scission, it became the cause of inner conflict.

Only someone who has successfully brought to mind the depth of indifference that is hidden away in the eternal will realize that it cannot have been the absolute beginning, for they will understand that the truly absolute beginning must much rather have been its opposite, the awakening of love, surging forth without any real relationship to anything that came before it. If we started out by saying that the primordial living being in its indifference was the first actuality, we will now have to add the caveat that a first actuality so conceived is actuality only in itself. With respect to anything else, it is no more than a seed, that is, no more than the first possibility of actual being. Yes, it precedes actual being as its potency or concept, but by no means as the creative act making it real. If we should attempt to determine the beginning of that act in accord to the duration of the condition that preceded it, then we would have to understand this original condition as if it itself were already an actually unfolded existence instead of being what it is: a state of self-absorption so complete that it could have no effect whatsoever on anything outside of it. Within that state, there is nothing to be found apart from the bottomless abyss of eternity, for there is no measure appropriate to it, no goal and no time by which it might be determined. The search for a beginning can therefore be nothing other than an eternal quest that springs forth out of itself.

If we have allowed ourselves on occasion to speak as if the original condition persisted in time, then this has to be understood in a metaphorical or mythical sense and not as part of philosophical science.

Anyone who might challenge us by saying that we have explained the origin of the world through sheer miracle would be saying the right thing. Is there anyone who believes that the world could have sprung forth without a miracle – indeed, without a whole long row of miracles? Up until the birth of the Son[1] everything is miracle, everything is eternity. Nothing whatsoever sprang forth through the effect of a preceding cause, but on the contrary everything arose in an eternal fashion.

Granted that the will that wills nothing is the highest, one has to recognize that there is no transition out of it; the first thing that follows it, the will that wills something, must beget itself. It must spring forth in an absolute way. And so if the eternal is eternal, it can precede everything that follows it only in the order of possibility. This is why the beginning of longing within it must be understood as an absolute beginning.

With that initial scission, whereby love seeks the beginning but does not find it, an inner time is posited in the eternal itself. This is the case, because time arises immediately through the distinction within the eternal of forces that are posited not simply in their unity but, because they are co-powerful, in their mutual independence. But time understood in this way can hardly be a time that is ordered and stays in place. Instead, in every moment it is forced by a new contraction to swallow again and again whatever it has just engendered. In this way, it becomes possible to posit that simultaneity that in every struggle gleams forth as space. For this reason it is also not truly time; it is not time that could find its real beginning and be pronounced and revealed. One might thus call it time with no beginning. Because it is in the eternal and can never show itself externally, it can also be called eternal time. But both of these, one will quickly notice, have thereby taken on a different meaning than usual.

The begetting of the Son through the power of the Father offers the first possibility of a real relationship. It is this moment that constitutes the first real beginning. For this reason the being of the Son is one with the beginning and the other way around.

What is thus required is a second personality, one different from the first, one capable of decisively cancelling the simultaneity of principles that are compacted in it. Only through it is being now posited as the first period or potency, standing in contrast with the present in which being is actively being. The unity of both of them, implicit already in the first period, can be freely and essentially unfolded in the future. Time, hidden away in eternity, is thus spoken forth and revealed by the second personality. The principles, simultaneously co-existing in eternity as potencies of being, are now invited to step forth as ages, actual periods of time.

Now for the first time, the true beginning has been found, and with it a beginning of time itself. It is simultaneously the beginning of the world, to the degree that a world is the always varied form of divine life, not as it is in itself but as it is in its revelation.

But this beginning is not a beginning that could ever cease to be the beginning. It is instead always emphatically an eternal beginning. For in every moment is born the divine Son, through whom eternity is opened up in time and spoken out. This genesis is never one that is over and done with, for it is an eternal genesis, one that is always happening. In every moment, just as in the first, the severity and reserve of the Father is overcome. This act, because it always and alone posits time in things, does not just happen once. It is an act that, always and according to its nature, precedes time itself.

This act, we have said, posits time in things. In relation to the things or to the world, time in its emerging beginning can by no means be thought of as external, as if things or the world could begin or exist *in it*. It is the nature of the world to be nascent, to be in beginning, whereby the world, as already established, is not the same as the totality, which can only be the one and can only be insofar as it is one. But such beginning is no beginning *in* time. It is easy enough to resolve the deception (though we can assume it is almost universal) that makes it seem as if the world – or at least each thing – were in time. Not only this or that thing, for example, one of the heavenly bodies or an organic growth, but quite simply everything has its own time in itself. What varies is whether it is straight away in the more unfolded time we are discussing now, the one that has been spoken forth, or whether it remains in the other time. For even if a thing appears to be without a vital inner time of its own, having undergone little in the way of differentiation, it will still be the case that it is not being governed by an external time outside of it. There is no thing that has its time outside of itself, for each thing has an inner indwelling time that was begotten with it and belongs to it.

The mistake of Kantianism with regard to time consists therein, that Kant did not recognize just how *universal* the subjectivity of time is. For that reason he accorded it the limited subjectivity that reduces it to a simple form of our own mental representations. But there are no things that originate in objective time, for *in* each and every thing time itself arises anew, springing forth immediately out of eternity itself. And if one cannot immediately say of everything, it has its being in the beginning of time, it is still the case that the beginning of time is in everything, and in everything it is as the same eternal beginning. For every individual thing arises through the same scission out of which the world itself arises, and thus emerges with its own middle point of time already from the beginning. Its time is in each moment its entire time. Although it comes to be in accord to the movement of one time to another, it is nevertheless not in time. A comparison of one time with another is possible only because outside of any individual thing there are other beings which likewise each have a time of their own. The illusory image of an abstract time arises first here, namely through the comparison and measuring of different times. While it is accurate to say that this image is a form of our mental representations, it by no means reflects something necessary and inborn. Instead, it is accidental and arbitrary, its truth simply a matter of convention. All of the objections that have ever been raised about the reality of time have really only been directed against this illusory picture of time.

The question, whether the world has existed for infinite time or whether it has existed only from a certain time, has been raised in every age, which offers the proof that the right answer has still never been given, as simple as it seems to be for those few who have found it. For it can be made clear to anyone that the concept of an infinite time is an incoherent concept. And yet the human understanding keeps coming back to it as long as its root has not been torn out. The root of the concept is what has been said above, that every beginning of time always presupposes before it a time that already was. In accord to the prevailing mechanical concept of time, this cannot be thought of as what has been split away from a preceding unity and immediately posited as past (as what was in an absolute sense), but rather as a time that has already actually elapsed. The result of this common viewpoint is that preceding every possible time one can always think of another time as already having flowed past. In this way, it will never ever be possible to think of a beginning of time.

If, however, after the dynamic explanation we have just now given, a beginning of time through a splitting into two is after all thinkable, then one need no longer ask such questions as 'when did time begin?' or 'how long has time already lasted?' This is the case, not because time does not in each moment have definite boundaries, but rather because time in each moment is the whole of time, that is, past, present and future. It does not start from the past, but rather from the middle point and in each moment stays the same as eternity. For given that each moment is the whole of time, one can only ask – not: how much time has already elapsed since the beginning, but rather – : how many different times have already come to be? From this it is easy enough to understand that, especially since each one of these moments is one complete time, the times as such can be viewed internally as containing an infinity that surpasses any possible number (just as any part of matter contains an inner dynamic that goes into infinity). Even so, it does not follow that viewed externally time can be understood as extending endlessly and without limit.

To comprehend that smooth continuity which one tries to express through the picture of a river of time, one has to understand that, because time is not a series of discrete parts showing themselves one after another, but instead is in every moment a whole, the reality is that whole follows whole. But this succession of times must itself surely be timeless, and can thus never in its turn be measured or determined in accord to any one time.

From this viewpoint we can see how questionable the familiar assertion of so-called critical philosophy is according to which no real succession can be thought without time. This is an assertion manufactured for the sake of preserving a mechanical explanation of the use of the understanding. On the other hand, it is contradicted even by sensible appearances. For precisely there, where according to the usual conception cause and effect are at play, one cannot envision time as somehow stepping *between* the two of them. The circles that are brought forth as a stone is thrown into the water are there, as effects, at the same moment with their cause: so too, then and there, the thunder with the lightning. In general it appears, however, that within each causal event a process unfolds that is similar to the process by which time itself is originally produced, an observation that sheds light on why the priority of what we just happen to call a cause is in fact a being-posited-as-past by the effect. This is a thought that is relevant to the laws that govern the communication of an impact and to other problems such as the way a cause decays or dissolves into an effect. But these are issues I leave for others to examine.

What occupies us here is a matter that has always been reckoned as among the most obscure. Indeed, as convinced as we are that we have come up with answers to questions that one has hardly even dared to pose, we want to acknowledge that our thoughts are anything but full and complete. There is still much that is miraculous left to discover. There are things we have touched upon here that can be drawn more sharply and brought closer to completion.

What does it mean, for instance, when we say that every possible particular time must be the whole time? We do not mean simply that it is whole in itself because it contains past, present and future all at once. For beyond that we also mean that it contains the whole of time as including what does not yet have real being (which perhaps more clearly could be called absolute time), and does so in a way that makes of itself a real picture of absolute time. The whole of time would first then truly *be* once it ceased coming to be and was thus no longer moving on toward the future. We can thus say: the future or the last time is the whole time. If we accept this to be true, then we can see that every possible time includes the whole time. For what it does not contain as present it still contains as past and as future. What each time includes, furthermore, is the same. For it distinguishes itself from what preceded it only by positing as partially past what this had posited as present, and positing as partially present what this had posited as still future. In the same way, though in reverse order, it distinguishes itself from the time that follows. In other words, each unique time presupposes time *as a whole*. If the whole of time did not precede it as an idea, it could not posit it as future. In that case, it could not posit itself, since in the absence of this determinate future, it would not be the determinate time that it is. But, even so, it presupposes the whole of time only in the form of an idea. If the completed whole were posited in it as actual, then it itself would not be the particular and determined time that it is.

Now, such a relationship of a particular to a whole is generally regarded as an organic relationship, for in an organism the particular requires for the sake of its own reality the whole as present in the idea. Time is thus overall and in everything organic. But if it is organic in everything, it is also organic in the particular. Any number of times, indeed, even infinitely many times, can presuppose in their turn a time that is (relatively) complete as constituting *their* unity, whereupon it is possible to envision an organic system of times that are inwardly infinite and dynamic, albeit finite and closed externally.

Without such an organism all of history would be an incomprehensible chaos. These unities of time are its ages. Each age represents in itself the whole of time, for every age begins ever again from a condition of greater or lesser indistinctness, regressing in part to the later times of previous ages, while on the whole still progressing.

But what is now the organizing principle of the various ages? Without a doubt, it can only be that principle which contains time as a whole. The whole of time, however, is the future. It is the Spirit that acts as the organic principle of the times. The Spirit is free from the opposition between the force of contraction in the Father and the force of expansion in the Son. Both attain complete equality first in the Spirit. He accords them both an equal right, for his life is eternally developed out of the Father through the Son. He relies on both equally for his existence. If the force of the Father is posited as past in relation to the Son, this by no means implies that it has been posited everywhere as nonbeing. It is only posited as nonbeing in the present; within the past it is posited as what is and indeed what is active. But it is not posited absolutely as past (for its overcoming through the Son always still continues). Instead, it is partly still present and partly still future. But the will of the Father in relation to the Son and of the Son in relation to the Father is the will of the Spirit. The Spirit recognizes the proper measure by which the eternal concealment of the Father should be opened and posited as past. The Spirit is thus the one who divides and orders the different times. For the variety and succession of times rests only on the difference of what in each is posited as past and as present and as future. Only the Spirit can investigate everything, even unto the depths of the divinity. In the Spirit alone dwells the knowledge of all things to come. He alone is allowed to lift the seal under which the future lies hidden away. Prophets are therefore driven by the spirit of God, for the spirit alone opens up the ages. It is then the task of the prophet to discern the way they cohere together.

Springing forth from the action and the counter-action of the forces of attraction and expansion in the Father and the Son, the divine life has times and periods of development just as do all things that are alive. The difference is only that God is the freest of all living beings. This is so true that the periods of his development can be said to depend alone on his freedom, whereas any other life faces involuntary constraints as it undergoes its development.

Every time or period of the divine revelation does, of course, represent a limitation within God as well. Does one want to deny that this is possible by resorting to the abstract and ungrounded concept of God as the being without limits? Measure is above all things the greatest. What is without limit was regarded by Plato – and by every higher spirit before him – as the principle of relative evil, whereas limit and measure were understood as belonging to the nature of the good. Once we refrain from appealing to such empty concepts as that of measureless infinity, common sense will enable us to recognize constraints on divine revelation in every moment.

[...]

The origination of space, which accompanies the emergence of visible things out of the invisible, shows itself in the most natural way when it appears in the tissues of organic beings as turgescence.[2] Space does not become, as one tends to imagine, as if (so to speak) it had been all at once poured out. Nor is it to be thought of as an emptiness that is endlessly spread out in all directions. Like time, it too arises from within out of the middle point of the force of resistance. This is its true essence. If it did not constantly strive against what spreads itself out, space would not in any way be possible.

In addition to this, we have to accord to the nature of space all of the determinations which we just accorded the nature of time, for example that things are not in space so much as space is in things and constitutes their measure-granting force. Every possible space is itself, moreover, the whole. And for that reason space is equally organic in all things great and small.

We reserve for ourselves the project of developing on a future occasion all of these determinations, each of which is rife with remarkable consequences.

Space as a whole is nothing other than the heart of divinity that, in its swelling fullness, is nonetheless always held back and pulled together by an invisible force.

In all visible things we recognize first the reality as such, after that their actuality or their external for-itself-being, and finally their mode of being, how they distinguish themselves intrinsically from other things. The reality can only be conferred by the creative force properly speaking, the actuality by the principle of articulate expression, and the mode of being by the inner essence insofar as it is free and soberly creative. The Father alone is the creator of things, the Son is the artisan that fabricates them, the Spirit the sculptor that gives them form.

A thing distinguishes itself modally (in terms of what kind of being it is) only by the degree in which the affirming principle is developed in it that raises it out of nonbeing, without, however, overcoming the negating force instantaneously and beyond all rule and measure. Instead, its progressive overcoming is governed by law. No middle member is jumped over and everything proceeds by degree and in a step-by-step fashion. It is this gradual overcoming that successively brings forth things according to sections and stages and distinctions, whereby it is necessary as always that the lower must go before the higher.

It is immediately obvious, insofar as exactly this incrementally unfolding repression of the negating force is in tandem with the elevation of the affirmative determines the sequence of times, that the sequence of things and the sequence of times is one. All things are only the fruit of their times. Each thing is indeed the fruit of a specific time. Only as such can things be comprehended.

However, the time that determines things, their kind, their character, and their entire nature, is repressed, over and over again, and they together with their time.

Because, however, time is organic overall and in everything as well as in individuals, and because each successive time embodies once again the unity of the time preceding it, all subsequent times reproduce the works of previous times, positing them now, however, as nonbeing, that is to say, as past, as subordinate in relationship to their own productions.

There is thus an eternal exchange between what arises and what disappears until the whole of time, embracing everything, and equal to eternity, is developed into one living being, which at the highest stage of the developmental process happens necessarily. Once this is attained, all the works of time receive their final confirmation. For after everything has been completely unfurled, the contraction, henceforth posited in its entirety as past, can once again operate in complete freedom.

After being has thus been unfolded to its highest point, and after it has been completely taken apart and brought to light by time, the contracting force emerges fully justified as the past that bears all things. The last effect through which the entire process closes itself off is this: that, as if in the ultimate grand finale, it posits as a unity everything that has been unfolded (without its being able to retract anything). In this way it brings forth the simultaneity between whatever has come into being, so that the fruits of different times live reunited in one time, assuming a concentric position like leaves and organs of one and the same blossom, all gathered together around one flaming centre.

In these ways, we have done our best to show how the archaic kingdom of the past, while being repressed by a higher force, is always simultaneously being progressively developed into the form of the present world.

Notes

1   *Editors' Note.* In the first draft of the *Ages of the World*, Schelling uses the trinitarian language of the Father, the Son and the Spirit to refer to the three potencies of being: contraction, expansion and the equipollence of the two.
2   *Translator's Note.* A medical term for swelling.

Presentation of the Purely Rational Philosophy (c. 1847)*

We may count on general approval if we say that something is material to the extent that we register in it something that remains, that stands still, held back from the goal and so averse to all movement; what overcomes this disinclination in the animal is no longer material. But the material is only a determination, an affection, of the Idea. [...] The Idea is not outside the organic being but within it. It is driven not consciously and purposively but simply by its nature, producing these accords insofar as it confirms the power of the contingent and protects the product against precisely this power. It is the Idea that, in a snail or some other animal standing at the same level, replaces the organ taken from it, the Idea that, when the life of an

*Translated by Iain Hamilton Grant from Lectures 18 and 19 in F.W.J. Schelling, *Sämmtliche Werke* (Stuttgart and Augsberg: Cotta, 1856–1861), Division Two, Volume One.

animal occupying a higher level is threatened by internal causes, makes the most intense exertions to save it.

We must, however, take one step at a time, and anticipate as yet nothing particular but remain in the universal. It is an axiom that what cannot go forward goes backwards. Something arrested in its natural motion retreats into itself without negating the preceding movement. The natural medium of both of these movements, proceeding (towards the end) and reverting, is extension, the next level after pure materiality, though this does not prevent there being positions (perhaps it would even be possible to prove that such positions must arise, i.e. where nature has first to prepare the material for a new creation) where, in place of actual extension there remain not so-called atoms, but the sheer potencies of extension. [...]

Extension, considered in actuality, is what appears as turgor in living beings, but it is nothing for itself, nothing without something that is extended, and is therefore in itself negation, the sheer potency of extension. Yet nothing in extension in general remains still. What cannot ascend into another in which it is true Being must seek to be for itself. What therefore is threatened with not-being will not be simply being but will be for itself. We are speaking of a will. This willing in things is what the original is, but not the original, only the aroused. In the world of Ideas as we present it, there was no reciprocal exclusion and the Heraclitean saying that nothing remains (itself, that is), everything makes way, is true in another sense than its author stated it concerning things that appear. In the intelligible world, every antecedent moment was determined to make room for another and to be taken up by it until the last into which everything should ascend. There was no space here, therefore, that each occupied to the exclusion of all others but only an indivisible Being, only a point, so to speak, but intelligibly containing everything and in its position. If however we think this line drawn through the whole as interrupted, in which case each either withdraws completely into non-being or has to assert itself, then each will take up a place for itself, i.e. exclude everything else from it and the space in which each is to the exclusion of everything else; this is not space in general but only sensible space. We have become all too familiar in recent times with space and time, such that we explain the former as the form of being outside itself and the latter as the form of being after another. For if this spatially external being and temporal sequence is not provided for in the intelligible world, then when the former takes place, a meaningless confusion must emerge and everything must be turned upside down: on the contrary, the strata of the earth which developed out of one another demonstrate a sequence that is so lawlike, and so greatly corresponds to the nature or Idea of each generation, that, in it, we are able to secure a recollection, as it were, of the world of Ideas. If the sensibly external, however, is without predetermination, there must already be complete confusion in the intelligible world, providing only that we give it an essential rather than the wholly inessential content of abstract concepts. But what, in this case, is separation, and what help can it be, since in all circumstances, only the inessential may issue from the inessential?

It has already been shown by way of our explication of the law of contradiction that there is already such a distinction amongst the principles, that, for example, a pure not-being cannot be in the same place as a pure being even in thought, since in thought each has its own place. But the same holds for the entire intelligible order of things, that each can only be in its determinate position, and conversely this determinate position can only receive this essence and none other.

We said that in the intelligible world every essence has its place by necessity, but it is not space that determines its position, but time. Each intelligible space is an organism of times, and this inner, thoroughly organic time is true time; the outer, which emerges from the fact that a thing is outside its true Where and not in a position it can remain, has rightly been called the emulator of the true (*aemula aeternitatis*), that is, the intelligible organism of time which can also be thought solely through eternity. For it leads each and everything again to its position and the place allotted it.

The contingent Where is bound up with contingent Being, with necessary unrest, i.e. movement, and the intelligible continuum transforms itself into sensible space, whose nature is complete indifference with respect to its content. But not every essence has an equal relation to space. It seems natural that those amongst them that are already in themselves or metaphysically more removed from materiality suffer less from the reverse movement than those in which the opposite is the case, and that those that seem therefore to have preserved their intelligible relation more are less subject to that contingent movement, which is set up by the fact that a thing finds itself outside its true Where, just as it seems that, amongst the planets, only a small shock is required to oust them from their place and transpose them into their orbital motion, through which they nevertheless affirm that place. Thus bound to the place, in general always at the same distance from others, as a whole uniformly moved, they appear to be sublime above the restlessness of the animate world, where in the animal kingdom at least the opposite takes place. Hence, as if seized by a soul's intuition, they can appear nearer the godhead, just as Aristotle himself seems in this respect closer to the ancient oriental picture that viewed the stars as servants at the mercy of the All-Highest whose throne they become and whose will comes to pass in the skies, while on earth another comes about. In fact, amongst everything visible, the stars are most like the Ideas according to their form and existence, and though they may be treated as partly consisting in corporeal things, what drives them, the true constellation in them, presents itself as purely intelligible. There is therefore one relation to space for these beings and another for one that has been torn from the universal, made into a world for itself and carries space within itself. The animate being is only bound to the planets by what is matter in it, but is, in its genuine self, free from place; although each individual plant is stitched into a definite place, it is completely indifferent to which place as such. Still more independent of space as such is the animal in which, with the preponderance in the soul of willing, the principle of selfhood, of being-for-itself, and hence independence from the universal, has reached full energy. It is only for reproductive purposes that the animal knows a territory, a place to remain where, so to speak, its selfhood dies and the individual enters the service of the species. The migratory bird returns from great distances to the same place for this purpose; even humanity, insofar as it has a home, has one only through birth, or to the extent that one is the founder of a new species [*eines neuen Geschlechts*].

It is already contained in the above that there is no staying in place even in sheer extension. For each demands not merely to be being, but to be being for itself, a whole for itself sealed against everything else. Nor therefore does it desire mere extension, rather extension sealed on all sides, i.e. to be a body. But the Idea alone is the whole, and even what appears will therefore only be a whole to the extent that it is itself an image of the Idea.

*

We have distinguished intelligible from sensible space. When everything perceptible is withdrawn from the latter, this gives rise to abstract or mathematical space, which is once again intelligible but is nevertheless sheer *hyle* [matter] – as Aristotle calls it, *intelligible hyle*.[1] It is 'hyle' because it accepts all determinations but is not itself the determinant; and 'intelligible' because these determinations are determinations of pure thought. There is therefore nothing that can be a principle in it, to which extent everything represented in space has only a material significance. Hence the Pythagoreans, and Plato after them, reckoned all extension, in a line or a geometrical figure, as merely material, while they correctly posited the *conceivable* in it as numbers. For them, the line according to its concept is only the first duplicity, surface the first triad, and the number four is that of the body, for more than four points are not required for a body of the simplest form.

It is to be expected that this enquiry will lead to a deduction of the three dimensions of the corporeal from one principle, which has been lacking in philosophy up to the present; even now, philosophy lags behind in grounding the three dimensions. Even Aristotle, to whom the principle of dimensions in the universal was no secret, did not seek to deduce the triad from its inner nature but rather, contrary to his habit, from universals lying entirely outside the thing. For he establishes this at the beginning of his book *On the Heavens*, or that there would be no magnitude without line, surface and body, just because three is always the number of the complete, which is why the Pythagoreans, to whom as a rule he is not wont to refer in this way, say that it is the number of the universe, for everything is held within beginning, middle and end. There is a departure from line to surface, and from surface to body, but no further *ekbasis* [going out] from the body, for a transition happens because of a lack and there can be no lack in what is complete. Later in time and against this entirely unsatisfactory deduction, Galileo, seeking to free himself from Aristotle's enchanted world, set down the geometrical proof that no more than three perpendicular lines may intersect in the same point. Previous philosophy has examined this question no further; for even Leibniz, who had so many occasions to do so, referring to Galileo, talks only of a geometrical necessity that certainly says there may be no *more* than three dimensions, but not that there are necessarily three.

Kant's construction of matter from two fundamental forces (a construction to which we might object that it offers no way to explain the specific manifold of matter) first provided more recent philosophy with the opportunity to revisit these dimensions. That is, since recent philosophy thinks the qualities of matters and bodies as determined by their various relations to the three major forms – magnetism, electricity, chemism – or, as they have been called, the categories of the dynamic process (this view received unexpected confirmation owing to recent results from the Voltaic pile and Davy's astute experiments), and as one should be persuaded moreover that the number and succession of these forms in nature could not be accidental but can be explained by the three dimensions of the corporeal, such philosophy had to turn once more to the question of the ground of the dimensions themselves. This is all the more the case once we have noticed that the real, primary significance of dimensions is only fully disclosed in organic nature. The inorganic body has neither right or left in itself, nor above and below, nor before and behind, rather, we determine these differences merely in relation to ourselves. That is, either we call 'right' what corresponds to our right, or if we think ourselves in a reverse position, we call 'right' what corresponds to our left, 'before' what is opposite to what is behind us, 'behind' what averts itself from us, without there being such distinctions in the objects themselves; for if we turn them round, the right has become left, and what was behind has come to be in front of us. At the deepest level therefore the three dimensions are so to speak only form or, as we might put it according to earlier accounts, intention without real content. Even with regular crystals, though some show the faint trace of a difference in their facets in relation to electricity or so-called light polarization, it depends on us what we will call right or left, above or underneath; and these distinctions acquire actual significance in organic but really only in animate bodies, amongst which in turn the human body counts as not merely formally but rather most positively as such a body, since it alone actually embodies the whole idea. The level of organic forms is in direct proportion to the separation and actual differentiation of the dimensions. The slightest change in proportion changes the entire type. The same muscles that draw an animal's head earthward are put, so to speak, into the past when brought further back, pointing the human head skyward. Through the entire ascending line of the animal kingdom we may note how the heart moves increasingly from the right or the middle towards the left. With this guiding thread in hand it becomes easier to demonstrate the progressive transformation of one and the same primal or proto-form through the entire series of organic beings, and leads to a thinking that opposes the drive to merely outward classification [...].

[...]

If we return to something that we regard as settled, independently of the present investigation, i.e. that the body is a whole that is complete in itself, combining the four principles, then a transition to the dimensions will be found without trouble, since the sequence and position of the principles relative to one another already entail that through its connection with the second, the first is not only connected to the second, but also to the third and through it to the fourth, which must be equally valid the other way round or in descending order. In this way, therefore, three connections arise that can only appear as so many dimensions in the material or the spatial can only appear as so many dimensions; just as indeed every dimension proves to be a pairing of two terms, superior and inferior, right and left, before and behind, giving the entire body. When it comes to the actual derivation however, the beginning will not be found without a prior dialectical exposition.

For everyone will be inclined to answer that length is the first dimension. But, as already noted, this is entirely undefined. For the pure line is the measure of every distance, and hence every dimension as well. The meaning of the question is which of the paired terms is first – above and below, right and left, or in front and behind? There is something else to consider here, namely that in every bond, one of the pair is considered more excellent than the other, or as Aristotle says, is 'the better',[2] the superior to the inferior, the right to the left, the before to the behind. Aristotle adds more to this when he defines only the nobler of each pair as the principle, in relation to which the other can only act as *matter*, and consequently not as being but as the patient. Now there may well be a similar relation amongst the bonded pairs such that in each of them, the consequent arises when its antecedent becomes matter or relative not-being. The characteristic of the first dimension would accordingly be that it has *both principles* in it, albeit not of equivalent standing, but rather with one subjugated to the other. Yet if we ask which one of the bonded pairs is the principle, we could not avoid saying that right and left have, for the most part, the appearance of principles. For the Pythagoreans, for instance, who sought to express the primordial contradiction in so many ways, as limit and unlimited, as straight to curved, as uneven to even number, never opposed the lesser good to the greater as inferior to superior, or as behind to before, but only as left to right. Aristotle even rebukes them for having called just this pair (right and left) the principle, but the four others, which they neglected, are no less principle-like (moreover he later indicates that they are more genuinely principles than the former). He himself, however, was as a rule careful to avoid calling the beneath or the behind a *principle*, and these certainly have less claim to this name than the left, because this is less materially conditioned than they are. And when we maintain that the contrast between left and right is sharper than that of above and below or before and behind, this is not based on the Pythagoreans' authority but on the far more ancient authority of the instinct that predominates in the development of language. This is proven by its more general application. For the sharpest contrast is indeed between what we want and what we do not want, not between what we want more and what we want less. We unconditionally call what we want 'right' – in the expression, 'this is right for me', for example. What we do not want is not right and is even 'left' [*links*][3] as in the expression, '*er nahm es links*' ['he took it wrongly'], i.e. contrary to how we wished him to. And there is exactly the same relation between the two principles that, as will be self-evident, are alone able to form the first antithesis as well as the first pairing. For according to our definition, the first principle relates to the second as the object that the second negates; but even to be negated, to be reduced to what *is* not or to potency, it must *be*. It is not in itself the left, therefore, but will only be posited as such; hence it is no less a *principle* in itself than the second. It need not be denied therefore that the left is also the reduced, the lesser or less noble, in relation to the right. But that its only relation to the right could be as inferior to superior, the behind to the before, would already be evident from the material difference between the higher and the lower in the plant (root here, blossom there), or between front and behind in humans, whereas the left eye, for example, is exactly the same as the right, in some cases even sharper.

But just this complete material indifference, which is perceived, at least on the exterior of the animal, between the right and left sides, now urges us to take a further step: this very equivalence requires a higher principle to decide between equal claims, especially since there is nothing in the object itself that would settle the matter, as absolute power allots the right to the right, the left to the left. And, following this decisive turn, we can be truly glad, as it were, that a principle emerged as necessary for us, independent of the object and impartial from the outset, acting equitably towards both principles. Having fulfilled its purpose by perfectly balancing the two, the principle, sublime above both, actualizes itself as two parallel structures. Accordingly, completely the same materially, the formal right of each is preserved as a principle for each as its right, since where there is no longer any material difference, the principle, albeit purely formal, remains. How else could we think to conceive this wonder, the wonder of consistently symmetrical formations, especially since the organs, the tools of motion and sense, including the brain, serve higher and no longer merely material ends. At this point, even Aristotle departs from us; for 'each (the right and the left) seeks the same as it'[4] (so runs the explanation) is in truth saying nothing. Nevertheless, to understand that there is no right or left without a *higher* has no need for such abstruseness at all; for even just spatially, for example, [...] in the line AB right and left are merely *potentia*, or, if you prefer, only exist for us; in order that it is actual in the object itself, we must assume something in the object which determines the right as the right and the left as the left. This determinant must lie outside AB, and can only be the higher in C. Thus it turns out that we are led to agree with Aristotle when he says that the higher is the principle of length, the above is prior to the right – prior, namely, in the order of *becoming*,[5] he deliberately adds, and hence incontrovertibly according to *actuality*. This does not rule it out that breadth is *potential* prior and, by being such, is the *lower*, which only makes a connection with the higher by having the antithesis, the first duality, emerge, becoming breadth in actuality so as to bond with the third (with the higher) and as we have seen, to eliminate not the duplicity but the (material) antithesis in it.

What was hitherto a merely dialectical path has thus led us to the true beginning, to the beginning of *evolution itself*, which *presupposes* the lower. If we are asked by what means this element is given in advance, the question recalls what we already know – the convulsion by which the Idea is lowered into materiality and only then strives again to reconstitute itself into the whole that alone is the image of the Idea, into the body – only by allowing the two principles, which are actually opposed to each other, to diverge. This 'below' is therefore one with the so-called prime matter, the *primum subjectum* [the first subject] that, concealed within everything corporeal as its constant ground, is one with the relative nothing or not-being from which everything becomes – the contingent that gives everything that has become from it its transient character and that, though difficult to conceive just because it is to be understood as the starting point, is precisely therefore not inconceivable. For it is only something inconceivable to those who view it as original, whereas, for us, it is something that is conceived, because it is something derived. In the course of this whole development, the different positions of matter give it different meanings, which neither Plato nor Aristotle distinguished, making their theories obscure in consequence. In its present position, it is only contingent matter that is at issue. It is not a principle here, but only a moment, a moment that is the first attempt at corporeal phenomena.

The first natural movement of what has descended into materiality is to revert towards principles – whereby, of course, dimensions emerge. When we consider that the below is nothing but the negation of every rising, that by nature it is what lies down (this is already implicit in other terms for it: *subjectum, hypokeimenon*); considering also that the horizontal dimension, breadth, is just the contrary of everything that is raised or vertical, then it is hardly surprising to say that the below is just *breadth itself*, the matter of breadth and hence unlimited and not yet limited and actual breadth, i.e. a dimension. In this sense, i.e. potentially, breadth is the first, prior to all. But the first movement is upward and the above cannot be reached from the beneath unless the antithetical principles separate or divide; hence the upward movement is essence, duality, emerging with breadth, actual breadth, the accidental, which is determined and limited only by the above, just as Aristotle says: the above is the determining nature, [...] the *eidos*, the below has a material nature, i.e. indeterminate, dyadic. Sideways movement is according to the above and below, and so is sustained by them. Only the vertical direction has an active, spiritual meaning, breadth only a passive, material one. The meaning of a human body is determined more by height than breadth. The first dimension (height) is that of difference, the second that of indifference and equivalence, i.e. matter.

[...]

Voluntary movement, however, does not simply arise with right and left, since otherwise it would also have to exist where, as in the organs discussed above, this antithesis has only as it were a figurative meaning. There is voluntary motion only with the introduction of the higher potency, which freely disposes of the two principles that operate outwards and within, and produces movements as it pleases. To freedom of movement there also belongs freedom in the direction of these movements, which for example is lost in the vertigo acquired by persistent movement around an axis in one direction. Exactly as in the principle of free movement itself, it seems that in the brain the various directions are weighed at the same time, so that allegedly, when the *pons varolii*[6] is damaged on one side, the animal falls into a rotatory movement that does not stop before the other side is similarly damaged. Total directional confusion will arise if a smaller or a larger part of the cerebellum is removed, but something quite unnatural occurs if the *medulla oblongata* is damaged, the complete destruction of which has total paralysis as its consequence. For in this case animals should move backwards, birds equally try to fly backwards, a movement that is contrary to nature according to Aristotle. For Aristotle gives the following relations for the various dimensions of free movement: deriving from the superior, the right side has the initiative and thence also its priority over the left, which is rather moved than moving; following the *what* and the *where from*, the *where to* is considered, and by nature all voluntary movement goes forwards.

[...]

Thus, if the three dimensions first acquire actual volume in the *animal*, it explains a well-known Platonic phrase from his own [Aristotle's] books called *Peri philosophias*, a phrase known to us only through Aristotle's mention of it, though in a more fragmentary manner than we might wish. Clearly the issue in it is not the world as a whole, as recent interpreters would like, but the animal. Plato has the animal itself emerge from the Idea of the One (which we earlier called the *whole Idea*) and the primary length, breadth and depth, and other bodies in an analogous or in the same way, from breadth and depth. Only analogously, because in them there is nothing genuinely distinctive of the animal. The animal itself is considered as something like the archetype in regard to other bodies; hence the world, in the expression which captured the learned imaginations of the Neoplatonist commentators, can only be something like the primary living being. The type of conjunction refers to a common concept which can here only be that of the body.

The third dimension first achieves complete *expression*, meanwhile, in humanity, because, in quadrupeds, multi-legged, and footless animals, before and behind collapse into length, *above* and *forward* are therefore not separated from one another, but are in the same line, where the difficulty of which we gave advance warning at the beginning arises. But everything falls into place the moment we imagine the animal standing upright and the horizontal spine as vertical.

Notes

1   Aristotle, *Metaphysics* VII.10 [1036a9-12].
2   Aristotle, *De partibus animalium* III.3 [665a23].
3   *Translator's Note.* Schelling's use of the term *das Linke* here exploits its meaning in phrases such as his next example ('*links nehmen*', i.e. 'to get it wrong') or 'to get out of bed on the wrong side' or *das linke Seite* (the left side).
4   Aristotle, *De partibus animalium*, III.7 [670a3-5].
5   Aristotle, *De caelo* II.2 [285a20-22].
6   *Editors' Note.* A part of the brainstem.

Further reading

Further consideration of Schelling's theories of space and time should begin with his 1843 lecture on the *Exhibition of the Process of Nature* (forthcoming in translation by Iain Grant), which is, in part, a detailed commentary on the first two antinomies of the *Critique of Pure Reason*. Moreover, it would be helpful to supplement the brief passage from the *Ideas* extracted above with the *Presentation of My System of Philosophy*, which covers in more detail the relationship between the three dimensions and the 'universal categories of physics'. Secondary literature in this area remains sparse in the English language, but some points of reference include:

G. Anthony Bruno, 'The Facticity of Time: Conceiving Schelling's Idealism of Ages.' In G. Anthony Bruno (ed.), *Schelling's Philosophy: Freedom, Nature, and Systematicity* (Oxford University Press, 2020), 185–208.

Drew Dalton, 'Being and Time for Schelling: An Exploration of Schelling's Theory of Temporality and Existence.' *Idealistic Studies* 38.3 (2008): 175–84.

Marie-Luise Heuser, 'Space Philosophy: Schelling and the Mathematicians of the Nineteenth Century.' *Angelaki* 21.4 (2016): 43–57.

Dalia Nassar, 'Pure versus Empirical Forms of Thought: Schelling's Critique of Kant's Categories and the Beginnings of *Naturphilosophie*.' *Journal of the History of Philosophy* 52.1 (2014): 113–34.

Judith Norman and Alistair Welchman, 'Creating the Past: Schelling's *Ages of the World*.' *Journal of the Philosophy of History* 4.1 (2010): 23–43.

Ben Woodard, *Schelling's Naturalism: Motion, Space and the Volition of Thought*. (Edinburgh University Press, 2019).

Part II

Philosophical methods

Part II

Philosophical problems

5

Intuition, construction and recollection

Introduction

As the opening chapters of this *Reader* demonstrate, Schelling is prone to avoid methodological prologues in order to leap straight into metaphysical speculation. Yet this does not mean he lacks a rigorous account of how one comes to know the fundamental structures of reality. Extensive treatments of the epistemological concepts of intuition, construction, exhibition, abstraction and recollection – as conditions of the possibility of coming to know anything properly at all – are to be easily located in his writings, alongside critiques of forms of knowing he deems inadequate. This chapter provides examples of Schelling's earlier reflections on method, from the 1790s through to the 1810s, where he is concerned with developing his own approach to epistemology in contradistinction to the other Idealists.

The term 'intellectual intuition' tends to dominate discussions of Schelling's approach to adequate knowledge, and it is certainly true that, at some periods during his early work, this concept is affirmed almost rhapsodically. The highpoint of this intuitionism is to be found in the opening to the 1795 *Of the I*, which is excerpted in Chapter 1 above, and we recommend turning back to this text in order to see Schelling's fullest early treatment of intuition. Another example is provided by the selection below from the *Lectures on the Method of Academic Study*, a course Schelling held in 1802 (and published the following year) and in which intellectual intuition is celebrated as the condition for accessing the absolute. Nevertheless, such affirmations of intuition need to be contextualized in terms of his far more complex and subtle methodological reflections developed in conversation with Kant and Fichte;

in particular, they need to be read alongside his interpretation of Fichte on intuition in the passage from the 1797 *Treatises Explaining the Idealism of the Science of Knowledge* and his interpretation of Kant's 'Discipline of Method' in the 1803 review, *On Construction in Philosophy* – both excerpted below.

Very early on – in 1800 – Schelling recognized that these key concepts of intuition and construction brought him into conversation with the Platonic tradition which conceives knowing in terms of *anamnesis* or recollection. He states in the *Universal Deduction of the Dynamic Process* of that year, 'The Platonic idea that all philosophy is remembering is true in this sense; all philosophizing consists in a remembering of the state in which we were one with nature.' In his middle period, this model of recollection is expanded upon and deepened, culminating in the Introduction to *The Ages of the World*, the third extant draft of which is the final text in this chapter.

Treatises Explaining the Idealism of the Science of Knowledge (1797)[*]

The main theorem of critical philosophy can be conveyed as follows: the *form* of our knowledge comes from *ourselves*, the *matter* of our knowledge is given to us *from outside*.

It is beneficial to have this *antithesis* stated generally. For although in our knowledge itself both form and matter are intimately united, it is clear that philosophy suspends this unity *hypothetically* in order to be able to *explain* it; and likewise, it is apparent that all philosophical systems, from the oldest times onwards, have considered form and matter as the two extremes of our knowledge.

It was soon found that *matter* is the ultimate substratum of all our *explanations* and so research into the source of matter itself was abandoned. But something else about things was also noticed – something which could no longer be explained from matter itself, but which required further explanation (e.g. general successiveness in nature; purposiveness; the order and system of the outside world determined by way of a complete linkage from beginning to end). These features hung together with the things themselves,

---

*Translated by Chelsea C. Harry from F.W.J. Schelling, *Sämmtliche Werke* (Stuttgart and Augsberg: Cotta, 1856–1861), Division One, Volume One – with thanks to Norman Schultz and Gottfried Heinemann.

such that one could think neither the things without these features, nor these features without the things. There arose, then, the demand for some kind of transfer from the intellect of the highest essence (e.g. a creator of the world) to these [things], but this failed to get at how any inseparable alliance emerged between [the things and their general features] – the kind which no speculative art can attain. In this way, all things, together with their features, were understood to originate from the *creative* power of a godhead; yet, while one can undoubtedly grasp how an external thing can be represented for a being with creative power, one cannot grasp how it can be represented for *another* being. Or in other words: even if we grasp the source of a world *outside ourselves*, we fail to grasp how the representation of this world came to be *in us*.

The ultimate aim must therefore be to explain, not how external things came to be independently from us – for, we do not possess any understanding of this, because they themselves are the ultimate substrate of all explanations of external events – but how a representation of these things came to be in *us*.

First, the question must be determined. Clearly, it is not only the *possibility* of a representation of external things in us, but also the *necessity* that must be explained. Furthermore, it must be explained not only how we become aware of a representation, but also why we are for this very reason compelled to relate it to an external object. For, we hold our knowledge to be *real* only insofar as it corresponds with the object. (The old definition of truth, it is the absolute correspondence of object and knowing, has long suggested that the object itself is nothing other than our necessary knowing.) For in speculation we are able to separate the two, but in our knowledge itself the two coincide entirely. It is the inability to distinguish the object from the representation while it is being represented that grounds the common understanding's belief in an external world.

The problem is therefore also this: to explain the absolute correspondence of the object and the representation, being and knowing. But now it is clear that, as soon as we *oppose* the object, i.e. the thing outside of us, and the representation (and we do it by posing this very question), no *unmediated* correspondence between the two is at all possible – giving rise to the attempts to mediate object and representation through concepts, to consider the former as *cause*, the latter as *effect*. Yet, with all these attempts, we never achieve what we actually wanted – identity of the object and representation; for that is what we must presume and what the common understanding has always presumed in all its judgements.

It is thus asked: whether such an identity of the object and the representation is in general possible? Simply put, it is only possible in one case: if such a being that looked at *itself* were to exist, then the one representing and that which is being represented, that which is intuiting and that which is intuited, would also exist at the same time. The only example we find of an absolute identity of a representation and of an object is thus *in ourselves*. What is alone unmediated, and through which one knows and understands immediately, is the I in us. I am compelled to ask with regard to all other objects: how is their *being* mediated by my *representation*? For [another] knowing subject, neither I nor matter is primary. I am primary only *for myself*; in me is the absolute identity of subject and object, of knowing and being. Since I know myself only *through myself*, it is absurd that the I still requires a predicate other than *self-consciousness*. Precisely in this consists the essence or being [*Wesen*] of mind – that it has for itself no other predicate than itself.

Thus, only in the self-intuition of a mind is there identity of representation and object. That is, in order to demonstrate the absolute correspondence of representation and object on which is based the reality of *all* of our knowledge, it would have to be *proven* that mind, when it intuits any object in general, only intuits *itself*. The reality of our knowledge is secured by this proof.

The question is, how does one prove it?

First, it is necessary that one obtains that position from which the subject and object in us, the one intuiting and that which is intuited, are identical. This can only occur by virtue of a free action.

Further: the *mind* is what is specified as *its own* object.[1] Mind must be an object *for itself*, yet it is not *originally* an object; it is rather an absolute *subject*, for which *everything* (including itself) is *object*. So it must be. An object is something dead, at rest. [...] [Therefore] mind is itself nothing other than an *eternal becoming*. (Thus is grasped the ongoing *advancement*, the progression, of our knowledge from dead matter to the idea of living nature). Mind must not be – but *become* – an object for itself. For precisely this reason all philosophy begins with deed and action, and mind cannot be an object (in itself) originally. *It only becomes object through itself, through its own action.*

Now what is (originally) object is as such necessarily also something *finite*. Because mind is not originally object, it cannot, in accordance with its nature, be originally finite. So, must it be infinite? This also seems problematic because it is *mind* only insofar as it becomes *object for itself*, i.e. insofar as it becomes *finite*. Thus, neither is it infinite without becoming finite, nor can it become finite (for itself) without being infinite. It is simply neither infinite nor finite. Hence, mind is the primordial *union of the infinite and finite* (a new definition of the mind's character).

From infinite to finite – no *passing over*! This was a principle of ancient philosophy. Earlier philosophers had at least sought to conceal this transition through images, hence the doctrine of emanation, a tradition from the most ancient world, and hence the inevitability of Spinozism from these inherited principles.

It was not until later ages that inane systems attempted to find intermediate links between the infinite and the finite. But between the two there could be no before or after; they found instead only *finite* things. The existence of finite things (thus also finite representations) cannot be explained by way of the concepts of cause and effect. With this insight all philosophy begins; for without it we would never have need to philosophize – without it all of our knowledge is empirical, advancing from cause to effect. The finite and infinite are *united originally* only in the *being* of an intellectual nature. In this absolute *simultaneity* of the infinite and finite lies the being of an *individual* nature (the ego). That it must be so follows from the possibility of *self-consciousness*, through which alone the mind is what it is. There is also possible an indirect proof for this. For either we are originally infinite, so we do not comprehend how finite representations and a finite succession of representations were created in us; or, we are originally finite, so it is inexplicable how an idea of infinity has come to be in us.

Further: the mind is everything only *through itself*, through its own *action*. Thus, there need to be actions originally opposed to it, or, if we consider its mere form, one opposed action would be originally *infinite*, the other originally *finite*. But the two should be distinguished only in their mutual relationship with each other.

Moreover, both these activities are originally united in me; but I know this only through the fact that I encompass the two in one action. This action is called *intuition* […]. With intuition consciousness is still not present, but without it no consciousness is possible. I can, to begin with, only distinguish in consciousness two of these activities: one is *positive* in nature, the other *negative*, one *fills*, the other *restricts* a sphere. The former is presented as activity from *outside*, the latter as an activity from *inside*. Everything that is (in the true sense of the word 'is') is only due to an *orientation towards itself* (which expresses itself through gravitational force in the dead object – which is not, but is simply there – and through the centripetal tendency of the world body in the world system). Mind is only by its orientation towards itself, through which it limits itself in its activity, or what is more, mind is itself no other than this activity and this limit, both as simultaneously thought.

By *limiting itself*, mind is at the same time *active and passive*, and because, without this action, there would likewise be no consciousness of our nature, this absolute unity of *activity* and *passivity* also takes on the character of the *individual* nature.

Passivity is nothing other than *negative* activity. An absolutely passive being is an absolute *nothingness* (a *nihil privativum*). Unnoticed, we have been led through our investigations to the most difficult problem in philosophy. In us no representation is possible without *passivity*, but even less so without *activity*. All philosophers have recognized this. It appears now that our *being* and *essence* are based on this original unity of activity and passivity, which belongs always to our being and essence, as well as, as will be shown in the future, to the determinate system of things. And because everything finite is only graspable through opposed activities – but these are originally united only in a mind – so it follows that all external existence comes forth from the self and is initially apparent in intellectual nature.

Intuition actively binds together activity and passivity. [...] The object of the intuition is thus nothing other than the mind *itself* in its activity and its passivity. But the mind, which intuits itself, cannot, at the same time, distinguish itself from itself – hence, the intuition of absolute identity of the object and the representation (and hence, as will soon be shown, the belief that reality is in the intuition alone, for now the mind does not yet distinguish what is real and what is not real).

But we know that we can distinguish the object and the representation, for we set out from this distinction. (Without it, there is no need to philosophize.) In order to distinguish the object and representation, we need to move beyond intuition.

This we can do only by abstracting from the product of our intuition. [...] That is, we could not *abstract* from the *product* of the intuition without acting freely, i.e. without the [mind's] original practice of *freely* repeating the intuition; and conversely, we would not be able to repeat this action *freely* without at the same time *abstracting* from its *product*. We could not thus abstract the action from the *product* without it *opposing* the free action (i.e. without giving it independence from our action, self-existence); and conversely, we could not oppose the product of action to our action without at the same time being free to act (i.e. without abstracting from it). Now only by our abstraction does the product become our action's *object*.

Only by my free action, insofar as it opposes an object, does *consciousness* arise in me. The object is now here, its origin lies for me in the past, beyond my current consciousness; it is here *without my making*. (Hence the impossibility to explain, from the standpoint of consciousness, the origin of objects.) I cannot act freely in abstraction, without opposing the object to myself, i.e. without feeling dependent on it. The object was but originally only in the intuition, absolutely undifferentiated from the intuition. Thus, I cannot freely *abstract* without feeling compelled with respect to the intuition, and conversely, I cannot feel compelled with respect to the intuition without at the same time abstracting freely.

I am becoming me, but I am not *conscious* of the intuition as I am abstracting from it. Thus, I will not be able to be *conscious* of the intuition without feeling myself *compelled* with respect to it. Conversely, I cannot feel myself compelled with respect to the objects [of intuition] without abstracting from them, i.e. without at the same time feeling free. Thus, I will also be *conscious* of my freedom only insofar as I feel myself restricted with respect to these objects. *There is no consciousness of objects without consciousness of freedom, no consciousness of freedom without consciousness of objects.*

By freely repeating the original practices of mind in the intuition, i.e. by abstracting, *concepts* arise. But, I cannot abstract without at the same time intuiting with consciousness, and vice versa; *hence, we are ourselves conscious of the concept only in contrast to the intuition and of the intuition only in contrast to the concept.*

[...]

In brief, because we ourselves are conscious of the concept only in opposition to the intuition, and we will be conscious of the intuition only in opposition to the concept, so the concept appears to us as dependent on the intuition, the intuition as independent from the concept, but the two are originally (before consciousness) *one and the same.*

An action, in respect to which we feel ourselves *free*, we call *ideal*; [an action] in respect to which we feel ourselves *restricted*, real. Hence, the concept seems to us *ideal*, the intuition *real*; but both only in mutual relationship with one another; for we are ourselves *conscious* of neither the concept without the intuition, nor the intuition without the concept.

Hence whoever remains at the standpoint of mere consciousness must necessarily argue: our knowledge is *part* ideal, *part* real; out of it will arise a fantastic system that can never explain how the ideal had become real or the real ideal. One who stands at a higher vantage point finds that there is *originally* no difference between ideality and reality, so that our knowledge is not in *part*, but *entirely and perfectly* ideal and real *at the same time*.

Originally the *practice* of the mind and the *product* of this practice are one and the same. But we can ourselves be conscious of neither the practice nor the products themselves without them opposing each other. The practice, abstracted from its product, is *purely formal*; the product, abstracted from the practice through which it arose, *purely material*.

Whoever only proceeds from consciousness (as a fact) will establish an inconsistent system, by force of which our knowledge is derived in part from unsubstantial forms and in part from formless things. In short, such a system will result from a principle which we have established above as the principal thesis of the newest philosophy:

'The *form* of our knowledge derives from *ourselves*; the *matter* is given to us from *outside*'.

We know that originally form and matter are one, that we could differentiate the two only because both exist through one and the same identical and indivisible action – we are familiar with only the single alternative: either both, matter and form, must be *given to us from outside*, or both, matter and form, must first come to be and spring forth *from us*.

If we accept the former, matter is something that is *in itself* and originally real. But matter is matter only insofar as it is an object (an intuition or an action). Were it something *in itself*, then it would have to be also something *for itself*; but this it is not, for it only ever is to the extent it is viewed from a being outside it.

But suppose it were something *in itself* – although it is absurd to say or even to think such a thing – we might not even be able to know what it is in itself. It seems that we would need to be matter ourselves in order to know it – but then, in order to know this being necessarily, we would nevertheless still need to be immaterial. So long as we *presuppose* that this being is something that *precedes* our knowledge, we do not even understand what we are saying. Instead of further groping around blindly at incomprehensible concepts, it is better to ask: what alone do and can we originally understand? But *originally* we only understand *ourselves*, and because there are only two conceivable schemas, one in which matter is the principle of mind, and the other which makes mind the principle of matter, so it remains for us to understand *ourselves*. Ultimately, this amounts to the contention that mind is not born of matter, but *matter born from mind* – a principle from which the transition to practical philosophy can very easily be made.

Note

1   Some fair-minded men, though they have nothing to say against the foregoing, will pick up, at least, on the word, *mind* [*Geist*]; and the Kantians (if they were to take seriously this criticism of their philosophy) will refuse it, or take it up in terms of doctrines that lie far below it, e.g. that it proceeds dogmatically or speaks of the mind as thing in itself, etc. Therefore, I have repeated many times, I call mind that which is *for itself* and not for another being; it is thus *originally* no *object* at all, let alone an object *in itself*.

Lectures on the Method of Academic Study (1803)*

Let us proceed at once to the pivotal issue upon which everything else turns. What is that issue? It is the idea of an intrinsically unconditioned knowledge, one and entire – the primordial knowledge, which in the phenomenal world exists only in separate branches, no longer as one single great tree of knowledge. As the knowledge of all knowledge, it must be based on the same assumption as every individual science. However we express this assumption – whether as adequacy of knowledge to its object or as the resolution of the particular in the universal or in some other formula – it is not conceivable without a higher assumption: true ideality is ipso facto true reality; there is no other ideality.

This essential identity of the real with the ideal cannot, strictly speaking, be proven even in philosophy: it is the assumption upon which all true science is founded. All that can be proved is that without it there can be no science, that the merest claim to knowledge implies search for this identity, for resolution of the real in the ideal.[1]

All universal laws of nature – such as the various sciences boast they have discovered – imply this identity; indeed, every effort to discover them

---

*Translated by E.S. Morgan from F.W.J. Schelling, *Sämmtliche Werke* (Stuttgart and Augsberg: Cotta, 1856–1861), Division One, Volume Five.

unconsciously presupposes it. Their aim is to resolve the concreteness and opacity of particular phenomena in a universal rational knowledge which should be self-evident and transparent. The validity of this presupposition is recognized in special fields with respect to particular cases, even though it is not understood and, consequently, not acknowledged in an absolute and universal sense, as it is in philosophy.

The geometrician more or less consciously bases his science on the absolute reality of the purely ideal when he proves that in any possible triangle the sum of the angles equals two right angles. To do this he does not refer to actually existing triangles but to the archetype. His insight is rooted in the nature of knowledge itself, which is purely ideal and thereby purely real. Even if we restricted the possibility of knowledge to merely finite knowledge, the empirical truth of the latter could never be accounted for by reference to any so-called object – for knowledge is already presupposed when we speak of an object. In fact, knowledge would be altogether inconceivable unless the intrinsically ideal, which in temporal knowledge appears in finite form, were not itself the reality and substance of things.

But this first assumption of all the sciences, this essential identity between the absolutely ideal and the absolutely real, is possible only because that which is the one is also the other. Now, this is nothing less than the Idea of the absolute – that is, in relation to the absolute, Idea is also Being. In other words, the absolute is the supreme presupposition of all knowledge, the first knowledge.

In virtue of this first knowledge, all other knowledge is in the absolute and is itself absolute. For, although primordial knowledge is originally present only in the absolute itself, it is also present in ourselves in the idea of the essence of all things and in the eternal idea of ourselves; and our total system of knowledge can be only a copy of that eternal knowledge. Needless to say, I am not referring to individual sciences insofar as they have separated from this total knowledge and moved away from their true archetype. Only knowledge in its totality can be a perfect reflection of the archetypal knowledge, but each single insight and every individual science are organic parts of this whole, and hence all knowledge that is not directly or indirectly related to primordial knowledge is without reality or meaning.

Our ability to engage in a given discipline with intelligence and the higher inspiration called scientific genius depends upon our ability to relate our particular insights to the original whole. Every thought not conceived in this spirit of unity and totality is intrinsically empty, of no account. Whatever cannot be incorporated into this active, living whole is dead matter to be eliminated sooner or later – such is the law of all living organisms. The fact is, there are too many sexless bees in the hive of sciences, and since they cannot be productive, they merely keep reproducing their own spiritual barrenness in the form of inorganic excretions.

Now that I have formulated the idea of the purpose of knowledge, I need not add anything concerning the dignity of science as such. Whatever norm for the development or study of science I may formulate in the following lectures originates in this one idea.

Historians of philosophy relate that Pythagoras changed into *philosophia* (the love of wisdom) the name of the discipline that until his time had been called *sophia* (wisdom), and that he justified the change on the grounds that God alone is wise. Whatever the historical accuracy of this story, the change and the alleged reason for it imply recognition that all knowledge is a striving for communion with the divine essence, for participation in the primordial knowledge of which the visible universe is the image and whose source is the fountainhead of eternal power. Accordingly, since all knowledge is one, and every branch of knowledge is a part of the whole, all sciences and kinds of knowledge are parts of philosophy, which is itself the striving to participate in primordial knowledge.

Everything, then, which springs directly from the absolute is itself absolute; it has no purpose outside itself, is an end in itself. Knowledge in its totality is one of the two aspects of the universe, and it is as absolute as the other aspect, Being or nature. In the domain of the real, finitude rules; in the domain of the ideal, infinitude; the former is what it is through necessity, the latter is to be achieved through freedom. Man – and the same is true of all rational beings – is intended in a sense to supplement the phenomenal world. The purpose of his activity is to develop that without which God's revelation is not total – for nature contains the whole of the divine essence in its real aspect. Man as a rational being is meant to express the image of the same divine nature as it is in itself, i.e. in its ideal aspect.

[...]

We have shown that mathematics is absolute knowledge only in the formal sense, and it will retain this formal character so long as its symbolism is not completely understood. The world of mathematics is merely a copy; the absolute identity of primordial knowledge is present in it only in a reflected form and, hence, separated from the rest. Only the science which deals directly with primordial knowledge as such can be absolute in every respect. The science which has no archetype except primordial knowledge itself is necessarily the science of all knowledge, that is, philosophy.

It cannot be our purpose here to convince everyone that philosophy is the science of primordial knowledge. All we can prove is that such a science is necessary and that any other definition of philosophy is not a definition of philosophy or even of any possible science.

Philosophy and mathematics are alike in that both are founded upon the absolute identity of the universal and the particular.[2] Hence, both are purely intuitive, since every relationship of this type is perceived through intuition. But whereas mathematical intuition is a reflected one, philosophical intuition is rational or intellectual intuition and identical with its object – with primordial knowledge itself. Philosophical construction interprets what is grasped in intellectual intuition. The particular identities, which, like the universal identity, express absolute primordial knowledge, can be grasped only in intellectual intuition, and in this sense are Ideas. Philosophy is therefore the science of Ideas or the eternal archetypes of things.

Without intellectual intuition no philosophy! Even pure space and time are not perceived in the ordinary consciousness; they, too, are grasped through intellectual intuition. However, because space and time are reflected in the sensible, the mathematician has the advantage of being able to visualize his objects; the philosopher lacks this advantage – intellectual intuition is his only guide. Those who do not have intellectual intuition cannot understand what is said of it, and for this reason it cannot be communicated to them. The minimum requirement is clear and genuine insight into the nothingness of all merely finite knowledge. Intellectual intuition can be developed; in the philosopher it must become his character, as it were – a regularly employed tool, a faculty for seeing things solely as they are in the Idea.

Notes

1 And vice versa, the possibility of fully translating the ideal into the real.
2 Does the geometrician see what is concrete in the actual circle? By no means; nor does he see in it only the universal concept. And yet he does see the universal in the particular. Thus he intuits only the absolute, the circle in itself, not the concrete circle. However, he does not eliminate the concrete, does not *negate* it, is merely indifferent to it – it has no bearing on his *cognition*.

On Construction in Philosophy (1803)*

Since philosophy can neither surpass the narrow limits of Kantian criticism, nor advance upon the path inaugurated by Fichte to a positive and apodictic philosophy without rigorously introducing the method of construction, the following text sketches and presents with the greatest clarity that central point upon which the scientific fulfilment of philosophy depends.

In the future, the doctrine of philosophical construction will constitute one of the most important aspects of scientific philosophy: it is undeniable that due to the lack of a concept of construction many [philosophers'] participation in the advances of scientific philosophy are hindered. The drive to a rigorous construction, developed from first principles, is the most powerful means against a certain false liberality that suffices for the 'great minds' of philosophy, who in the guise of philosophizing pander to mere reasoning. Construction is a powerful means against the muddle of all perspectives which confuses the true and false and makes them indistinguishable.

Some philosophical efforts, since they do not embark on this path and revolt against the attempt at a scientific construction, keep themselves in a certain superficial blindness to the relation [of matter and form]. Thus, especially in philosophy, matter and form must be indivisible to the extent that a system that neglects the side of form must neglect content to the same degree. Philosophy is not at all concerned with what is known, but rather the grounds on which it is known. Until one has pushed through to the absolute itself, the slogan of the sceptics, that every reason can be set over against another reason, will certainly and necessarily have its place. One cannot deny that isolated true philosophical propositions result even from systems that are disordered and contradictory with respect to form; in such systems the propositions are without any scientific worth, having neither sense nor content. The feeling of truth in the singular accompanied by the total confusion of the whole produces the most narrow self-righteousness and obstinate resistance to learning. There is no other means than form to convince these people of the total nullity of their philosophy and help them break through [to the absolute], if this is even possible.

Form, then, which on the one hand protects philosophers from errors and deviations, is, on the other hand, a very important weapon, even the

---

*Translated by Andrew A. Davis and Alexi I. Kukuljevic from F.W.J. Schelling, *Sämmtliche Werke* (Stuttgart and Augsberg: Cotta, 1856–1861), Division One, Volume Five.

only weapon, against half-philosophy and non-philosophy, both of which make no claim to form without thereby exposing their complete lack of it.

Furthermore, no philosophy can be counted as true and absolute without proving that it has acquired absolute form. Since no such philosophy may yet exist, no philosophical orientation or striving can be taken as the true one, if it has not had insight into the *indivisibility of essence and form* and made this into its lodestar and principle.

The great example that Spinoza bequeathed philosophy, through his usage of the geometrical method, instead of spurring on the perfection of that method, actually had the opposite effect. The world, which did not understand this great mind, searched for the source of its errors in the form [of geometrical method], ascribing to it a certain affinity with fatalism and atheism.

If Spinoza erred, it is because he did not go far enough back in his construction, and if he did not neglect the form, he certainly neglected the pure ideal side of philosophy. The same is true of both dogmatism and the geometrical method: there is an external and internal, a formal and essential dogmatism. Essential dogmatism has only one distinguishing feature; it is the use of the form of reflection of the absolute. This essential dogmatism conflicts with the inner spirit of Spinozism, which is a system at the antipodes of dogmatism. This can be shown even without taking into account the proofs that one could extract from his texts. Spinoza could not avoid formal dogmatism; his philosophy lacks the necessary element of scepticism: since philosophy is completely in the region of the infinite such that it does not have a point above itself, as does mathematics, from which it can reflect, but rather unifies all points of reflection in itself, its own essence must always accompany it. Philosophy is not only a knowing, but always and necessarily at the same time a knowing of this knowing, not in endless procession, but an always present infinity.

We will not speak of the *Wolffian* philosophy which is in every respect dogmatic, or of its soulless and spiritless application of an external form of the geometrical method from which no idea of construction can be awakened.

We turn to *Kant*, who grasps the demonstrative method in philosophy only in the spirit of dogmatism and as logical analysis. He dedicated only a portion of his doctrine of method to the critique of the use of demonstrative method in philosophy.

Kant is perhaps the first to grasp the universal concept of construction deeply and truly philosophically.[1] He consistently describes construction as the identification of *concept* and *intuition* and thereby lays claim to a non-empirical intuition that must express itself, on the one hand, as an intuition that is singular and concrete and, on the other hand, as a construction of a concept that is universally valid for all possible intuitions belonging under the same concept. Regardless of whether the object that corresponds to the universal concept 'triangle' is projected in pure or empirical intuition, its ability to express its concept without compromising its universality remains the same because the empirical intuition itself will only be seen in and for itself through the activity of the construction of the concept.

To this extent, Kant has completely expressed the idea of construction and the ground for all evidence. If he thereafter denies the concept of construction in philosophy, since philosophy only has to do with pure concepts which have nothing to do with intuition, and nevertheless attributes the non-empirical intuitions of mathematics to construction, it becomes clear that Kant has only actually evaluated the *empirical* side [of construction], the relation to the sensible, which others had missed. For if philosophy is limited to pure concepts without intuition, it would then follow, if it could be proven, that there can be no *non-empirical* intuitions that fit philosophy's concepts. Kant denies non-empirical intuitions to philosophy, because they would have to be intellectual intuitions, and according to his opinion all intuition is necessarily sensible. However, it is clear that in mathematical intuition the absolutely *universal*, the pure unity of the universal and the particular, is not sensible, but rather purely intellectual. He thus places the singularity of mathematical intuition completely in the relation to the sensible. Or since mathematics involves *sensibly* reflected intellectual intuitions, a non-empirical, i.e. intellectual intuition must be added to the particularity of sensible intuition *as such*, in order to advance a mathematical construction.

Since Kant grants a non-empirical intuition to geometry, he cannot then establish an absolute difference between mathematics and philosophy through this non-empirical intuition. Such a difference requires a non-empirical intuition that cannot be given. The difference between the two lies much more in the fact that the mathematician makes use of intellectual intuitions reflected in sensibility and the philosopher makes use of intellectual intuitions reflected purely and in themselves. Kant's grounding of geometry in space and arithmetic in time expresses the totality of intellectual intuition, for geometry in the finite and for arithmetic in the infinite. The reasons internal to Kant's whole philosophy that make intellectual intuition absolutely and intrinsically inaccessible to him, are in part well enough known and in part will be clarified in what follows.

Let us not speak of the contradictions Kant finds himself in through the rejection of construction and pure intellectual intuition. His *transcendental imagination*, his *pure synthesis of apperception*, requires the reality of such an [intellectual] intuition. Kant often remarks in the *Critique of Pure Reason* that concepts are only mediated representations of objects, and without unity with these objects are totally empty, and yet philosophy itself is limited to discursive concepts. In order to avoid these contradictions, we must ask what advantages mathematics has over philosophy that make it capable of an expression of intellectual intuition in sensibility. Clearly nothing remains but the possibility that [the mathematician] can place appearances into a construction without the aid of intellectual consciousness, thus requiring the accidental [and] external support of sensible intuitions. But then, the true philosopher would not envy the advantages of the mathematician and Plato would certainly not have said: it is necessary for the philosopher to know geometry *in order to see the essential and to lift himself out of the changing flux.*

The geometer has the advantage that, besides the image that commands his attention, there is at the same time a sign that fixes his otherwise flowing activity and by which he can uncover the errors of his conclusions. This advantage is noticeably diminished in the other branch of mathematics, in which there is no image of the object, but only a sign and relationships of quantity. In algebra only relations of relations are observed. On the other hand, it may be expected that a universal symbolic or characteristic is to be invented even outside the special symbolic and characteristic presentation of mathematics. And so the idea that Leibniz had already advanced is realized. That certain steps have already been taken, which prove the possibility of such an invention, can be easily shown.

The primary reasons, expressed even by Kant, why dominant public opinion opposes construction *in philosophy* and thereby opposes philosophy itself as a science, are as follows.

The first reason is the absolute opposition of the universal and the particular, which, as Kant recognizes, is suspended for mathematics but still holds for philosophy. Kant writes, 'Mathematical knowledge observes the universal in the particular' while philosophy observes *the particular only in the universal*.'[2] There are several observations to be made here. First, since every true identity of the universal and the particular is in itself *intuition*, there is no reason to negate intuition because in one case the particular is presented in the universal and, in the other case, the universal is presented in the particular. Rather, what follows is that there are two different *kinds* of intuition. If one understands by universal the pure understanding's [universality] or the discursive universal, it is easy to show that even these *two kinds* of *intuition* are given in both branches of mathematics. Arithmetic expresses the particular (the relation of singular quantities) in the universal, geometry expresses the universal (the concept of figure) in the particular. Thus it is evident that all oppositions made possible through the antithesis of the universal and the particular fall under mathematics itself and that philosophy is not in opposition to mathematics. Construction can be divided into philosophical and mathematical sides and in philosophy it achieves a point of absolute indifference. More specifically, when each side must be *either* a presentation of the universal in the particular *or* the particular in the universal, then philosophy is *neither* of these, but rather the *presentation of their unity in absolute indifference*, while these sides appear divided in mathematics.

There is another idea of the universal, which Kant did not know or explicitly accept, but which he nevertheless takes up unwittingly from the tradition as an explanation of philosophy. Namely, that philosophy can be seen as a *presentation of the particular in the universal.*

In this case, the universal is the essential and absolutely universal, not the concept, but the idea, if we think of the universal and particular as reflective oppositions in the Kantian sense. For its part, this shows how the particular, in the sense that it is presented in geometry, besides grasping the particular as a formal factor, also grasps the universal in itself. In this sense, the universal as the unity of the universal and particular in itself is already an object of intuition, which, understood intellectually, is the idea. But Kant does not take it in this sense, so he cannot explain philosophy as the presentation of the particular in the universal.

Even the distinctions made above between geometry and arithmetic, namely that one presents the universal in the particular and the other the particular in the universal, occur, to speak more specifically, not in the view of construction itself as such, but in other relationships, for construction as such is in mathematics and philosophy always the absolute and *real* equalization of universal and particular. The particular in geometry is not the empirical triangle sketched upon a piece of paper, but, according to Kant himself, *the triangle of pure intuition.* Construction has only this triangle of pure intuition in view; the empirical is related accidentally, as an *accidens*, upon which construction does not reflect. *This* particular is however already the particular *presented in the universal* and insofar as it is an idea, or the real universal itself, it has an *essential* unity and not merely a formal unity.

It is certainly odd that Kant shows philosophers a geometrical concept in order to enter into competition with the geometer over its construction.

> Suppose a philosopher be given the concept of a triangle and he be left to find out, in his own way, what relation the sum of its angles bears to a right angle. He has nothing but the concept of a figure enclosed by three straight lines, and possessing three angles. However long he meditates on this concept, he will never produce anything new. He can analyse and clarify the concept of a straight line or of an angle or of the number three, but he can never arrive at any properties not already contained in these concepts. The geometer alone can take up these questions.[3]

This is every bit as clever as when on the contrary he demands that the geometer construct an idea, e.g. Beauty, Right, Equality, or Space. The geometer would doubtless meet with no more success as the philosopher did in his construction of the triangle. It is as if one gave paints and paint brushes to the musician to develop music, or musical notes and instruments to the sculptor in order to sculpt and out of the resulting impossibility, prove the non-existence of their art.

It follows from this position that the philosopher after Kant could only approach his work analytically, given the concepts to which he is constrained. Is this truly Kant's opinion, or has this later chapter forgotten the previous chapters?

However, more in line with the spirit of Kant's own system are other statements that these are nothing but repetitions of the same old opposition of discursive concepts to intuition, unity to multiplicity.

All *a priori* multiplicity is already given to mathematics, but for philosophy there remains nothing but *pure understanding* on the one hand and *empirical multiplicity*, on the other hand, which as empirical, however, is excluded from it [philosophy]. Philosophy proceeds with completely empty hands, that is, with an empty understanding. With an undetermined multiplicity as its material, philosophy would construct *without an object*. That is, philosophy does not construct at all.

Put in another way: philosophy has *no other a priori* concepts than those [obtained from] the synthesis of possible intuition (which is merely a *possibility* of intuition) with which one can make synthetic *a priori* judgements but cannot construct. It is true that nothing can be constructed *with* these concepts, but one can construct the concepts themselves, though not insofar as they are *synthetic* and therefore discursive concepts which oppose the actuality of the intuition. These concepts will not be constructed in any other way than as ideas, the concept of cause and effect, e.g. in the idea of the absolute unity of possibility and actuality, which has possibility and actuality itself in the idea of the absolute unity of subjective and objective, etc.

All of these statements are necessary for the view that nothing exists in human minds but empty concepts, empirical intuitions and between them an absolute hiatus. Kant cannot justify his own procedure in this part of the Doctrine of Method, namely how he himself arrived at these synthetic concepts. It is true that Kant did not construct these synthetic concepts, but grasped them analogically from experience. It is unthinkable that Kant could have consciously made this presupposition: there is no higher source of the cognition of concepts, from which the concepts could be grasped *a priori*, necessarily and truly. The retrogression of construction – or because this is not granted – of thinking as such cannot stop until it reaches the point at which constructing and constructed, thinking and thought come together as one. Only this point can be called the *principle* of construction. This is not the case with every concept. Without doubt, philosophical reflection thinks something else in these concepts than whatever thinks *from* them; what for the Kantian analytic is actually *the constructed*. These concepts may be principles for the latter, but not the former. Everything that cannot be circumscribed by the aforementioned conjunction [of constructing and constructed] falls outside the jurisdiction of construction, or philosophy as such.

Thus concepts, which are themselves the constructed, or at least do not have the character of a principle of construction or a *means* of construction, prove that one cannot advance from the merely reflected and deduced and even if the reflection and deduction is completely true, one cannot construct *with* these concepts. Not even the geometer constructs *with* the concept of the triangle, the square, etc., for then there would be as many and as various evidences as constructions. These are all themselves the constructed from the *perspective* of the geometer's presentation. Should the geometer construct *with* these concepts, he would fare no differently than in the aforementioned outline of the philosopher.

There is only one principle of construction, *one* [principle] *with which* we construct in both mathematics and philosophy. For all the geometer's constructions, this principle is the homogenous, absolute unity of space and for the philosopher it is the absolute unity of the absolute. As has been said, only one thing is constructed, namely *ideas*, and everything that is deduced is not constructed as deduced but rather in its idea.

Perhaps this is expressed nowhere more immediately and judiciously than in Kant's reasoning about philosophical construction. His *Critique of Pure Reason* only deals with the *understanding* and after that, when he pressed on to the true objects of philosophy, the realm of ideas, he had only the highly confused reports of others.

[…]

It is necessary that Kant, who only gave his pure concepts of the understanding possibility, look for an actuality outside of the concepts. For in construction, there is given not merely a relative or purely ideal possibility but an absolute possibility. With the idea of construction, [an] author commits himself to absolute idealism. If the question concerns absolute reality, then it is given immediately with absolute ideality. If the discussion concerns, as it seems, external necessity as a condition of empirical actuality, then this can never be demonstrated as such in the idea, for it becomes *empirical actuality* by removing itself from the idea. Even the general laws, according to which this empirical actuality changes by so removing itself to this and no other determination, can only be constructed in the idea.

Kant yanks up the last anchor of the fantastical hope that science can ground itself in the intellectual world when he shows that none of the three parts that ground mathematics, namely definitions, axioms and demonstrations, can be accomplished or imitated by philosophy. It would be a noteworthy undertaking to investigate the extent to which axioms and definitions ground mathematics. The sceptics directed their strongest doubts against these grounds of mathematics. When one can define a straight line and a circle, but cannot account for their genesis, how does that amount to a proof of the grounds [of mathematics]? How do I even arrive at two or more things, in order to create the axiom that establishes that two things, which are similar to a third, are similar to each other or concerning the concepts of the whole and the part, that the whole is larger than the part? As one can see, these questions lead to an infinite regress, this possibility proves that axioms and definitions are not, as Kant imagined, true *principles*, but that they are *limit points* of principles and of science. They are limit points of a return to an absolute origin. Each subordinate science, e.g. physics, requires these limit points, through them a science isolates itself and develops itself for itself. How could that which makes up the mere limitation of a science become the measure of the thoroughness of a science, and, moreover, be the science of all sciences? Precisely because philosophy is completely *in* [the domain of] *absolute knowing*, it is not bound by these limitations. It must construct construction itself, as well as define definition.

Notes

1   *Editors' Note.* The remainder of this passage closely engages with the detailed claims Kant makes in the Discipline of Pure Reason of his *Critique of Pure Reason.*
2   *Editors' Note. Critique of Pure Reason,* A714/B742.
3   *Editors' Note.* Critique *of Pure Reason,* A716/B744.

The Ages of the World, 3rd version (1815)*

What is past is known, what is present is discerned, what is future is divined.

The known is retold, the discerned is represented, the divined is foretold.

The conception of science hitherto accepted was that it is a mere consequence and development of its own concepts and thoughts. The true conception is that it is the development of a living, actual essence, which is represented in it.

It is a distinction of our times that this essence has been restored to science, and indeed, it may be asserted, in such a way that science cannot easily lose it again. Now, since the dynamic spirit is at last awakened, it is not too harsh to condemn any philosophizing which does not draw its power from that spirit, and to consider it as a vain misuse of the noble gift of thought and speech.

The living reality of the highest science can only be primal living reality, the essence, which is preceded by nothing else and which is thus the oldest of all beings.

There is nothing before or outside this primal living reality by which it might be determined. Therefore, in so far as it develops itself, it can only do so freely, by its own impulse and volition, purely by itself, yet just on this account not lawlessly but only according to law. There is no arbitrariness in it; it is a nature in the most complete meaning of the word, just as man is a nature without prejudice to his freedom, nay, owing to his freedom.

After science has achieved objectivity with respect to the object, it seems a natural consequence that science seek objectivity also with respect to form.

---

*Translated by Frederick de Wolfe Bolman, Jr. from F.W.J. Schelling, *Sämmtliche Werke* (Stuttgart and Augsberg: Cotta, 1856–1861), Division One, Volume Eight.

Why has this remained impossible until now? Why cannot that which is known, even in the highest science, be related with the same directness and simplicity as every other known thing? What holds back the anticipated golden age when truth again becomes fable and fable truth?

A principle which is outside and above the world must be conceded to man. For how could he alone of all creatures retrace the long course of developments from the present back into the deepest night of the past, he alone ascend to the beginning of the ages, if there were not in him a principle of the beginning of the ages? Drawn from the source of things and akin to it, the human soul has a co-knowledge of creation. In the soul lies the highest clarity of all things, and the soul is not so much knowing as itself knowledge.

In man, however, the supramundane principle is no longer free in its primordial purity, but is bound to another, lesser principle. This other is itself something which became, and therefore is by nature unknowing and obscure, and it necessarily also obscures the higher principle with which it is bound. To be sure, in that lesser principle there lies a recollection of all things – their original relationships, their becoming, their significance. But this archetype of things slumbers in the soul like an obscured and forgotten, even if not completely obliterated, image. Perhaps it would never awaken again, if the divining and yearning toward discernment did not lie in that same dark region. But the higher principle, incessantly besought by this lower about its elevation, observes that the lower principle is not added to the higher in order that the latter may remain fettered by it, but in order that the higher itself may have another in which it can view itself, represent and become intelligible to itself. For everything lies in the higher without distinction, that is, as one; but it can make distinguishable, express, interpret in the other that which is one in the higher itself. Thus there is in man one thing which must again be brought to mind, and another thing which brings it to mind; one thing in which lies the answer to every question of research, and another thing which brings forth this answer from it. This other is free with respect to all things and is able to think all things, but it is bound by that innermost one, and can believe nothing true without the assent of this witness. On the other hand, the innermost is originally bound and cannot develop itself; but it becomes free through the other and discloses itself to the same. Therefore both principles alike long intensely for the separation – the higher principle in order that it may return home to its original freedom and become manifest to itself,[1] the lower principle in order that it may conceive of the higher and likewise, although in a quite different way, come to know.

This separation, this duplication of ourselves, this secret intercourse in which there are two essences, an asking one and an answering one, an ignorant one which, however, seeks knowledge, and a knowing one which, however, does not know its knowledge – this silent dialogue, this inner art of conversation, the peculiar secret of the philosopher, is that of which the external, therefore called dialectic, is the imitation. But where this inner art has become mere form, it is the empty semblance and shadow of itself.

Thus, according to its nature, everything known is retold. The known, however, is not something lying finished and ready to hand from the beginning but something always first arising from within by an altogether characteristic process. The light of science must arise by inner separation and deliverance before it can illuminate. What we call knowledge is just striving after conscious recollection, thus more an aspiring after knowledge than knowledge itself; for which reason unquestionably the name philosophy has been given to it by that great man of antiquity. For the belief, cherished from age to age, of being able to turn philosophy at last into actual knowledge by means of dialectic, of considering the most perfect dialectic as science itself, betrays not a little narrowness, since indeed just the presence and necessity of dialectic prove that it is still in no way actual knowledge.

The philosopher, however, is in this regard in no different situation from another historian. For even the latter must win what he desires to know from the statements of original documents or the memory of living witnesses; and he needs great art of discrimination or criticism in order to separate the false from the true, the wrong from the right, in the preserved traditions. Also, he greatly needs that discrimination in himself, whence the customary saying, he must try to free himself from the concepts and peculiarities of his own age, and also much else of which it would be too much of a digression to speak here.

Everything, absolutely everything – even what is by nature external must previously have become inward for us before we can represent it externally or objectively. If the ancient era, whose image he wishes to sketch for us, does not dawn again within the historian, then he will never truly, never plastically, never vitally represent it. What would all history be if an inner meaning did not come to its aid? It would be what it is for so many who know, to be sure, most of what has happened, but who understand not the slightest thing about real history. Not only human events, but even the history of nature has its monuments, and one can indeed say that neither passes from any stage in its broad path of creation without leaving behind something as a mark. These monuments of nature for the most part lie open to view, are repeatedly investigated, in part actually deciphered; and yet they do not speak to us, but remain dead, until that succession of actions and productions has become inward for man. Thus everything remains incomprehensible for man before it has become inward for him, that is, has been led back to just that innermost part of his nature which is for him, as it were, the living witness of all truth.

Now there have always been some who thought that it is possible to set aside that subordinated part[2] and to annul all duality in one's self, so that we would be, as it were, only inwardly, and live altogether in the supramundane, discerning everything immediately. Who can entirely deny the possibility of such a transposition of man into his supramundane principle, and therefore an elevation of the powers of mind into vision itself? From time to time, every physical and moral whole requires a reduction to its innermost origin for its preservation. Man rejuvenates himself again and again and is blessed anew by feeling the unity of his nature. Particularly the person seeking knowledge continually draws fresh power in just this way. Not only the poet but also the philosopher has his ecstasies. He needs them in order to be preserved against the forced concepts of an empty and inspirationless dialectic by the feeling of indescribable reality of those higher ideas. But to demand the continuity of this state of vision, which is at odds with the nature and character of the present life, is another matter. For however we may consider life's relation to its innermost origin, it always comes back to this, that what was indivisibly together in the origin unfolds and is spread out piece by piece in this present life. We do not live in vision; our knowledge is piecework, that is, it must be produced piece by piece in a fragmentary way, with divisions and gradations, all of which cannot occur without reflection.

Therefore the goal is also not attained by mere vision. For in vision, in and by itself, there is no understanding. In the external world everyone sees more or less the same thing, and yet not everyone can express it. In order to complete itself, each thing runs through certain moments – a series of processes following one another, in which the later always involves the earlier, brings each thing to its maturity. The peasant as well as the scholar, for example, sees this process in the plant, and yet does not really know it, because he cannot keep the moments apart, cannot observe them severally, in their mutual contrast. Just in this way man is able to run through, and, as it were, immediately experience in himself that series of processes whereby the infinite manifoldness is finally born out of the highest simplicity of being; indeed, to speak accurately, he must experience it in himself. But all experiencing, feeling, intuiting, merely as such, is mute and needs a mediating organ in order to attain expression. If the one having vision lacks the mediating organ, or if he intentionally thrusts it from himself in order to talk immediately from vision, then he loses the criterion which he needs, he is united with the object, and is like the object itself for a third person. Just for this reason he is not master of his thoughts, and yet he strives in vain to express the inexpressible without any certainty; what he hits upon he hits upon without being sure of it, without being able to place it firmly before himself and inspect it again in the understanding, as if in a mirror.

That relatively external principle is thus at all costs not to be given up; for everything must first be submitted to real reflection in order to attain the highest expression. Here is the boundary between theosophy and philosophy, which the lover of knowledge will try to keep pure. The former has just as much advantage in depth, fullness and vitality of content over the latter, as the real object over its image, nature over its representation; and of course the two become incomparably disparate if a dead philosophy, seeking the essence in forms and concepts, is taken for comparison. Therefore the preference of the inwardly disposed for theosophy is just as easily explained as the preference for nature in contrast to art. For theosophical systems have this advantage over all systems previously current, that in them at least there stirs a nature, even if not one which is master of itself; in the other systems, on the other hand, there is nothing but affectation and vain artifice. But the fullness and depth of life are just as attainable for science, correctly understood, as nature is for correctly understood art; only more slowly, more indirectly, and by gradual progress does that science attain to fullness and depth of life, so that the knower always remains different from his object, and the latter, on the other hand, also remains separated from him, and becomes the object of a deliberate, tranquilly enjoying contemplation.

All science must thus pass through dialectic. Another question, however, is this: Does the time never come when knowledge becomes free and living, as does the image of the ages for the historian, who no longer thinks of his researches when he is expounding it? Can the memory of the primordial beginning of things never again become so living that science, since it is history in substance and in name, could be so in its outer form too, and the philosopher able to return to the innocence of history, like the divine Plato, who is dialectical throughout the entire series of his works, yet becomes historical in each at the summit and last stage of transfiguration?

It seems reserved for our age at least to open the way for science to attain this objective form. So long as science restricts itself to the inward, the ideal, it lacks the natural means of external representation. Now, after long wanderings, it has regained the memory of nature and of nature's former unity with knowledge. But the matter did not rest there. Hardly had the first steps of reuniting philosophy and nature taken place, when one had to acknowledge the great antiquity of the physical, and how the physical, far from being the last, is rather the first from which everything, even the development of the divine life, originates.[3] Science no longer takes its origin from the remoteness of abstract thoughts in order to descend from these to natural objects; but conversely, originating from the unconscious presence of the eternal, knowledge leads this presence up to the highest transfiguration in a divine consciousness. The most supersensible thoughts now receive physical power and life, and, conversely, nature becomes more and more the visible impress of the highest concepts. In a short time the contempt with which, after all, only the ignorant still look down on everything physical, will cease, and the expression will once more be true: The stone which the builders rejected has become the cornerstone. Then general acknowledgement, so often sought in vain, will come of its own accord. Then there will no longer be any difference between the world of thought and the world of reality. There will be one world, and the peace of the golden age will make itself known for the first time in the harmonious union of all sciences.

With such prospects, which the present book will try to justify in more than one way, an oft-considered essay which contains some preparation for that future objective presentation of science may well venture forth. Perhaps he will yet come who is to sing the greatest heroic poem, comprehending in spirit what was, what is, what will be, the kind of poem attributed to the seers of yore. But this time has not yet come. We must not misconstrue our age. Heralds of it, we do not want to gather its fruit before it is ripe, nor to misunderstand what is already ours. It is still an age of struggle. The goal of the search is not yet reached. We cannot be narrators but only explorers, weighing the pro and con of each opinion until the right one stands firm, indubitable, rooted forever.

Notes

1   *Marginal Note.* Thereby transplanting itself again into its original and innate knowledge.
2   *Marginal Note.* The external tool.
3   *Marginal Note.* How, even if the last with regard to dignity, it may be the first with regard to all development.

Further reading

Schelling's reflections on methodology are scattered throughout his early work – from the 1794 essay, *On the Possibility of a Form of Philosophy in General*, to the 1800 polemic, *On the True Concept of Philosophy of Nature*, the first sections of the 1802 *Further Presentations* and the opening pages of the 1804 *Philosophy and Religion*. In the English-language scholarship, the following works are worth consulting on the issues raised by the above texts:

Daniel Breazeale, '"Exhibiting the Particular in the Universal": Philosophical Construction and Intuition in Schelling's Philosophy of Identity (1801–1804).' In Lara Ostaric (ed.), *Interpreting Schelling: Critical Essays* (Cambridge University Press, 2014), 91–119.

G. Anthony Bruno, 'The Appearance and Disappearance of Intellectual Intuition in Schelling's Philosophy.' *Analecta Hermeneutica* 5 (2013): 1–14.

Chelsea C. Harry, 'Situating the Early Schelling in the Later Positive Philosophy.' *Comparative and Continental Philosophy* 6.1 (2014): 6–15.

Alberto Toscano, 'Philosophy and the Experience of Construction.' In Jane Norman and Alistair Welchman (eds), *The New Schelling* (Continuum, 2004), 106–27.

Michael G. Vater, 'Intellectual Intuition in Schelling's Philosophy of Identity, 1801–1804.' In Christoph Asmuth et al. (eds), *Schelling: Between Fichte and Hegel* (Grüner, 2000), 213–34.

Jason M. Wirth, *The Conspiracy of Life: Meditations on Schelling* (SUNY Press, 2003), Chapter IV.

6

Reason and experience

Introduction

As became clear in Chapters 4 and 5 of this book, Schelling is a 'post-Kantian' philosopher not only because he is philosophizing after Kant, but because he is often addressing distinctly Kantian problems. One of Kant's central aims in the first *Critique* is to develop a system of philosophy that can steer a third way between rationalism and empiricism while recognizing the importance of both reason and experience in the formation of knowledge. This chapter presents Schelling's views about the relationship between reason and experience.

Schelling addresses the relationship between a priori and a posteriori knowledge in various texts. *Is a Philosophy of History Possible?* (1798) – the first text in this chapter – explores the significance of the a priori/a posteriori distinction for the topic of history. In the *Introduction to the Outline* (1799), he argues that knowledge of the strictly rational forms structuring reality is not only unopposed to empiricism but requires experimentation. And in the later philosophy, he makes this thought of the complementary relationship between reason and experience the principle of the entire system. Indeed, in lectures such as those on the *System of Positive Philosophy* (1832/3) and the *Philosophy of Revelation* (1842/3) (both of which are excerpted below), Schelling argues that philosophy can only become a true science if it pursues two distinct yet closely related paths of enquiry: a rationalist demonstration of the fundamental essences or forms of reality (i.e. the 'potencies') and an empirical-historical confirmation that those forms *actually exist*. The former path is identified as 'negative philosophy' and the latter 'positive philosophy', and Schelling insists upon the profound importance of both. That being said, one of Schelling's major arguments in the late work is that, for too long, philosophers have ignored the actual, historical manifestation of the rationally necessitated 'essences' or 'potencies' which structure the realms of nature and spirit. In fact, looking back on his own, earlier work from the perspective of the late philosophy, Schelling claims that texts such as the 1801 *Presentation* are strictly 'negative', i.e. motivated by reason alone. The late Schelling is therefore intent upon discovering a philosophical method that will attend to history and, in particular, to the event or historical act that grounds the rational structure of reality. He discusses this topic in a lecture on *The Source of the Eternal Truths* (1850) – the fifth and final text presented in this chapter.

Is a Philosophy of History Possible? (1798)*

Proposition: There is no possible philosophy of history. One way of proving this proposition would be to show that the concept of history contains some property that contradicts this combination, and so it must be asked: what does one usually understand by the concept of history?

Understood etymologically, history [*Geschichte*] is knowledge of what has happened [*das Geschehene*]. As such, it has as its object not things that remain and persevere, but rather those which change and develop over time. Yet the sphere specified by this definition is still infinitely broad in comparison to the ordinary concept of history, and so we must turn to individual examples in an attempt to further narrow down the concept of history.

Nature is the epitome of all that happens [*alles Geschehenden*] and thus qualifies as the object of history. At the same time, not every natural occurrence is historical [*historisch*] in character. It is true that we find natural occurrences recorded in the annals of history; they thus contain accounts of the great flood, of earthquakes, etc. Yet it is easy to see that:

1. All such occurrences are included in history not as natural *phenomena*, but rather as natural *episodes* which have affected humans qua natural beings. The appearance of a comet may figure in a chronicle from the barbarian era, but it has no place in a *history*, except to the extent that it exercised some influence on the actions of the people alive at the time. In this way, historians can talk about meteors that were thought to foretell Caesar's death, or of the lunar eclipse that Columbus prophesied on the island of Hispaniola.

---

*Translated by Benjamin Berger and Graham Wetherall from F.W.J. Schelling, *Sämmtliche Werke* (Stuttgart and Augsberg: Cotta, 1856–1861), Division One, Volume One.

2. The inclusion of natural occurrences in history can only be attributed to people's *ignorance*. For if they had known how to explain, e.g. visible meteors, etc., they would not have believed them to be omens of future destinies; and how else is it to be explained that everyday natural occurrences receive no mention in history? If the very first man had recounted the history of his first day on earth, he would certainly have begun with the magnificent spectacle of the sunrise (just as we begin with the emergence of the world from chaos). And if one of those ephemeral insects which come into being in the morning and perish in the evening were to leave behind the story of its own life, would it not recount the course of this star in historical terms?

Therefore: *occurrences that are witnessed recurring with periodic regularity do not belong to history*, even if one does not *apprehend* the rule of this recurrence (for one still presupposes it); and all the less so when one does apprehend the rule! (This makes clear from the outset that history cannot move in *periodic circles*, as Mendelssohn believed,[1] but that it must *advance*.)

The course of the stars, their periodic appearance, etc., belongs to *history* for human beings only for as long as they have not observed the underlying regularity. Where they succeed in completely determining this regularity, there is no longer any history of the heavens. Since we have learned to calculate solar eclipses, they have ceased to be the object of history. We record the eruptions of fire-spewing mountains; if it were possible to observe some law behind their recurrence, and eventually even to work it out, we would have no need for such records. If the return of a comet could be calculated more accurately, we would not need to wait for history to confirm it. Thus: *that which can be calculated a priori, or which occurs according to necessary laws, is not an object of history; and conversely, that which is an object of history cannot be calculated a priori.*

The description of nature has hitherto been known as *natural history*, and not entirely without reason. For since it cannot presume to establish its system as a faithful copy of nature, in this context, every new discovery is a *historical* discovery, i.e. an unforeseen augmentation; and since some varieties of animal and plant can be found for which the existing system contains no corresponding genus, a discovery of this kind can only be appended *historically*.

Meanwhile, if it should ever prove possible to raise natural *history* up to a *system* of nature, there would nonetheless still remain a space for a *natural history* in the proper sense of the term. We now find ourselves at a point from which our entire investigation must be illuminated.

Nonetheless, it is (from the viewpoint of physics) a very bold hypothesis, which some may find verges on being venturesome, to claim that all individual organizations merely denote different stages of the development of one and the same organization, in which case, the archetype of them all would have to occupy the centre of our present system of nature. Yet even if we abandon this idea, there still remains a different, less bold hypothesis, namely: that the present state of organic nature is very different from its original state. It is not only the remains of extinct creatures that provide historical evidence for this hypothesis (as if nature had conceived its original construction on too large a scale or too imperfectly for this specific distance from the sun ... from which one could conclude that its original design endures on other planets ...). Additionally, one is driven to this conclusion by, on the one hand, the interest of reason, which demands the greatest unity in the greatest manifoldness, and, on the other, the observation of common properties among various creatures belonging to different types. For if one were to assume an original mutability of organic nature, one could thereby dramatically reduce the number of original genera and (as Kant already did with the human species) trace back apparently different kinds to varieties of the same genus.

Whichever of these two ideas were realizable, carrying either of them out would lead us to a natural history in the proper sense of the term. According to the first, we would conceive of nature in its freedom – how it develops a primordial organization in all possible directions (which for precisely that reason could no longer exist anywhere); how it here suppresses one force at the expense of the others; and how, with a lesser or greater intensity of organic forces, it establishes an equilibrium of organic forces, whether they be of lesser or greater intensity. In this case, one would furthermore have the advantage of being able to trace back the outward diversity of earthly creatures, in consideration of the number, size, structure and function of the organs, to an original, inner difference in relation of organic powers (of which they would only be the outward phenomenon). – In the other case, we would have to take as our basis not a single archetype common to all organizations, but rather common archetypes for various kinds now understood as separate, which would owe their origin to a gradual *deviation* from the original brought about by particular natural influences.

The fact that such an account of nature would be a *natural history* can only follow from the fact that, here, we see nature in a state of freedom, yet not of lawlessness; for, although all its products have arisen through *deviations*, they are nonetheless deviations from an *ideal*, whose limits it never transgresses.

In this way, we have arrived at a proposition whose significance for our investigation will only become completely clear in the following, namely: *there is only history where there is an ideal, and where infinitely manifold deviations* from this ideal occur at the individual level, and yet always in complete *congruence with this ideal* at the level of the whole. This proposition makes clear in advance that history is only possible for beings that express the character of a *genus*; and hence it is from this proposition alone that we will be able to justify representing the human race in history as *a totality*.

We return now to our actual object. Insofar as we assume that nature's productions are guided by an archetype that it follows, there is an appearance of freedom in nature, but nothing more than an appearance. – (Whence this appearance originally came forth into nature can only be deduced in a philosophy of nature.) – And so there is only ever an appearance *of natural history*. Nonetheless, this analogy assists us in reaching the following insight: that history in the single, truest sense only takes place where it is absolutely impossible (i.e. impossible for every degree of cognition) to determine a priori the course taken by a free activity (for it may be that apprehending the course of nature's free activities as necessary a priori is relatively impossible, i.e. impossible for us, but not *absolutely* impossible).

If we summarize our findings so far, we are left with following propositions:

1. *That which is not progressive cannot be an object of history.* The concept of *progression* must be more precisely defined. For example, although a series of actions takes place within it, mechanism is not *progressive*, since these actions move in a circle, such that every such cycle of actions can be counted as a single (constantly repeated) action. – For the same reason, there is no *history of animals*, except in the improper sense. *First*, there is no history of the individual animal (as such). For it is enclosed within a circle of actions, beyond which it never steps; what it is, it is forever and what it will be is predetermined by laws of a mechanism which, while certainly of a higher order, are nonetheless still inviolable. The history of a human being, however, is not predetermined; human beings can and should create their own history. For this is the character of the human being: although its history *should* be orderly at a practical level, for this very reason, it cannot be orderly from a theoretical point of view. – It is only analogously that one can speak of a history of those animals that possess a *technical drive*, e.g. a history of beavers, of bees, etc. Some think they perceive an analogue to freedom in the productive industriousness of such animals, yet this too is an illusion, for if we could identify the inner mechanism of their organic forces,

all contingency of their products would vanish. – (There need not necessarily be a history of a poem which is written in a genuinely poetic way).

For the same reason, there is no *history of the animal kingdom*, or of animal kinds in general, because the *genus* does not *develop*, because each *single* individual *perfectly* expresses the concept of the genus, because *each* single one realizes the ideal of its genus; because therefore no realization in an infinite succession of generations is conceivable, and thus too no transmission from kind to kind, no building on the foundation of what came earlier, no increase of the predecessors' achievements, no transgression of the limit at which those predecessors came to a halt – none of this is conceivable in such a succession.

2. *Where there is mechanism, there is no history, and conversely, where there is history, there is no mechanism.* Can we imagine, for example, the history of a clock that (in accordance with the unity of its principle) runs at a steady rate? We cannot, for two reasons: first, because there is no freedom of the principle within it; and, additionally, because there is no manifold of action within it, as we see in it only one and the same repeated occurrence. Thus, a man who lived by the clock and who became a machine himself ('he ate, drank, took a wife and died') is not a suitable object [of a history] – nor even for a story.

If we bring these two principles together into a general expression, we get the following principle:

3. *For anything that admits of an a priori theory, no history is possible*, and conversely, *only that which does not admit of an a priori theory has a history*. As such, if man has a history (*a posteriori*), he has it only because he does not have a history (*a priori*); in short, because he does not bring his history with him, but produces it himself.

Before we make further deductions from this principle, we might be allowed a few further comments.

The sense of our claim is that, for us, everything that cannot be determined *a priori* becomes history. It is therefore not a matter of whether something has a specific mechanism or occurs in accordance with certain laws, but rather whether we can *apprehend* this mechanism and whether we can *specify* its laws. As such, the poet, for example, can *deliberately* turn something that is not history into history, presenting a necessary occurrence as contingent (instead of relating it to the universal natural mechanism). This is why one permits the historian (who is always also a *poet*) a kind of *superstition*; for if he understands his art, he will not simply incorporate natural occurrences into his history without suggesting [the presence of] something more than just nature (a higher, yet concealed hand). In all sciences, *history* has preceded *theory*. In this way, Greek mythology (wherever it may have first emerged) was originally nothing other than a historical schematism of *nature* (prior to any attempt to explain nature). – As such, any doctrine concerning things belonging to a supersensible world becomes a history (since we have no natural laws for this world); and every religion which is theoretical passes over into mythology; it will and should always remain mythology and will never become anything else (for it can only have poetic truth, and it is only true as mythology).

The more the limits of our *knowledge* expand, the narrower the limits of *history* become (which is why, in some people, the sphere of their historical knowledge stands in an inverse relation to their actual knowledge; – for how few people know what knowing means!). – Thus, from another perspective, the fact that we have history is a measure of our limitations. For if we had ever fulfilled our complete task, and realized the absolute, then for both individuals and the whole species, there would be no other law than the law of its perfected *nature*, and all history would thus cease. This is why every representation of an absolute state of reason inevitably brings with it a sense of boredom (such as the performance of a play in which only perfect beings appear, or the reading of a novel – like those by Richardson[2] – where ideal men appear, or of a Christian heroic poem, in which angels – by far the most boring of all beings – play the main roles). – As such, if we posit an absolute that falls *outside of ourselves,* it could have no history. Our own history would thus be a mere illusion, and the freedom simulated to us by the happy dream of our limitation would with regard to this essence (which we do not know) be ironclad necessity. This is why there is no freedom in dogmatism, but only fatalism, and conversely, why the philosophy that commences with *freedom* annuls all absoluteness that falls beyond us.

Therefore, if the human being can only have a history insofar as this history is not determined *a priori*, it also follows from this that the idea of an *a priori* history is self-contradictory; and, if the *philosophy of history* is nothing other than a science of history *a priori* – then a philosophy of history is impossible. Which is what we set out to prove.

Notes

1   *Editors' Note.* Schelling is referring here to Moses Mendelssohn's anti-progressive, cyclical theory of history, which can be found, among other places, in *Jerusalem,* trans. Allan Arkush (Waltham, MA: Brandeis University Press, 1983), pp. 96–7.

2   *Editors' Note.* Samuel Richardson (1689–1761), author of epistolary novels, such as *Pamela*.

Introduction to the Outline of a System of the Philosophy of Nature (1799)[*]

§ 3 Philosophy of Nature is Speculative Physics

Our science, as far as we have gone, Is thoroughly and completely realistic; it is therefore nothing other than physics, it is only *speculative* physics. In its tendency it is exactly what the systems of the ancient physicists were, and what, in more recent times, the system of the restorer of Epicurean philosophy is, i.e. *Lesage's* mechanical physics,[1] by which the speculative spirit in physics, after a long scientific sleep, has again for the first time been awakened. It cannot be shown in detail here (for the proof itself falls within the sphere of our science) that on the mechanical or atomistic basis that has been adopted by Lesage and his most successful predecessors, the idea of a speculative physics cannot be realized. For, inasmuch as the first problem of this science, that of inquiring into the *absolute* cause of motion (without which Nature is not in itself a finished whole), is absolutely incapable of a mechanical solution. Because mechanically motion results only from motion to infinity, there remains for the real construction of speculative physics only one way open, the dynamic, with the presupposition that motion arises not only from motion, but even from rest; we suppose, therefore, that there is motion in the rest of Nature, and that all mechanical motion is the merely secondary and derivative motion of that which is solely primitive and original, and which wells forth from the very first factors in the construction of a Nature overall (the fundamental forces).

In making clear the points of difference between our undertaking and all those of a similar nature that have hitherto been attempted, we have at the same time shown the difference between speculative physics and so-called empirical physics; a difference which may principally be reduced to the fact that the former occupies itself solely and entirely with the original causes of motion in Nature, that is, solely with the dynamical phenomena;

---

[*]Translated by Keith R. Peterson from F.W.J. Schelling, *Historisch-kritische Ausgabe*, ed. Wilhelm G. Jacobs und Paul Ziche (Stuttgart: Frommann-Holzboog, 2001), Series One, Volume Seven.

the latter on the contrary, inasmuch as it never reaches a final source of motion in Nature, deals only with the secondary motions, and even with the original ones only as mechanical (and therefore likewise capable of mathematical construction). The former, in fact, aims generally at the inner clockwork and what is *nonobjective* in Nature; the latter, on the contrary, only at the *surface* of Nature, and what is *objective* and, so to speak, *outside* in it.

§ 4 On the Possibility of Speculative Physics

Insofar as our inquiry is directed not so much upon the phenomena of Nature as upon their final grounds, and our business is not so much to deduce the latter from the former as the former from the latter, our task is simply this: to erect a science of Nature in the strictest sense of the term; and in order to find out whether speculative physics is possible, we must know what belongs to the possibility of a doctrine of Nature viewed as science.

(a) The idea of knowledge is here taken in its strictest sense, and so it is easy to see that, in this use of the term, we can be said *to know* objects only when they are such that we see the principles of their possibility, for without this insight my whole knowledge of an object, e.g. of a machine with whose construction I am unacquainted, is a mere seeing, that is, a mere conviction of its existence, whereas the inventor of the machine has the most perfect knowledge of it, because he is, as it were, the soul of the work, and because it preexisted in his head before he exhibited it as a reality.

Now, it would certainly be impossible to get a glimpse of the internal construction of Nature if an invasion of Nature were not possible through freedom. It is true that Nature acts openly and freely; its acts however are never isolated, but performed under the concurrence of a host of causes which must first be excluded if we are to obtain a pure result. Nature must therefore be compelled to act under certain definite conditions, which either do not exist in it at all, or else exist only as modified by others. – Such an invasion of Nature we call an experiment. Every experiment is a question put to Nature, to which it is compelled to give a reply. But every question contains an implicit *a priori* judgement; every experiment that is an experiment, is a prophecy; experimenting itself is a production of phenomena. The first step toward science, therefore, at least in the domain of physics, is taken when we ourselves begin to produce the objects of that science.

(b) We *know* only the self-produced; knowing, therefore, in the *strictest* sense of the term, is a *pure* knowing *a priori*. Construction by means of experiment is, after all, not an absolute self-production of the phenomena. There is no question that much in the science of Nature may be known comparatively *a priori*; as, for example, in the theory of the phenomena of electricity, magnetism and even light. There is such a simple law recurring in every phenomenon that the results of every experiment may be told beforehand; here my knowing follows immediately from a known law without the intervention of any particular experience. But whence then does the law itself come to me? We suggest that all phenomena are correlated in one absolute and *necessary* law, from which they can all be deduced; in short, that in natural science all that we know, we know absolutely *a priori*. Now, that experimentation never leads to such a knowing is plainly manifest from the fact that it can never get beyond the forces of Nature, of which it makes use as means.

Since the final *causes* of natural phenomena are themselves not phenomenal, we must either give up all attempt ever to arrive at a knowledge of them, or else we must altogether put them into Nature, endow Nature with them. However, that which we put into Nature has no other value than that of a presupposition (hypothesis), and the science founded upon it must be equally as hypothetical as the principle itself. It would be possible to avoid this only in one case, i.e. if that presupposition itself were involuntary, and as necessary as Nature itself. Assuming, for example, what must be assumed, that the sum of phenomena is not a mere world, but of necessity a Nature (that is, that this whole is not merely a product, but at the same time productive), it follows that in this whole we can never arrive at absolute identity, because this would bring about an absolute transition of Nature as productive into Nature as product, that is, it would produce absolute rest. Such a wavering of Nature, therefore, between productivity and product, will necessarily appear as a universal duplicity of principles, whereby Nature is maintained in continual activity, and prevented from exhausting itself in its product; and universal duality as the principle of explanation of Nature will be as necessary as the idea of Nature itself.

This absolute hypothesis must bear its necessity within itself, but it must, besides this, be brought to an empirical test; *for, inasmuch as all the phenomena of Nature cannot be deduced from this hypothesis as long as there is in the whole system of Nature a single phenomenon which is not necessary according to that principle, or which contradicts it, the hypothesis is thereby at once shown to be false*, and from that moment ceases to have validity as a hypothesis.

By this deduction of all natural phenomena from an absolute hypothesis, our knowing is changed into a construction of Nature itself, that is, into a science of Nature *a priori*. If, therefore, such deduction itself is possible, a thing which can be proved only by the deed, then too a doctrine of Nature is possible as a science of Nature; a system of purely speculative physics is possible, which was the point to be proved.

Note. There would be no necessity for this remark if the confusion that still prevails in regard to ideas perspicuous enough in themselves did not render some explanation with regard to them requisite.

The assertion that natural science must be able to deduce all its principles *a priori* is in a sense understood to mean that natural science must dispense with all experience, and, without any intervention of experience, be able to spin all its principles out of itself; an affirmation so absurd that the very objections to it deserve pity. – *Not only do we know this or that through experience, but we originally know nothing at all except through experience, and by means of experience,* and in this sense the whole of our knowledge consists of the judgements of experience. These judgements become *a priori* principles when we become conscious of them as necessary, and thus every judgement, whatever its content may be, may be raised to that dignity, insofar as the distinction between *a priori* and *a posteriori* judgements is not at all, as many people may have imagined, one originally cleaving to the judgements themselves, but is a distinction made solely *with respect to our knowing*, and the *kind* of our knowledge of these judgements, so that every judgement which is merely historical for me – i.e. a judgement of experience – becomes, notwithstanding, an *a priori* principle as soon as I arrive, whether directly or indirectly, at insight into its internal necessity. Now, however, it must in all cases be possible to recognize every natural phenomenon as absolutely necessary; for, if there is no chance in Nature at all, then likewise no original phenomenon of Nature can be fortuitous; on the contrary, for the very reason that Nature is a system, there must be a necessary connection, in some principle embracing the whole of Nature, for everything that happens or comes to pass in it. – Insight into this internal necessity of all natural phenomena becomes, of course, still more complete, as soon as we reflect that there is no real system which is not, at the same time, an organic whole. For if, in an organic whole, all things mutually bear and support each other, then this organization must have existed as a whole previous to its parts; the whole could not have arisen from the parts, but the parts must have arisen out of the whole. It is *not, therefore*, that WE KNOW *Nature* as *a priori*, but *Nature* IS *a priori*; that is, everything individual in it is predetermined by the whole or by the idea of a Nature generally. But if Nature *is a priori*, then it must be possible to *recognize* it *as* something that is a priori, and this is really the meaning of our affirmation.

Such a science, like every other, does not deal with the hypothetical or the merely probable, but depends upon the evident and the certain. Now, we may indeed be quite certain that every natural phenomenon, through whatever number of intermediate links, stands in connection with the last conditions of Nature; the intermediate links themselves, however, may be unknown to us, and still lying hidden in the depths of Nature. To find out these links is the work of experimental research. Speculative physics has nothing to do but to show the need of these intermediate links;[2] but since every new discovery throws us back upon a new ignorance, and while one knot is being loosed a new one is being tied, it is conceivable that the complete discovery of all the intermediate links in the chain of Nature, and therefore also our science itself, is an infinite task. – Nothing, however, has more impeded the infinite progress of this science than the arbitrariness of the fictions by which the lack of profound insight was so long doomed to be concealed. The fragmentary nature of our knowledge becomes apparent only when we separate what is merely hypothetical from the pure outcome of science, and then set out to collect the fragments of the great whole of Nature again into a system. It is, therefore, conceivable that *speculative* physics (the soul of true experimentation) has, throughout all time, been the mother of all great discoveries in Nature.

Notes

1   *Editors' Note.* Georges-Louis Le Sage (1724–1803), an eighteenth-century physicist whose mechanical physics Schelling discusses in a number of texts, including the *First Outline* itself.

2   Thus, for example, it becomes very clear through the whole course of our inquiry, that, in order to render the dynamic organization of the Universe evident in all its parts, we still lack that *central phenomenon* of which Bacon already speaks, which certainly lies in Nature but has not yet been extracted from it by experiment.

Lectures on the System of Positive Philosophy (1832/3)*

The question is [now to be] posed: what is *opposed* to pure thinking? I answer: in general that which is *experiential*. In experience is found that supplement that we lacked in the concept of the *pure* subject. Insofar as this subject excludes everything experiential, we could call this system in the most general sense the *system of pure rationalism* – evidently not in a theological, but a philosophical sense. The opposite of pure rationalism is expressed, as *empiricism*. – I mean here empiricism as a philosophical principle, insofar as it claims that the (highest) object of philosophy is *experiential*. I do not mean that this empiricism claims merely the objects of philosophy are (in the ordinary sense) experiential; objects of experience are accepted in all systems of philosophy. This is not what is at stake. Empiricism as a philosophical system can only be called such, not when it admits merely empirical objects in general, but [when it] claims that the *genuine object of philosophy* is not to be determined through *mere thinking* and posited in mere thinking; rather, when it wills that this object is an *experiential* one. This *genuine* object of philosophy is however not some individual being, but the *prius of all being* to which all other being is related as posterius.

It seems obvious that what is the *prius* of all being could itself be nothing experiential, and this silent and basic reflection has led many in philosophy on the path of that abstraction for which Kant was responsible. This abstraction was the main reason for that path along which only the pure subject remains. However, the question that concerns us in this transition (to empiricism) is whether it is so completely unthinkable that the prius of all things is not *also an experiential*, therefore a *positive* being [*Seiendes*]?

True knowledge is only in experience. This is the principle of empiricism. However, we have also claimed that what is posited in thinking by means of a merely necessary development is known genuinely only through a *non-knowing knowledge*. The [true] relation is now to be shown. Above all, the whole limited concept of empiricism must be eliminated. One must, for example, differentiate between what is the object of actual experience and

---

*Translated by Lydia Azadpour and Daniel Whistler from F.W.J. Schelling, *Grundlegung der Positiven Philosophie: Münchner Vorlesung WS 1832/33 und SS 1833*, ed. H. Fuhrmans (Turin: d'Erasmo, 1972), Part One, Lectures 33 and 34, and Part Two, Lecture 23.

what is *by its nature* actual experience. There is within nature a lot which is not the object of an actual experience. Every pre-human catastrophe, for example, without humans having been there to perceive it, is by its nature an experiential event. However, the question is: *beyond* the circle of sensible experience, does everything experiential stop *or not*? – then one will say: experience lying beyond that limit can be accessed merely by thinking, from which every free act is excluded. However, this view, which excludes everything experiential from that region, contradicts all those views that extend *decision* and *activity* beyond the sensible world. For example, among those views that explain the world through *real* process belongs the doctrine of emanation. This bears witness to the need for a *historical* explanation of the world. If we posit Christianity [and its fundamental thesis] that the world is a production of free personality, then there is no doubt that this decision must be realized *solely through experience*, i.e. a posteriori. If now the *highest* [object] of philosophy is to grasp the world as something *freely* posited and produced, then philosophy, in obtaining its highest goal, seems to obviously become a *science of experience*, insofar as it no longer excludes the experiential. Therefore, in *this* case empiricism is not silenced in the face of rationalism, but it has first to undertake its investigation in opposition to rationalism.

In this regard, all delusions were established in Germany by means of the definition of philosophy as *that science which begins from scratch*.

But in what sense? Is that prius by its own nature something *positive*, or does one demand of *such* a beginning that it be posited only through pure thinking? – The presupposition that the prius of philosophy must be of such a nature that it can come to pass only in pure thinking has produced the most negative philosophy. This demand presupposes that the concept of experience and the absolute prius are mutually exclusive.

But how is the prius and the above definition meant? The definition says only in general: philosophy must depart from scratch, *from the absolute prius*. But it leaves the nature of the prius undetermined. The concept of the absolute prius and the concept of the experiential are in no way mutually exclusive concepts. The same thing can be known from an a priori and an a posteriori perspective. The artist possesses a science of his work a priori, while others obtain some familiarity with it only a posteriori. The above definition therefore contains nothing more than this: philosophy must deduce everything *from scratch*, from the beginning, [deriving] the implications it has developed from that beginning. However, it posits nothing certain about how that beginning is constituted, just as little as it posits something certain about the type and nature of this emergence. Therefore, whoever posits the logic of this beginning a priori commits, in respect to that definition, the grossest *petitio principii*. He assumes what is in question. With that demand to withdraw into pure thinking there is already expressed [the assumption] that the true beginning cannot be a *free* personality. How can one begin with such a denial, before the opposite has even been considered? *Our* interpretation is, therefore, that philosophy proceeds from a *positive* prius, i.e. from the *absolutely positive*, which is only knowable by means of the fact that it is, i.e. *a posteriori* in a general sense.

*

That in the world everything is determined by pure thinking – this is rationalism's view. To this presupposition can only be opposed the claim that the highest is itself something *empirically determinable*, its activity something experientially knowable, i.e. an actual *activity*. We have called this claim or the system appropriate to it *empiricism*, to which we do not mean to connect the common idea.

God is – by means of the fact that he is a personality – already no mere abstract thing, but something knowable through experience [...]. If therefore empiricism is itself thought as a philosophical system, then it is to be differentiated from rationalism in a material respect through the assertion of a highest principle which is *not* a mere abstraction or pure concept.

Here the idea emerges: It was earlier remarked that the positive is that which transcends mere *thinking*. Therefore, we are searching in positive philosophy for an empirically-determinable highest. So now the question is how positive philosophy is differentiated from empiricism.

It seems that the two are one and the same. This is, however, not my view. In order to show the difference between the two, I must repeat what was said earlier about the ways and means to bring about positive philosophy. If they are different, they can only be formally differentiated. We explained that the completed positive science would only be that which is attained going out from God to other being, i.e. the being of the world. In so claiming, we presuppose that [this being] must have *proceeded* from God. However, it was claimed that the absolute prius could not itself be known from a prius. If, however, God is this absolute prius itself, then it follows that God is only knowable a posteriori. It would therefore follow that [this being] cannot proceed immediately from God, that a positive philosophy in the indicated sense is impossible ([since] known a priori means to be explained from a prius).

In order to meet this objection, one must direct attention to the word 'know'. Knowing always encompasses being [*Sein*] within itself. That which is not a being [*nicht-Seiende*] is not known, but either merely thought or not thought. Knowledge of a thing does not merely contain the concept of a thing, but at the same time its *existence*.

That a freely acting personality could be known as being only by means of its acts – this is completely certain. Now, however, it must be remembered that it has not been a matter of proceeding from the already *known* highest, but only from its concept. Our view was: it should proceed from its concept – hence its existence should be proven through the actuality of its action.

Philosophy looks for and wants in the beginning the whole and complete being [*Seiende*]. In this way, a relation to the world is not yet assumed at all at first. That this whole and complete being [*Seiende*] is at the same time the prius of another – this is shown or made manifest only *subsequently*. Therefore: the objection is thus removed. Positive philosophy in no way proceeds from the already-*known* highest, but only from the concept of that highest.

Now it needs to be made clear how rationalism, empiricism and positive philosophy – [since] by these three concepts all possible systems are encompassed for us – it should be made clear how these three concepts relate to each other.

[...]

After the concept of empiricism as a philosophical system had been initially determined in terms of empiricism wanting a prius that is *not* posited in mere thinking, but knowable experientially, it was found that empiricism is not differentiated from the positive system in this respect. There must be a merely formal difference. Formally, empiricism is differentiated from both rationalism and positive philosophy provisionally through the fact that empiricism proceeds not from the concept of existence, but, on the contrary, from what exists in experience, in order to attain from being the mere concept of the positive. For such empiricism, it is not a matter of being [*Sein*] (for it proceeds from being [*Sein*]), but only a matter of the concept. What for positive philosophy is *the point of departure* is the *goal* for empiricism. If the posterius were to contain the concept of the prius in a specific way, then the posterius is proof of the existence of the prius; for example, if a human author was capable of recording in his work such an expression of his inner self that, from this work, one could create the completely determinate concept of the author, then the existence of this determined author would be given. Empiricism does not ask primarily whether something of which it possesses the concept exists, but it asks what truthfully exists in what is assumed to exist, i.e. it looks for the concept of the *truthfully* existing in existence.

By presupposing the existence of the empirical world, it presupposes the existence of what in the world *truthfully* exists, and therefore the *concept* of the same. Its question is only what there genuinely is, what in this empirical world is a *truthful* being [*Seiende*]. *Its movement is a regressive one.*

By contrast, the movement of positive science is a *progressive* one, which has existence as its goal. Only the concept can be proven regressively; since *being* [*Sein*] must be presupposed. Existence can only be progressively proven, and so consequently the concept must be presupposed.

One can go either *forwards* from the concept to being or *backwards* from being [*Sein*] to the concept. Rationalism and positive philosophy are materially opposed, but they are formally in agreement: both go from prius to posterius. By contrast, conventional empiricism is different from both rationalism as well as positive philosophy, and insofar as the progressive belongs to the concept of positive philosophy, empiricism can also be called *negative* philosophy, like all rationalisms, for pure rationalism is no less *negative* philosophy in opposition to the positive.

Positive science is science *beginning from scratch* in relation to the world. Positive science proves the *existence* of thought in its *highest* concept. By contrast, empiricism proceeds from the posterius. The *terminus ad quem* [endpoint] is not existence, but concept. What is gained from *its* scientific work is not existence, but only the nature or the concept of what *genuinely* exists. This definition, in virtue of which existence is wholly excluded from the goal of empiricism and only the concept is explained, is important, because it shows the difference between pure empiricism and other forms of argumentation, which move from its presuppositions to the existence of an intelligent creator of the world, as in the physico-theological proof.

Of the same kind is the so-called cosmo-theological argument which likewise possesses a fact resting on induction. The other premise is that a *regressus in infinitum* [infinite regress] is impossible. Only then is the existence of the cause inferred. In complete opposition to this, it is for *pure* empiricism only a question of the concept. *Pure* empiricism is, as such, pure analysis.

By rationalism I no longer understand subjective rationalism, but objective rationalism in which, as one says, reason is conscious of its being. However, *we* assume a philosophy which is differentiated from rationalism by the fact that it has a principle *not* posited through pure thinking. Rationalism and positive philosophy are consequently materially opposed. On the contrary: what they have in common is that both go from the concept to being. Customary empiricism is doubly opposed to rationalism –

materially, because it wants something experiential; formally, because it is regressive, while rationalism is at least supposedly progressive. Empiricism also possesses the same formal opposition to positive philosophy. That is: it is regressive, while the latter is *progressive*.

Positive philosophy, once established, would contain both opposites *within itself*. For that very reason it would appear outside all opposition. It would have taken possession of the negative itself through pure thinking. Positive philosophy does not share with rationalism the relation of exclusion that the latter has with empiricism. It is, if one likes, super-naturalism. However, for this reason it contains [empiricism] within itself as something that has been overcome.

However, even though it is formally different from empiricism, [positive philosophy] is in the most peaceful and friendly agreement [with empiricism] materially. Positive philosophy can give [empiricism] its due. It recognizes its claims against rationalism.

From time immemorial, noble and free spirits – peering out from under the bondage of arid rationalism – have fled to the domain of empiricism. Nowadays, only contemptible concepts are bound up with this word. However, this opposition, this uprising of empiricism against the yoke of exclusive rationalism has been ever beneficial and breathed new life into science. After the limitations of all-smothering rationalism, it is again beneficial to be able to view the world in general as *fact* once more. It is beneficial that, as physicists do with individual appearances, the philosopher can search out the *all-explaining cause* of the appearance of the world.

[...]

True empiricism thus does not necessarily deny everything supernatural. Beginning with Kant it has become customary to explain everything supersensible as *super*-empirical. After Kant, God has taken refuge in pure thinking, posited in a way that excludes *all* experience. However, such an empiricism that denies everything supersensible was *not* the empiricism of a Bacon, of a Pascal, or of a Newton. Read the final *Scholia in [Newton's] Philosophiae Naturalis Principia Mathematica* and the letters exchanged between Leibniz and Clarke (Newton's pupil). Even John Locke believed that he was not committed to excluding God because of his empiricism.

The true principle of empiricism, *genuine* empiricism, is what infers the existence of God as much as all other personalities from *experiential* marks. – (Whoever wants to obtain a correct feeling for the true standpoint of empiricism should read, for example, Locke and David Hume's writings.)

*

In philosophy everything obviously depends on how one begins.

It can be remarked that, in terms of the beginning, what characterizes positive philosophy is that it *proceeds* from a mere concept to the being of what is thought in the concept.

[...]

However, the difficulty is to reach such a positive prius; a difficulty that was the reason why philosophy has remained so firmly in the negative. The decided and decisive step of Descartes, in breaking from scholastic philosophy, stimulated the idea of a genuinely real-philosophy. This idea has been the implicit orienting [principle] of all modern philosophy. In Descartes, the idea of a real-philosophy was indeed not articulated, but was at the very least stimulated. After philosophy posits for itself the requirement *to begin wholly from scratch* and with the object, to be a priori science, then everything depends on how one tries to take possession of this point of departure, this prius. An objective prius that lay in the object itself was attained. But to this requirement there was immediately bound another requirement that this prius must be immediately certain, [a prius] in view of which being is to be posited immediately with thinking. This was to be achieved in no other way than by refusing to ascribe the being that it genuinely could have to every being that was actual, positive and expressing something different from itself. And thus the requirement for immediate certainty led straight to negativity. By the cumulative development of this negativity, there came the realization that *this* was not the prius we *genuinely* wanted. If, however, the genuinely-desired one is the *positive prius*, then it can only be one that is *experientially* cognizable.

At this point empiricism emerged as the rival to philosophy. In empiricism, the next [step] was to assume – retaining the ascription of *immediate* certainty – that the positive prius could be an object of immediate experience – hence could be an empirically immediate certainty. This was the presupposition of mysticism, in the narrower sense, which in Jacobi does not even overcome this immediate empirical certainty and so does not get beyond the principle at all, such that it is neither progressive nor scientific. It therefore does not belong to the history of philosophy as such. Daring mystics or theosophers – like Jakob Böhme – overcome immediate empirical certainties, but in so doing form, as it were, merely a drunken, self-enclosed, conceptless and senseless world.

It remains now to explain this positive prius itself as a certainty that is merely empirically mediated. The empiricism that we could call *scientific* realizes that this positive prius cannot be determined as an empirically *immediate* certainty, for it is for us empirically *immediate* certainty only in the world. Hence, we want to try to draw this concept out from the being of the world, but not in a rational direction where one begins from the concept of the prius and derives being as the immediate consequence, insofar as it is viewed as posterius. Here being was something genuinely *a priori*, something known from its concept. In the concept of regressive empiricism, on the contrary, *being* as logical principle has been assumed, but not the concept of the *genuine, actual* prius; rather, the being of the *world* immediately at hand in experience was made into the logical prius. However, if it were possible through analysis of the empirically given being and of its progressive spiritualizations to draw out the concept of the actual prius in a really convincing manner, then this being itself would be proven *a posteriori*, i.e. the being *of this* prius. In the rational procedure, being was an *a priori* certainty, thus only an immediate certainty, because it supposedly followed immediately from the concept. However, it is thus a merely negative prius. In regressive empiricism, the discovered prius is positive and its being was only an *a posteriori* certainty.

Now, then, it has been shown that the concept of the prius discovered in this way is not the concept of the *absolute* prius but only the *relative* prius, or – if we use the word in its precise sense – it is not the absolute, but only the *relative concept of God*; and it was this remark that drove us beyond empiricism.

In order to begin philosophy wholly from scratch, we must also have the whole absolute, self-contained *concept, free from every relation.* This is the first thing we *genuinely* want.

Now, our entire critique of rationalism and empiricism has shown that the being of this desire is knowable neither a priori nor a posteriori. Not a priori, since our concept lacks the appropriate being; a priori I produce being merely as something negative. But also not a posteriori: since here the concept is lacking, just as before being had been; here I possess the *relative* concept alone and, to this extent, I have yet to prove the being of the genuine desire.

What else remains then? Where there no longer remains knowledge, there is nonetheless *willing*. Therefore, to begin, there remains the consideration of the concept as something merely *willed* – hence, philosophy is begun from this willing itself – and this agrees with the very term 'philosophy' which contains a willing that alone distinguishes philosophy from all other sciences. For instance, in the beginning, geometry does not know where it wants to arrive and come to an end. Even if it assumed that Euclid's claims in Book 11 are its goal, it still could not anticipate the inception of this claim. Because of the fact that philosophy begins with a determinate intention, it is to be distinguished from other sciences. '*I want*,' says the philosopher, '*the absolutely self-contained concept excluded from any relation*.' This expression also signifies: 'I want the whole and perfect being [*Seiende*].' For only this is the absolutely self-contained, free from all relation. Every other concept has at the very least one relation to something supplementary.

First of all – and this is, we are claiming, the first stage of progressive philosophy – it is asked what pertains to the fact that something is the complete and *perfect* being [*Seiende*]. Here philosophy is still enclosed in mere pure thinking. However, I want it to *be*. And now we see that it is not to be known a priori as an entity. But a posterius is not yet available to us. Consequently, it is evidently only explainable in its being, if, according to its concept, it *can* give itself such a posterius from which its actual being is to be known. I say if this absolutely self-contained prius *can* give itself such a posterius, from which its actual existence could thereupon be known. And this is because whether it *will* give itself this posterius cannot be seen from the concept. However, it is possible to ask what consequence it *could* have according to its concept. I then trace this consequence which it *can* give itself; and presupposing precisely this consequence and no other, if it is to be found in the immediate experience of the actual world, then the being [*Sein*] of the perfect being [*Seienden*] has been proven and indeed proven a posteriori; however, not regressively, nor as one usually understands a posteriori; rather, this being of the absolute prius is proven *progressively a posteriori* through the derivation of the consequence as given in immediate experience from the concept. I discover in the concept the possibility that the prius gives itself a consequence, I then determine the character of this consequence. If now the character of this consequence is so constituted that it coincides completely with the actual world, then it is a proof of the actual existence of this absolute prius, and indeed a proof a posteriori. However, it is not a regressive-a posteriori proof; rather, this being [*Sein*] itself first emerges as a derivation from the absolute prius. And when this occurs, when the being of this absolute self-contained prius is proven, everything I wanted from philosophy has been realized. And this describes the whole of the philosophy that I call *positive*, about which I want merely to add a few provisional remarks.

The following has now been determined: 1) the relation of positive philosophy to both rationalism and empiricism. Consider the two end-points around which everything moves – the concept and the existence of something – then it is at bottom a matter in all philosophy of whether one goes from concept to being or from being to concept. If you posit the two end-points 'concept' and 'being', then rationalism proves being a priori, immediately from the concept, while empiricism, on the contrary, tries to prove the concept from experience a posteriori. However, positive philosophy reverses what *is* in rationalism and empiricism. It establishes the concept a priori. *Departing* from what it *wants* as the prius, it differentiates itself from empiricism. However, it does not prove being or existence from the concept, but through experience and, in this sense, a posteriori. That it, therefore, does not prove being a priori is what differentiates it from rationalism. But just as it *differentiates* itself from both, so too it has something *in common* with both: with rationalism the departure from the concept, with empiricism the proof of being from experience. It therefore unites the opposites, but in so doing stands *above* both. One could call also call positive philosophy *a priori empiricism*. Since it proves [the point] from which it departs only empirically, it at once includes empiricism within itself and, as it were, reconciles with it. Such a sublation of the two external opposites is also an external sign that positive philosophy could be true.

2) The whole positive philosophy is really nothing other *than a proof of its principle*. Its principle is not something proven in advance that leaves us no freedom. A great difference emerges from the fact that positive philosophy does not have the existence of finite things as the object of its proof, like earlier forms [of philosophy]. Things enter into positive philosophy only in virtue of the proof that the positive prius *actually exists*. It is only a matter of the existence of the absolute prius, not of things. The expression 'a priori empiricism' does not mean that in it the empirical is derived a priori, but that, in it, the prius is grounded *empirically*. Positive philosophy has an empirically grounded – and for that reason not abstract but experiential – positive prius, and, as it were, the more experiential it is, the further science is progressed. Negative philosophy, which derives the empirical from the prius, can accordingly only have a negative prius. *Positive, a priori philosophy is that [philosophy] which has something as principle that is only proven by act.*

Lectures on the Philosophy of Revelation (1842/3)*

The knowledge in which rationalism has its essence is to be called *substantial* to the extent that it excludes all *actus*. Rationalism can generate nothing through an action, that is, through a free creation; it is familiar only with pure essential relations. Everything merely follows from it *modo aeterno*, eternally, which means in a merely logical manner, through immanent movement. [...] The substantial movement in which rationalism is confused starts out from a negative *prius*, for example, starts out from something nonexistent that must first move itself into being [*Seyn*]; but the historical philosophy starts out from something positive, that is, from an existing *prius* that does not first have to move itself into being. This *prius* thus posits only with *complete* freedom without being somehow required by its nature to posit a being.

[...]

The question now, however, is in which way the science we have proposed – the positive philosophy – is a philosophy and in which way it will become a science.

If among the categories that stand at our behest for the designation of philosophical doctrines, empiricism can be opposed to nothing other than rationalism, then positive philosophy, as the antithesis of rationalism, will nevertheless be incapable of denying that it is also in some way and in some sense empiricism as well. The question thus returns to what type of relation the positive philosophy will have to experience: the same as that of a mystical doctrine, or an entirely different relation? What is common to all of these mystical doctrines is that they *start out* from experience – from something that occurs in *experience*. *What* this experience is is entirely irrelevant, for example, whether it starts out from the appearance or the miracles of Christ (as in an earlier time, when there was such a mindless historical theology, which avoided every contact with philosophy to the extent that it believed it could eliminate all philosophical arguments for the existence of God and could best prove the existence of God through the miracles of Christ), whether it proceeds from the presence of an

---

*Translated by Bruce Matthews from Lectures 7 and 8 in F.W.J. Schelling, *Sämmtliche Werke* (Stuttgart and Augsberg: Cotta, 1856–1861), Division Two, Volume three.

exuberant feeling in us that is only to be satisfied through an existing God, or whether it proceeds from an immediate intuition of the divine – each of these always starts out from something given in immediate or mediated experience. I would now like only to briefly state – for it extends as far as a preliminary distinction, and we are concerned only with a preliminary distinction – that the positive philosophy starts out just as little from something that occurs merely in thought (for then it would fall back into the negative philosophy) as it starts out from some being that is present in *experience*. If it does not start out from something that occurs in thought [*im Denken Seyende*] and, thus, in no way from pure thought, then it will start out from that which is before and external to all thought, consequently from being [*Seyn*], but not from an empirical being. For we have already excluded this, in that empirical being is external to thought only in the very relative sense, to the extent that *every* being that occurs in experience inherently carries with it the logical determinations of the understanding, without which it could never even be represented. If positive philosophy starts out from that which is external to all thought, it cannot begin with a being that is external to thought in a merely relative sense, but only with a being that is *absolutely* external to thought. The being that is external to all thought, however, is just as much beyond all experience as it is before all thought: positive philosophy begins with the *completely transcendent being* [*Seyn*] and it can no longer be just a relative prius like the potency that serves as the basis of the science of reason. For precisely as potency – as *nonbeing* – it has the necessity to pass over into being, and, thus, I call it the merely relative *prius*. If that being from which positive philosophy proceeds were also merely relative, then the *necessity* of passing over into being would inhere within its principle. Thus, through this principle, that being would be subordinated to the thought of a necessary movement and, consequently, the positive philosophy would fall back into the negative. If, therefore, the relative *prius* cannot be the beginning of the positive philosophy, then it must be the absolute prius, which has no necessity to move itself into being. If it passes over into being, then this can only be the consequence of a free act, of an act that can only be something purely empirical, that can be fully apprehended only a posteriori, just as every act is incapable of being comprehended a priori and is only capable of being known a posteriori.

The positive philosophy is not empiricism, at least insofar as it does not start out from experience – neither in the sense that it presumes to posses its object in an immediate experience (as in mysticism), nor in the sense that it attempts to attain to its object through inferences drawn from something given in experience, such as an empirical fact (for I must still exclude even this to distinguish positive philosophy from rational dogmatism that, in its proof for the existence of God, makes partial use of empirical facts, such as the purposive arrangement of nature). But if positive philosophy does not start out from experience, then nothing prevents it from going toward experience, and thereby proving a posteriori what it has to prove, that its *prius* is God, that is, that which is above being. For what it begins with is a priori – but a priori it is not God, only a posteriori is it God. That it is God is not a *res naturae*, something that is self-evident, but is a *res facti*, and can therefore only be proved factually. It is God. This proposition does not mean the concept of this *prius* is equal to the concept of God. It means that this *prius is* God, not according to its concept, but according to its reality. Of course, if positive philosophy does not start out from experience, then it must be an a priori science. To this extent it is thus again no different from the negative philosophy, for what we have ascribed to the positive philosophy also holds for the negative, namely, that it does not start out from experience but goes *toward* experience. They do indeed relate in this way, but the difference is this: positive and negative philosophy each has a position toward experience, but each is different. For the latter experience confirms but does not *prove* [*erweisend*]. Rational philosophy has its truth in the immanent necessity of its progress; as we said earlier, it is so independent of existence that it would be true even if nothing existed. If that which actually occurs in experience agrees with its constructions then this is something gratifying, something to which the construction indeed refers, but with which it does not really *prove* anything. The position of positive philosophy is entirely different. It enters into experience itself and grows, as it were, together with it. It too is an a priori science, but the *prius* from which it proceeds is not simply *before* all experience, so that it must necessarily move forward into experience, but rather it is *above* all experience, and thus there is no *necessary* transition into experience for this *prius*. From this *prius*, positive philosophy derives in a free thought and in an evidentiary sequence that which is a posteriori or that which occurs in experience, not as what is possible, as in the negative philosophy, but as what is real. It derives it as what is real, for only as such does it have the meaning and the force of proof. So that I make myself completely clear: not the absolute *prius itself* will be proved (this is above all proof, since it is the absolute and through itself indubitable beginning), thus, not it itself (the absolute *prius*) will be proved, but rather what the consequences are that follow from this, these must be *factually* proved, and only thereby do we prove the divinity of that *prius* – that it is God, and that *God* therefore exists. Consequently, we will say that the *prius*, whose *concept* is such and such (that of what is above being), will be *capable* of having *such* a consequence (we will not say that it will necessarily *have* such a consequence, for then we would fall back again into necessity, that is, *fall back into a movement* determined solely by concepts. We should rather only say it can have such a consequence *if it wishes*, since the consequence is contingent on its will). This consequence, however, really exists (*this* proposition is one founded now in experience: the existence of such a consequence is a datum, a fact of experience). This datum, thus, shows us – the *existence* of such a consequence shows us – that the *prius* itself also *exists in the way* we have *conceived* it, that is, that God exists. You see that in this manner of argumentation the *prius* is always the point of departure, that is, it always remains the *prius*. The *prius* will be known from its consequences, but not in a way such that the consequences had *preceded* it. The preposition 'a' in 'a posteriori' does not in this instance signify the *terminus a quo*; in this context 'a posteriori' means '*per posterius*': through its consequence the *prius* is known. To be known a priori means just this: to be known from and out of the *prius*; what is known a priori is, thus, that which a *prius* possesses and from which it is known. The absolute *prius*, however, is what has no *prius* from which it can be known. To be the absolute *prius* means, therefore, not to be known a priori. Here, in the positive philosophy, lies the real empiricism insofar as that which occurs in experience itself becomes an element of and an assistant to philosophy.

To express this distinction in the sharpest and most concise manner: the negative philosophy is *a priori empiricism*, it is the *Apriori* of what is empirical, but, for this very reason, it is not itself empirical. Conversely, the positive philosophy is an empirical *Apriori*, or it is the empiricism of what is a priori insofar as it proves that the *prius per posterius* exists as God.

From the perspective of the world, positive philosophy is an a priori science, which is nonetheless derived from the absolute *prius*; from the perspective of *God*, it is a posteriori science and knowledge.[1]

The experience towards which positive philosophy proceeds is not just of a *particular kind*, but is the entirety of all experience from beginning to end. What contributes to the proof is not a part of experience, but all of experience. For precisely this reason, though, this proof *itself* is not just the beginning or a part of a science (least of all some type of syllogistic proof posited at the apex of philosophy), it is the entire science, that is, the entire positive philosophy – and this is nothing other than the progressive, strengthening with every step, and continually growing proof of the actually existing God. Because the realm of reality in which this proof moves is not finished and complete – for even if nature is now at its end and stands still, there is, nonetheless, still the unrelenting advance and movement of history – because insofar as the realm of reality is not complete, but is a realm perpetually nearing its consummation, the proof is therefore also never finished, and for this very reason this science is only a *Philo-sophie*. For the science of reason is *philosophy* to the extent it seeks and possesses only at its terminus that which is the object of the most supreme knowing (that is, the *sophia* [wisdom]) and possesses this only at the end of its path in a *concept*. The *other* side, which has the task of reaching this not merely as an object found or remaining to be known or cognized, but as an object actually known and cognized, the positive side is *philosophy* since it achieves its goal only when the proof is provided not in its individual components, but rather only in its continual development. [...] This entire philosophy is, therefore, an always advancing knowledge, always nothing other than a *philo-sophia*, never rigid or stagnant, and, thus, in this sense, a dogmatic science. For this reason, however, even this proof is only a proof for those who want to think and move forward, and, thus, only for the *wise*. It is not like a proof of geometry, with which one can coerce those of even the most limited abilities, and even the dumb, whereas I can coerce no one to become wise through experience if he does not want to, and this is why the psalm says: 'the foolish speak in their hearts: there is no God.'[2]

The positive philosophy is the truly free philosophy; whoever does not want it should just as well leave it alone. I propose it to everyone freely. I only maintain that if one wants the actual chain of events, if he wants a freely created world, and so on, he can have all of this only via the path of such a philosophy. If the rational philosophy satisfies him, and he longs for nothing beyond it, then he should just as well stay with it, only he must give up the desire to possess within the rational philosophy that which it by no means can possess, namely, the real God, the actual chain of events, and a free relationship of God to the world. The confusion that now reigns over this matter must cease. No one can appreciate the rational philosophy more than I; indeed, I would consider university students lucky if there was again a purely rational philosophy taught in the schools. For I do not concede that those who now boast of being rationalists are indeed rationalists; they are instead nothing less than this: those who produce a repulsive mixture of rational and suprarational philosophy, whereby neither of the two is done justice.

*

It is a proud name with which [negative philosophy] is entitled to adorn itself when it calls itself the science of reason. But what is its content as such a science? Properly speaking, only the constant *overthrow* of reason. And its result? Simply that reason, inasmuch as it merely takes itself as its source and principle, is capable of no *actual* knowledge. For that which always simultaneously becomes what is and what is knowable for it is something that goes beyond reason, namely experience, which it must leave to another science. In this advance, then, reason possesses nothing *on its own account*, it only watches as its content *dissipates*, and even with the one that remains, *it* can – on its own account – begin nothing or bring this one thing together with its content to knowledge. To the extent that the positive philosophy brings to knowledge precisely that which remained in the negative as something incapable of being known, to this extent it is precisely the positive philosophy that straightens out reason *contorted* by the negative, in that it helps bring it to the actual *knowledge* of that which it had become acquainted with as its singular, *enduring* and inviolable content. If the negative philosophy would have remained alone and by itself, if it would have had no positive result for reason *itself*, then this knowing reason would have remained unsatisfied regarding its own content and would have departed empty-handed. In the positive philosophy, the negative triumphs as the science in which thought, after it has liberated itself from its immediate, that is, accidental content, first really attains its goal whereby its necessary content becomes dominant, and upon which thought now looks on in freedom (for previously, thought did not see this necessary content in freedom, since the accidental content, so to speak, stood between reason and its necessary content). Therefore, in its truth, that is, to the extent it is *philosophy*, the negative is itself positive since it posits the latter outside itself, and, thus, there is *no longer* a duality. From the very beginning our earliest aspirations have sought a positive philosophy. History shows how late the origins of all purely rational inquiries are and how early the human spirit concerned itself with representations that, considered from the rational standpoint alone, are transcendent. The positive philosophy is the one philosophy that has always and originally been wanted, but because it was unsuccessful or was sought for in the wrong manner it prompted the *critique* from which, in exactly the same manner as I have shown, the negative philosophy then emerged as a philosophy that has its worth and meaning only *as* negative, that is, insofar as it does not want to be positive itself, but rather posits the positive outside itself. [...]

The rational philosophy does not concern itself with what really exists, with that which has the capacity to exist. The ultimate that can exist, however, is *the* potency that is no longer potency but, rather, since it is being itself, is pure *actus*; for this reason we could call it the *existing* potency [*die seyende Potenz*]. Yet this ultimate is, for the present, only a concept in the negative philosophy. But certainly it can be asked, and it can always be considered a priori, *in what way* this ultimate can exist. Here it becomes immediately clear that the potency, which is not a potency, but is rather itself the *actus*, does not exist via the transition *a potentia ad actum*. *If* it exists, then it can only *be* a priori, having being as its *prius*. We could, therefore, also call it the inverted capacity to be, namely, that capacity to be in which the potency is the *posterius* and the *actus* is the *prius*.

Notes

1   One usually understands by a posteriori knowledge that type in which one, for example, infers backwards from the effect to the cause. The order of the proof here is the reverse of the actual matter, for the effect is as such only the conclusion, only the result; the cause, however, precedes it, it is the antecedent. In such an inference, what is the consequence according to its nature becomes something artificial in order to benefit the proof, and is, thus, accepted as what is logically antecedent (and for precisely this reason the proof means an a posteriori proof, i.e. a proof in which what is actually the *posterior* is made into the logical *prius*, into the point of departure). Conversely, that which is the antecedent according to its nature – the cause – here in the proof becomes a logical conclusion, a consequence. In the positive philosophy, however, this is not an a posteriori proof in the usual sense of the word, for we progress not from the effect to the cause, but, conversely, from the cause to the effect; the cause, which according to its *nature* is that which precedes, is in this way here also the *prius* of the proof. It follows from this (natural) arrangement of cause and effect that here, while the *causa* (God) a posteriori or *per posterius* is proved or demonstrated, the conclusion (the world) is deduced or comprehended a priori.

2   *Translator's Note.* Psalm 14:1.

On the Source of the Eternal Truths (1850)*

The question that I intend to discuss today was already treated by the philosophy of the Middle Ages; and still further back it is connected with the greatest investigations of philosophical antiquity. Taken up again by Descartes and Leibniz, this question entered a fresh stage owing to the new philosophical movement introduced by Kant – a movement which, undeterred by interruptions and momentary detours, has never been sidetracked from its true goal – so that now perhaps the issue is closer to resolution than ever before.

The question I am referring to concerns the so-called eternal or necessary truths, in particular their *source*. But this is the simplest way of expressing the matter: More fully stated it treats *de origine essentiarum, idearum, possibilium, veritatum aeternarum* [of the origin of essences, ideas, possibilities, eternal truths]. All these are regarded as equivalent expressions. For with regard to the essences, it was held to be an indisputable principle that *essentias rerum esse aeternas* [the essences of things are eternal]. Contingency (*contingentia*) is exclusively concerned with the *existence* of things: For example, this plant existing here in this place, or now in this instant, is contingent; whereas the *essence* of the plant is necessary and eternal, incapable of being otherwise, either just so or not at all. From this it is self-evident that the *essentia rerum* [essence of things] are also the same as the *Ideas* more or less as Plato conceived them. Since, moreover, actuality has no bearing on essence, in that the essence remains the same whether the thing is actually present or not (just as the essence of a circle is not altered in the slightest by the circumstance that I actually construct one), it is thus understandable that the realm of essences is also the realm of possibilities, and that what is only possible in a certain way is also *necessarily* the case. This leads directly to the fourth expression, that of necessary or eternal truths.

Ordinarily the latter expression is used only of mathematical truths, but the concept is much broader. If, like Kant, we conceive of the highest Idea of reason as the completely determinate concept of all possibilities, then there will also be a science which distinguishes these possibilities and makes them

*Translated by Edward A. Beach from F.W.J. Schelling, *Sämmtliche Werke* (Stuttgart and Augsberg: Cotta, 1856–1861), Division Two, Volume One.

comprehensible by means of a thinking activity that leads them out of their potentiality and lets them become *actual* in thought. Mathematics does the same thing, for example, when it takes something that is merely *in potentia* [potentially] (*qua* capacity) in a figure – as in a right triangle, the relation of the legs to the hypotenuse is implicit as a potential – just so, I was saying, mathematics finds this relation by means of a thinking activity. 'It is evident,' says Aristotle, 'that that which is merely *qua* potency, is discovered by means of transformation into *actus*'.

This is the path of every pure or merely rational science. Now, in the highest Idea of reason even the plant will indisputably be predetermined; and it will not be absolutely impossible to proceed from the first possibilities, those that can be classed as fundamental principles, to the multiply conditioned and complex possibility of the plant. This will, I maintain, not be *absolutely* impossible. For at stake here is by no means what may be possible *for us*, but rather what is possible *in itself*. What is possible for us is everywhere dependent on many very contingent conditions. The assistance of experience for such derivations is indispensable *for us* (a higher spirit might perhaps dispense with it). But experience is an ever continuing, never completed process, and also the range wherein our fundamentally limited mental capacities can be applied is very much conditioned by contingencies.

Assuming, however, what in general ought to be assumed as possible and never abandoned, that a continuous progression is discoverable from the highest Idea of reason all the way down to the plant as a necessary moment of the same; then in this context the plant is nothing contingent any longer, but is rather itself an eternal truth. And I will not pronounce the judgement that one would have to make of the natural scientist to whom this is irrelevant and whose research is unaccompanied by the constant awareness that what concerns him is not something merely contingent and insignificant for reason, but rather the sort of thing that, from the broad (even if, to him, incomprehensible) perspective has a necessary place and therewith an eternal truth.

Having now, as I believe, sufficiently established the extension of the *object* in question, I come next to the motivating *occasion*, and will first of all show what induced the Scholastics to concern themselves with the *source* of the eternal truths.

This occasion, then, was that eternal, i.e. necessary truths, could not derive their sanction from the divine *will*; for if determined through divine *pleasure* alone, they were contingent truths that could also just as well be untruths. Consequently, it was necessary to recognize a source of such truths that was independent of the divine will; and likewise there had to be something independent of the divine will wherein the possibilities of things had their ground.

For Thomas Aquinas, to be sure, the possibility was still in the *essentia divina* [divine essence] itself, namely in that aspect which one thought of as *participabilis s. imitabilis* [participable or imitable]. A trace of this conception is still to be found in Malebranche. In these expressions one easily detects the Platonic *methexis* [participation], as well as the term which the Pythagoreans more frequently employed, *mimesis* [imitation].

But who does not immediately perceive that here the capacity of the things themselves to participate in, or imitate, the divine essence – wherein the *possibility* of the things was supposed to consist – has covertly been smuggled into a capacity *of the divine essence*: viz., to permit them to participate in, or to imitate, itself? Thereby the possibility on the side of the things would not be explained at all. It was therefore inevitable that one would eventually recognize an original possibility within the things themselves, which was not only independent of the divine will but also of the divine essence.

Such a possibility was affirmed by the Scotists, who were forced into it, as a disciple of Leibniz expresses it, 'forced to admit some unknown principle of the reality of essences, a principle distinct from God and coeternal as well as co-necessary to him, from which would depend the necessity and eternity of the essences.' Incidentally, this *nescio quod* [unknown something] could well have resolved itself up to a certain point even by means of the expressions Scotus used. Scotus spoke of an *ente diminuto, in quo possibile constitutum sit* [a lesser entity, in which the possible would be constituted]. *Ens diminutum* in the Latin of Scotus indisputably signifies nothing other than what is [determinate] being (*das Seiende*) in a merely subordinate sense. In the same way Aristotle, too, distinguishes the *protos on*, the primary being, from the merely *hepomenos on*, that being which is posited merely as the consequence and supplement of another; just as he distinguishes the *energeia on* [actual being] from the merely *hylikos on* [material being], and makes the latter equivalent to the *dynamei on* [potential being] or the *me on* [not-being] (carefully to be distinguished from the *ouk on*, which is the absolute non-being, or nothing at all).[1] Thus, regarding the material nature of this co-posited being there surely was no doubt. What was unresolved, and remained unresolved even into our own time, consisted not in its constitution, but rather in the fact that this secondary being, though in its own nature merely an ability-to-be (*Seinkönnendes*), yet had to have some sort of a relationship to God.

Now, however, there came *Descartes*, who sliced the knot in his own way – that is, violently – in that he stipulated the opposite: According to him, the mathematical as well as the other so-called eternal truths are established by God and no less dependent on the divine will than are all other creatures. Descartes's own words in one of his texts are the following: 'In my Physics I treat the metaphysical questions, especially this one: the mathematical truths, which you call eternal, I claim to have been established by God and dependent on him no otherwise than the created bodies are dependent.' One could attempt to interpret these words in such a way as to deny only that the eternal truths are independent of the divine *knowledge* (in opposition to those Scotists who taught that the eternal truths would persist even if there were no understanding at all, not even God's). However, this interpretation is contradicted by another statement of the philosopher, viz.: 'In God it is one and the same thing to will and to know, so that whatever he might will he would identically know, and just as identically (namely, because he wills it) the thing is true.'

The next consequence to emerge out of this claim would be, as for mathematics, that it is merely an empirical science: For that which is the result of a will (and accordingly is contingent, since it might equally well not be the case) can only be experienced and not known, as one says, *a priori*. This is already contradicted, however, by the fact that there is in *experience* no [mathematical] point, nor is there in actuality any line that is perfectly straight or without breadth; and from this it would in any case follow that regarding the first principles or premises of geometry something else is in play than experience alone. I say 'in any case,' for in making the general observation that mathematics is an *a priori* science we have still not disposed of the matter; but I cannot here embark on the special enquiry concerning the genesis of mathematical truths, and must reserve this topic for another opportunity.

However, what most of all contradicts the assertion (i.e. that mathematical knowledge would only be true in consequence of the divine will) is the entire nature of mathematics. For wherever the *will* intervenes, there it is a question of *actuality*. Yet it is evident that geometry, for example, concerns itself not with the actual, but with the possible triangle; and none of its propositions have the meaning that it *actually* is such and so, but rather that it *could not be* otherwise; and that the triangle, for example, is only possible on the condition that the sum of its angles equals two right angles. Of course, from thence it follows too that the triangle will be just *so*, if it Is, but that it Is is regarded as a matter of complete indifference.

To be sure, this conclusion about mathematics is something that Descartes would have been the least likely to admit. But it is not any the less true on that account that [the conclusion] ineluctably follows from his drawing the eternal truths out of the divine will, and that with this supposition all eternally valid truth would be removed from the sciences. One could, like Pierre Bayle, draw from Descartes's assertion the conclusion that $3 + 3 = 6$ is only true where and for as long as it pleases God, that it may perhaps be untrue in other regions of the universe, and next year may even cease to be true for us.

The situation would have more serious consequences if the doctrine were carried over into the ethical and religious domain. This was done by certain theologians of the Reformed Church, who allowed themselves to be led by the teaching of the *decretum absolutum* [absolute decree] all the way to the belief that the distinction between good and evil is nothing objective in itself, but established only through the divine will. Especially from this side the above-mentioned Bayle has attacked Descartes, in words that Leibniz found not unworthy of quoting in a passage of his *Theodicy*, and which I may also repeat here. He says:

> A great many of the most serious authors declare themselves to be in favour of the proposition that there is in advance of every divine decree and independent of the same a good and an evil *in the nature of the things themselves*. As proof of this opinion they make especial use of the dreadful consequences following from the opposite teaching; but there is a directly telling argument from metaphysics. It is a *certain* thing that God's existence is not a consequence of his *will*: He *exists*, [but] not because he *wills* it; and if it is just as little the case that he is almighty or all-knowing because he wills to be such, then in general his will can only extend to beings that are *outside* him, [and] furthermore, *only* to the fact *that* [each given being] Is, but not to whatever belongs to its *essence*. God, if he wished, could have made matter, humankind, the circle, *non*-actual; but it was impossible for him to make them actual without providing them with their essential properties, which thus were not dependent on his will.[2]

One ought not to take colorful speech too literally; else one could suppose that Bayle's words implied the opinion that the existence of God is an eternal truth in the same sense that $3 + 3 = 6$ is such – an opinion that one might find oneself just as tempted to contradict as was [a certain] abbot of a cloister in response to an over-eager teacher, who [so the story goes] had gotten so carried away as to assert that God's existence is as certain as $2 \times 2 = 4$; a claim which [the abbot] reproved with the retort that God's existence is far more certain than 2 x 2 = 4. I understand completely if, as is further reported, the audience laughed at this statement; and I also realize that to this day there are plenty of people who cannot comprehend how anything could be more certain than 2 x 2 = 4. Without wishing to investigate this expression further, it is clear that there are *different orders* of truths, and that the truths of arithmetic and mathematics in general cannot have *unconditional* certainty, if only for the reason that these sciences (as I already explained in my earlier lectures on Plato) work with presuppositions that *they themselves* cannot justify; and therewith, so far as their worth and validity is concerned, they acknowledge a higher court of appeal. A further indication is that there is much they know only through experience: e.g. concerning even and odd, derivative and prime numbers, for which they still have not even discovered a law of reciprocal intervals.

Leibniz then declares himself in agreement with Bayle concerning the independence of the eternal truths from the divine will; but he does not agree with the most extreme among the Scotists, and not at all with those who affirm a realm of eternal truths independent of God *in every sense*, or a *nature of things* for itself and outside of every relationship with God. If the will of God is capable only of being the cause of the actuality of things, then the source of their possibility cannot also be in this will; but just as little can [this source] be something unconditioned by God and in every respect independent. Says Leibniz (in the *Theodicy*):

> In my opinion the divine will is the cause of the actuality of things, but the *divine understanding* is the source of their possibility. It is *this* that constitutes the truth of the eternal truths, without the will's having any role therein. All reality (thus, he means, even that which we must attribute to the eternal truths) must be grounded on something that exists. [...]³

[...] But now concerning this understanding – how does it *relate* to the eternal truths? Either it determines from itself, and without being bound to anything, what in the things should be necessary and eternal. In this case there is no seeing how it is any different from the will, so that here too it could be said: *Stat pro ratione voluntas* [let the will stand in place of reason]. If it is the understanding of God that, without being determined or restricted by anything, thinks out the possibilities of things (which in the actuality become necessities), then by this means one will still not have circumvented caprice. Or if this is the meaning: The understanding does not create the possibilities, it finds them before it, discovers them as already being there, – then there must be something distinct from this understanding and presupposed by it, wherein these possibilities are grounded and wherein it beholds them. This something, however, which we would thus be conceiving of as independent of the divine understanding and to which we would have to suppose the latter itself bound – what should we call it? As the source of the *universal* and *necessary* in the things, it can itself no longer be anything individual, as we must conceive the understanding to be; for also the Leibnizean expression, *l'entendement divin* [the divine understanding], can only be understood of a divine faculty. To be independent of everything individual, indeed even opposed to this, to be itself the Universal and seat of the universal and necessary truths – all this can only be said of *Reason*. We would thereby be referred to an eternally existing Reason independent of the divine will, a Reason whose limits or laws the divine understanding, in its own productions or projections, could not overstep. But once having come to this point, and beguiled by the universal that rises above everything individual – should we remain at this point, and not rather seek to rid ourselves entirely of the individual? And this so much the more as, when one distinguishes between this reason and God, two mutually independent beings must be postulated, neither of which is derivable from the other; whereas science insists first and above all on the unity of principles. Why not, therefore, affirm that God himself is nothing other than this eternal Reason – an opinion which, once it has been adopted among clever people as incontrovertible and self-explanatory, spares them endless difficulties and removes all perplexities at a single stroke?

One may perhaps object to this account of the progression that it is too much of a leap and ejects us out of the Leibnizian period immediately into the present. For the system in which Reason is all is surely the most recent. But from this the intended conclusion would not follow. In the period from Leibniz up to Kant rationalism was the *universal* mode of thinking; it just was not represented yet by any philosophical system (for in those days, as is well known, a system was lacking). Consequently, it was compelled to prove itself in a more popular style by launching into theology. This theological rationalism, which to be sure was not yet itself cognizant of what in the final analysis it wanted, emerged (this can be demonstrated with historical precision) directly out of the Wolffian school. But although this rationalism has only quite recently succeeded in establishing itself as a philosophical system – owing, to be sure, to the later developments – it nevertheless has its actual roots not in this, but in the preceding period. [...]

A great and unavoidable difficulty, however, clings even to this outcome. For just as, on the one hand, the divine will alone does not explain the necessary and universal features of things, it is equally impossible for pure reason alone to explain the contingent and actual features of things. To achieve this end, no other alternative would seem to remain than to suppose that reason would become untrue to itself and experience a fall from itself, [to imagine] that the very same idea which first had been represented as the most perfect and for which *no* further dialectical progress would be feasible – that this idea, without having in itself any grounds to do so, and truly, as the French say, *sans rime ni raison* [without rhyme or reason], should disintegrate itself into this world of contingent things that are opaque to reason and in active opposition to the concept. [...]

To return to Leibniz, this much is clear: In order to avoid the sheer impossibility of a total dependence and a total independence, Leibniz postulates two distinct faculties in God. But would it not be simpler and more natural to seek the cause of the various relationships to God in the nature of that *nescio quod* [I know not what] itself, which is supposed to contain the ground of all possibility and as it were the stuff, the material for all possibilities? And [is it not the case that this ideal ground], by the same token, can itself only be a possibility, hence only the *potentia universalis* [universal potentiality], which as such differs *toto coelo* [completely and utterly] from God? Must not [this *potentia universalis*] also, according to its essence, that is, considered purely logically, be independent of that Being of whom all traditions unanimously agree that he is *pure Actuality* – Actuality in which there is nothing of potentiality?

To this extent the relationship is still a purely logical one. But now, how will the real relationship be represented? Simply thus: That which comprehends all possibility, as itself merely possible, will be incapable of *self-being* and only be able to be in the mode of relating itself as mere material to another [pure Actuality], which is its being and over against which it [the pure potentiality] appears as that which is not through itself. I offer these characterizations without further ado, because they are all based on well-known Aristotelian propositions. *To hylikon oudepote kath' hautou lekteon* [the hyletic, which is only capable of a material being, cannot be said of itself, it can only be said of another], to which other it therefore belongs. For if I *say* (predicate) B of A, then I am saying that A *is* B. That other, however, which *is* this (the [potentiality] incapable of self-being), that would have to be the self-being, and indeed in the highest sense *the Self-Being* – God. The real relationship then would be that God *is* that being which is not for itself and which now, insofar as it is – *Is*, namely, in the only way it can be – will appear as the *ens universale* [universal being], as the essence in which all essences, i.e. all possibilities, are.[4]

[…]

God contains in himself nothing except the pure thatness (*Daß*) of his own being (*Sein*); but this, that he *Is*, would be no *truth*, if he were not *Something* – Something, to be sure, not in the sense of a [determinate] being (*ein Seiendes*), but in the sense of the [determinate] all-being (*das alles Seiende*) – if he did not have a relation to thought, a relation not to a *concept* but to the *concept of all concepts*, to the *Idea*. Here is the true place for that [principle of the] unity of being and thought which, once expressed, has been used in quite diverse ways. For it is easy to extract bits and pieces from a system when one lacks an overview of it, and when it is perhaps far from having been developed as it ought, but it is difficult to cover over its flaws by means of such scraps and, in doing so, to avoid applying them to the wrong places. It is a long path to the highest opposition, and anyone who wishes to speak about this should ask himself twice whether he has traversed this path. The unity intended here reaches all the way to the highest opposition; thus, that [unity] is also the final limit, is that beyond which one cannot pass.

In this unity, however, the priority does not lie on the side of thought; being (*das Sein*) is the first, thinking only the second or following. This opposition is likewise that of the universal and the absolutely individual. But the path does not go from the universal to the individual, as people generally seem to hold nowadays. Even a Frenchman who, moreover, has gained a mastery of Aristotle's achievement, attaches himself to this general opinion when he says: *le général se réalise en s'individualisant* [the universal realizes itself in individualizing itself].[5] It would be difficult to say whence the universal would acquire the means and the power to realize itself. What one should say, rather, is that the individual (*das Individuelle*) – and indeed, especially what is the individual in the highest sense – realizes itself, i.e. makes itself intelligible, or enters into the sphere of reason and knowledge, inasmuch as it generalizes itself, or makes the universal, all-comprehending essence its own, clothes itself with it.

Notes

1   *Editors' Note*. As early as the *Freedom* essay of 1809, Schelling held on to this distinction between *me on* or being-as-nothing and *ouk on* or non-being.

2 Leibniz, *Theodicy*, [...] § 183.
3 Leibniz, *Theodicy*, § 184.
4 *Translator's Note.* Observe Schelling's very specialized and unique usage of the word 'is' in this context. The appeal to Aristotle notwithstanding, one should bear in mind that what guides Schelling's argument is a highly personalized adaptation of the Greek philosopher's ideas. In the above passage, Schelling is effectively distinguishing between the 'is' of predication (applicable to all determinate possibilities) and another, more fundamental sense of 'is.' The latter is like the 'is' of existence, but more than that, it is the 'Is' (pure Act) that gives existence to Itself as well as to finite entities.
5 *Translator's Note.* Probably Victor Cousin (1792–1867) is meant.

Further reading

For further reading on the relationship between reason and experience, we first recommend that one turn to the extracts from the 1801 *Presentation* which can be found in this book. In the *Presentation* – along with the other texts of the so-called 'identity philosophy' – Schelling develops a philosophical system that is meant to be fully rational in its exhibition of the essential structures of reality; this is Schelling at his least empiricist. Schelling's *On the History of Modern Philosophy*, a series of lectures delivered in the 1830s, provides further context and detail regarding the turn to experience in the later philosophy.

In-depth discussions of Schelling's understanding of reason and experience can be found in the following secondary literature:

Edward Allen Beach, *The Potencies of God(s): Schelling's Philosophy of Mythology* (SUNY Press, 1994), Part II.
Emil L. Fackenheim, *The God Within: Kant, Schelling, and Historicity*, ed. John Burbidge (University of Toronto Press, 1996), Chapter VII.
Marcela García, 'Schelling's Late Negative Philosophy: Crisis and Critique of Pure Reason.' *Comparative and Continental Philosophy* 3.2 (2011): 141–64.
Christopher Lauer, 'Spinoza's Third Kind of Knowledge as a Resource of Schelling's Empiricism.' *Pli* 18 (2007): 168–81.
Christopher Lauer, *The Suspension of Reason in Hegel and Schelling* (Continuum, 2010).

Marcia Sá Cavalcante Schuback, 'The Work of Experience: Schelling on Thinking beyond Image and Concept.' In Jason M. Wirth (ed.), *Schelling Now: Contemporary Readings* (Indiana University Press, 2005), 66–83.

Tyler Tritten, *Beyond Presence: The Late F.W.J. Schelling's Criticism of Metaphysics* (De Gruyter, 2012).

7

System

Introduction

In 1781, at the end of the *Critique of Pure Reason*, Kant articulated the demand for philosophy to become systematic in a chapter on The Architectonic of Pure Reason:

> In accordance with reason's legislative prescriptions, our diverse modes of knowledge must not be permitted to be a mere rhapsody, but must form a system. Only so can they further the essential ends of reason. By a system I understand the unity of the manifold modes of knowledge under one idea.[1]

Within the German philosophical context, this ideal of a properly unified system stuck, even if Kant's own attempts at determining *the* systematic form of philosophy did not. Any post-Kantian philosopher worthy of the name was invested in such an ideal, but – again – none of them agreed on how this term 'system' should be defined.

Despite not being as prone as the other Idealists to philosophize about philosophy – i.e. to explicitly set out metaphilosophical positions illuminating his own practices – Schelling often made an exception when it came to thinking through the concept of the system. From his very first essay – *On the Possibility of a Form of Philosophy in General* – the question of the proper organization of knowledge is central to his philosophical project, and, despite all the significant differences between the genres in which he chooses to present philosophy, these presentational choices are almost always intended as means for the communication of a system. It is for this reason that 'system' remains such a common reference point in the titles of his publications: *First Outline of a System of the Philosophy of Nature*

(1799), *System of Transcendental Idealism* (1800), *Presentation of My System of Philosophy* (1801), *Further Presentations of the System of Philosophy* (1802), *System of Philosophy in General and the Philosophy of Nature in Particular* (1804), *System of the Ages of the World* (1827–8), *System of Positive Philosophy* (1832–3).

The aim of this chapter is to introduce readers to some of Schelling's more explicit attempts to characterize the philosophical system, both in the context of contemporaneous trends in German Idealism and in the context of the demands of his own intellectual vision and practice. Hence, the following includes:

1 A critique, in Letter Five of the *Philosophical Letters on Dogmatism and Criticism*, of overenthusiastic interpreters of the *Critique of Pure Reason* who understood Kant as providing *the* system of philosophy, as opposed to the groundwork from which *all* systems should be produced, including both realist and idealist systems.

2 One of his most orthodox accounts of systematic philosophy as oriented around a central grounding principle in the *System of Transcendental Idealism*, namely, the coincidence of nature and the self – a view that has significant consequences for how he conceives the relationship between the philosophy of nature and transcendental idealism.

3 His interrogation of the capacity of philosophy to incorporate everything into a system, even the spirit world of supernatural truths, as illustrated in an essay that is sometimes treated as an Introduction to *Clara* but was meant to introduce a treatise entitled the *Presentation of the Transition from a Philosophy of Nature to a Philosophy of the Spirit World*.

4 His most demanding re-figuration of the system as a work of freedom in an extract from his 1820–1 Erlangen Lectures (*Initia Philosophiae Universae*) that has come to be dubbed *On the Nature of Philosophy as Science*.

Note

1   Immanuel Kant, *Critique of Pure Reason*, trans. Norman Kemp Smith (Basingstoke: Palgrave Macmillan, 2007), A832/B860.

Philosophical Letters on Dogmatism and Criticism (1795)*

Nothing, it seems to me, proves more strikingly how little of the *spirit* of the *Critique of Pure Reason* the majority have grasped than the almost universal belief that the *Critique of Pure Reason* belongs to one system alone, since it precisely must be the peculiarity of a critique of reason *that* it can favour *no* system exclusively, but rather must either truly establish, or at least prepare, a canon for *all*. Of course, the universal methodology belongs to a canon for *all* systems as a necessary part, but nothing worse can befall such a work than if one takes the method that it sets up for *all* systems as the system itself.

After such long dispute over the purpose of that great work, it seems presumptuous to offer one's own opinion beyond that. But perhaps that question which so bothers foes and friends of the *Critique* is all the more securely answered the more one reverts from the first impression. It is not such a rare case in human life that one takes the prospect of a future possession for the possession itself!

If without presumption I may impart to you my own conviction, it is that the *Critique of Pure Reason* is not destined to establish any one *system* exclusively – much less to establish that crux between dogmatism and criticism, which I have tried to characterize in my previous letters. Rather, as far as I understand it, it is destined precisely to deduce from the essence of reason the possibility of two directly opposed systems and to establish a system of criticism (conceived in its completion) or, better said, of idealism as well as, directly opposing it, a system of dogmatism or of realism.

When the *Critique of Pure Reason* spoke against dogmatism, it spoke against dogmaticism, i.e. against a system of dogmatism erected blindly and without prior investigation of the faculty of cognition. The *Critique of Pure Reason* taught dogmaticism how it could become dogmatism, i.e. a firmly established system of objective realism. You may be predisposed to judge this statement as entirely contrary to the spirit of the *Critique*, and your judgement would seem all the more natural to most inasmuch

---

*Translated by G. Anthony Bruno from the Fifth Letter in F.W.J. Schelling, *Sämmtliche Werke* (Stuttgart and Augsberg: Cotta, 1856–1861), Division One, Volume One.

as the statement appears at least to be contrary to its letter. Permit me, then, to remind you, *by anticipation*, of a part of the *Critique* that, notwithstanding all the disputes about it, has until now been least elucidated: I mean the part that deals with *things in themselves*. If one believes that the *Critique of Pure Reason* should only establish criticism, it is on this very point, as far as I can see, that it cannot be saved at all from the reproach of inconsistency. Presupposing, however, that the *Critique of Pure Reason* belongs exclusively to no system, one will soon have discovered the reason why it left the two systems of idealism and realism standing side by side. It applies to both, to the system of criticism and to that of dogmatism, but criticism and dogmatism are nothing other than idealism and realism systematically conceived.[1] Anyone who reads attentively what the *Critique* says about practical postulates will certainly admit that it reserves a field in which dogmatism can safely and durably erect its edifice. Many opponents of criticism have asserted this because, like friends of criticism, they stopped short at the exterior of method, asserting that criticism distinguishes itself from dogmatism solely by a differing method. And how have the so-called followers of critical philosophy responded? For the most part, they were modest enough to acknowledge that what distinguishes their criticism consists merely in method, that they merely *believe* what the dogmatist imagined he *knew*, and that the main advantage of the new method (for it is all about no more than such *advantages!*) consists solely in the stronger influence that through it the doctrines of dogmatism gain upon morals.

It may, after all, remain the glory of our age to have excellently applied the new method for the purpose of dogmatism: a future age may have in store the merit of completing the opposite system in its whole purity. After all, we may continue to work at a system of dogmatism; only let no one sell us their dogmatic system for a system of criticism on account of having borrowed its canon from the *Critique of Pure Reason*.

The *Critique*, which furnished the method of practical postulates[2] for two entirely opposed systems, could not possibly go beyond this mere method; since it must be adequate for all systems, it could not possibly determine the *peculiar* spirit in a *particular* system. In order to maintain that method in its universality, it had to retain that method in that indeterminacy which excluded neither of the two systems. Indeed, according to the spirit of the age, the method had to be applied by Kant himself to the *newly* founded system of dogmatism rather than to the system of criticism *first* founded by him.

The *Critique of Pure Reason* (allow me to press on in my conclusions) is therefore the only work of its kind because it applies to all systems – or, since all remaining systems are more or less only faithful replicas of the two main systems, applies to both systems – whereas any attempt beyond mere critique can only belong to one of the two systems.

The *Critique of Pure Reason, as such*, must therefore be incontrovertible and irrefutable, whereas every system, if it deserves this name, must be refutable by a *necessarily* opposing system. The *Critique of Pure Reason*, as long as there is philosophy, will stand alone, while each *system* will tolerate another directly opposed to it. The *Critique of Pure Reason* is incorruptible through individuality, and therefore valid for all systems, whereas every *system* bears the stamp of individuality on its face because none can be completed otherwise than *practically* (i.e. subjectively). The more closely a philosophy approaches a system, the greater share *freedom* and *individuality* have in it and the less claim it has to universal validity.

The *Critique of Pure Reason* alone is or contains the actual doctrine of science because it is valid for all *science*. After all, *science* may rise to an absolute principle and it *must* do so if it is to become a *system*. But the *doctrine of science* cannot possibly establish an absolute principle in order to become a *system* (in the narrower sense of the word) – neither an absolute principle nor a definite and complete system – for it must contain the canon for all principles and systems. But it is time to return from our digression.

If the *Critique of Pure Reason* is the canon of all possible systems, then it had to deduce the necessity of practical postulates from the idea of a system *as such*, not from the idea of a *particular* system. Hence, if there are two wholly opposed systems, the method of practical postulates cannot possibly belong to one of them exclusively; for the *Critique of Pure Reason* has first of all proved from the *idea* of a system as such that no system – whatever its name – is, in its completion, an object of *knowledge*, but only an object of a practically necessary yet *infinite* activity. What the *Critique of Pure Reason* deduces from the essence of reason is what every philosopher who was guided by the regulative idea of a system, perhaps without clearly grasping its ground, had already applied in establishing his system.

Perhaps you remember our question: why did Spinoza present his philosophy in a system *of ethics*? Certainly he did not do so in vain. Of him, one can really say: 'he lived in his system'. But surely he also thought of it as more than a theoretical castle in the sky, in which a spirit like his could hardly have found the calm and the '*heaven in understanding*' in which he so visibly lived and moved.

A *system* of knowledge is either a stunt or intellectual game (as you know that nothing could be more repugnant to the serious spirit of Spinoza) – or it must *obtain* reality, not by a theoretical, but by a practical faculty; not by a cognitive, but by a *productive, realizing* faculty; not by *knowledge*, but by *action*.

One will say: 'But that is the distinguishing character of dogmatism, that it is occupied with mere intellectual games.' I know well that such is the common language of those who have so far continued to dogmatize on Kant's behalf. But a mere intellectual game never amounts to a system. – 'We meant precisely that there *shall* be no system of dogmatism: the only possible system is that of criticism.' As for myself, I believe that there is a system of dogmatism as well as a system of criticism. I even believe that, in criticism itself, I have found the solution of the riddle as to why these two systems must necessarily exist side by side, why, as long as finite beings still exist, there must also be two directly opposing systems, and why, finally, no human can convince himself of any system at all except *practically*, i.e. by realizing one of the two *in himself*.

Consequently, I believe that I can also explain why, for a spirit who has made itself free and who owes *its* philosophy only to itself, nothing must be more unbearable than the despotism of narrow minds who cannot tolerate another system beside their own. Nothing more disgusts the philosophical mind than when it hears that henceforth all philosophy shall lie captive in the fetters of a single system. Such a mind has never felt itself to be greater than when it beheld an infinity of knowledge. The whole dignity of his science has consisted in just this, that it would never be complete. The moment he believed he had completed his system, he would become unbearable to himself. He would in that moment cease to be *creator* and be degraded to an instrument of his system.[3] – How much more unbearable would he find the thought if another wanted to impose such a thing on him?

The highest dignity of philosophy is precisely that it expects everything of human *freedom*. Hence, nothing can be more pernicious to philosophy than the attempt to confine it within the limits of a system universally valid in theory. Whoever undertakes such a thing may have a sagacious mind, but the *true* critical spirit is not upon him. For this spirit means to quell the vain passion of demonstrations in order to save the *freedom* of science.

How much more merit for true philosophy, then, lies in the sceptic who declares war on every universally valid system in advance. How much more than in the dogmaticist, who henceforth lets all spirits swear to the symbol of a *theoretical* science. As long as the sceptic stays in his boundaries, i.e. as long as he does not dare to encroach on the field of human freedom, so long as he believes in infinite truth yet also in *infinite enjoyment*, in progressive, self-acquired truth, who would not revere in him the true *philosopher*?[4]

Notes

1   By the way, I believe that these names should soon be abandoned and replaced by more definite terms. Why should we not denote both systems by their names – dogmatism as the *system of objective realism* (or of subjective idealism), criticism as the *system of subjective realism* (or of objective idealism)? (Evidently, the *Critique of Pure Reason* allows objective and subjective realism to exist in speaking of appearances grounded by things in themselves.) – It seems to be a very small merit to improve the terminology notwithstanding that for many, or even most, more depends on words than on concepts. If, after the appearance of the *Critique*, circulation had not been obtained for the terms 'critical philosophy' and 'criticism', one likely would sooner have abandoned the opinion that the *Critique of Pure Reason* establishes only one system (that of the so-called criticism).

2   *Editors' Note.* Kant's postulates of practical reason – especially those of God and immortality – were one of the most fiercely contested areas in the early reception of the critical philosophy. During the mid-1790s, Schelling was particularly horrified at the use made of them by some of his teachers at Tübingen to justify old orthodoxies through the Kantian apparatus.

3   As long as we are engaged in the realization of our system, there can be only *practical* certainty of it. Our pursuit to complete it realizes our knowledge of it. If we had solved our entire task at any single moment of time, the system would become an object of *knowledge* and would thereby cease to be an object of *freedom*.

4   *Philosophy*, an admirable word! If this author has a vote, he casts it for the retention of this old word. For, as far as he sees, our whole knowledge will always remain *philosophy*, i.e. always merely progressing knowledge, whose higher or lower degrees we owe only to our *love* for wisdom, i.e. to our freedom. – Least of all would he wish to displace this word through a philosophy that has for the first time undertaken to save the freedom in philosophizing from the presumptions of dogmaticism, through a philosophy that presupposes the self-achieved freedom of the spirit and that therefore will be eternally incomprehensible for every slave of system.

System of Transcendental Idealism (1800)*

§ 1. Concept of Transcendental Philosophy

1. All knowledge is founded upon the coincidence of an objective with a subjective. – For we *know* only what is true; but truth is generally taken to consist in the coincidence of presentations with their objects.

2. The intrinsic notion of everything merely objective in our knowledge, we may speak of as nature. The notion of everything subjective is called, on the contrary, the self, or the intelligence. The two concepts are mutually opposed. The intelligence is initially conceived of as the purely presentative, nature purely as what can be presented; the one as the conscious, the other as the non-conscious. But now in every *knowing* a reciprocal concurrence of the two (the conscious and the intrinsically non-conscious) is necessary; the problem is to explain this concurrence.

3. In knowing as such – *in the fact of* my knowing – objective and subjective are so united that one cannot say which of the two has priority. Here there is no first and second; both are simultaneous and one. – Insofar as I *wish to explain* this identity, I must already have *done away with* it. To explain it, inasmuch as nothing else is given me (as explanatory principle) beyond these two factors of knowledge, I must necessarily *give priority* to one over the other, *set out* from the one, in order thence to arrive at the other; from *which* of the two I start, the problem does not specify.

4. Hence there are only two possibilities.

A. *Either the objective is made primary, and the question is: how a subjective is annexed thereto, which coincides with it?*

The concept of the subjective is not contained in that of the objective; on the contrary, they exclude one another. The subjective must therefore be *annexed* to the objective. – The concept of *nature* does not entail that there should also be an intelligence that is aware of it. Nature, it seems, would exist, even if there were nothing that was aware of it. Hence the problem can also be formulated *thus*: how does intelligence come to be added to nature, or how does nature come to be presented?

---

*Translated by Peter Heath from F.W.J. Schelling, *System des transzendentalen Idealismus*, ed. Ruth-Eva Schulz (Hamburg: Felix Meiner, 1957).

The problem assumes nature or the *objective* to be *primary*. Hence the problem is undoubtedly that of *natural science*, which does just this. That natural science in fact – and without knowing it – at least *comes close* to the solution of this problem can be shown briefly here.

If all *knowing* has, as it were, two poles, which mutually presuppose and demand one another, they must seek each other in all the sciences; hence there must necessarily be *two* basic sciences, and it must be impossible to set out from the one pole without being driven toward the other. The necessary tendency of all *natural science* is thus to move from nature to intelligence. This and nothing else is at the bottom of the urge to bring *theory* into the phenomena of nature. – The highest consummation of natural science would be the complete spiritualizing of all natural laws into laws of intuition and thought. The phenomena (the matter) must wholly disappear, and only the laws (the form) remain. Hence it is, that the more lawfulness emerges in nature itself, the more the husk disappears, the phenomena themselves become more mental, and at length vanish entirely. The phenomena of optics are nothing but a geometry whose lines are drawn by light, and this light itself is already of doubtful materiality. In the phenomena of magnetism all material traces are already disappearing, and in those of gravitation, which even scientists have thought it possible to conceive of merely as an immediate spiritual influence, nothing remains but its law, whose largescale execution is the mechanism of the heavenly motions. – The completed theory of nature would be that whereby the whole of nature was resolved into an intelligence. – The dead and unconscious products of nature are merely abortive attempts that she makes to reflect herself; inanimate nature so-called is actually as such an immature intelligence, so that in her phenomena the still unwitting character of intelligence is already peeping through. – Nature's highest goal, to become wholly an object to herself, is achieved only through the last and highest order of reflection, which is none other than man; or, more generally, it is what we call reason, whereby nature first completely returns into herself, and by which it becomes apparent that nature is identical from the first with what we recognize in ourselves as the intelligent and the conscious.

This may be sufficient to show that natural science has a necessary tendency to render nature intelligent; through this very tendency it becomes *nature-philosophy*, which is one of the necessary basic sciences of philosophy.

B. *Alternatively, the subjective is made primary, and the problem is: how an objective supervenes, which coincides with it?*

If all knowledge rests upon the coincidence of these is undoubtedly the supreme problem for all knowledge; and if, as is generally admitted, philosophy is the highest and foremost of all sciences, we have here undoubtedly the main problem of philosophy.

However, the problem only requires an explanation of the concurrence as such, and leaves it completely open as to where explanation starts from, as to which it should make primary and which secondary. – Yet since the two opposites are mutually necessary to each other, the result of the operation is bound to be the same, whichever point we set out from.

To make the *objective* primary, and to derive the subjective from that, is, as has just been shown, the problem of *philosophy of nature*.

If, then, there is a *transcendental philosophy*, there remains to it only the opposite direction, that of *proceeding from the subjective, as primary and absolute, and having the objective arise from this*. Thus nature-philosophy and transcendental philosophy have divided into the two directions possible to philosophy, and if all philosophy must go about *either* to make an intelligence out of nature, *or* a nature out of intelligence, then transcendental philosophy, which has the latter task, is thus *the other necessary basic science of philosophy*.

§ 2. Corollaries

In the course of the foregoing, we have not only deduced the concept of transcendental philosophy, but have also furnished the reader with a glimpse into the entire system of philosophy; this, as we see, is constituted of two basic sciences which, though opposed to each other in principle and direction, mutually seek and supplement one another. Here we shall not set forth the entire system of philosophy, but only one of the basic sciences, and the derived concept thereof will thus first receive a more exact characterization.[1]

1. If the *subjective* – the *first* and only ground of all reality – is for transcendental philosophy the sole principle of explanation for everything else (§ 1), then it necessarily begins with a general doubt as to the reality of the objective.

Just as the nature-philosopher, directed solely upon the objective, has nothing he more dearly wishes to prevent than an admixture of the subjective into knowledge, so the transcendental philosopher, by contrast, wishes nothing more dearly than to avoid an admixture of the objective into the purely subjective principle of knowledge. The means of separation lie in absolute scepticism – not the half-scepticism which merely contends against the common prejudices of mankind, while never looking to fundamentals, but rather that thoroughgoing scepticism which is directed, not against individual prejudices, but against the basic preconception, whose rejection leads automatically to the collapse of everything else. For in addition to the artificial prejudices implanted in mankind, there are others far more fundamental, laid down in us not by art or education, but by nature herself; prejudices which, for everyone but philosophers, serve as the principles of all knowledge, and for the merely self-made thinker rank even as the touchstone of all truth.

The one basic prejudice, to which all others reduce, is no other than this: *that there are things outside us.* This is a conviction that rests neither on grounds nor on inferences (since there is not a single reputable proof of it) and yet cannot be extirpated by any argument to the contrary (*naturam furca expellas, tamen usque redibit*[2]); it makes claim to *immediate* certainty, since it assuredly relates to something entirely different from us, and even opposed to us, of which we understand not at all how it enters into immediate consciousness; and hence it can be regarded as nothing more than a prejudice – innate and primary, to be sure – but no less a prejudice on that account.

The contradiction, that a principle which by nature cannot be immediately certain is yet accepted as blindly and groundlessly as one that is so, is incapable of resolution by the transcendental philosopher, save on the presupposition that this principle is not just covertly and as yet uncomprehendingly connected with, but is identical with, one and the same with, an immediate certainty, and to demonstrate this identity will in fact be the concern of transcendental philosophy.

2. But now even for the common use of reason, nothing is immediately certain save the proposition *I exist*; which, since it actually loses its meaning *outside* immediate consciousness, is the most individual of all truths, and the *absolute preconception*, which must *first* be accepted, if anything else is to be certain. – The proposition *There are things outside us* will therefore only be certain for the transcendental philosopher in virtue of its identity with the proposition I exist, and its certainty will likewise only be *equal* to the certainty of the proposition from which it borrows its own.

Transcendental cognition would thus differ from ordinary cognition on two counts.

First, that the certainty that external things exist is for it a mere prejudice, which it goes beyond, in order to discover the grounds thereof. (It can never be the transcendental philosopher's business to demonstrate the existence of things-in-themselves, but merely that it is a natural and necessary prejudice to assume that external objects are real.)

Second, that it separates the two propositions, *I exist*, and *There are things outside me*, which in ordinary consciousness are fused together; setting the one before the other, precisely in order to prove their identity, and so that it can really exhibit the immediate connection which is otherwise merely felt. By this very act of separation, if complete, it shifts into the transcendental mode of apprehension, which is in no way natural, but artificial.

3. If only the subjective has initial reality for the transcendental philosopher, he will also make only the subjective the immediate object of his cognition: the objective will become an object for him indirectly only, and whereas in ordinary cognition *the knowing itself* (the act of knowing) vanishes into the object, in transcendental cognition, on the contrary, the object *as* such vanishes into the act of knowing. Transcendental cognition is thus a knowing of knowing, insofar as it is purely subjective.

Thus in intuition, for example, only the objective element attains to ordinary consciousness, the intuiting itself being lost in the object; whereas the transcendental mode of apprehension merely glimpses the intuited through the act of intuiting. – Again, ordinary thinking is a mechanism governed by concepts, though they are not distinguished *as* concepts; whereas transcendental thinking suspends this mechanism, and in becoming aware of the concept as an act, attains to the *concept of a concept*. – In ordinary action, the *acting itself* is lost sight of in the object of action; philosophizing is likewise an *action*, yet not only an action but also at the same time a continuous *scrutiny of the self* so engaged.

The nature of the transcendental mode of apprehension must therefore consist essentially in this, *that even that which in all other thinking, knowing, or acting escapes consciousness and is absolutely non-objective, is therein brought to consciousness and becomes objective – it consists, in short, of a constant objectifying-to-itself of the subjective.*

The transcendental artifice will thus consist in the ability to maintain oneself constantly in this duality of acting and thinking.

§ 3. Preliminary Division of Transcendental Philosophy

This division is *preliminary*, because the principles of division can only be first derived in the science itself.

We revert to the concept of the science.

Transcendental philosophy has to explain how knowledge as such is possible, it being presupposed that the subjective element therein is to be taken as dominant or primary.

It therefore takes as its object, not an individual portion, nor a special object of knowledge, but *knowledge itself* and *knowledge as such*.

But now all knowledge reduces to certain primordial convictions or primordial prejudices; transcendental philosophy must trace these individual convictions back to one fundamental conviction; this one, from which all others are derived, is formulated in the *first principle of this philosophy*, and the task of finding such a principle is nothing other than that of finding the absolute certainty whereby all other certainty is mediated.

The division of transcendental philosophy itself is determined by those original convictions whose validity it vindicates. These convictions must first be sought in the common understanding. – And if we thus transport ourselves back to the standpoint of the common outlook, we find the following convictions deeply rooted in the human understanding.

A. That there not only exists a world of things outside and independent of us, but also that our presentations are so far coincident with it that there is *nothing else* in things save what we attribute to them. This explains the constraint in our objective presentations, that things should be unalterably determined, and that our own presentations should also be mediately determined by this determinacy of things. This first and most fundamental conviction suffices to determine the first task of philosophy: to explain how our presentations can absolutely coincide with objects existing wholly independent of them. – The assumption that things are just what we take them to be, so that we are acquainted with them as they are *in themselves*, underlies the possibility of all experience (for what would experience be, and to what aberrations would physics, for example, be subject, without this presupposition of absolute identity between appearance and reality?) Hence, the solution of this problem is identical with *theoretical* philosophy, whose task is to investigate the possibility of experience.

B. The second and no less basic conviction is this, that presentations, arising *freely and without necessity* in us, pass over from the world of thought into the real world, and can attain objective reality.

This conviction is in opposition to the first. The first assumes that objects are *unalterably determined*, and thereby also our own presentations; the second assumes that objects are *alterable*, and are so, in fact, through the causality of presentations in us. On the first view there is a passage from the real world into the world of presentation, or a determining of presentation by an objective; on the second, there is a passage from the world of presentation into the real world, or a determining of the objective by a presentation (freely generated) in ourselves.

This second conviction serves to determine a second problem, namely how an objective can be altered by a mere thought, so that it perfectly coincides therewith.

Upon this conviction the possibility of all free action depends, so that the solution of this problem is identical with *practical philosophy*.

C. But with these two problems we find ourselves involved in a contradiction. – *B* calls for a dominance of thought (the ideal) over the world of sense; but how is this conceivable if (by *A*) the presentation is in origin already the mere slave of the objective? – Conversely, if the real world is a thing wholly independent of us, to which (as *A* tells us) our presentation must conform (as to its archetype), it is inconceivable how the real world, on the contrary, could (as *B* says) conform itself to presentations in us. – In a word, for certainty in theory we lose it in practice, and for certainty in practice we lose it in theory; it is impossible both that our knowledge should contain truth and our volition reality.

If there is to be any philosophy at all, this contradiction must be resolved – and the solution of this problem, or answer to the question: *how can we think both of presentations as conforming to objects, and objects as conforming to presentations?* is, not the first, but the highest task of transcendental philosophy.

[...]

§ 4. The Organ of Transcendental Philosophy

1. The sole immediate object of transcendental concern is the subjective (§ 2); the sole organ of this mode of philosophizing is therefore *inner sense*, and its object is such that it cannot even become, as can that of mathematics, an object of outer intuition. – The mathematical object is admittedly no more located *outside* the knowing-process than that of philosophy. The whole existence of mathematics depends upon intuition, and so it also exists only in intuition, but this intuition itself is an external one. The

mathematician, furthermore, is never concerned directly with intuition (the act of construction) itself, but only with the construct, which can certainly be presented externally, whereas the philosopher looks solely to the *act of construction itself*, which is an absolutely internal thing.

2. Moreover, the objects of the transcendental philosopher exist not at all, save insofar as they are freely produced. – One cannot be compelled to such production, as one can, say, by the external depiction of a mathematical figure, be compelled to intuit this internally. Hence, just as the existence of a mathematical figure depends on outer sense, so the entire reality of a philosophical concept depends solely on *inner sense*. The whole object of this philosophy is nothing else but the action of the intellect according to determinate laws. This action can be grasped only through immediate inner intuition on one's own part, and this too is possible only through production. But that is not all. In philosophizing, one is not simply the object of contemplation, but always at the same time the subject. Two conditions are therefore required for the understanding of philosophy, *first* that one be engaged in a constant inner activity, a constant producing of these original acts of the intellect; and *second*, that one be constantly reflecting upon this production; in a word, that one always remain at the same time both the intuited (the producer) and the intuitant.

3. Through this constant double activity of producing and intuiting, something is to become an object, *which is not otherwise reflected by anything*. – We cannot here demonstrate, though we shall in the sequel, that this coming-to-be-reflected of the absolutely non-conscious and non-objective is possible only through an *aesthetic act* of the imagination. This much, however, is apparent from what we have already shown, namely that all philosophy is *productive*. Thus philosophy depends as much as art does on the productive capacity, and the difference between them rests merely on the different direction taken by the productive force. For whereas in art the production is directed outwards, so as to reflect the unknown by means of products, philosophical production is directed immediately inwards, so as to reflect it in intellectual intuition. The proper sense by which this type of philosophy must be apprehended is thus the *aesthetic* sense, and that is why the philosophy of art is the true organon of philosophy (§ 3).

From ordinary reality there are only two ways out – poetry, which transports us into an ideal world, and philosophy, which makes the real world vanish before our eyes. – It is not apparent why the gift for philosophy should be any more widely spread than that for poetry, especially among that class of persons in whom, either through memory-work (than which nothing is more immediately fatal to productivity), or through dead speculation, destructive of all imagination, the aesthetic organ has been totally lost.

4. It is needless to linger over the commonplaces about a native sense of truth, since we are wholly indifferent to its conclusions, though one might ask what other conviction could still be sacred to one who takes for granted the most certain of all (that there are things outside us). – Let us rather take one more look at the so-called claims of the common understanding.

In matters of philosophy the common understanding has no claims whatever, save that to which every object of enquiry is entitled, namely to be *completely accounted for*.

Thus it is no concern of ours to prove the truth of what it takes to be true; we merely have to lay bare the inevitability of its delusions – It is agreed that the objective world belongs only to the necessary limitations which make self-consciousness (the I am) possible – for the common understanding, it is sufficient if, from this opinion itself, the necessity of its own view is again derived.

For this purpose it is necessary, not only that the inner workings of our mental activity be thrown open, the mechanism of necessary presentation unveiled, but also that it be shown by what peculiarity of our nature it is ordained, that what has reality merely in our intuition is reflected to us as something present outside us.

Just as natural science brings forth idealism out of realism, in that it spiritualizes natural laws into laws of mind, or appends the formal to the material (§ 1), so transcendental philosophy brings forth realism out of idealism, i*n that it materializes the laws of mind into laws of nature,* or annexes the material to the formal.

On the Necessity and Character of a Supreme Principle of Knowledge

1. It will be assumed meantime as a hypothesis, that there is indeed reality in our knowledge, and we shall ask what the conditions of this reality may be. – Whether there is *actually* reality in our knowledge will depend on whether these initially inferred conditions can be actually exhibited later on.

If all knowledge rests upon the coincidence of an objective and a subjective (§ 1), the whole of our knowledge consists of propositions which are not *immediately* true, which derive their reality from something else.

The mere putting-together of a subjective with a subjective gives no basis for knowledge proper. And conversely, knowledge proper presupposes a concurrence of opposites, whose concurrence can only be a *mediated* one.

Hence there must be some universally mediating factor in our knowledge, which is the sole ground thereof.

2. It will be assumed as a hypothesis, that there is a system in our knowledge, that is, that it is a whole which is self-supporting and internally consistent with itself. – The sceptic denies this presupposition, like the first, and like the first it can be demonstrated only through the fact itself. – For what would it be like, if even our knowledge, and indeed the whole of nature (for us) were internally self-contradictory? – Let us then *assume* merely, that our knowledge is a primordial whole, of which the system of philosophy is to be the outline, and renew our preliminary enquiry as to the conditions of such a whole.

Now every true system (such as that of the cosmos, for example) must contain the ground of its subsistence within *itself*; and hence, if there be a system of knowledge, its principle must *lie within knowledge itself*.

3. *There can only be one such principle.* For all truth is absolutely *on a par*. There may certainly be degrees of probability, but there are no degrees of truth; one truth is as true as another. But that the truth of all propositions of knowledge is absolutely equal is impossible, if they derive their truth from different principles (or mediating factors); so there can only be one (mediating) principle in all knowledge.

4. This principle is the mediating or indirect principle in every science, but the immediate and direct principle only of *the science of all knowledge*, or transcendental philosophy.

Notes

1   Only on completion of the system of transcendental philosophy will one come to recognize the necessity of a nature-philosophy, as a complementary science, and thereupon desist from making demands upon the former, which only a nature-philosophy can satisfy.

2   *Editors' Note.* A slight misquotation from Horace, *Epistles*, Book I: 10: 'Drive nature out with a pitchfork, it'll come right back.'

Presentation of the Transition from a Philosophy of Nature to a Philosophy of the Spirit World (1810?)*

Ever since the peaceful harmony broke up in which the sciences lived not so long ago, philosophy can be characterized as an intense striving toward the spiritual that decidedly lacks a corresponding capacity to rise to it.

Through its name the old metaphysics declared itself to be a science that followed in accordance with, and that to some extent also followed from, our knowledge of nature and improved and progressed from that; thus in a certain competent and sound way that is of service only to those who have a desire for knowledge, metaphysics took the knowledge that it boasted in addition to physics. Modern philosophy did away with its immediate reference to nature, or didn't think to keep it, and proudly scorned any connection to physics. Continuing with its claims to a higher world, it was no longer metaphysics but hyperphysics. Only now did its complete incapacity for its proposed aim emerge. Because it wanted to spiritualize itself completely, it first of all threw away the material that was absolutely necessary to the process and right from the very beginning it kept only what was spiritual. But what is to become of the spiritual if it is spiritualized again? Or if we want everything spiritual to be within nature already, what do we have left for the spirit world?

These remarks will serve to make comprehensible the strange phenomenon that just when philosophy wanted to take its highest approach to the spiritual, it sank to the very bottom and became more and more inadequate and incapable in relation to all higher objects. After a period of seeing this happen, it finally came to be felt intensely that there was nothing else left for philosophy to do than to testify against itself – not only to recognize its spiritual impotency, but also to demonstrate the obviousness of such. Meanwhile, this conclusion was also used to drive the spiritualization yet another degree further away. It was not enough, one said, to have given up the connection to what is objective or to insensible nature, if so coarse a concept

---

*Translated by Fiona Steinkamp from F.W.J. Schelling, *Sämmtliche Werke* (Stuttgart and Augsberg: Cotta, 1856–1861), Division One, Volume Nine.

as that of knowledge were still tolerated within the subjective. Knowledge itself was still too solid; spiritualization would be perfect only when, instead, a tender, fleeting spoor of a feeling or hunch alone remains; that is, when the subjective is subjectified again. Since then one party occupied itself with offering a surrogate of the spirit (of knowledge) rather than the true spirit; the surrogate supposedly being somehow more spiritual than the spirit itself. And so, whereas previously a virtue was made of necessity, a virtue was now made of ignorance.

In this state of affairs there was indeed no other means of restoring philosophy than by calling it back to earth – albeit not from heaven, which it had renounced, but from that empty space in which it was suspended between heaven and earth. This happened through the philosophy of nature. Nevertheless, it was only to be expected from the general order and run of things that the spiritualizers of this time would clamour that this beginning was bringing philosophy down, denying everything spiritual, even denying what was holy and divine.

Yet right from the start nature was explained only as one side of the universe, with the spirit world opposed to it. Thus, even the philosophy of nature was given always as only one side of the larger picture, and the central role of philosophical science resided in scientifically explaining the contradictions and connections between nature and the spirit world. Now that we have satisfactorily undertaken this exercise in our first steps in philosophy, it can be predicted that to those philosophers this beginning appears to be one that is superficial, fanciful even, and in any case unnatural. For doesn't it so happen that as soon as their own concepts and theories go beyond nature, these too take on a truly unnatural character and thereby prove themselves ineffectual for daily life? Yes, here those philosophers will become friends with those with whom they previously professed to be in conflict but with whom they are really more united than they themselves believe; I mean those who can't hear the words 'spirit world' without getting caught up in their own particular fear of 'spirit.' This sickness in its strongest form may rise to fear and to granting only that man's own innermost being is spirit, but in its weakest form limits itself to a concern with cutting oneself off from the spirit world completely and ensuring there is no belief in any spirit other than one's own and those of one's contemporaries.

Now the adherents of both philosophies would have the completely wrong idea of our undertaking if they thought that here the spirit world is to be brought immediately to light in some way or even brought only to articulation, for our express intention is only scientifically to show the natural field's transition to the field of the spiritual world. Thus, insofar as nature is our starting point, it would be best for them to see this treatise as a purely physicalistic one and to grasp the idea that just as in the physical [world] it has been possible to bind earth to heaven through the law of gravity, and just as we may flatter ourselves for having placed the golden chain of universally-extending light in friendly concourse with the distant stars that barely come to view even when we equip our eyes with the strongest means, so too within the spiritual [world] a tie may be found going out from nature through which our as yet merely earthly sciences could continually rise up toward heaven, for heaven does indeed appear to be their true fatherland.

For now it is up to them to deny such an upward growth of nature into the spiritual world, and they will deny it. However, unless they deny the existence of a spirit world altogether – a debate which is not our concern here – they admit that nature is subordinate to the spirit world. Thus, in relation to the higher the subordinate has at some point its limit; somewhere it has a definite end. Now, how can they believe that the subordinate can find its goal and be closed, unless the last thing that it brings forth from itself is already something that goes beyond it and that belongs to it only with the subordinate part of its essence, just as man is in relation to the earth? And in being the rung to it, mustn't the lower thereby be in a natural relation to the higher?

Thus, before they can raise their usual complaints against this undertaking, they will first have to prove that there is such a chasm between nature and the purely spiritual world as they assume, or at least they will have to knock down our proofs that there is a natural connection between them. Only with this qualification do we consider it possible to do justice to the proposed exercise. We ourselves recognize that any knowledge that doesn't develop purely from what is present and real is one that is superficial and that has to lead to fanciful imagination and error. Just because of that we declare that however far we may care to drive the edifice of our thoughts in what follows, we will still only have achieved something if the temple whose last spire disappears into an inaccessible light is, at its very deepest foundation, wholly supported by nature.

On the other hand, we will thus certainly dare to take on whatever he who knows of a sound basis permits us to do, and we will be able to explain higher things with more certainty than has been possible until now. A person earns, so to speak, the right to the most spiritual objects only when he has already taken care to understand their opposite. In his undertakings, even scientific ones, man errs not through what he undertakes to do, but in the way he does it; namely by not taking his knowledge step by step; meanwhile nothing is in fact denied, not even within science, to him who meets that condition. A tree that draws strength, life and substance into itself from the earth may hope to drive its topmost branches hanging with blossom right up to heaven. However, the thoughts of those who think from the beginning that they can separate themselves from nature, even when they are truly spiritually and mentally gifted, are only like those delicate threads that float in the air in late summer and that are as incapable of touching heaven as they are of being pulled to the ground by their own weight.

Fully conscious of the scientific means required by the nature of our procedure, we won't bring anything into play that isn't essential or that could otherwise lead us astray.

In this discourse one will rarely find flights of imagination, particularly ones sought within the external, or find those certain lighthearted talks about the immortality of the soul that both writers and public alike seem so very much to enjoy. We don't want to excite people's opinions or foster a fanciful imagination, for these always arise mainly out of the shortcomings or inadequacies of science. If science remains silent about the things man finds to be the most essential of all, then people must indeed come to their own aid. How far ahead they are of the educated in their certitude of thought! Our moralistic and other proofs for the immortality of the soul would not suffice for the people. Common sense comprehends that the true basis that persuades it [that sense] of some kind of existence must at the same time necessarily give us knowledge of how that existence is constituted, and common sense will consider any basis for which this is not the case to be invented and artificial rather than one that is true and natural. But even now it still holds, as it has for ages, that the scholars have thrown away the keys to knowledge and although they themselves don't go therein, they refuse to let in those who wish to enter. Even the refuge in the truths of revelation – which was the last refuge that remained to the people – is taken from them, with the teachers of these truths interpreting them either literally or only in a general, moralistic sense. The learned know in what kind of light they appear when a real sense is attached to these truths and the physical relationship is given. The chasm between revelation and science comes about just because the former contains all truths within it, truths pursued from the very beginning and to a degree of individual certainty that our philosophy, forever drifting about in generalities, could not yet achieve.

Thus, one shouldn't suspect those seeking certainty of knowledge, even in the most spiritual objects, of fanciful imagination or of trying to lead people to so imagine; rather, one should suspect those who work against that certainty, even if they should do so with the pretext of having a sense that supersedes science itself. When superstition completely overlooks the natural connection of things, nonbelief results; and it results from the suffocation of the divine stirring in its innermost being, the suffocation itself resulting from nonbelief's not being able to set natural mass into motion, from its being unable to transform that mass into a living, progressive surge up to the spiritual. Belief, which acts as the opposite of science, is in exactly the same situation. But it is impossible for a belief that follows from an initial nonbelief and that shares the same starting point as nonbelief to be a true one.

But, even looking at it purely from a formal standpoint, the real dreamers are without doubt those who regard the world of science as a great empty space wherein each person in his own peculiar way can record whatever takes his fancy. They are those who have no idea of how to go back to the basics and construct anything systematically. They are those who, when they ask themselves what they know with certainty from their philosophical endeavours, have to admit, if they are at all honest with themselves, that they do not even know so much as is required, for example, for taking notes from a book in some language or other, whereby one must know whether one should read from left to right or, as in Hebrew, from right to left.

Insofar as his concern is purely to achieve an effect, an author can hardly fail to achieve his aim with a subject that bears a manifold and intimate relationship to the deepest feelings of human kind, if he knows how to introduce these feelings in an unobtrusive and pleasant way. However, he who tries to produce these feelings by using precise-scientific insight must wish to silence them from the beginning. The inclination will become naught, even if a justifiable longing is accorded to it; with his scientific earnestness increasing with the magnitude of the subject, he will ask only about whatever can be ascertained scientifically and will deny himself for the sake of the invaluable gain of an everlasting truth. The deepest feeling is fully confirmed only within a science that does not combine with that feeling; a combination of the two is scorned by both. He only hopes that he will never find himself in contradiction with faith, hope and love; and he never will have a low opinion of anything that is inspired by them just because he can't scientifically justify it, if, like the poet, we may suppose that in those bright realms there is a word for every beautiful and pleasant feeling. But, although faith, hope and love are that innermost, sacred essence that gives all works of science and art their last transfiguration, in their more intimate nature they have to appear as one or the other to be a visible principle.

In taking responsibility for conveying our thoughts in a more accessible form, too, we will favour the stricter form and we will, where possible, give an example in this treatise of a method that differs from those heretofore in so far as it is quite inseparable from its content, with the method being given through the content, as the content is through the method. Unavoidably, more than a few of its formulae have been most shamefully misused (whose innermost being no one has yet completely penetrated), by treating what is most living mainly with reason. On the other hand, we have noticed that in cases of real investigation where, perhaps without knowing it, the formulae have been conceded to have a certain influence, the method proves itself to be more beneficial than the usual one; proving that in various areas the current standing of science is beginning to call for this method. Whoever wants to change this method mustn't attack the spiritless use of it, nor in any way the method itself; he must attack the substance.

On the Nature of Philosophy as Science (1821)*

The idea or the endeavour of finding a system of human knowledge, or, put differently and more appropriately, of contemplating human knowledge within a system, within a form of coexistence, presupposes, of course, that originally and of itself it does not exist in a system, hence that it is an *asystaton* [something that is non-systematic] – something whose elements do not coexist, but rather something that is in inner conflict. In order to recognize this *asystasy*, this non-existence, this disunity, this *bellum intestinum* [civil war], so to speak, in human knowledge (for this inner conflict must become apparent), the human spirit must already have searched in every possible direction. Hence in Greece, for example, the idea of the system had to be preceded by a) the simple physicists, who believed that everything can be explained in terms of natural causes, b) Anaxagoras' dualism, and c) the Eleatics' doctrine which, in order to resolve all existing conflicts, posited mere *unity*, while it would be equally legitimate to posit opposition or disunity, and while the true system can only be the one that establishes the

---

*Translated by Marcus Weigelt from F.W.J. Schelling, *Sämmtliche Werke* (Stuttgart and Augsberg: Cotta, 1856–1861), Division One, Volume Nine.

unity of unity and opposition, i.e. the one that shows how unity can coexist with opposition and opposition with unity, and how the one is indeed necessary for the benefit of the other. All this had to take place before even the true *idea* of a system could appear in Plato. In terms of time, then, the systems are prior to the system. The need for harmony arises first of all in disharmony.

Finally, for there really to be an endeavour to find a system, one must have come to see that this conflict between opinions is not something incidental, grounded in subjective imperfections such as superficial or erroneous thinking by individuals, or, as some shallow minds would have it, in mere logical fabrications. One must have understood that this conflict has an objective basis, that it is grounded in the nature of the matter itself, namely in the primary roots of all existence. One must have given up all hopes that this conflict, this *bellum omnium contra omnes* [war of all against all], might come to an end, that one individual view could become absolute master over the others, that one system could subjugate the others. This can, of course, often seem to be the case. For although all exclusive systems have in common that they are not the system and that they are therefore something partial or subordinate, one of them can still be on a higher level than another. Or actually – for this deserves to be explained more precisely – the problem has to be understood in the following way. Within all contradictions between the systems, there is ultimately only one great contradiction, one original discord. This can be expressed by saying that according to one assertion A equals B, and according to the other it equals C. Now it can happen that both systems, the one positing A = B and the one positing A = C, have to be comprehended as competing on a very subordinate level. In the meantime, someone appears who goes beyond this subordinate standpoint, and who, rather than putting forth something that could unify A = B with A = C on a higher level, only repeats A = B, but on a higher level, raising it to a higher power. Frequently, however, this onesidedness becomes even more accentuated, for once the analysis begins, it naturally follows its course and finally reaches the point where it is a matter of individual choice. Thereby, however, we only admit that neither is the absolute master of the other. If, however, A = B has really advanced (without being otherwise essentially altered), while A = C has not advanced, then A = B openly becomes the master of A = C. This does not last very long, though, as A = C will become aware of its disadvantage and will also advance, such that, again, but only at the higher standpoint, the two confront each other in just the same way as on the lower.

Another, even more incidental possibility is the following: if A = B and
A = C perfectly balance each other, the outcome will depend on which of
the two is the better combatant. Alas, this is the kind of victory that does not
decide anything.

Hence, one system can become the other's master only in appearance
and for a short time, while in reality or in the long run it is impossible.
Each system actually has the same authority, the same claim to validity, and
this insight has to precede the system in the wider sense – the system *par
excellence*. So long as the materialist does not acknowledge the legitimacy of
the intellectualist, or the idealist the legitimacy of the realist, the system *kat'
exochen* [*par excellence*] is inconceivable. I wish to point out, by the way, that
only those systems which constitute genuine elements of our intellectual
development are mentioned here, as opposed to those which are only so
called by their authors; even to consider such people capable of an *error*
would be to give them too much credit. Those who can *err must* at least
be on some track. But those who never even set out and just stay sitting at
home, cannot err. Those who dare set out to sea can certainly, due to storms
or by their lack of skill, lose their way and be led astray, but those who
never even leave port and whose entire endeavour, rather, consists in not
leaving port and in preventing philosophy from ever beginning, by endless
philosophizing about philosophy, those, of course, have no dangers to fear.

Hence the idea of the system as such presupposes the necessary and
irresolvable conflict of the systems: without the latter the former would not
arise.

Philosophy has often been reproached for this asystasy, this inner conflict.
Kant, in various parts of his writings, as well as others later, for the purposes
of instruction and improvement, compared metaphysics unfavourably with
mathematics. 'Look here,' they say, 'how in geometry, for example, everyone
is in agreement, going back to Euclid and beyond him to Thales and to
the Egyptian priests, while in philosophy the motto is still: *quot capita, tot
census*, as many systems as there are heads, and every day brings a new one.'
Concerning those systems that spring up overnight, I have already given
my opinion. If one holds philosophy in low esteem, however, because it has
systems and geometry does not, then I say: certainly there are no systems
in geometry, because there is no system – and there must be systems in
philosophy precisely because there is a system. It is as though one preferred
a stereometrically regular crystal to the human body for the reason that the
former has no possibility of falling ill, while the latter hosts germs of every
possible illness. Illness is related to health, namely, in roughly the same way

as the individual system is related to the system *kat' exochen* [*par excellence*]. In the human organism as well, doctors distinguish between different systems. Now, if someone suffers from one of these systems, or if one of these systems is particularly prominent, then they are tied to that system, restrained in their freedom, and are actually its slave. Healthy individuals do not feel any of these systems in particular. They do not *know*, as we say, that they have a digestive, etc., system; they are free from all systems. Why? Not because those systems would not be part of their organism, as this would not serve much to their benefit, but because they each live only in the whole, in the total system, in which all individual systems, so to speak, fall silent and become impossible (the word 'healthy' probably means the same as *whole*). The same happens in philosophy. Those who manage to get through to the end find themselves in complete freedom, they are free from the systems – *above* all systems.

We have, then, determined the following by this point. 1) The *external possibility of the system,* the matter, so to speak, the fabric of it, is precisely that irresolvable inner conflict in human knowledge. 2) This conflict must have become apparent; it must have shown itself and developed in every possible direction. 3) One must understand that there is nothing accidental in this conflict and that everything is grounded in the primary principles themselves. 4) One must give up the hope of ever terminating this conflict by having one system become master over another. If, however, a one-sided subjugation of one by the other is impossible then 5) we must not – and this is a new element – we must not imagine finding a unity in which they all *annihilate* one another either, because in this way, too, the concept of the system would perish, and the task consists precisely in having them all truly *coexist*. In the first case (where they would annihilate one another), instead of the system, one would only be confronted with a bottomless pit into which everything sinks and within which nothing can be distinguished any longer. The systems, however, are not supposed to be annihilated, they are supposed to coexist, like the different systems of one organism, and in this coexistence they are supposed to produce a perspective that goes beyond the individual systems, a healthy perspective which gives pleasure to man, the same way as in a healthy human body all differences between the organs and functions blend into *one* inseparable life whose feeling is well-being.

[...]

So far I have talked about the external reason of the system, or about the ambition of regarding human knowledge in a system – in coexistence. This external reason is a conflict in human knowledge which is, in itself, irresolvable. I have not demonstrated or proven it; I have presupposed it and I had to presuppose it. Instead of the system itself; I would have otherwise also had to present the preparations – the propaedeutic – for it. Namely, the best propaedeutic is the one which follows the necessary contradiction in which the awakening consciousness, or the awakening reflection, gets entangled, and the one which follows it from its primary roots, through all its branches, towards the desperation which, so to speak, forces man to form the idea of a superior whole. In this superior whole, by coexisting, the conflicting systems create a higher consciousness that frees man from all systems again, that takes him beyond all systems. This is actually the purpose of mere dialectics, and although dialectics is by no means the science itself; it is nevertheless the preparation for it.

So, the external reason for the system is an original *asystasia* [asystasy] of human knowledge. But what is the *principle* of its possibility? We do grasp the desirability of such a whole that brings all conflicting elements into harmony, but how is it possible and which presuppositions make it conceivable? The first presupposition for it is indisputably 1) the general idea of progression, of *movement* within the system. For it is certainly impossible that conflicting assertions could be true, as one would commonly say, *at the same time* – namely at one and the same evolutionary moment. It is quite possible, though, that at a certain point in the evolution, the statement 'A is B' is true, while at another 'A is not B' is true. Here the movement keeps conflicting statements separate. 2) This movement, however, requires a subject of movement and of progress, understood as that which moves and progresses, and about this subject two assumptions are made. a) It is only *one* subject that proceeds through everything. For if there were one subject in B and another in C, then B and C would be completely separated and there would be no connection. In the same way as it is only one and the same subject that lives in the different elements of an organism, so it has to be only one subject that proceeds through all the aspects of the system – it is not true, however, that therefore the elements through which it proceeds are one and the same also. But b) this one subject must proceed through everything and cannot remain in anything. For wherever it would remain, life and evolution would be inhibited. *Proceeding through everything and not being anything,* namely not being anything such that it could not also be something else – this is the requirement.

What is this subject that is in everything and that does not remain in anything? What should we call it? (Let me remark in passing, this question is identical to the common question of what the principle of philosophy is. The principle of philosophy is something that is not only principle at the beginning and then ceases to be principle. It is something always and everywhere, in the beginning, middle and end, equally principle. Furthermore, others also used to conceive of this principle as a supreme law. Since philosophy was regarded only as presenting a chain of laws deriving from one another, it was thought that there must be a supreme element in this chain – a first law, from which a second one is derived, and from this a third, and so on. In this way, Descartes had a supreme law in his *cogito ergo sum.* Fichte: I am I. In a living system, however, one that is not a sequence of laws, but of aspects of progression and evolution, the existence of such a supreme law is out of the question.) *What* then is the system's principle, the one subject that proceeds through everything and does not remain in anything? What should we call it, what can we say about it? First, we want to see what the question itself, *What is* it?, means. 'To characterise it as *something* that it really is.' Now, this is easy. Should I say then: A is B? Of course! But it is not only B. What I require, then, is that it be more precisely determined, I require that its concept be paraphrased within fixed limits, that it be *defined.* If one requires a definition, then one wants to know what the subject definitely is, and not merely what it is in such a way that it could also be something else, or even the opposite of it. [...] Geometry = definable science. When we look at philosophy as the subject, however, things are very different. It is simply indefinable. For i) it is nothing – not *something,* and even this would at least be a negative definition. But it is also not nothing, i.e. it is everything. Only it is nothing individual, static, particular; it is B, C, D, and so on, only in so far as each of these elements belongs to the flow of an inseparable movement. There is nothing that it would be and nothing that it would not be. It is in constant motion, it cannot be restricted to one form, it is the incoercible, the ungraspable, the truly infinite. Those who want to gain a command of the completely free and self-generating science must rise to its level. Here we have to depart from everything finite, from everything that is still an entity, and our last attachments must dwindle. Here we have to leave *everything* – not only, as one commonly says, wife and children, but that which merely *exists,* even *God.* For from this standpoint God, too, is only an entity. Here, where we first mention this concept (God), we may use it as the supreme example for demonstrating what was said earlier. We said: there is nothing that the absolute subject would not be, and there is nothing that this subject would be. Namely, the absolute subject is not not God, and it is not God either, it is also that which is not God. Hence, in this respect it is above God – since one of the most splendid mystics of early times dared speak of a superdivinity, this will also be permitted to us too. I want to make this point here, so that the Absolute – that absolute subject – will not be straightforwardly mistaken for God. This distinction is very important. Those, then, who want to find themselves at the starting point of a truly free philosophy, have to depart even from God. Here the motto is: whoever wants to preserve it will lose it, and whoever abandons it will find it. Only those who have at one time abandoned everything and have themselves been abandoned by everything, those for whom everything has been lost, and who have found themselves alone, face-to-face with the infinite (a decisive step which Plato compared with death) - only they have reached the ground in themselves and have become aware of the depths of life. That which Dante saw written on the door of the inferno must be written in a different sense also at the entrance to philosophy: 'Abandon all hope, ye who enter here.' Those who look for true philosophy must be bereft of all hope, all desire, all longing. They must not wish anything, not know anything, must feel completely bare and impoverished, must give everything away in order to gain everything. It is a grim step to take, it is grim to have to depart from the final shore. This we can infer from the fact that so few have ever been capable of it. How high does Spinoza rise when he teaches us that we ought to separate ourselves from all particular and finite things and to reach for the infinite. And how deeply does he sink again when he turns this infinite into a substance, i.e. into something dead, stagnant. When he tries to explain this substance as the unity of the realms of extension and thought, it is as if he attaches two weights with which he drags substance down completely into the finite sphere. Fichte, he who stood here on this spot before I did, and who was the first to take up again the emphatic call for freedom, he to whom philosophy is indebted for being able to start freely and from the beginning again, did something similar in our time. Far below himself he saw all existence, existence which for him was merely an inhibition of free activity. However, when all external and objective existence disappeared for him, in the moment when one expected him to go beyond all mere existence, he clung to his own self. Those who want to climb up to the free ether, however, have to abandon not only objects, but also themselves. Man is granted, by means of a great resolution in the middle of time, the opportunity to begin his moral life anew. Should this not also be possible in the spiritual realm? In this case, however, he would quite simply have to be born again.

[...]

Resolutely and categorically we said to ourselves that the absolute subject was the indefinable, the ungraspable, the infinite. Precisely in doing so, however, we acted against our own maxim, namely that nothing can be affirmed of this absolute subject without qualification, without the opposite being possible also. This must also be applied to the concept of the indefinable. For it is not indefinable in such a way that it could not also become definable, not infinite in such a way that it could not also become finite, and not ungraspable in such a way that it could not also become graspable. And if, gentlemen, *you* firmly keep this in mind, *you* have the positive concept. Namely, in order to be able to adopt one form it must of course be beyond all form, though its positive element is not that it is beyond all form or ungraspable, but, rather, that it can adopt a form, that it can make itself graspable, thus that it is free to adopt or not to adopt a form. For even at the very outset, it was not claimed that it was simply without shape or form, but only that it did not remain in any particular form, was not tied down by any given one. Hence, we explicitly presupposed that it *would* adopt a certain form. For only in adopting and then successfully divesting itself of each form, does it present itself as in itself ungraspable, infinite. It would not be free, however, to divest itself of each form if it had not been free from the very beginning to adopt or not to adopt form. I say from the very beginning – for after it has adopted form once, it might not be able to break through to its eternal freedom again immediately, but, rather, only by going through all forms. Originally, however, it is free to adopt or not to adopt a form. I do not, however, wish to express it like this: it is that which is free to adopt form. For this way freedom would appear as a *quality*, presupposing a subject different from and independent of it. Freedom, however, is the *essence* of the subject, or the subject itself is *nothing but the eternal freedom*.

Further reading

Whenever Schelling presents philosophical material, he is implicitly saying something about his conception of the philosophical system (or systems); and, as this suggests, many of his remarks on systems are scattered throughout his writings – often to be found in prefaces, footnotes or codas. For example, in addition to the passages excepted above, the concluding history of systems in *Bruno* or the final remarks on the 'oldest system' of nature in the *Philosophical Investigations into the Essence of Human Freedom* would be particularly useful starting points. For those interested in the later Schelling, it is worth turning to Chapter 6 of this book, where he discusses the systematic relationship between negative and positive philosophy.

In terms of the secondary literature, the following are pertinent:

Paul Franks, *All or Nothing: Systematicity, Transcendental Arguments and Skepticism in German Idealism* (Harvard University Press, 2005).

Martin Heidegger, *Schelling's Treatise on the Essence of Human Freedom*, translated by Joan Stambaugh (Ohio University Press, 1985).

Gregory Moss, 'Free Thinking in Schelling's Erlangen Lectures.' In Gregory Moss and Robert Scott (eds), *The Significance of Indeterminacy* (Routledge, 2018), 84–103.

Tilottama Rajan, 'Philosophy as Encyclopedia: Hegel, Schelling, and the Organization of Knowledge.' *The Wordsworth Circle* 35.1 (2004): 6–11.

Tilottama Rajan, 'Excitability: The (Dis)Organization of Knowledge from Schelling's *First Outline* (1799) to *Ages of the World* (1815).' *European Romantic Review* 3 (2010): 309–25.

Dale Snow, *Schelling and the End of Idealism* (SUNY, 1996), Chapter Five.

8

History of philosophy

Introduction

When Schelling was called to the University of Berlin in 1841 as the new Chair of Philosophy, it was – to a large extent – a result of the renown that his ever-developing critique of Hegel had gained during the 1830s in Munich. Moreover, those who attended the notorious lecture course of 1841/2 on the philosophy of revelation – from Kierkegaard to Engels – did so in eager expectation of either celebrating or resisting (and at times both) the destruction of the Hegelian system. Schelling's late diagnosis of Hegel as a negative (or logical) philosopher who transcended the strict limits of the field to attempt to speak of actuality remains his most influential argument, and the main reason why his work refuses to be shoehorned into a neat, progressive narrative running from Kant through to Hegel; nevertheless, his rigorous engagement with the Hegelian corpus is only one example among many of his sustained considerations of other philosophies. Schelling devotes significant attention to Plato, Aristotle, Bruno, Bacon, Descartes, Spinoza, Malebranche, Newton, Leibniz, Wolff, Kant, Herder, Jacobi and Fichte, as well as numerous others – and this chapter seeks to showcase a small portion of his engagement with the history of philosophy.

Schelling's forays into the history of philosophy should not be understood to be separate from the Schellingian system of philosophy itself. While some of his most rigorous commentaries on texts from the history of philosophy, such as his student notes on Plato's *Timaeus* (the opening extract of which is below), predate this period, it was in Summer 1801 that Schelling began to use a narrative of the history of philosophy as a prologue to his system – a pedagogical entry-point for his students. And, over the years, this prologue grew exponentially, such that, by the 1830s, the system itself is often presented by means of such a narrative: the 1833/4 Munich lectures on the history of modern philosophy (sections of which are anthologized as the third text below) are a good example of this, as are the opening lectures of the 1842/3 lecture course on the philosophy of revelation, from which we anthologize one example of Schelling's Hegel-critique (the fourth text below). Throughout this period, Schelling also wrote occasional pieces devoted to figures in the history of philosophy whose legacy remained contentious, such as the obituary he wrote on Kant's death, reproduced below.

In all these texts, Schelling is explicitly or implicitly concerned with showing how the history of philosophy has led to the need for his own philosophical endeavours, and so these forays into the history of philosophy are significant reference points for understanding Schelling's claim to the uniqueness of his position vis-a-vis his intellectual peers and forebears.

'Timaeus' (1794)*

Plato states the basic principle according to which one must judge the manner of presentation in the *Timaeus* at 28c: 'Now to discover the poet and father of this all is quite a task, and even if one discovered him, to speak of him to all men is impossible.'

This main principle is initially stated at 27d–28a: 'What is it that always is and has no becoming; and what is it that comes to be and never is? Now the one is grasped by intellection accompanied by a rational account, since it's always in the same condition; but the other in its turn is opined by opinion accompanied by irrational sensation, since it comes to be and perishes and never genuinely is.' Plato explains the *on* [what is] at this point as something that is the object of pure intellect, that which is pure and perfectly discernible and not simply an object of uncertain and imperfect opinion. These are all distinctive features that match the ideas of pure understanding and pure reason. But he explains *gignomenon* [that which is generated] (that is, the empirical, which has arisen through experience) through that which is only an object of opinion and something independent of ideas, and, what's more, even an intuition that contradicts the ideas. (The ideas, among which Plato understands the pure concepts of the power of representation, contradict intuition, insofar as they lie outside the sphere of intuition, and do not in

---

*Translated by Adam Arola, Jena Jolissaint and Peter Warnek from F.W.J. Schelling, *Timaeus* (1794), ed. Hartmut Buchner (Stuttgart: Frommann-Holzboog, 1994).

the least belong under the objects of intuition. Intuition itself, considered as such, is independent of all ideas.)

[…]

'Again, starting from these things, there's every necessity that this cosmos here be the likeness of something' (29a–b). It is at this point that Plato first comes to the principle that the world would have to be the imitation of some kind of archetype. Since Plato makes the world subordinate to the extent that he does, insofar as it was visible, and even attributes to it an existence that is merely present to the senses – and since he views it therefore (as a mere object of the senses) as entirely heterogeneous to all forms – he could not possibly view the form of the world in its regularity and lawfulness as *inherent* in matter itself, nor as a form that was brought forth from matter. He must have held that this form of the world is in its essence something wholly other and distinct from all matter. Accordingly, he locates it in the intellect, and describes it as something to be grasped only by the understanding; and because he could find the cause of this connection between form and matter neither in the one nor in the other alone, nor in both together (for he saw these [regularity and unruliness] as two things constantly striving against one other), therefore some third was necessary (see the *Philebus*) that unified each with the other, or, in other words, 'gave to the world a form, which was an imitation of the original, pure form of the understanding.'

'What moved the maker of the world to bring it forth?'

[…]

One has to distinguish in Plato two different kinds of ideas (something that, to my knowledge, has not yet taken place):

1   Those ideas that ground the world with respect to its materiality.
2   Those ideas that ground the world with respect to its form, that AS SUCH pertain to no particular objects at all. (For example, the idea of the good, of quantity, quality, causality, and so on.)

The key to the explanation of the entirety of Platonic philosophy is noticing that Plato *everywhere carries the subjective over to the objective*. It is from this that the principle arose in Plato that *the visible world is nothing but a copy of the invisible world* (though this principle is present long before him). But no philosophy could have come from this principle, if the philosophical ground for it weren't already in us. This means, namely, insofar as the whole of nature, as it appears to us, is not only a product of our *empirical receptivity*, but is rather actually the work of our power of representation – to the extent that this power contains within itself a pure and original foundational form (of nature) – and insofar as the world belongs in representation to a power that is higher than mere sensibility and nature is exhibited as the stamp of a higher world which the pure laws of this world express. The discovery of nature's legislation as it is prescribed by pure understanding can prematurely lead one to the idea that the visible world is the stamp of one that is invisible, something that leads to fanaticism as soon as one extends this stamping to the intuitions (with regard to their matter), and to the extent that one then believes, with regard to the mere lawfulness of nature as such, that it has its ground in humanity itself.

Plato now assumes:

1 That the world, with respect to its lawfulness, is an expression of a higher lawfulness.
2 That every *living being of the world* is grounded in an idea, which holds the character of the whole genus, without it being the case that the idea is ever completely arrived at through a particular kind of being.

Had Plato assumed that every worldly being is grounded objectively in an invisible, albeit physically existing, grounding being that contains what is distinctive to its whole genus, this would have been fanaticism – that is, it would have been the carrying over of the merely sensible, of what *merely* belongs to the empirical intuition, onto the supersensible. But Plato is indeed constantly protesting against this very opinion; and it is astonishing that one for so long has wanted to foist upon him the concept of a physical existence precisely there where he most forcefully, most emphatically and most clearly makes evident his own opposition to this.

Plato only accepted the ideas that grounded worldly beings *to the extent that* these ideas could be the object of pure thinking, the expression of the pure form of the power of representation. He thus had to accept the ideas that *as such* ground the objects only insofar as these are also dependent mediately or immediately upon the pure form of the understanding. If we recall his theory of the origin of the world, this becomes clear to us at once. Plato assumed, after all, a pre-existing matter, but one that had absolutely no determinate empirical form. For a proof of this see 51b–52a. Thus, according to his theory, insofar as all worldly beings were the work of the *demiurgos*, they did not belong to *matter*, but rather to the *form* with which the *demiurgos* brought it into unity. Matter in and of itself could not bring forth any *zoa* [living things], for this was the work of the master builder of the world, who brought the form *of the understanding* into unity with matter, and thereby brought into being not only the *universal* lawfulness of nature but also the lawfulness of the individual products themselves. Or, to put it another way, he made the *universal* laws of nature harmonize with the productivity of the individual ordered products. Every individual worldly being was thus not the work of *matter*, but rather actually a product of the *concordance of an individual pure law* to a whole – that is, it was the work of an idea, a *representation* of the concordance of an individual pure law to a whole. Moreover, if this concordance of a pure law with the productivity of a whole takes place for its part according to rules, then the concordance of this law itself was for its part not a work of matter, but rather a work of a pure form of *unity*, a work of an *intelligence*.

Furthermore, we have to remember that Plato viewed the entire world as a *zoon* [living thing], that is, as an organized being, thus as a being whose parts are possible only through their relation to the whole, whose parts are reciprocally related against each other as means and end, and thus which reciprocally bring themselves forth according to both their form and connectedness.[1] We must keep in mind that we, according to the subjective orientation of our power of knowing, simply cannot think the emergence of an organized being otherwise than through the causality of a concept or idea; we must think that everything that is contained within a being must be determined a priori and – just as the particular parts of the organized being bring themselves reciprocally in relation to each other and so bring forth the whole – on the contrary, the idea of the whole must be thought as determining a priori and in advance the form and parts in their harmony.[2]

Plato could thus assume that the ideas ground natural beings; and it was even necessary for him to make such an assumption. But these ideas are, namely, also only *ideas*, that is, the ideas of natural beings, only *zoa noeta*, only the originary images, in which reason comes to think itself, as if in outline, as the form that is in concordance with a whole and an end.

It was one of Plato's great ideas, and one which easily could have led him to flights of fancy, to seek the harmony of natural beings, not only in their relation to each other, but also in each individual as it relates to itself, and not along the path of empirical research, but in the investigation into the pure form of the power of representation. It is no wonder that he expressed himself with regard to this noble idea in a language that sailed far beyond all other philosophical language. No wonder that the work of his language is itself philosophically inspired; such a discovery of a supersensible principle of the form and harmony of the world in ourselves necessarily had to give rise to this inspiration. But precisely the inspired insight into this noble principle that lies beyond all sensibility caused him to express himself so strongly and forcefully, such that it really cannot be comprehended how one so often attributes to him the assertion of a physical existence of these ideas. For he directly presents the form of their existence in direct opposition to the form of all physical existence.

Equally impressive to him had to be the observation that all natural beings, grounded in a concept in us, a concept that express the form of every individual object that belongs to that concept, are to be arrived at, however, not through an individual, but rather only through the *genus*. He was able to think such a concordance of all beings in one concept in no other way than through the causality of a *concept* as it intentionally grounds the artful knowing of the master builder of the world, but also as it is able to contain a universality that is sufficient for all *in concreto* individual presentations of this universality, yet without being wholly expressible by any one of them. Such a concept could not be the work of matter, but had to be the product of a pure form of the understanding, through which matter first became capable of exhibiting the concepts. This is elaborated in the passage cited by Pleßing[3] in § 46. For if the form of unity, which ultimately gathers together every object, was the original form of the divine understanding, then the concept of all individual objects in their universality had to be present in the divine understanding before the objects could be brought forth.

A universal concept (even one in accord with pure rules independent of experience), at least as it is available to us in human understanding, can emerge only empirically. But insofar as Plato views all concepts as derivative in relation to a supreme intelligence, as the form of a highest understanding, in which the ideal of the world was grounded, he nevertheless had to regard these universal concepts as original concepts that are present prior to all experience. They do not first emerge through the objects of sensible intuition, but rather they themselves make sensible intuition first possible, because the individual objects of the world can only arise through the causality of the concepts that are already at hand, so that an empirical understanding through comparison and abstraction could again discover these concepts in the objects. The concepts had to be present in order to be able grant to objects some indication of their heritage and in order to leave a lasting mark of their origination. The universal concepts had to be present in a higher intelligence, because they were the condition of the possibility of universal law, according to which humans establish their empirical research.

[...]

According to Plato, the form of this inquiry would be a pure and *original* form without which no empirical inquiry would be possible. It would thus be a form which was also originally present in divine understanding, then imposed upon matter by the *demiurgos*, and imparted to human understanding as pure original form. This becomes clearer still in the following passage:

> This form is a gift from the gods to humans which was once sent by Prometheus along with the purest fire of the heavens. For this reason the ancients (humans greater and nearer to the gods than us) also bequeathed to us the legend that from out of unity and manifold (the many) everything that ever was became present, in that it united within itself what is unbounded (*apeiron*, the universal) and what is limited (*to peras*, the particular): such that we also, with this arrangement of things, presuppose one idea for every object and ought to seek it out. The gods who instruct, instruct us to think, to learn, and to teach according to this.[4]

The idea of the connection between the unity and the manifold, or the many, is the one dominant idea throughout all of Plato that he applies not only logically, but rather also as a natural concept (in these dialogues namely, for example, in the passage cited above). It is everywhere considered as one form that embraces of the whole of nature, and through its application upon formless matter not only are individual objects brought forth, but rather also the relation of objects to each other and their subordination to genera and kinds becomes possible.

In all these ways Plato must hold that every object corresponds to an original idea in divine understanding. This idea embraces all the individual kinds, and can exist only insofar as it comes to be in divine understanding, not first through an abstraction from individual objects but rather by first making these objects possible. It can be only by being ungenerated, indestructible and utterly not subordinated to the form of time.

According to this, the world as a great *zoon* [living thing] would have to be grounded in an idea in divine understanding, an idea that would not only exhibit a particular genus or kind of organic being, but rather would be able to serve as the universal idea of all beings. Just as there is only one idea of the world, so too could there be only one visible world. ('For since the god wanted to make it as similar as possible to the most beautiful things intellected and in all ways complete, he constructed it as an animal visible and one, holding within itself all those animals that are akin to it according to nature' [30d–31a]). Here one can clearly see what Plato understands by the archetype that grounds the world. Namely, that it is nothing other than an *idea*. For only the idea of the world is necessarily *one*. But then Plato says that the visible world is a copy of the perfect archetype, and on *account of this* can be only one. In passing, he states what has already been assumed, that the archetype of the visible world is only one. However, had he not understood this to be an idea, then he could not have assumed it. For only the *idea* of the world necessarily imposes itself as the form of *unity*; the reason for this is that this idea itself only properly emerges through the form of absolute unity that is grounded in the power of representation. Precisely in this way, however, what once again becomes apparent is the carrying over of the subjective onto the objective that holds sway throughout the whole of Platonic philosophy. For the world is only properly a unity as a *representation in us*. This is because the subjective form of reason is everywhere ascending to absolute unity, and thus because every part of the world that can be considered as a *particular* world of reason ascending without hindrance to the unconditioned is likewise formed into a representation of the whole. That Plato's reasoning arises from attending to the particular way our reason proceeds is evident from the following passage at 31a. Here he says, 'For that which embraces all the intelligible animals (however many they are) wouldn't ever be second in company with another one.' (But this can only be said of the intelligible world insofar as it is present in the form of the power of representation, and thus it can only be said of the idea of the world.) 'For again there would have to be another animal surrounding them both, of which both would be a part.' (A completely straightforward description of the procedure of reason, clear evidence that Plato only speaks of an *idea* of the world.) 'And then this cosmos would be more correctly spoken of as copied no longer from those two but from that other one which embraced them' (31a). (Again, a description of the way in which reason *subjectively* generates the idea of the world.)

Notes

1   See Kant's *Critique of Judgement*, § 65.
2   Ibid.
3   *Editors' Note.* F.V.L. Pleßing (1749–1806) was a late eighteenth-century commentator on Plato, to whom Schelling responds critically throughout his own commentary. In 1788–90, Pleßing published a two-volume work on ancient philosophy, the first volume of which is entitled *Plato's Metaphysical Philosophy*.
4   *Philebus*, 16c–e.

Immanuel Kant (An Obituary) (1804)*

Although he died in old age, *Kant* still did not outlive himself. He outlasted his fiercest opponents, in part physically but above all morally, and the fire of further advancements has only served to separate out the pure gold of his philosophy from the dross of the age, and present it in pure brilliance. The public effect of a great writer is always determined partly by his relations of opposition and partly by those of agreement with his times. The first relation is, as a rule, the beginning, but sooner or later turns into the other. Every extreme, according to a law of nature, demands its opposite, and, for a spiritually and morally disintegrated and dissolute age, this could have nothing but the beneficial effect of returning back into coherence with the rigidity of so wonderful a spirit. After a period which could only produce eclectic and desultory philosophies in which objects of speculation – known solely by means of tradition – were condemned by common human understanding, the inner unity, the strong connection of a [body of] work cast as from one mass – [a body of work] which returns to the sources of all knowledge, without any regard for its content – is worthy by the fact of its form and intention alone of serious and high reverence. In particular, the youth feel themselves irresistibly drawn to it, and are overjoyed – as at the most lucky find – at the form through which it restores treatments not only of the objects of knowledge, but also of life, with ease and with more reason than before. In the midst of the most bitter controversies and counter-controversies, the time came for that moment when *Kant*, in complete harmony with his age and for Germany, appeared as the highest herald and prophet of its spirit. This is nothing less than the seemingly superficial claim that the great event of the French Revolution afforded him by itself *the* universal and public effect which his philosophy would never have afforded in itself. Not without noting in this a certain fate did many of his enthusiastic followers wonder at the coincidence of both upheavals, which were of equal worth in their eyes, not realizing that it was one and the same long-dormant formative spirit which manifested itself – according to differences in nation and circumstance – there in a real and here in an ideal revolution. Just as it was a consequence of the Kantian philosophy that in Germany a judgement was formed so quickly on the Revolution, so too,

---

*Translated by Lydia Azadpour and Daniel Whistler from F.W.J. Schelling, *Sämmtliche Werke* (Stuttgart and Augsberg: Cotta, 1856–1861), Division One, Volume Six.

on the contrary, a convulsion was produced in which all prior principles – the conviction of an eternal, self-subsistent foundation to justice and the social constitution – became a matter for all, and made knowledge of the Kantian philosophy, which was, in the highest instance, held in sufficient esteem to decide on this, into a requirement for the people of the world and men of state. – The conciseness of its ethical formulae, through which one could decide with the greatest precision on moral cases, the rigour of the ethical and judicial principles that it advocated, just like the way it had of giving proofs raised above all dependence on experience – all this found its reference-point, its parallel and the purest material for application in the great moral spectacle of the era. – If, with the ebb of the Revolution, the Kantian system also seemed to have embarked [on its ebb], then the experts looked for the reason not so much in the falling away of contingent factors which maintained everyone's interest in it, but far more in an actual, inner agreement and likeness between the two, since both had in common a merely negative character and an unsatisfactory solution to the conflict between abstraction and reality, which was just as insurmountable in speculation as it had been for everyone in practice.

If the public effect of a philosophy is to be assessed by its influence on other doctrines, *Kant* lay the ground for a new way of considering things not only in the moral and political sciences, but directly and indirectly in most of the others. Similarly to his compatriot *Copernicus* who displaced movement from the centre to the periphery, he first reversed the ground of representation, according to which the subject [had been] passively and quietly receptive and the object active – a reversal which passed through all branches of knowledge like an electric effect.

It is not our intention here to precisely evaluate Kant's service to science: more interesting for our purpose is the impression of his personality, which has been left out of his works. It has often been remarked that, in his mind, the idea of the whole of his philosophy does not precede the parts, but rather the latter precede the former, and the whole thereby arises more atomistically than organically. Constrained by his teaching position to lecture on speculative philosophy, he spent a number of years merely sceptical of then-dominant Wolffian-Baumgartian concepts, since the infinite honesty and sincerity of his spirit prevented him from appeasing himself with that dogmatism, as others had. Yet he must already have grasped the main ideas of his critique with a fair amount of clarity in the 1770s, since they are to be found in a very popularized form in that well-known conversation in *Hippel's Lebenslaufen in aussteigender Linie* which appeared at that time, in which the *Dean of the Philosophy Faculty* is not only a scientific, but also a personal portrait of Kant.[1]

If one asks why *Kant* is usually felt to be superior to most of his opponents, among whom the most recent, *Jacobi*, was not lacking in acerbity, then one would have to recognize the reason for this in the above-mentioned *philosophical sincerity* which he himself so unwillingly found lacking in most other philosophers and which he praised as the first virtue. In it, the clear naivety of his mind recognizes and despises all trickery, all sham and empty superficiality. It is clear from the procedure of his work, as when he unintentionally arrives at his results and even from many expressions, that he proceeds almost against his inclination and concerns himself with the abstract investigations his critique contains only in consideration of practical utility. This [critique] seems to have been for him more a means of freeing himself from philosophy and therefore was for him a necessary transition from the 'thorny paths of speculation'[2] to the fruitful fields of experience, on which, as he gave clearly to understand, his happier successors could wander alone in the wake of his efforts. His mind was in general not, as he is commonly represented, of the difficult, deep-sensing kind (in his *Anthropology* he himself makes fun of such traits which, according to him, signify only melancholy), but of the easy and carefree type. One recognizes already from his earliest productions, e.g. the *Observations on the Feeling for the Beautiful and the Sublime*, a tendency to French elegance and the social wit of that nation – hence, his own love for vibrant conviviality, his taste for the joys of a table enlivened by intellect, for which he turned down no opportunity, his inexhaustible knowledge of humorous incidents and witty anecdotes, of which a few are preserved in his *Anthropology* next to many comments of less value.

Thus, in a way a *philosophe malgré lui* [philosopher despite himself], *Kant's* true geniality is necessarily misjudged when he is customarily considered *only* as a philosopher. Without doubt, however, precisely only a man of this type of mind was capable of achieving a lasting victory over dogmatism and of so purely brightening the philosophical horizon that had been beclouded by this philosophy. The old, serene Parmenides, as he is depicted by Plato, and the dialectician Zeno would have happily recognized in him their intellectual progeny, if they had beheld his artfully worked *antinomies*, those ever-lasting monuments of victory over dogmatism and eternal propylaeum to the true philosophy.

Irrespective of the fact that his philosophy developed in parts, his spirit shows *a natural and unhindered drive for totality*, which he attained in his sphere. His later speculative investigations were, excepting those that relate to society and life, pre-eminently scientific, and, with the same exceptions, he was mostly attracted to them until his power of thought began to fail. His *theory* and *history of the heavens* is prized more than others (which is not saying very much) because of its prediction of a planet beyond all the others then known, because of its almost accurate definition of Saturn's orbit, prior to any observation of it, and because of the bold thoughts proposed primarily on the systems of fixed stars, the Milky Way and nebulae: several years later, through Lambert's *Cosmological Letters* in which they are repeated without any mention of *Kant*, they were made famous, even if they were more pleasing for the imagination than grounded in reason. Even more valuable than all this was the bold impetus of his mind in looking for the ground underlying the above determination of a world-system and its movement in the realm of matter and its natural forces, as opposed to the Newtonians who looked to divine omnipotence.

To his theoretical critique of reason, as the formal side, he later added his *Metaphysical Foundations of Natural Science* as the real [side], but without being able to develop this division fruitfully into the true unity of the principles of both parts and turn natural science into *philosophy* of nature, and also without managing to pursue the universal to the point of perfect harmony with the particular. Even in 1801 he was still working in the few hours left him by his power of thinking on a work: *Transition from Metaphysics to Physics*, which, had age allowed him to complete it, would without a doubt have been of the highest interest. His ideas about organic nature were separated from general natural science, and in his *Critique of Teleological Judgement* are set forth without any connection to it.

Moreover, his mind illuminated the wide field of *history* with many enlightening thoughts, but was inhibited by the contemporary idea of the continual progress of mankind.

The *naivety* irradiating from all his works, through which was often divulged the goodness of his temperament no less than the depth of his spirit – a not-uncommon divine *instinct* that orients him with certainty – is particularly recognizable in his *Critique of Aesthetic Judgement*. It is explainable only in terms of the purity of a truly independent mind and the great talents of a clear spirit: owing to the deepest vilification of art, [art] had been completely forgotten or misjudged – notwithstanding that unique mastery which appeared in *Winckelmann* and *Goethe* – due to an age partly dissipated in empty sentimentality, partly craving the rough, material excitement of [art], and partly demanding ethical improvement or, at the very least, instruction or other uses from it. But [Kant] raised himself to the idea of art in its independence from every other end than what lies in itself, he exhibited the unconditionality of beauty and he demanded naivety as the essence of artistic genius. This was doubly worthy of admiration, since both the natural inclination of his mind and the circumstances of his life (he never went further than a few miles from his native Königsberg) hindered him from achieving any more significant historical knowledge of the fine works of the figurative arts than of the poetic arts, among which for him *Wieland's* poetry (the furthest limit of his acquaintance with German poetry) and *Homeric* poetry came to stand on roughly the same level. When he says in his explanation of his doctrine of genius: 'No *Homer* or *Wieland* can show how his ideas, rich in fancy and yet also in thought, arise and meet in his mind; the reason is that he himself does not know',[3] it is difficult to know whether to be more amazed at the naivety with which Homer is invoked in an elucidation of the (modern) concept of genius or at the good-naturedness of claiming of *Wieland* that *he himself could not know* how his fanciful ideas came together in his head – something which, according to the judgement of experts on French and Italian literature, *Wieland* was able to know very precisely. – As is well-known, this very good-naturedness subsequently served him badly.

Leaving aside the above, it is undeniable that only since *Kant* and because of him has the essence of art come to be expressed scientifically. Truly without knowing it, he handed down concepts which unlock the meaning of and form judgements about past beauties, as well as authenticity, in German art; and, like what is most vital in science, the bold impetus that his critique took on in his last years can be attributed indirectly to its effect.

This indirect relation to all later thought in a way completes him and preserves the purity of his appearance. He lay the *boundary* between two epochs in philosophy – one of which he finally put an end to, the other of which he prepared the way for negatively by prudently limiting his goal to the critical alone.

Undistorted by the gross features produced by the misunderstandings of those who under the name of commentators and followers were caricatures of him or bad plaster-casts, as well as by those who attacked him with the anger of bitter adversaries, the image of his spirit, in its utter uniqueness, will shine throughout the future of the philosophical world.

[…]

In the remembrance of *his* nation, to which he can alone truly belong in spirit as in temperament, will Kant eternally live as one of the few intellectually and morally great individuals in whom the German spirit has vividly shown itself in its totality. AVE SANCTA ANIMA.

Notes

1   *Translators' Note.* This is a reference to the 1781 autobiography of Theodor von Hippel the Elder (1741–1796), a Prussian satirical writer and friend of Kant.
2   *Translators' Note.* A citation of the famous passage from the second-edition Preface to Kant's *Critique of Pure Reason*.
3   *Translators' Note.* A quotation from Kant, *Critique of Judgement*, § 47.

Lectures on the History of Modern Philosophy (1833/4)*

Descartes

The history of modern European philosophy is counted from the overthrow of scholasticism until the present time. Renatus Cartesius (René Descartes), born 1596, the initiator of modern philosophy, a revolutionary, in the spirit of his nation, began by breaking off all connection with earlier philosophy, by rubbing out, as if with a sponge, everything that had been achieved in this science before him, and by building it up again from the beginning, as if no one had ever philosophized before he did. The necessary consequence of such a total tearing away was, though, that philosophy regressed, as if into a second childhood, a kind of immaturity which Greek philosophy had already almost surpassed with its first steps. On the other hand, this regression to simplicity could be advantageous to the science itself; it withdrew thereby from the breadth and extension which it had already received in antiquity and in the middle ages, almost to a single problem, which now, by successive expansion, and after everything was prepared for it in detail, has grown into the great, all-inclusive task of modern philosophy. It is almost the first definition of philosophy to offer itself if one says philosophy is the science which begins absolutely at the beginning. It had, therefore, already to have a big effect, even if one only began at the beginning in the sense that one did not presuppose anything from previous philosophy and did not presuppose that *it* proved anything.

---

*Translated by Andrew Bowie from F.W.J. Schelling, *Sämmtliche Werke* (Stuttgart and Augsberg: Cotta, 1856–1861), Division One, Volume Ten.

The Greek Thales is supposed to have asked what the First and the Oldest in the whole nature of things was. Here, beginning at the beginning was meant objectively. But Descartes only asks: 'What is the First *for me*?' and to that he could, of course, only answer: 'I myself, and even then I myself at the most with respect to *being*.' To this first, immediate certainty all other certainty for him was only subsequently to attach itself, everything was only to be true to the extent that it connected to that immediate certainty. But obviously the proposition: *I am* is at the most the starting point for me – and *only* for me; the connection which results from the attachment to this proposition or to the immediate consciousness of one's own being can, therefore, always only be a subjectively logical one, i.e. I can always only infer: to the extent to which I certainly am, I must *assume* as certainly that *A, B, C*, etc., are. But how *A, B* and *C* are really connected to each other, or with their *true* principle, or even only how they are connected to the I am itself, is not shown at all. Philosophy achieves here, therefore, no more than a merely subjective certainty, and a certainty not about the kind of existence [of the subject] (which alone is really dubious), but only about the existence of everything outside the subject. This much [about Descartes] in general.

[...]

What must be most important for us, and it is primarily because of this that I have tried to give an idea of Descartes's philosophy, is precisely the introduction of that *ontological argument*. Descartes has become decisive for the whole of subsequent modern philosophy, far less for what he said otherwise about the beginnings of philosophy than for the setting up of the ontological proof. One can say: philosophy is still now occupied with disentangling and explaining the misunderstandings to which this argument gave rise. This argument is also curious because, among the classic proofs by which the existence of God used to be proven in ordinary metaphysics, it was always in first place until Kant. It is important to note that this argument was not recognized at all by the scholastics. For, although Anselm of Canterbury had already advanced a similar argument, Thomas Aquinas most emphatically contradicted him. The so-called ontological proof became primarily an object of the Kantian critique, but neither Kant nor any of his successors hit upon the correct point. The main objection to the Cartesian proof which was primarily raised by Kant depends upon the already-mentioned incorrect idea that the argument is supposed to be as follows: I find in me the idea of the perfect being, but existence is itself a perfection, therefore existence is also of its own accord included in the idea of the perfect being. Here, then, the minor proposition of the conclusion is denied. It is said that existence is not a perfection. A triangle, e.g. does not become any more perfect by existing, or, if this were the case, then I should also have to be allowed to conclude that the perfect triangle must exist. What does not exist, it is said, is neither perfect nor imperfect. Existence only expresses the fact that the thing, i.e. that its perfections, *are*. Therefore existence is not one of these perfections, but it is that without which neither the thing nor its perfections are. But I have already remarked that Descartes does not infer in *this* manner. Rather, his argument goes as follows: it would contradict the nature of the perfect being to exist just contingently (as, e.g. my own existence is simply contingent, precarious and for this reason doubtful in *itself*), therefore the most perfect being can only exist necessarily. There would, I suggest, be no objection to this argument, particularly if one agrees that the concept of necessary existing should be understood to mean merely the opposite of contingent existing. But the conclusion of Descartes is different. Let us repeat again the whole syllogism. The perfect being *cannot* exist only contingently, thus can only exist necessarily (major proposition); God is the perfect being (minor proposition), therefore (he ought to conclude) He *can* only exist necessarily, for this alone is inherent in the premises; instead of this, though, he concludes: therefore He necessarily exists, and, it is true, thereby apparently brings out the fact that God exists, and seems to have proven the existence of God. But it is something completely different whether I say: God can only exist *necessarily,* or whether I say: He necessarily exists. From the First (He *can* only exist necessarily) only follows: therefore He exists necessarily (n.b., *if He exists,* but it does not at all follow *that* He exists). In this, therefore, lies the mistake of the Cartesian conclusion. We can also express this mistake like this. In the major proposition (the perfect being can only exist *necessarily*), it is only a question of the *manner* of existence (it is only stated that the perfect being could not exist in a contingent *manner*), in the conclusion, however, it is no longer a question of the *manner* of existence (in this case the conclusion would be correct) but of existence at all, therefore there is *plus in conclusione quam fuerat in praemissis* [more in the conclusion than there was in the premises], i.e. a logical law has been broken, or the conclusion has an incorrect form. That *this* is the real mistake I can also prove by the fact that Descartes himself *directly* infers in several places, or, for the time being at least, infers *only* in the manner I have shown. In an essay with the title 'Rationes Dei existiam etc. probantes ordine geometrico dispositae', the conclusion is as follows: Therefore it is true to say of God that in Him existence is a necessary existence *or* (he adds) that *He exists*. The latter, though, is something completely different from the former and cannot be regarded as equivalent to it, as is suggested by the 'or'. (Descartes himself is well aware that in his concept of the perfect being only the *manner* of existence is determined.) Thus he says in the same account: in the concept of a limited, finite thing, merely possible or contingent existence is contained; in the concept of the perfect thing, therefore, is contained the concept of necessary and perfect existence. At another point, in his fifth Meditation, he carries out the conclusion as follows: I find in me the idea of God no differently or in the same way as I find the idea of any geometrical figure or of a number, *nec*, he immediately continues, *nec minus clare et distincte intelligo, ad ejus naturam pertinere, ut semper existat* [nor do I understand any less clearly and distinctly that it belongs to His nature that He *always* exists]. (Take good note of this *semper* [always]; here he does not, then, say, *ad ejus naturam pertinere, ut existat*, but only *ut semper existat*.) From that it merely follows that God, if He exists, only *always* exists, but it does not follow *that* He exists. The true meaning of the conclusion is always only: *either* God does not exist at all, or, if He exists, then He *always* exists necessarily, i.e. not contingently. But it is clear that His existence is not proven thereby.

With this critique of the Cartesian argument we admit, though, that, if not the existence, then the *necessary* existence of God is proven – and this *concept* is now really the one which has had the most decisive effect for the whole subsequent period of philosophy.

[...]

Spinoza

If one recalls the Cartesian system in its true constitution, then one *longs* for a better, more beautiful, more reassuring form, which is then at once to be found in Spinozism.

Spinoza, who can be regarded as pupil and immediate successor of Descartes, born in Amsterdam in 1632, had already, before he set up his real system, worked on the Cartesian system, but in the direction or with the aim of giving it a really objective context. The decisive move to his own system took place when he made what was First *in itself* into the sole point of departure, but also took no more of this into consideration than could be known with certainty, namely necessary existence. Spinoza retained from the Cartesian concept, in which God was still more than the necessarily existing being, no more than *this* definition; God was for him *only* the necessarily existing being; he cut off all reflections in Descartes which preceded this concept, and began at once with a definition of substance, by which he understood precisely, *ad cujus naturam pertinet existere* [to whose nature it belongs to exist], or *id, quod cogitari non potest nisi existens* [that which cannot be thought if it does not exist], that which cannot at all, without there being a contradiction, be thought as not being [*nicht seyend*]. To the extent that Spinoza determined that which exists necessarily as substance, and indeed as absolute, general substance, one can clearly see that he had thought that which exists necessarily first as the general subject of being [*Seyn*], which, if just thought as such, is not yet being [*das Seyende*], but only the prerequisite, the possibility of being [*Seyn*], as, e.g. the person who is thought of as the subject of illness is not for that reason really ill, but only the person who can be ill. Individual real things are not at all the subject of being itself [*des Seyns selbst*], although they are in being [*seyend sind*]; they are in being [*sind seyend*] only by participation in being [*Seyn*], not by the fact that they could not not be at all, for they rather *cannot* be, because their being [*Seyn*] is attached to being in a *particular* way [*das so Seyn*]. We must, of course, ascend to that of which not just being in a *particular* way, but of which being at all [*das Seyn überhaupt*] can be predicated, *cujus actus est existere* [whose act is to exist], and only this is the general or absolute subject of being [*Seyn*], which we also call *being itself* [*das Seyende selbst*]. One can attempt to hold onto it purely and abstractly, where it is still the *Prius* of being; here it would then be being [*das Seyende*] just in thought, which only has a being [*Seyn*] in thinking (in this sense, unity of thinking and being – namely taken negatively, in the sense that being is not outside thought, thus not transitive being, but just immanent being); but, as was already said, it cannot be held onto in this narrowness, it is not just in the *logical* sense, it is also in the transitive sense that which cannot not be, and however early I may arrive, before I have had time to think, so to speak – *before* all thinking, it is to me, or *I find* it already, as being [*das Seyende*], because it, as the subject of all being [*alles Seyns*], is precisely that which is according to its *nature*, and is never to be thought as not being.

This, then, is the origin of the Spinozist concept, which, as the history of philosophy shows, has been until the present time the point around which everything moves, or rather the imprisonment of thought, from which thought has sought to emancipate itself by the succeeding systems without yet being able to do so. It is the concept by virtue of which there is in God *explicite* – expressly – neither will nor understanding, according to which He really is only that which blindly exists – we can also say: that which exists in a subjectless way, namely because He has gone over wholly and completely into being [*Seyn*]. In possibility there is still a *freedom* from being, thus also against being. But in this case possibility is swallowed by being. *Because* that First is that which can *only* be (and not also that which is able *not* to be), it is for that reason that which *only* is [*das nur Seyende*], i.e. being [*das Seyende*] which is by the exclusion of all non-being – by the exclusion of all potentiality – of all freedom (for freedom is nonbeing). Accordingly it is being [*das Seyende*] without potentiality, and, in *that* sense, powerless being, because it absolutely does not have the power of another being [*Seyn*] in itself. Spinoza calls God *causa sui* [cause of itself], but in the more narrow sense that He Is through the sheer necessity of His essence, without being able to be held onto as being able to be (as *causa*); the cause has completely merged into the effect, and behaves only as *substance*, against which His thought can do nothing. For surprised, as it were, by blind being [*Seyn*], as the unexpected, which no thought can anticipate (whence *this* being really is the *existentia fatalis* [fatal existence], the system is itself fatalism), overtaken, I say, by being [*Seyn*], which blindly descends upon Him, which swallows its own beginning, He even loses consciousness, all power and all freedom of movement in relation to this being. It is because of this that one can admittedly also attribute to Spinozism that calming effect, which, among other things, Goethe praised in it; Spinozism is really the doctrine which sends thought into retirement, into complete quiescence; in its highest conclusions it is the system of perfect theoretical and practical quietism, which can appear beneficent in the tempestuousness of a thought which never rests and always moves; as Lucretius describes the state of such a peace; *Suave mari magno*, it is sweet to watch the distress of others in a wild sea from a distant bank – *magnum alterius spectare laborem*,[1] not that one enjoys other people's misfortunes, but because one feels oneself free from this torment. It is unquestionably the peacefulness and calm of the Spinozist system which particularly produces the idea of its *depth*, and which, with hidden but irresistible charm, has attracted so many minds. The Spinozist system will also always remain in a certain sense a *model*. A system of freedom – but with just as great contours, with the same simplicity, as a perfect counter-image of the Spinozist system – this would really be the highest system. This is why Spinozism, despite the many attacks on it, and the many supposed refutations, has never really become something truly past, never been really overcome up to now, and no one can hope to progress to the true and the complete in philosophy who has not at least once in his life lost himself in the abyss of Spinozism. [...] But if we now ask at which price that deep calm of the Spinozist system is bought, we must answer: at the price that God is just substance, not free cause, and that even *things* can only relate to Him as to substance, not as to cause. God is not the freely creating or producing spirit which can work outside Himself, outside His immediate being [*Seyn*]; He is completely confined in His being [*Seyn*] which precedes all thought, thus things as well can only be *in* him, only be particular forms or ways in which the divine being presents itself; not that God Himself would be limited thereby, but that every thing only expresses in itself the immediate divine essence in a particular and determinate way. Even though God Himself is not limited by these forms, to the extent to which He himself goes beyond them, one still naturally demands to know how these limitations of being get into God. All Spinoza answers to this is that those affections, and thus the things, belong to the nature of God in the same way as the affections of the triangle follow from the nature of the triangle and belong to it, i.e. there is not a free but a *necessary* connection between God and things. But he does not show the nature of this necessary connection. He admittedly does assume mediating elements between the things themselves and God, i.e. he does not let the things arise *immediately* out of God. As such, one might think it possible that he provides some constant sequence of moments or transitional points by virtue of which a comprehensible move from the highest idea to the things, not just to things at all, but to things constituted in *that* particular way, could be proven. But it is like this with regard to those transitional elements. He posits, as the first mediations between God and things, infinite extension and infinite thought, which, as he says, are the immediate attributes of God or of the infinite substance, i.e. the forms in which the substance immediately exists (for one cannot explain the concept of attributes in any other way). For him thinking and extension are, therefore, the two immediate and – each in its own way – equally infinite forms in which the absolutely infinite substance exists, which, to the extent to which these are the two immediate forms of its *being* [*Seyn*], is itself neither thinking nor extended. Here, it now seems, Spinoza would have to be brought back to the concept of substance in and before itself and would have to come to an explanation of the attributes. Substance is for him *causa sui*, cause of itself. This *causa sui* could be explained as that which posits itself. That which posits itself, one could continue, can only posit itself as existing in the two forms of *thinking* and *extension*, roughly in the manner, as it has later been said, that what posits itself posits itself necessarily (a) as object (this would in Spinoza be infinite extension), (b) as subject (this would be Spinoza's infinite thought). But that way one would be giving determinations to it which have only emerged in a later development, and would thereby have removed his peculiarity and his individual position in the history of science. The substance of Spinoza is a subject-object, but one in which the subject gets completely lost.

Note

1   *Editors' Note.* A partial quotation from Lucretius; in English the full passage reads, 'How delightful it is when on the great sea, the winds have raised the waters, to witness the perils of another from the land.' *De rerum natura* II.1-2.

Lectures on the Philosophy of Revelation (1842/3)*

It was to be expected that precisely at that moment when the negative and the positive should have become forever divorced – thus at the moment of the formation of the purely negative philosophy – that the positive had to appear even more forcefully and establish its own legitimacy. And if earlier I had had the clear presentiment that on the other side of this *Critique*, which had destroyed the dogmatizing philosophy, a different one must arise, and, indeed, a dogmatic philosophy that would not be touched by it, then it is easy to imagine how when that rational system, prepared by Kant and now brought to its full manifestation and liberated from all contingencies, stood before my eyes as a real system, that this same sight must have weighed on my heart all the more heavily. The more purely the negative philosophy was put forth, the more forcefully the positive had to rise up in contrast to it, and it seemed as if nothing had been done as long as this had not been discovered as well. Perhaps this will explain how, almost immediately after the first presentation of that system that had developed out of the *Critique*, this philosophy[1] was more or less abandoned by its founder and left for the time being to those who stood ready to appropriate it, who, as Plato would say, were drawn by the brilliance of the vacated position to pounce on it with zeal. For myself, this philosophy had really only been a transition. [...]

---

*Translated by Bruce Matthews from Lecture 5 in F.W.J. Schelling, *Sämmtliche Werke* (Stuttgart and Augsberg: Cotta, 1856–1861), Division Two, Volume Three.

The *true* improvement to my philosophy could partly have been to have restricted it precisely to only a logical meaning. Hegel, however, made much more specific claims than his predecessor did to have comprehended the positive as well. In general, one has made altogether false concepts about the relationship between these two thinkers. One believes that the former [Schelling himself] was angry with the latter [Hegel] for having gone beyond him. But exactly the opposite is the case. The first, who still had much to overcome (about which one nowadays no longer knows anything) and had to master all the material that the latter found already subdued in the concept, could certainly put up with being corrected by the latter. Even if those elements of Hegel's overall approach that were particularly hostile to all that is meaningful and inspired could not be hidden from me, I nonetheless also saw how that same approach opposed with vigor, and for the true benefit of rigorous thinking and science, much of what he found before him in that time that was spuriously brilliant, really weak – yes, even childish – and that misled through an ostensible conviviality. While others just floundered about, he at least held tight to the method as such, and the energy with which he carried out a false system – although mistaken, it was nonetheless a system – had it been turned to what is correct could have contributed a priceless largess to science. As I saw then, it is precisely this aspect that mostly accounts for his influence, in that those who praised him most fervently always removed a few platitudes and slogans, rarely spoke of specifics, but always emphasized that his philosophy is a *system*, and indeed a complete system. On the one hand, this unconditional demand for a system expresses the heights to which the philosophical science has been elevated in our time; one is convinced that nothing more can be known in its singularity, but rather only in its context and as part of a great, all-encompassing totality. On the other hand, there are many who want to be finished at any cost and feel childishly delighted to subscribe to a system, thereby elevating their own importance; primarily because of this, it is always such a deplorable affair when the labels of party or sect come into use or are again accepted as valid. For I have had the opportunity to see some whom on their own meant nothing, but when they called themselves a liberal or a monarchist sympathizer fancied both themselves and others to actually be something.

Not everyone, by the way, is called upon to be the creator of a system. It requires an artistic sensibility to remain within the borders of what is natural and to keep oneself from being carried away by the pursuit of closure to absurd or bizarre conclusions. Hegel, who in the details is so sharp, was abandoned by this artistic sensibility by nothing so badly as when he moved on into the whole, for otherwise he would have detected the interruption of movement that takes place for him between the *Logic* and the *Philosophy of Nature*; from the manner alone, in which the latter was pieced onto the former, he should have seen that he was not on the correct path. I do not belong to those who look for the source of philosophy exclusively in feeling, but for philosophical thinking and invention, as for the poetic or artistic, feeling must be the voice that warns of the unnatural and indistinct, and many a path that leads to error will be spared those who listen to it for the very reason that this sensibility shuns that which is artificial and can only be achieved through laborious and unclear compositions. The philosopher who really wants a completed system must see far out into the distance, not just stare myopically at details and what lies nearby.

The earlier philosophy [i.e. Schelling's early philosophy] could not present itself as an *unconditional* system in the sense of Hegel's, but one could not, for this reason, reproach it for not being a system at all. It did not first need *to be* systematized, since it was born a system; its peculiarity consisted precisely in the fact that it is to be a system. Whether the external presentation was held to be more or less academic could appear as inconsequential: the system resided in the *subject matter*, and whoever had the subject matter had for precisely this reason the system as well. Yet it could not achieve closure as an absolute system that leaves nothing outside itself, and as long as the positive philosophy had not been created, it could do just as little to prevent another thinker from advancing this system as philosophy *per se*. At first, Hegel seemed to realize the *purely logical* nature of this science. Yet if he were serious about its purely logical meaning, then logic for him could not be just a *component*. This entire philosophy, even those philosophies of spirit and nature undertaken by his predecessor [Schelling himself], had to be logical for him, that is, they had to be logic, and yet what he specifically proposed as logic must not be something so misguided as it is in his hands. Instead of using the true and real logic as a foundation from which one could have advanced, he hypostatized the concept with the intent of providing the logical movement – which, however independent one takes it to be of everything subjective, can nonetheless always exist only in *thought* – with the significance of an objective movement, nay, what is more, of a *process*. So little had he freed himself from what is real, and which had impeded his predecessor, that he in fact *affected* what is real with expressions taken from that predecessor, which were in no way made for his standpoint. In the transition to the philosophy of nature, which can occur only hypothetically in a philosophy that remains purely negative (whereby even nature is preserved in its sheer possibility, with no attempt to explain it as a reality, a task which must be reserved for an entirely different facet of philosophy), he helps himself to such expressions – for example, the idea *resolves* itself; nature is a *fall* from the idea – that either say nothing, or, according to his intent, should be *explanatory* and thus include something real, an actual process, a happening. Thus, if the error of the first presentation was not to have placed what is positive *outside* itself, so this was surpassed by the ensuing (Hegelian) presentation, but only through the perfection of that error.

I return to the opinion that some have formed as they heard from afar of the positive philosophy, namely that it should take the *place* of the negative entirely, and should thereby supplant and nullify the latter. Thus was it never intended, and so easily will a creation like that of this philosophy never surrender, a philosophy that since then has determined itself for me as the negative. It was a beautiful time in which this philosophy arose, when through Kant and Fichte the human spirit released itself to a real freedom toward all being and justifiably saw to ask not what is but what *can* be, and when Goethe also shone forth as the sublime paradigm of artistic perfection. The positive philosophy, however, could not have been discovered and developed without a corresponding advance in the negative, which is now capable of an entirely different presentation than forty years ago. Although I know that this simple, easy, and nonetheless magnificent architectonic, insofar as with the very first thought it crossed over into nature, and, thus, proceeding from the broadest basis, culminated in a peak that soared up into the heavens – I know that this architectonic, in its *perfect* execution, particularly in the countless details of which it is capable and, indeed, even demands, all of this is only comparable to the works of the old German architecture, which cannot be the work of one person, of one individual, and, for that matter, not even of one epoch. Yet even the Gothic cathedrals, left uncompleted in an earlier age, were taken up again by a later progeny and constructed according to their principle. Although aware of this, I nonetheless hope not to withdraw from this world, without having also consolidated the system of the negative philosophy in its true foundation, and as far as it is now possible for me, to have further developed it.

From what has been said, it becomes immediately clear how superfluous it was to want to defend the rational or negative philosophy against me or bring it to bear upon me, as if I no longer wanted to know anything about a philosophy of pure reason. Those people, incidentally, who believed themselves called to do this and, in particular, those who believed they must undertake a defence of the Hegelian philosophy against me in this regard, did this, at least in part, not to somehow oppose the positive philosophy, but, on the contrary, they themselves *also wanted* something of the sort. Only they were of the opinion that this positive philosophy must be constructed on the basis of the Hegelian system and can be constructed on no other. Moreover, they thought that the Hegelian system lacked nothing more than for *them* to carry it on into the positive, and this, they thought, can happen in a continuous advance, without interruption and devoid of any setbacks. They proved through this that, firstly, they had never had a correct concept of the preceding philosophy, otherwise they would have known that this philosophy was in itself a closed and fully consummated system. A totality that had a *true* end, that is, an end beyond which one could not, according to circumstances or conditions, again move, but rather one that must remain the end. Secondly, they proved that they did not even know about the philosophy that they wanted to improve and expand, the Hegelian, since this philosophy had no need to be extended by them to the positive because it had, on the contrary, already done that on its own. Its error consisted precisely in this; it wanted to be something that, according to its nature and heritage, it could by no means be, namely, to be a dogmatic philosophy. In particular, it was their opinion (probably derived from dubious hearsay) that the positive philosophy begins with the personal God, and the personal God was that which they thought to acquire through the advancement of the Hegelian philosophy as the *necessary* content of reason. They did not know, therefore, that Kant along with the philosophy that followed from him already had God as the *necessary* content of reason: about this there was no quarrel and no doubt, for it was no longer a question of *content*. As far as Hegel is concerned, yes, he indeed boasted that he had God at the end of philosophy as absolute *spirit*. But can one think of an absolute spirit that would not simultaneously be an absolute personality, a consciousness absolutely aware of himself? Perhaps they meant this absolute spirit is just not a freely acting personality, the freely acting creator of the world, or any such thing. This of course could not be the spirit who first comes at the end, *post festum* [after the fact], after everything has been done, and who has nothing other to do than take up into himself all those extant moments of the process that are before and independent of him. And yet it was precisely this that even Hegel had finally sensed, and in later addendums he allowed this absolute spirit to freely decide to create a world, to externalize itself with freedom into a world. Yet these addendums came too late even in this respect. They could not say that at the creation of the world the Hegelian philosophy is an impossible thought, since after all they wanted to achieve the same thing with precisely this philosophy. Their imagined improvement of the Hegelian philosophy was thus quite actually, as one says, *moutarde après diner* [mustard after dining], and one would now truly have reason to assume that Hegel would be against his students. One must have been no less inclined to defend him against the insult that was done to him, when others with melodramatic phrases – those sentimental, pietistic phrases capable of arousing only disgust in that powerful thinker – sought to make his philosophy accessible to a portion of the public by forcing ideas taken from elsewhere into a narrow vessel, which always failed to hold them.

The main argument of those defenders of Hegel, who at the same time want to be his reformers, is this: a rational philosophy is something intrinsically necessary and particularly indispensable to the *foundation* of a positive philosophy. Against this, one might now say that the negative as well as the positive is necessary for the *consummation* of philosophy. The positive is necessary not in *that* sense that they imagine it, however, in which the negative founds it; also, it would not be just a continuation of the negative, since in the positive there occurs an *entirely* different *modus progrediendi* [mode of proceeding] as that in the negative, in that, here, even the form of the development is completely reversed. That the negative should found the positive philosophy would only be necessary if the negative philosophy handed over to the positive its object as something that is already cognized, with which it could only then begin its operations. But such is not the case. That which will be the proper object of the positive remains stuck in the preceding philosophy as that which is no longer capable of being known. For in the negative philosophy everything is knowable only to the extent that it has a *prius*, yet this final object does not have a *prius* in the sense of everything else, since here the matter is turned on its head: that which in the purely rational philosophy was the *prius* here becomes the *posterius*. In its culmination, the negative philosophy itself contains the demand for the positive, and the philosophy that is aware of itself, and understands itself completely, certainly *has* the need to posit the positive outside itself. In this sense, one could say that, from its perspective, the negative grounds the positive but could not say that the converse is true, however, that the positive likewise has the need to be grounded by the negative. The foundation that we of course recognize from the *perspective* of the negative (but not of the positive) philosophy is not to be understood as though the end of the negative philosophy would be the beginning of the positive. This is not so. The former hands over its final concept to the positive only as a demand, not as a *principle*. Yet, one will say, then it is nonetheless grounded by the negative to the extent it receives this demand from it. Quite right, but the positive philosophy must, entirely on its own, supply the means to satisfy this demand. If the negative arrives at the demand for the positive, this occurs only in its *own* interest that it completes itself – but not as if the positive had the *need* to receive this demand from it or to be grounded by it. For the positive can begin purely of itself with even the simple words: I want that which is *above* being, that which is not merely being, but rather what is more than this, the *Lord* of Being. Since it begins with a wanting, it is already justified as philosophy, that is, as a science that itself freely determines its object, a philosophy that in itself, and even according to its name, is a wanting. It can therefore also receive this demand *solely* from itself, and, likewise, it can provide itself with its own actual beginning. For this beginning is of the type that requires no foundation: it is that which through itself is the certain and absolute beginning.

Note

1   *Editors' Note.* A reference to Schelling's own earlier philosophy of identity.

Further reading

Many of Schelling's post-1801 works contain substantive narratives of the history of philosophy – and, in particular, the full versions of the last two works excerpted above (Schelling's *Lectures on the History of Modern Philosophy* and *Lectures on the Philosophy of Revelation* [published under the title of *The Grounding of Positive Philosophy*]) should be consulted, as should Bowie's and Matthews's significant introductions to the respective volumes. Other pertinent discussions of Schelling's relation to the history of philosophy include:

Andrew Bowie, *Schelling and Modern European Philosophy* (Routledge, 1993), Chapter VI.
Marcela García, 'How to Think Actuality? Schelling, Aristotle and the Problem of the Pure *Daß*'. *Kabiri* 1 (2018): 37–46.
Stephen Houlgate, 'Schelling's Critique of Hegel's *Science of Logic*.' *The Review of Metaphysics* 53.1 (1999): 99–128.

Bruce Matthews, *Schelling's Organic Form of Philosophy: Life as the Schema of Freedom* (SUNY Press, 2012), Chapter IV.

Sean J. McGrath, 'On the Difference between Schelling and Hegel.' In Joseph Carew and Sean J. McGrath (eds), *Rethinking German Idealism* (Palgrave, 2016), 247–70.

Alessandro Medri, 'The Role of Aristotle in Schelling's Positive Philosophy.' *Review of Metaphysics* 67.4 (2014): 791–810.

Karin Nisenbaum, *For the Love of Metaphysics: Nihilism and the Conflict of Reason from Kant to Rosenzweig* (Oxford University Press, 2018), Chapter IV.

Fred Rush, 'Schelling's Critique of Hegel.' In Lara Ostaric (ed.), *Interpreting Schelling: Critical Essays* (Cambridge University Press, 2014), 216–37.

John Sallis, 'Secluded Nature: The Point of Schelling's Reinscription of the *Timaeus.' Pli* 8 (1999): 71–85.

Part III

The ideal world

9

Freedom

Introduction

It is typically assumed that the Idealists are primarily concerned with the *ideal* world, i.e. the world of the mind and of practical action. Although arguments of varying degrees of success have been made to support this interpretation of Kant, Fichte and Hegel, the same cannot be said for the mature Schelling, who states again and again that the ideal world is only intelligible upon a more fundamental consideration of the *natural* world. Hence, we present Schelling's texts on the ideal world as the third and final part of this volume. This should not, however, suggest that the ideal world is philosophically insignificant in Schelling's eyes. On the contrary, Schelling is deeply concerned with the nature of the mind and the distinct experience of humanity, including the aesthetic, religious and political dimensions of human existence. And at the centre of all ideal or spiritual activity, for Schelling, is *freedom*.

According to Schelling, freedom is not simply *opposed* to determinism or necessity, but is rather a distinctive *kind* of necessity, namely, a necessity that issues from the human individual. In this regard, Schelling is similar to other German Idealists. Yet Schelling insists that there is something overly formalistic about the conception of freedom championed by Kant, Fichte and Hegel. This criticism is clearly articulated in one of Schelling's most celebrated works, the 1809 *Philosophical Investigations into the Essence of Human Freedom*, in which he argues that freedom cannot be reduced to the formal structure of self-determination but that it involves the concrete possibility of determining one's personal character as *good* or *evil*.

This chapter contains the key passage of the *Freedom* essay, which includes Schelling's critique of earlier philosophical accounts of freedom and evil, his own account of what evil *is* (and, less explicitly, what goodness is) and, finally, his account of how the capacity for evil (and, by extension, goodness) distinguishes the human from other forms of life. Schelling's insights about the nature of human freedom are not, however, exhausted in the *Freedom* essay, and this chapter provides some of the context to – and indeed preparation for – the definitive account of freedom Schelling offers in the *Freedom* essay. It therefore includes extracts from: (i) the *Philosophical Letters on Dogmatism and Criticism* (1795), which uses the dialectic of freedom and necessity in Greek tragedy as a springboard to think through, more generally, what it means to be a free subject; (ii) the *System of Transcendental Idealism* (1800), an influential attempt to solve 'the problem of transcendental freedom' which Schelling considers a weakness of all early German Idealist philosophizing; and (iii) the *System of Philosophy in General and the Philosophy of Nature in Particular* (1804), Schelling's most Spinozist moment in ethics, in which freedom and necessity are equated and identified further with acting in accordance with the divine.

Philosophical Letters on Dogmatism and Criticism (1795)*

It has often been asked how Greek reason could bear the contradictions of their tragedy. A mortal – destined to be a criminal, fighting *against* this fate, and yet terribly punished for the crime, which was a work of fate! The *ground* of this contradiction, that which made it bearable, lay deeper than one would seek it. It lay in the strife of human freedom with the power of the objective world, in which, if that power is superior – a fate – the mortal *necessarily* succumbs. And yet, because he did not succumb *without a struggle*, he had to be *punished* for his defeat. That the criminal, who succumbed only to the superior power of fate, was still *punished*, was a recognition of human freedom, an *honour* due to freedom. Greek tragedy honoured human freedom by letting its hero *fight* against the superior power of fate. In order not to leap over the limits of art, it had to let him *succumb*. But in order to remedy this humiliation of human freedom, extorted through art, it also

---

*Translated by G. Anthony Bruno from the Tenth Letter in F.W.J. Schelling, *Sämmtliche Werke* (Stuttgart and Augsberg: Cotta, 1856–1861), Division One, Volume One.

had to let him *atone* for the crime committed by *fate*. As long as he is still *free*, he holds out against the power of fate. As soon as he succumbs, he ceases to be free. Succumbing, he still accuses fate for the loss of his freedom. Even Greek tragedy could not reconcile freedom and ruin. Only a being *deprived* of freedom could succumb to fate. It was a *sublime* thought, to suffer punishment willingly even for an *inevitable* crime, so as to prove one's freedom even by the very loss of this freedom, and to go down with a declaration of free will.

Here, too, as in all instances, Greek art is *standard*. No people has remained more faithful than the Greeks to the character of humanity, even in art.

As long as man remains in the realm of nature, he is *master* of nature, in the most proper sense of the word, just as he can be *master* of himself. He assigns to the objective world its definite limits, over which it may not step. In *representing* the object to himself, in giving it form and consistency, he masters it. He has nothing to fear, for he himself has set limits to it. But as soon as he suspends these limits, as soon as the object is no longer *representable*, that is, as soon as he himself has strayed beyond the boundaries of representation, he finds himself lost. The terrors of the objective world overtake him. He has suspended its bounds; how should he overpower it? He can no longer give form to the limitless object, hovering indeterminately before him; where shall he bind it, where seize it, where set boundaries to its superior power?

As long as Greek art remains within the limits of nature, which people is more natural? Yet, as soon as it leaves those limits, which is more terrible![1] The invisible power is too sublime to be bribed by flattery, its heroes too noble to be saved by cowardice. There is nothing left but – struggle and ruin.

But such a struggle is thinkable only for the purpose of tragic art. It could not become a system of action for that very reason, since such a system would presuppose a race of titans, and, without this presupposition, would doubtless be the great destruction of humanity. If it were really the destiny of our race to be tormented by the terrors of an invisible world, would it not be easier to tremble at the faintest notion of freedom, cowed by the superior power of that world, than to go down fighting? In fact, the horrors of the present world would torment us more than the terrors of the coming world. The man who would obtain his existence in the supersensuous world by begging becomes the pestilence of humanity in this world, raging against himself and others. Power in this world will compensate him for the humiliation in that world. Waking up from the delights of that world, he returns to this one to make it a hell. It would be fortunate were he to be lulled in the arms of that world in order to become a moral *child* in this.

It is the highest interest of philosophy to awaken reason from its slumber, by means of that unchangeable alternative which dogmatism offers to its confessors. If reason can no longer be awakened by this means, then at least one can be sure of having tried the *utmost*. The attempt is all the easier, since that alternative, as soon as one tries to account for the ultimate grounds of one's knowledge, is the simplest, most comprehensible, most primordial antithesis of all philosophizing reason. 'Reason must renounce either an objective intelligible world or a subjective personality; either an absolute object or an absolute subject – freedom of will.' Once this antithesis is definitely established, the interest of reason also demands that the utmost care is taken to ensure that the sophistry of moral indolence does not draw a new veil over it that would deceive humanity. It is a duty to uncover the whole deception, and to show that any attempt at making it bearable to reason can succeed only through new deceptions that keep reason in constant ignorance and hide from it the last abyss into which dogmatism, as soon as it proceeds to the last great question (to be or not to be?), must inevitably fall.

Dogmatism – this is the result of our collective investigation – is irrefutable *theoretically* because the dogmatist leaves the theoretical realm in order to complete his system *practically*. Hence it is practically *refutable* if one realizes *in oneself* an absolutely opposing system. But it is irrefutable for him who is able to realize it *practically*, who can bear the thought of working at his own annihilation, of abolishing every free causality in himself, and of being the modification of an object in whose infinitude he will sooner or later find his own (moral) ruin.

What, therefore, is more important for our age than to no longer cloak these results of dogmatism, to no longer veil them under ingratiating words, under deceptions of indolent reason, but rather to expose them as distinctly, as obviously, as frankly as possible. In this alone lies the last hope for the redemption of humanity, which, after having long borne all the shackles of superstition, may finally find *in itself* what it sought in the objective world, in order to turn from the boundless debauchery of an alien world to its own – from selflessness to selfhood – from the enthusiasm of reason to the freedom of will.

Individual delusions had vanished by themselves. The age seemed to wait only for the ultimate grounds of all those delusions to disappear. It had corrected individual errors; now the last point on which everything hinged was to fall. The disclosure seemed to be expected when others interfered who, at the very moment when human freedom should complete its last work, invented new delusions in order to blunt the bold decision even before the execution. The weapons slipped from the hand, and bold reason, which had destroyed the delusions of the objective world, whined childishly at its own weakness.

Why do you who believe in reason indict it for being unable to work at its own destruction, for being unable to realize an idea whose actuality would destroy everything that you yourself have so laboriously erected? That the others do it, those who have always been at variance with reason and whose interest demands its indictment, does not surprise me. But that you yourself should do it, you who praise reason as a divine faculty in us! – How would you assert *your* reason against that *highest* reason, which obviously could leave only the most absolute passivity for limited, finite reason? Or, if you presuppose the idea of an objective God, how can you speak of *laws* brought forth by reason *from itself*, since autonomy alone can attain to an *absolutely* free being? In vain, you imagine that you can save yourself by presupposing that idea only *practically*. Because you presuppose it only *practically*, it threatens your moral existence all the more certainly with ruin. You indict reason for not knowing of things in themselves, of objects of a supersensuous world. Have you never – not even dimly – suspected that it is not the weakness of your reason, but the absolute freedom in you that makes the intellectual world inaccessible to any *objective* power; that it is not the limitation of your knowledge, but your unlimited freedom that has confined the objects of cognition to the limits of mere appearances?

Note

1   The Greek gods were still within nature. Their power was not *invisible*, nor inaccessible to human freedom. Human wisdom often won a victory over the physical power of the gods. The very bravery of Greek heroes often terrified the Olympians. But for the Greeks the actual *supernatural* begins with *fate*, the invisible power that no natural power can access and over which even the immortal gods have no power. – The more terrible they are in the realm of the supernatural, the more natural they are themselves. The sweeter a people dreams of the supersensuous world, the more despicable and unnatural it is itself.

System of Transcendental Idealism (1800)*

We think it not unnecessary to warn the reader in advance that what we here seek to establish is, not a moral philosophy of any kind, but rather a transcendental deduction of the thinkability and explicability of moral concepts as such; also, that we shall conduct this enquiry into that aspect of moral philosophy which falls within the scope of transcendental philosophy at the highest level of generality. This we shall do by tracing back the whole to a few principles and problems, while leaving the application to particular problems to the reader himself, who in this way may most easily discover, not only whether he has grasped our transcendental idealism, but also, which is the main thing, whether he has equally learned to make use of this type of philosophy as an instrument of enquiry.

First Proposition. Absolute abstraction, i.e. *the beginning of consciousness, is explicable only through a self-determining, or an act of the intelligence upon itself.*

Proof. We presume that the meaning of the term *absolute abstraction* is already understood. It is the act whereby the intelligence raises itself absolutely above the objective. Since this act is an absolute one, it cannot be conditioned by any of the preceding acts, and thereby the concatenation of acts, wherein each succeeding one is necessarily made through that which preceded it, is as it were broken off, and a new sequence begins.

That an act does not follow from a preceding act of the intelligence means that it cannot be explained from the intelligence, insofar as it is this particular one, and insofar as it acts in a particular way; and since it must be explicable as such, it is so only from the absolute in the intelligence itself, from the ultimate principle of all action therein.

That an act is explicable only from the ultimate in the intelligence itself must (since this latter is nothing else but its original duality) mean the same as this: the intelligence must determine itself to this act. Thus the act is admittedly explicable, though not from a determinacy of the intelligence, but from an immediate self-determining.

But an act whereby the intelligence determines itself is an act upon itself. Hence absolute abstraction is explicable only from such an act of the

---

*Translated by Peter Heath from F.W.J. Schelling, *System des transzendentalen Idealismus*, ed. Ruth-Eva Schulz (Hamburg: Felix Meiner, 1957).

intelligence upon itself, and since absolute abstraction is the beginning of all consciousness in time, the first beginning of consciousness is also explicable only from such an act, which is what we had to prove.

First Corollary. This self-determining of the intelligence is called *willing*, in the commonest acceptation of the term. That in every willing there is a determining of self, or at least that it appears to be an act of this sort, is something that everyone can demonstrate for himself through inner intuition; whether this appearance is truthful or deceptive is of no concern to us here. Nor indeed are we speaking of any determinate act of will, in which the concept of an object would already be present, but rather of a transcendental self-determining, or of the original act of freedom. But what this self-determination may be is inexplicable to anyone who does not know of it from his own intuition.

[…]

There is no command, no imperative, of happiness. It is senseless to suppose one, for that which happens of itself, *i.e.* according to a natural law, is in no need of being commanded. This inclination to happiness (as we have called it for brevity, the further development of this concept being the concern of moral theory) is nothing else but the objective activity, directed to something independent of willing, and again become objective to the self; an urge which is therefore as necessary as the consciousness of freedom itself.

Thus the activity, whose immediate object is pure self-determining itself, cannot come to consciousness save in contrast to an activity whose object is something external, to which it is quite blindly directed. As necessarily, therefore, as there is a consciousness of willing, a contrast must exist between what is demanded by the activity which becomes an object through the moral law, and is directed solely to self-determining as such, and what is demanded by the natural inclination. This opposition must be real, that is, both actions – that which is commanded by the pure will become an object to itself, and that which is called for by the natural inclination – must present themselves in consciousness as equally possible. By the laws of nature, therefore, no action could be forthcoming, for they each cancel out the other. So if an action results, and it does so as surely as consciousness persists, this action cannot result from natural law, that is, necessarily, and hence is due solely to free self-determination; it results, that is, from an activity of the self which, in that it wavers in the middle between what we have so far called the subjective and the objective, and determines the one by the other, or the other by the one, without itself being again *determined*, brings forth the conditions under which, as soon as they are given, the action, which is always merely the *determined*, results entirely blindly and seemingly of itself.

This opposition of equally possible actions in consciousness is therefore the condition under which alone the absolute act of will can again become an object to the self itself. But now this *opposition* is precisely what turns the absolute will into *choice*, so that *choice* is the appearance we were seeking of the absolute will – not the original willing itself, but the absolute act of freedom become objectified, with which all consciousness begins.

That a freedom of the will exists is something the ordinary consciousness can be persuaded of only through the act of choice, that is, by the fact that in every willing we are aware of a choice between opposites. But now it is argued that choice is not the absolute will itself, for this, as demonstrated earlier, is directed only to pure self-determining as such; it is, rather, the appearance of the absolute will. So if freedom = choice, then freedom too is not the absolute will itself, but merely the appearance thereof. Thus of the will absolutely regarded it cannot be said that it is either free or not free, since the absolute cannot be thought of as acting from a law that was not already prescribed to it by the inner necessity of its own nature. Since, in the absolute act of will, the self has as its object only self-determining as such, no deviation from this is possible for the will in its absolute sense; if it can be called free at all, it is thus *absolutely* free, since that which is a command for the will that appears is, for the absolute will, a law that proceeds from the necessity of its own nature. But if the absolute is to appear to itself, it must figure to itself as dependent in its objective upon something else, something alien to it. This dependence, however, does not belong to the absolute itself, but merely to its appearance. This alien factor, on which the absolute will is dependent for purposes of appearance, is the natural inclination, in contrast to which alone the law of the pure will is transformed into an imperative. In its absolute sense, however, the will has originally no other object save pure self-determining, that is, itself. So nor can there be any obligation or law for it, *demanding* that it *be* an object to itself. Hence the moral law, and freedom, insofar as it consists in choice, are themselves merely conditions for the appearance of that absolute will, which is constitutive of all consciousness, and to that extent also a condition of the consciousness that becomes an object to itself.

Now by this result, without actually meaning to, we have simultaneously resolved that notable problem which, so far from having been settled, has so far scarcely been properly understood – I mean the problem of transcendental freedom. In this problem it is not a question whether the self is absolute, but whether, insofar as it is *not absolute*, insofar as it is *empirical*, the self is free. But now it appears indeed from our solution, that just precisely insofar as the will is *empirical*, or *appears*, so to that extent it can be called *free* in the transcendental sense. For insofar as it is absolute, the will itself transcends *freedom*, and so far from being subjected to any law, is in fact the source of all law. But insofar as the absolute appears, it can only do so, in order to appear *as* absolute, in the form of choice. This phenomenon of choice can therefore no longer be explained objectively, for it is not anything objective, having reality *per se*, but is rather the absolute subjective, the intuition of the absolute will itself, whereby the latter becomes, *ad infinitum*, an object to itself. But this very appearance of the absolute will is in fact true freedom, or what is commonly understood by the term *freedom*. Now since, in free action, the self intuits itself *ad infinitum* as absolute will and in its highest power is itself nothing else but this intuition of the absolute will, the aforementioned appearance of choice is likewise as certain and indubitable as the self itself. – Conversely, also, the phenomenon of choice can be thought of only as an absolute will, though a recurring revelation of the absolute will within us. It should be noted, however, that if we had sought to infer backwards from the phenomenon of choice to that which lies at the root of it, we should assuredly have had difficulty in ever hitting upon the correct explanation of it, though Kant, in his Doctrine of Law, has at least pointed to the contrast between the absolute will and the faculty of choice, even if he does not yet give the true relationship of the one to the other. And this, then, is a new proof of the superiority of a method which presupposes no phenomenon as *given*, but first becomes acquainted with each of them through its grounds, as though it were totally unknown.

And now by this we also resolve all the doubts which could be drawn, say, from the common assumption that the will is free, concerning the claim put forward earlier, that the objective self which appears to engage in action is in itself merely intuitant. For it is not that *merely* objective self, operating quite mechanically in both action and intuition, and in all free action *determinate*, to which the predicate of freedom is ascribed; it is rather that self which wavers between subjective and objective factors of willing, determining one by the other – viz. *the self-determinant of the second order* – to which alone freedom is and can be attributed, in that the objective self, which in regard to freedom is merely the determined, still continues, in and for itself or regardless of the determinant, to remain what it was before, namely a mere intuiting. Thus if I reflect merely upon the objective activity as such, the self contains only natural necessity; if

I reflect merely upon the subjective activity, it contains only an absolute willing which by nature has no other object save self-determining as such; if I reflect finally upon the activity determinant at once of both subjective and objective, and transcending them both, the self contains choice, and therewith freedom of the will. From these different lines of reflection arise the various systems concerning freedom, of which the first absolutely denies freedom; the second posits it simply in pure reason, *i.e.* in that ideal activity directed immediately to self-determining (by which assumption we are compelled, in all actions determined contrary to reason, to postulate an utterly groundless quiescence of the latter, whereby, however, all freedom of the will is actually done away with); the third view, on the other hand, deduces an activity, extending beyond both the ideal and the objective, as that alone to which freedom can belong.

Nor, indeed, for this absolutely determining self, is there any predetermination, since this applies only to the intuiting, objective self. The fact that for the latter all action, insofar as it passes over into the external world, is predetermined, can no more prejudice the absolutely determinant self, superior as it is to all appearances, than does the fact that everything in nature is predetermined; for in the relation to the free self the objective self is a mere appearance, having no reality in itself, and like nature is merely the external basis of its action. For from the fact that an action is predetermined for appearance, or for the purely intuitant activity, I cannot infer back to its also being so for the free activity, since the two are wholly unequal in dignity; so that while the merely apparent is certainly quite independent of the determinant which does not appear, the latter is equally independent of the former, and each acts and proceeds on its own account, the one from free choice, the other, having once been so determined, entirely in accordance with its own peculiar laws; and this mutual independence of each from the other, despite their consilience, is in fact rendered possible only through a *preestablished harmony*. Here, therefore, is the point of first entry of the predetermined harmony we earlier deduced between the freely determinant and the intuitant, in that each of them is so separated from the other, that no reciprocal influence of one on the other would be possible at all, unless a conformity between them were set up by something lying outside them both. But what this third thing may be, we have absolutely no means of explaining at present, and must be content to have given merely a preliminary indication and presentation of this point, the most elevated of our whole enquiry, and to await its further elucidation by the investigations that are to follow.

We shall merely observe, that if there is even a predetermination for the freely determinant, such as we have certainly maintained in the foregoing, insofar as we have required an original negation of freedom as necessary for individuality, and indirectly for the interaction between intelligences, this predetermination is itself actually thinkable in turn only through an original act of freedom, which admittedly does not attain to consciousness, and concerning which we must refer the reader to Kant's enquiries into original evil.

System of Philosophy in General and the Philosophy of Nature in Particular (1804)*

§ 302 *A free cause can only denote that which, in virtue of the necessity of its essence, without all other determination, acts according to the law of identity.*

Since each effect which does not follow from the essence of a thing follows necessarily from something foreign to it, lying external to it, i.e. the cause for such an effect would be determined through another cause which would in turn be determined through another. It was therefore not free, but compelled. However, the effect which follows purely from the essence of a thing *as such* can follow from this according to no other law than that of absolute identity, since the essence of each thing is, in itself and considered apart from all affections and determinations, absolute substance itself. However, this acts – as has already been initially demonstrated in the general [case] – not so that it determines itself or is produced out of itself, but in virtue of the pure necessity of its nature, according to the law of identity alone. Thus a free effect is (1) only that which follows from the essence of a thing alone and (2) that which follows from this according to the law of identity.

Therefore, the usual concept of a free *self-determination* is discarded; since from the essence of a thing as essence nothing can follow according to the law of causality, even itself; it is not necessary to determine itself, for it is absolute identity. If it determines itself, and in such a way as is assumed

---

*Translated by Lydia Azadpour and Daniel Whistler from F.W.J. Schelling, *Sämmtliche Werke* (Stuttgart and Augsberg: Cotta, 1856–1861), Division One, Volume Six.

in the concept of a free self-determination, [i.e.] such that the determined is equal to it not in itself but only through the act of determining, then it does not act according to the pure law of identity. For this is to be in fact the case, then the determined must harmonize in itself with the determining *in activity*, and this is because both are one and the same thing – as, in God, the affirming corresponds to the affirmed and is equal to it – not because the former is determined through the latter, but because both are one and the same, namely God.

Free self-determination is therefore a contradiction, because, in absolute free activity, the determined and determining are not differentiated into two, but are one and the same, just like the essence of a circle and the property of all points on the periphery being equidistant from the centre are not differentiated into two, but are only one and the same, and the latter flows from the former not through mediation, but immediately, according to absolute identity. Free activity, or, since this is really a pleonasm, *activity* in general, therefore is only true when what follows from a thing follows from its essence in virtue of the law of identity. From which it can be seen that all other freedom except that in the divine is nothing, and God alone can truly be called free. For God's activity is the very essence of God, and vice versa, and nothing can follow from it which does not follow from the idea of that essence alone and is not equal to it.

§ 303 *Only such an activity which follows with absolute necessity from the essence of the soul or, what is the same, from the divine insofar as it is the essence of the soul is an absolutely free activity.*

This follows from the previous two propositions. For all positing, all affirmation, which does not follow from the essence of the soul is = an inadequate idea, therefore = a passion, a not-acting. What is free, however, is, according to the above, only such an activity that follows from the essence of a thing in virtue of the necessity of its nature alone, and therefore, in relation to the soul, only that activity which follows from the essence of the soul, i.e. from God insofar as he is the essence, the ground, the in-itself of the soul.

§ 304 *Absolute cognition and absolute activity are one and the same, merely viewed from different sides.*

For, according to § 300, the essence of the soul is the principle of all absolute cognition, or the essence of the soul is rather itself only this absolute cognition, and nothing else. Only in absolute cognition is thus the soul truly free. However, all truly free activity is nothing but an absolute affirmation, i.e. an affirmation which follows from the essence of the soul just as it follows from this essence that I eternally cognize A as = A.

The difference made between activity and cognition is a mere difference of potency, i.e. inessential.

Just as I cognize and affirm in absolute knowledge or in absolute contemplation the finite immediately as something infinite, so *activity* is conversely an affirmation of the infinite as something finite, of the ideal as something real, which must flow with the same necessity from the essence of the soul as the knowledge that the finite, the real is = the ideal.

The essence of the soul is one. There are no faculties which somehow reside in the soul, neither a particular faculty of cognition nor a particular faculty of will, as false psychological abstraction claims; rather, there is only one essence, only one in-itself of the soul, in which everything that abstraction separates is one and the same; and only what originates from this in-itself of the soul, whether in knowledge or in activity, is absolute, is true, is at once free and necessary.

The abstraction that has perverted science – as always, I call abstraction the separation of things from totality – the abstraction therefore, from which all error in science, all one-sided and false systems were born, is also the death of all true activity and the source of most errors about the nature of activity.

The idea that there is one thing that cognizes in us and another which acts has first and foremost led to the idea that there is a freedom independent of necessity. The separation of activity from cognition is the fall of freedom from necessity itself, as if the former could exist for itself. If truthfulness (the ground of all virtue) is the unity of activity and cognition, then the separation of the two is the first lie, and our contemporary morality is only this continual lie – that is, believing in, requiring and praising a virtue which does not have its source in the essence of human nature and does not flow from the necessity of the same divine principle from which science flows, or, conversely, it is belief in a cognition which is not immediately as such also activity. (In this whole presentation, I must presuppose that *you* hold primarily to the proofs of our claims alone without falling into error through objections which can appear contrary to them.)

§ 305 *In the soul as such there is no freedom; rather, only the divine is truly free, as well as the essence of the soul insofar as it is divine.* (However, in this sense there is also no individual.) – To ascribe freedom to the human soul is to misleadingly suggest that one ascribes a particular will as an individual faculty to it, which is a mere product of the imagination. In the soul as such we truly find nothing but individual acts of willing; however, external to these individual acts of willing, there is as little of a particular *will* as there is a particular extension external to individual extended things or a particular corporeality outside of corporeal things. Individual acts of willing are necessarily determined each time in the soul as soul and are therefore not free, not absolute. This is to be perceived quite generally.

That is, the soul (as such) is to be understood as a mode of infinite affirmation which relates to a particular thing, so that what holds for it also holds for the thing itself. Thus, just as in every moment the latter is determined to *be* what it is, or to move in the way that it *moves*, so too [the same holds] necessarily for the soul as soul. In the soul as such, there is therefore no freedom of willing.

Outside of all determinability through causal connection, there lies only what is the absolute prius of all time – the eternal, the essence of the soul. However, the essence of the soul is divine; thus only the divine as the essence of the soul is absolutely free; man is not free considered for himself alone, but, considered according to himself and his individual life, he falls prey to necessity and fate to the extent that he separates *his* freedom, as his, from the divine. Man is not free for himself; only activity which stems from God is free, in the same way as only a similar kind of knowledge is true.

[...]

§ 307 *Freedom which is ascribed to the individual as individual is no freedom but a mere tendency to be absolutely in itself what in itself is nothing and the unfolding of which follows with necessity as immediate fate.* – Most think of freedom as nothing but choice, i.e. a capacity to do what one likes; even virtue is only choice for them, and they value this freedom as the highest good of mankind. Yet, that this choice is no freedom could be taught by mere experience. For those who mostly believe themselves to act according to their likes, they are mostly driven to act by means of affections of desire, hate and passion in general. Just as certainly, no one is virtuous who is not capable of a divine necessity which takes possession of him.

The above principle, which we have to explain and prove, follows from the fact that everything in infinite substance has a double life, a life in substance and a life in itself. This life in itself becomes equivalent to that in substance in reason, and the essence of reason is thus both mostly in itself and at the same time absolutely in the absolute. In other words: *in [reason] the necessity of natural things becomes equivalent to absolute freedom.* However, this freedom is, as is self-evident from the above viewpoint, nothing in separation from necessity. Now, it is indeed through the life in the absolute, i.e. through necessity, that there is the possibility to be in itself; however, the actuality of this being-in-itself is, when separated from its *possibility* (necessity), immediately nothing, as all actuality separated from its possibility is nothing in itself and is no true actuality. The immediate fate of freedom as choice, as being-in-itself, is therefore implicated in nothingness and finitude, in that necessity which can be to the existent only a contingent existence, i.e. in the empirical.

[...]

§ 308 *All truly free, i.e. divine, activity is of itself in harmony with necessity.* – For truly free activity is solely that which follows from the essence of the soul just like adequate ideas follow from it, i.e. such an activity which as such is simultaneously necessary.

In God there is absolute harmony of necessity and freedom, God is absolutely free, since everything follows from the idea of his essence without any determination internal or external to him. God is not moved by an imperative through an intention, through the good which he presupposes: he is absolutely good in virtue of the nature of his essence. God's activity is thus, as absolutely free, simultaneously absolutely necessary.

In ourselves, there lies that harmony of necessity and freedom – that is, it lies at the source of adequate ideas in the eternity of the soul. It is necessary that consciousness of this point continually escapes men when they are acting, since their activity, their striving after something external rests on the determinate separation of freedom from necessity. This is because [men] fancy themselves to be free, whereas only an eternal and absolute necessity acts in them. They do not become aware that the point for which they are ultimately striving – that is, to posit their freedom in harmony with necessity – necessarily escapes them in their activity, that it does not lie *before* them, but *behind* them, and that they must first stand still in order to find it. Most, however, never come to a standstill, never arrive at the divine prudence by means of which man incorporates the infinite into himself and grounds his life in the eternal. When someone has attained this point, there too is happiness and true rest; heaven arches forth for him as the clear image of totality, and like the North Star for the sailor through the groundless deep, so the eternal identity of this point shines for him through all the storms and changes of life. It comforts us, it forever raises us above all empty longing, fear and hope, to know that we do not act, but that a divine necessity acts in us – a necessity by which we are brought to our goal and with which nothing that follows from absolute freedom can stand in contradiction; since it is itself this absolute freedom.

Nothing in us which follows from adequate ideas, from the cognition of God, can resist this necessity or be annihilated by it, and with difficulty is a man great through deeds or thoughts if he does not cognize this necessity and, in this sense, become a fatalist. That is, it is impossible that either mere empirical lawfulness which considers man's own activities from the moment they pass over into the external world or freedom of the will is enough for such a man. [...]

The only true system for activity is the unconditional belief – i.e. not an indubitable truth, but fast confidence – in absolute necessity which acts in *everything* (and is at the same time free). In this alone [is] the holiness that mankind requires.

[...]

§ 311 *There is no absolute morality in the sense that it could be considered as a matter of reward or work of individual freedom.*

That is, if morality were claimed to be a reward for man, then it would have to be a matter of his choice, of acting rightly or not and choice is also all individual freedom. But as long as man has a choice about right deeds or not, he cannot be called moral in the absolute sense; his activity might well be right, but he is not himself moral in the absolute sense. He is moral in this sense – that is, virtuous – only by means of an absolute binding of his will, as a result of which doing the opposite of right is impossible for him. However, this binding cannot be of a finite, nor of a psychological kind; hence, it cannot come from the soul, not from individual freedom, but, rather, from what is above the soul, from what overpowers it with divine force, from the absolute which is its essence.

[...]

§ 314 *For he who is in identity with God, there is as little imperative as there is reward, but he acts according to the inner necessity of his nature. –* Since (1) for God there is no imperative (imperative is announced through an ought, i.e. it presupposes the possibility of deviation from it, both the concept of good and of evil); therefore there is no [imperative] for him who is in identity with God. (2) God is to be considered as one and the same, both absolute freedom and absolute necessity in a fully equal way: where therefore there is absolute freedom, there is also absolute necessity; therefore, that person who is in identity with God equally acts absolutely freely and absolutely necessarily [...]

Remark. The doctrine that mankind should act morally from mere respect for the moral imperative would be wholly correct, if it were in general correct that the highest mankind could attain was *morality*. Rather, the higher goal of mankind's striving is that what is right transforms itself into a *law* of his nature, and that he fulfils his duty not from mere respect, but from love and the force of the inner necessity of his nature. Without the immediate enjoyment of morality as bliss, man would only exist morally from menial subjection under the law, without love, pleasure or beauty.

Philosophical Investigations into the Essence of Human Freedom and Related Matters (1809)*

Here, then, once and for all our definite opinion about Spinozism! This system is not fatalism because it lets things be conceived in God; for as we have shown, pantheism does not make formal freedom, at least, impossible. Spinoza must then be a fatalist for another reason, entirely independent of this. The error of his system is by no means due to the fact that he posits all *things in God*, but to the fact that they are *things* – to the abstract conception of the world and its creatures, indeed of eternal Substance itself, which is also a thing for him. Thus his arguments against freedom are altogether deterministic, and in no way pantheistic. He treats the will, too, as a thing, and then proves, very naturally, that in every case of its operation it must be determined by some other thing, which in turn is determined by another, and so forth endlessly. Hence the lifelessness of his system, the harshness of its form, the bareness of its concepts and expressions, the relentless austerity of its definitions; this admirably in accord with the abstract outlook. Thence also, quite consistently, his mechanistic view of nature. Or can one doubt that even a dynamic conception of nature must necessarily bring about an essential change in the basic views of Spinozism? If the doctrine that all things are conceived in God is the basis of the entire system, it must at least first be vitalized and cut loose from abstractness before it can become the principle of a system of reason. [...] Spinozism in its rigidity could be regarded like Pygmalion's statue, needing to be given a soul through the warm breath of love: but this comparison is imperfect, as Spinozism more closely resembles a work of art which has been sketched only in its most general outlines and in which, if it were endowed with a soul, one would still notice how many

---

*Translated by James Guttmann from F.W.J. Schelling, *Sämmtliche Werke* (Stuttgart and Augsberg: Cotta, 1856–1861), Division One, Volume Seven.

features were lacking or incomplete. It could more readily be compared to the most ancient likenesses of the divinities, which seemed all the more mysterious the fewer the features of individual lifelikeness apparent in them. In a word, it is a onesidedly realistic system, and although this expression sounds less damning than 'pantheism', it nevertheless describes the peculiar nature of this system far more correctly, and is, moreover, not now used for the first time. It would be tedious to repeat the many explanations concerning this point which are to be found in the author's[1] earliest writings. The expressed intention of his efforts was a mutual interpenetration of realism and idealism. Spinoza's fundamental concept, spiritualized by the principle of idealism (and changed at one essential point) was given a vital basis through the more elevated way of regarding nature, and through the recognized unity of what is dynamic with what is spiritual and emotional. From this there developed a philosophy of nature, which as a mere physics could indeed stand by itself, but which was always regarded, with respect to the whole of philosophy, as merely one of its parts (that is, its real part) and which would permit of being raised into a genuine system of reason only by first being completed by an ideal part wherein freedom is sovereign. In this freedom, it was declared, the final intensifying act was to be found through which the whole of nature found its transfiguration in feeling, in intelligence and, ultimately, in will. – In the final and highest instance there is no other Being than Will. Will is primordial Being, and all predicates apply to it alone – groundlessness, eternity, independence of time, self-affirmation! All philosophy strives only to find this highest expression.

It is to this point that Idealism has raised philosophy, up to our time; and only at this point are we really able to take up the investigation of our subject, since it could by no means be our purpose to take account of all those difficulties which can be raised (and have already been raised) against the concept of freedom on the basis of the one-sidedly realistic or dogmatic system. However, high as we have been placed in this respect by Idealism, and certain as it is that we owe to it the first formally perfect concept of freedom, Idealism itself is, after all, nothing less than a finished system. And as soon as we seek to enter into the doctrine of freedom in greater detail and exactitude, it nonetheless leaves us helpless. As regards systematic completeness, we observe that in an idealism which had been formulated into a system, it would by no means suffice to declare that 'Activity, life and freedom are alone true reality.' For even Fichte's idealism, subjective idealism, (which does not understand itself) can go this far. Rather it is required that the reverse be proved too – that all reality (nature, the world of things) is based upon activity, life and freedom, or – in the Fichtean expression – that not only is the Ego all, but on the other hand, all is Ego. The thought of making freedom the sum and substance of philosophy has emancipated the human spirit in all its relationships, and not only with respect to itself and has given to science in all its parts a more powerful reorientation than any earlier revolution. The idealistic conception is the true initiation into higher philosophy in our time and especially into a higher realism. If only those who sit in judgement on this realism, or appropriate it, would reflect that freedom is its most essential presupposition, in what a different light would they then regard and comprehend it! Only he who has tasted freedom can feel the desire to make over everything in its image, to spread it throughout the whole universe. Whoever does not approach philosophy in this way, merely follows others and copies what they do without feeling why they do it. But it will always remain strange that Kant, after first distinguishing the things-in-themselves from appearances only negatively, as being independent of time, and later, in the metaphysical explications of his *Critique of Practical Reason,* treated independence-of-time and freedom as correlative concepts, did not proceed to the thought of transferring this only possible positive conception of *per-se-ity* [the property of existing through itself] to things. By doing this he would immediately have raised himself to a higher standpoint, above the negativity which is characteristic of his theoretical philosophy. But, on the other hand, if freedom is the positive conception of *per-se-ity* as such, then the investigation of human freedom is again thrown back into generality, since intelligibility, upon which freedom alone was based, is then also the essence of things-in-themselves. Mere idealism is therefore not adequate to show the specific differentia, *i.e.* the precise distinctiveness of human freedom. Similarly, it would be a mistake to believe that pantheism has been put aside and destroyed by idealism; an opinion which could only issue from confusing it with one-sided realism. For it is immaterial to pantheism, as such, whether many individual things are conceived in an absolute substance or many individual wills are conceived in one primal will. In the first case it would be realistic, in the second, idealistic; but its fundamental concept remains the same. From this very fact it can be seen in advance, that the most profound difficulties which lie in the concept of freedom will be as little solvable through idealism, taken in itself, as through any other incomplete system. For idealism supplies only the most general conception of freedom, and a merely formal one. But the real and vital conception of freedom is that it is a possibility of good and evil.

This is the point of profoundest difficulty in the whole doctrine of freedom, which has always been felt and which applies not only to this or that system, but, more or less, to all: To be sure it applies most strikingly to the concept of immanence, for either real evil is admitted, in which case it is unavoidable to include evil itself in infinite substance or in the primal will, and thus totally disrupt the conception of an all-perfect Being; or the reality of evil must in some way or other be denied, in which case the real conception of freedom disappears at the same time. But the difficulty is no slighter if even the faintest connection is assumed between God and the world-order. For even if this is limited to a mere *concursus,* so-called, or to that necessary cooperation of God in the activity of his creatures (which must be assumed because of the essential dependence of the latter upon God, even if freedom is otherwise asserted) then God undeniably appears as co-author of evil. For permitting an entirely dependent being to do evil is, after all, not much better than cooperating with it in causing evil. Or, again, the reality of evil must be denied in some way or other. The proposition that all that is positive in creatures comes from God, must be asserted in this System too. Now if it is assumed that there is something positive in evil, then this positive also comes from God. It may be objected to this, that what is positive in evil, insofar as it is positive, is good. Evil does not disappear in this way any more than it is explained. For if that element in evil which has *being* is good, whence, then, comes that *wherein* it has its being, the *basis* which really constitutes the evil? An assertion quite different from the foregoing (though often, and recently, confused with it) is the statement that in evil there is nothing at all positive, or – otherwise expressed – that evil does not exist at all (not even in connection with or through something else which is positive) but that all actions are more or less positive, and that the difference between them is a mere plus or minus of perfection. In this view no antithesis is established, and all evil disappears entirely. This would be the second possible position with regard to the statement that everything positive has its source in God. Then the power manifest in evil would indeed be relatively less perfect than the power in goodness, but in itself or without regard to this comparison it would itself be perfect and, like all perfection, would thus have to be derived from God. That which we call evil is only a lesser degree of perfection, which seems a defect only in our comparison but is none in nature. It cannot be denied that this is Spinoza's real opinion. Someone might try to escape from this dilemma by answering: That which is positive, derived from God, is freedom, which in itself is indifferent to good and evil. However, if he does not think of this indifference in a merely negative way but as a vital, positive power for good and evil, then it cannot be understood how a power for evil can come from God who is regarded as utter goodness. As may be said in passing, it becomes clear in this connection, that if freedom really is what it must be in consequence of this conception (and it undoubtedly is) then the above attempt to deduce freedom from God is probably not correct either. For if freedom is a power for evil it must have a root independent of God. Compelled by this argument one may be tempted to throw oneself into the arms of dualism. However, if this system is really thought of as the doctrine of two absolutely different and mutually independent principles, it is only a system of self-destruction and the despair of reason. But if the radical principle of evil is thought of as in any sense dependent on the good, then the whole difficulty of the derivation of evil from goodness is, to be sure, concentrated on a single being, but the difficulty is rather increased than diminished in this way.

[...]

Every being which has arisen in nature [...] contains a double principle which, however, is at bottom one and the same regarded from the two possible aspects. The first principle is the one by which they are separated from God or wherein they exist in the mere basis of things. But as an original unity exists between that which is in the basis, and what is prefigured in understanding, the second principle, which by its own nature is dark, is at the same time the very one which is revealed in light, and the two are one in every natural object, though only to a certain extent. For the process of creation consists only in an inner transmutation, or revelation in light of what was originally the principle of darkness since understanding or the light which occurs in nature is actually only searching in the depths for that light which is akin to it and is turned inward. The principle of darkness, insofar as it was drawn from the depths and is dark, is the self-will of creatures, but self-will, insofar as it has not yet risen to complete unity with light, as the principle of understanding cannot grasp it and is mere craving or desire, that is blind will. This self-will of creatures stands opposed to reason as universal will, and the latter makes use of the former and subordinates it to itself as a mere tool. But this will becomes one whole with the primal will or reason when, in the progressive transformation and division of all forces, there is totally revealed in light the inmost and deepest point of original darkness, in One Being. The will of this One Being, to the extent to which it is individual, is also a particular will, though in itself or as the centre of all other particular wills it is one with the primal will or reason. This elevation of the most abysmal centre into light, occurs in no creatures visible to us except in man.

In man there exists the whole power of the principle of darkness and, in him too, the whole force of light. In him there are both centres – the deepest pit and the highest heaven. Man's will is the seed – concealed in eternal longing – of God, present as yet only in the depths, – the divine light of life locked in the deeps which God divined when he determined to will nature. Only in him (in man) did God love the world, – and it was this very image of God which was grasped in its centre by longing when it opposed itself to light. By reason of the fact that man takes his rise from the depths (that he is a creature) he contains a principle relatively independent of God. But just because this very principle is transfigured in light – without therefore ceasing to be basically dark – something higher, the *spirit*, arises in man. For the eternal spirit pronounces unity, or the Word, in nature. But the (real) Word, pronounced, exists only in the unity of light and darkness (vowel and consonant). Now these two principles do indeed exist in all things, but without complete consonance because of the inadequacy of that which has been raised from the depths. Only in man, then, is the Word completely articulate, which in all other creatures was held back and left unfinished. But in the articulate word the spirit reveals itself, that is God as existing, in act. Now inasmuch as the soul is the living identity of both principles, it is spirit; and spirit is in God. If, now, the identity of both principles were just as indissoluble in man as in God, then there would be no difference – that is, God as spirit would not be revealed. Therefore that unity which is indissoluble in God must be dissoluble in man – and this constitutes the possibility of good and evil.

We expressly say – 'the possibility of evil,' and for the present seek only to make comprehensible the divisibility of the principles. The reality of evil is the subject matter of quite another inquiry. That principle which rises up from the depths of nature and by which man is divided from God, is the selfhood in him; but by reason of its unity with the ideal principle, this becomes *spirit*. Selfhood *as such*, is spirit; or man as an egocentric, particularized being (divorced from God) is spirit – the very relation [to God] constitutes personality. But by reason of the fact that selfhood is spirit, it is at the same time raised from the level of the creature to a higher level. It is will beholding itself in complete freedom, no longer the tool of the universal will operating in nature, but above and outside all nature. Spirit stands above light as in nature it raises itself above the unity of light and the principle of darkness. Thus, by being spirit, selfhood is free from both principles. However this selfhood, or self-will, only becomes spirit (and, accordingly, only becomes free and superior to nature) by being really transformed into the primal will (light), so that it indeed remains (as self-will) in the depths (because there must always be a basis) – just as in the transparent body the material which has been raised to identity with light does not therefore cease to be matter, the principle of darkness, except as being the bearer and, so to speak, the container of the higher principle of light. But selfhood can separate itself from light since it possesses spirit (because this is sovereign over light and darkness) – provided, indeed, it is not the spirit of eternal love itself. Self-will may seek to be, as a particular will, that which it is only in its identity with the universal will. It may seek to be at the periphery that which it is only insofar as it remains at the centre (just as the quiet will in the calm depths of nature is also universal will precisely because it stays in the depths). It may seek to be free as a creature, (for the will of creatures is, to be sure, beyond the depths, but in that case it is also a mere particular will, not free but restricted). Thus there takes place in man's will a division of his spiritualized selfhood from the light (as the spirit stands above light) – that is, a dissolution of the principles which in God are indissoluble. If, on the contrary, man's self-will remains in the depths as the central will, so that the divine relation of the principles persists (as, for example, the will in the centre of nature never exalts itself above light but remains below it as the basis in the depths), and if the spirit of love rules [in the will] in place of the spirit of dissension which wishes to divorce its own principle from the general principle, then the will exists in divine manner and condition. But that evil is this very exaltation of self-will is made clear from the following. Will, which deserts its supernatural status in order to make itself as general will also particular and creature will, at one and the same time, strives to reverse the relation of the principles, to exalt the basis above the cause, and to use that spirit which it received only for the centre, outside the centre and against the creature, which leads to disorganization within itself and outside itself. Man's will may be regarded as a nexus of living forces; as long as it abides in its unity with the universal will these forces remain in their divine measure and balance. But hardly does self-will move from the centre which is its station, than the nexus of forces is also dissolved; in its place a merely particular will rules which can no longer unite the forces among themselves as before, but must therefore strive to form or compose a special and peculiar life out of the now separate forces, an insurgent host of desires and passions – since every individual force is also an obsession and passion. This is possible inasmuch as the first nexus of forces, the foundation of nature, persists even in evil. As a genuine life could only exist in the original relationship, there thus arises a life which is indeed a life, but is false, a life of lies, a growth of disquiet and corruption. The most appropriate comparison is here offered by disease, which is the true counterpart of evil and sin, as it constitutes that disorder which entered nature through a misuse of freedom. Disease of the whole organism can never exist without the hidden forces of the depths being unloosed; it occurs when the irritable principle which ought to rule as the innermost tie of forces in the quiet deep, activates itself, or when Archaos is provoked to desert his quiet residence at the centre of things and steps forth into the surroundings. So, on the other hand, all radical cure consists in the reestablishement of the relation of the periphery to the centre, and the transition from disease to health can really only take place through its opposite, that is through the restoration of separate and individual life to the inner light of the being, whence there recurs the division (crisis). Local disease also occurs only because some entity whose freedom or life exists only so that it may remain in the whole, strives to exist for itself. Disease is indeed nothing essential and is actually only an illusion of life and the mere meteoric appearance of it – a swaying between being and non-being – but nonetheless announces itself in feeling as something very real. Just so is the case of evil.

In recent times this only correct conception of evil as consisting of a positive perversion or reversal of the principles, has been advanced especially by Franz Baader who has expounded it through profound physical analogies, especially those of disease. All other explanations of evil leave the understanding and moral consciousness alike dissatisfied. They all rest at bottom on the denial of evil as a positive antithesis, and its reduction to the so-called *malum metaphysicum* [metaphysical evil] or the negative concept of the imperfection of the creature. It was impossible, says Leibniz, that God should grant man all perfection without making himself God; the same applies to created beings in general; and on this account it was necessary to bring about various grades of perfection and all sorts of limitation thereof. If one asks what is the source of evil, the answer is: in the ideal nature of the creature, insofar as it is dependent on the eternal verities contained in divine reason but not on God's will. The realm of eternal verities is the ideal cause of evil and good, and must be put in the place of the 'matter' of the ancients. There are, to be sure, he says in another place, two principles, but both exist in God and they are reason and will. Reason yields the principle of evil, though it does not thereby itself become evil; for it presents all natures as they are in accordance with the eternal verities; it contains in itself the basis for the admission of evil, whereas will is directed only towards the good. This sole possibility was not of God's making, since reason is not its own cause. This distinction of reason and will as two principles in God, by means of which the original possibility of evil is made independent of divine will, is in accord with the suggestive thought of this man, [Leibniz]; and the conception of reason (divine wisdom) as something to which God himself is related passively rather than actively, points to something deeper. Nevertheless the evil which could be derived from this exclusively ideal basis turns out to be something merely passive – limitation, insufficiency, deprivation – concepts which are completely at odds with the actual nature of evil. For the mere consideration of the fact that man, the most perfect of all visible creatures, is alone capable of evil, shows that this basis can by no means consist of insufficiency or deprivation. According to the Christian view, the devil was not the most limited but rather the least limited of creatures.[2] Imperfection, in the general metaphysical sense, is not the common character of evil, as it often manifests itself united with an excellence of individual powers which must less frequently accompanies the good. The basis of evil must therefore not only be founded on something inherently positive, but rather on the highest positive being which nature contains. This, indeed, is the case in accordance with our views since it lies in the manifested centre or primal will of the first basis. Leibniz tries in every way to make comprehensible how evil could arise from a natural insufficiency. The will, he says, strives towards the good in general, and must seek perfection whose highest measure is in God; but if it remains entangled in the voluptuousness of the senses with a loss of higher value, this very lack of further effort is the privation which constitutes evil. Otherwise, he suggests, evil requires a special principle as little as do cold or darkness. That which is affirmative in evil is only incidental, like force and efficacy in cold; freezing water cracks the strongest container, and cold nevertheless actually consists in a decrease of motion. However since deprivation is nothing in itself and, in order even to become noticeable, requires something positive in which it becomes apparent, the difficulty now occurs of explaining the positive factor which must after all be assumed in evil. As Leibniz can only derive this from God, he finds himself obliged to make God the cause of that which is material in sin, and to ascribe only its formal aspect to the original limitation of the creature. He seeks to explicate this relationship by means of the conception which Kepler discovered, of the natural inertia of matter. This, he says, is the complete picture of an original limitation of the creature, which precedes all activity. If two different bodies of unequal mass are moved by the same impulse with unequal velocities, then the case of the slowness of the motion of the one is not in the impulse but in the peculiar tendency to inertia innate in the matter, that is, in the inner limitation or imperfection of matter. But in this connection it should be remarked that inertia itself cannot be thought of as a mere deprivation, but that it is indeed something positive, namely an expression of the inner selfhood of the body, the force through which it seeks to maintain itself in its independence. We do not deny that metaphysical finitude can be made comprehensible in this way, but we do deny that finitude in itself is evil.[3]

This type of explanation is after all drawn from that lifeless conception of the positive, in accordance with which only deprivation can be contrasted with it. There is, however, an intermediate concept which provides a real contrast to it and which is far removed from the concept of mere negation. This is derived from the relationship of the whole to the individual, of unity to multiplicity, or however one wishes to express it. The positive is always the whole or unity; that which is contrasted with it is division of the whole, discord, ataxia of forces. The identical elements which existed in the unified whole are in the divided whole; the matter in both is the same – from this aspect evil is no more limited or worse than good; but the formal aspect of the two is totally different and it is this very form which comes from the essence or positive factor itself. Thus there must necessarily be a positive character in evil as in the good, but in the former it is one opposed to the good, which transforms its normal temperature into distemper. It is impossible for dogmatic philosophy to recognize this character since it has no conception of personality, that is of selfhood elevated to spirituality, but only an abstract concept of the infinite and the finite. Thus if someone wished to reply that discord is precisely a privation, namely a deprivation of unity, nevertheless this concept would be insufficient even if the general conception of deprivation contained the concept of the dissolution or division of unity. For the division of forces is not in itself discord but the false unity of forces which can only be called a division in relation to true unity. If unity is completely dissolved, then conflict is thereby dissolved too. The end of disease is death, and no single tone can make a discord by itself. But just to explain this false unity requires something positive which must accordingly and of necessity be assumed in evil, but which will remain inexplicable as long as a root of freedom is not recognized in the independent basis of nature.

The Platonic view, insofar as we can judge it, will best be discussed in considering the question of the actuality of evil. The notions of our age, which takes a far easier view of this point and carries its humanitarianism to the extent of denying evil, have not even the slightest connection with such ideas. According to current views the sole basis of evil lies in the world of the senses or in animality or the earthly principle, since they do not contrast Heaven with Hell, as would be proper, but with Earth. This notion is the natural outcome of the doctrine in accordance with which freedom consists in the mere mastery of the intelligent principle over the desires and inclinations of the senses, and the good is derived from pure reason. Accordingly it is obvious that evil can have no freedom (since the inclinations of the senses are here sovereign) or – to speak more correctly – evil is completely lost sight of. For the feebleness and inefficacy of the reasonable principle can indeed be a basis for the lack of good and virtuous actions, but it cannot be a basis for actions that are positively bad as opposed to virtue. But if it is granted that passion or a passive attitude to external impressions involves evil actions with a kind of necessity, then, in performing them, man himself would be only passive. That is, evil would have no meaning from the point of view of the agent (i.e. subjectively) and as whatever follows from natural determination, objectively considered too, cannot be evil, evil would have no meaning at all. But to say that the reasonable principle is ineffective in evil, explains nothing either. For why does it not exert its power? If it prefers to be ineffective, then the basis of evil is in this preference and not in the world of the senses. Or if it can in no way conquer the opposing power of the latter, then we have here mere feebleness and insufficiency but nowhere evil. Thus, in accordance with this explanation there is but one will (if, indeed, it can be so called) and no dual will. And the adherents of this view could in this regard be called Monotheletes, for since the names of Arian, etc., have happily been introduced into philosophic criticism we can also take this name from Church History, though in a different sense. But just as it is nowise the intelligent principle, or the principle of life, in itself which operates in the good, but only this principle combined with selfhood, that is, elevated to spirit; in the same way evil is not derived from the principle of finitude in itself, but only from the dark or selfish principle which has been brought into intimacy with the centre. And just as there is an ardour for the good, there is also an enthusiasm for evil. That dark principle is indeed effective in animals too, as in every other natural being; but in them it has not yet been born to light as in man, it is not *spirit* and understanding but blind passion and desire; in short no degeneration, no division of principles is possible here where there is as yet no absolute or personal unity. In animal instinct the unconscious and the conscious are united only in a specific and definite fashion which for this very reason is unalterable. For because of this, because they are only relative expressions of unity, they are subject to it, and the force which operates in the depths receives the unity of the principles which is appropriate to it in ever the same measure. Animals can never escape from unity, whereas man can deliberately cut the eternal nexus of forces. Wherefore Franz Baader is right in saying that it would be desirable if the rottenness in man could only go as far as animality; but unfortunately man can only stand above or beneath animals.

Notes

1   *Editors' Note.* That is, Schelling's.
2   In this connection it is striking that the scholastics were not the first to designate evil as a mere privation, but that a number of the earlier Church Fathers, especially Augustine, did so. [...]
3   For the same reason every other explanation of finitude, for instance by the concept of relations, must be inadequate as an explanation of evil. Evil is not derived from finitude in itself, but from finitude which has been exalted to independent being.

Further reading

The concept of freedom appears throughout Schelling's writings, and not only in his discussion of the human individual; he also attends to forms of freedom that can be seen in natural and divine activity. It is therefore important to read Schelling's discussion of human freedom in light of his more general metaphysical reflections, many of which can be found in Part One of this book. Beyond this volume, the first place one should turn for his account of human freedom is the *Treatise Explicatory of the Idealism in the Science of Knowledge* (§§ 3-4), translated by Thomas Pfau in *Idealism and the Endgame of Theory*. The following elucidate Schelling's understanding of human freedom:

Charlotte Alderwick, 'Atemporal Essence and Existential Freedom in Schelling.' *British Journal for the History of Philosophy* 23.1 (2015): 115–37.

Joseph A. Bracken, 'Freedom and Causality in the Philosophy of Schelling.' *The New Scholasticism* 50.2 (1976): 164–82.

Peter Dews, *The Idea of Evil* (Wiley-Blackwell, 2013), Chapter 2.

Sebastian Gardner, 'The Metaphysics of Human Freedom: From Kant's Transcendental Idealism to Schelling's Freiheitsschrift.' *British Journal for the History of Philosophy* 25.1 (2017): 133–56.

Michelle Kosch, *Freedom and Reason in Kant, Schelling, and Kierkegaard* (Oxford University Press, 2006), Chapters 3–4.

Werner Marx, *The Philosophy of F.W.J. Schelling: History, System, and Freedom*, translated by Thomas Nenon (Indiana University Press, 1984).

Frank Schalow, 'The Dialectic of Human Freedom: Schelling on Love and Evil.' *Philosophy and Theology* 8.3 (1994): 213–30.

Alan White, *Schelling: An Introduction to the System of Freedom* (Yale University Press, 1983).

Slavoj Žižek, *The Abyss of Freedom* (University of Michigan Press, 1997).

10

Art and mythology

Introduction

In 1796 or thereabouts, Schelling – then at university in Tübingen – sat down with his former roommates, Hegel and Hölderlin, and penned a two-page prospectus that has come to be known as 'The Oldest System Programme of German Idealism'. It reads, in part:

> I am convinced that the highest act of reason, which, in that it comprises all ideas, is an aesthetic act, and that *truth and goodness* are united like sisters *only in beauty* – The philosopher must possess just as much aesthetic power as the poet. […] Poetry thereby obtains a higher dignity; it becomes again in the end what it was in the beginning – *teacher* of *(history) the human race.* […] Monotheism of reason and the heart, polytheism of the imagination and art, that is what we need! First I will speak about an idea here, which as far as I know, has never occurred to anyone's mind – we must have a new mythology; this mythology must, however, stand in the service of ideas, it must become a mythology of *reason.* Until we make ideas aesthetic, i.e., mythological, they hold no interest for the people.[1]

What is here programmatically sketched recurs in more nuanced ways throughout Schelling's reflections on philosophy, art and mythology. On the one hand, the earlier Schelling draws close to romanticism in his insistence on art, literature and myth as capable of expressing fundamental truths that substantially aid the philosophical endeavour. On the other hand, the later Schelling – from his 1816 address on *The Deities of Samothrace* through to his final lectures on the philosophy of mythology – discerned in myths not some allegorical representation of an esoteric truth, but the literal structure of the emergence of consciousness and, indeed, that of being itself.

This chapter charts Schelling's trajectory from his interest in the artistic form of mythology to his concern with the mythological content of art. It begins with (i) his clearest account of the significance of artistic creation for the philosophical system found at the end of the 1800 *System of Transcendental Idealism,* before turning to (ii) his most sustained attempt to understand all art forms – and their mythological content – from a philosophical or absolute point of view in his *Lectures on the Philosophy of Art* of 1802–4. The third text reproduced below is (iii) a speech given to the Bavarian Academy of Sciences in October 1807 in celebration of King Maximilian I Joseph of Bavaria's name day, entitled, *On the Relationship of the Plastic Arts to Nature* – a speech which combines Schelling's aesthetic interests with his philosophy of nature, resulting in his most sophisticated account of the categories of 'life', 'force' and 'formation' in artistic creation. The final text then turns to (iv) Schelling's peculiar conception of 'tautegory' – here formalized in his lectures on the philosophy of mythology in a way consonant with his earlier remarks on mythology in the lectures on the philosophy of art. For Schelling, myths are tautegorical to the extent that they are to be understood as entirely self-referential, rather than representing some external meaning; this necessitates a hermeneutic shift away from questions of hidden meanings to the idea that myths are the actual performances through which the genesis of gods – and consciousness of those gods – takes place.

Note

1   'The Oldest Systematic Program of German Idealism', *Philosophy of German Idealism: Fichte, Jacobi, and Schelling,* ed. Ernst Behler (New York: Continuum, 1987), p. 162.

System of Transcendental Idealism (1800)*

§ 1. Deduction of the Art-Product as Such

The intuition we have postulated is to bring together that which exists in separation in the appearance of freedom and in the intuition of the natural

---

*Translated by Peter Heath from F.W.J. Schelling, *System des transzendentalen Idealismus,* ed. Ruth-Eva Schulz (Hamburg: Felix Meiner, 1957).

product; namely *identity of the conscious* and the *unconscious* in the *self*, and *consciousness of this identity*. The product of this intuition will therefore verge on the one side upon the product of nature, and on the other upon the product of freedom, and must unite in itself the characteristics of both. If we know the product of the intuition, we are also acquainted with the intuition itself, and hence we need only derive the product, in order to derive the intuition.

With the product of freedom, our product will have this in common, that it is consciously brought about; and with the product of nature, that it is unconsciously brought about. In the former respect it will thus be the reverse of the organic natural product. Whereas the unconscious (blind) activity is reflected out of the organic product as a conscious one, the conscious activity will conversely be reflected out of the product here under consideration as an unconscious (objective) one; whereas the organic product reflects its unconscious activity to me as determined by conscious activity, the product here being derived will conversely reflect conscious activity as determined by unconscious. To put it more briefly: nature begins as unconscious and ends as conscious; the process of production is not purposive, but the product certainly is so. In the activity at present under discussion, the self must begin (subjectively) with consciousness, and end without consciousness, or *objectively*; the self is conscious in respect of production, unconscious in regard to the product.

But now how are *we* to explain transcendentally *to ourselves* an intuition such as this, in which the unconscious activity operates as it were, through the conscious, to the point of attaining complete identity therewith?

[…]

This unknown, whereby the objective and the conscious activities are here brought into unexpected harmony, is none other than that absolute which contains the common ground of the pre-established harmony between the conscious and the unconscious. Hence, if this absolute is reflected from out of the product, it will appear to the intelligence as something lying above the latter, and which, in contrast to freedom, brings an element of the unintended to that which was begun with consciousness and intention.

This unchanging identity, which can never attain to consciousness, and merely radiates back from the product, is for the producer precisely what destiny is for the agent, namely a dark unknown force which supplies the element of completeness or objectivity to the piece-work of freedom; and as that power is called destiny, which through our free action realizes, without our knowledge and even against our will, goals *that we did not envisage*, so likewise that incomprehensible agency which supplies objectivity to the conscious, without the cooperation of freedom, and to some extent in opposition to freedom (wherein is eternally dispersed what in this production is united), is denominated by means of the obscure concept of *genius*.

The product we postulate is none other than the product of genius, or, since genius is possible only in the arts, the *product of art*.

The deduction is concluded, and our next task is simply to show by thoroughgoing analysis that all the features of the production we have postulated come together in the aesthetic. The fact that all aesthetic production rests upon a conflict of activities can be justifiably inferred already from the testimony of all artists, that they are involuntarily driven to create their works, and that in producing them they merely satisfy an irresistible urge of their own nature; for if every urge proceeds from a contradiction in such wise that, given the contradiction, free activity becomes involuntary, the artistic urge also must proceed from such a feeling of inner contradiction. But since this contradiction sets in motion the whole man with all his forces, it is undoubtedly one which strikes at *the ultimate in him*, the root of his whole being. It is as if, in the exceptional man (which artists above all are, in the highest sense of the word), that unalterable identity, on which all existence is founded, had laid aside the veil wherewith it shrouds itself in others, and, just as it is directly affected by things, so also works directly back upon everything. Thus it can only be the contradiction between conscious and unconscious in the free act which sets the artistic urge in motion; just as, conversely, it can be given to art alone to pacify our endless striving, and likewise to resolve the uttermost contradiction within us. Just as aesthetic production proceeds from the feeling of a seemingly irresoluble contradiction, so it ends likewise, by the testimony of all artists, and of all who share their inspiration, in the feeling of an *infinite* harmony; and that this feeling which accompanies completion is at the same time a *deep emotion*, is itself enough to show that the artist attributes that total resolution of his conflict which he finds achieved in his work of art, not to himself [alone], but to a bounty freely granted by his own nature, which, however unrelentingly it set him in conflict with himself, is no less gracious in relieving him of the pain of this contradiction.

[...]

If we are to seek in one of the two activities, namely the conscious, for what is ordinarily called *art*, though it is only one part thereof, namely that aspect of it which is exercised with consciousness, thought and reflection, and can be taught and learnt and achieved through tradition and practice, we shall have, on the other hand, to seek in the unconscious factor which enters into art for that about it which cannot be learned, nor attained by practice, nor in any other way, but can only be inborn through the free bounty of nature; and this is what we may call in a word, the element of *poetry* in art.

It is self-evident from this, however, that it would be utterly futile to ask which of the two constituents should have preference over the other, since each of them, in fact, is valueless without the other, and it is only in conjunction that they bring forth the highest. For although what is not attained by practice, but is born in us, is commonly regarded as the nobler, the gods have in fact tied the very exercise of that innate power so closely to a man's serious application, his industry and thought, that even where it is inborn, poetry without art engenders, as it were, only dead products, which can give no pleasure to any man's mind, and repel all judgement and even intuition, owing to the wholly blind force which operates therein. It is, on the contrary, far more to be expected that art without poetry should be able to achieve something, than poetry without art; partly because it is not easy for a man to be by nature wholly without poetry, though many are wholly without art; and partly because a persistent study of the thoughts of great masters is able in some degree to make up for the initial want of objective power. All that can ever arise from this, however, is merely a semblance of poetry, which, by its superficiality and by many other indications, *e.g.* the high value it attaches to the mere mechanics of art, the poverty of form in which it operates, etc., is easily distinguishable in contrast to the unfathomable depth which the true artist, though he labours with the greatest diligence, involuntarily imparts to his work, and which neither he nor anyone else is wholly able to penetrate.

But now it is also self-evident that just as poetry and art are each individually incapable of engendering perfection, so a divided existence of both is equally inadequate to the task. It is therefore clear that, since the identity of the two can only be innate, and is utterly impossible and unattainable through freedom, perfection is possible only through genius, which, for that very reason, is for the aesthetic what the self is for philosophy, namely the supreme absolute reality, which never itself becomes objective, but is the cause of everything that is so.

§ 2. Character of the Art-Product

a) The work of art reflects to us the identity of the conscious and unconscious activities. But the opposition between them is an infinite one, and its removal is effected without any assistance from freedom. Hence the basic character of the work of art is that of an *unconscious infinity* [synthesis of nature and freedom]. Besides what he has put into his work with manifest intention, the artist seems instinctively, as it were, to have depicted therein an infinity, which no finite understanding is capable of developing to the full. To explain what we mean by a single example: the mythology of the Greeks, which undeniably contains an infinite meaning and a symbolism for all ideas, arose among a people, and in a fashion, which both make it impossible to suppose any comprehensive forethought in devising it, or in the harmony whereby everything is united into one great whole. So it is with every true work of art, in that every one of them is capable of being expounded *ad infinitum*, as though it contained an infinity of purposes, while yet one is never able to say whether this infinity has lain within the artist himself, or resides only in the work of art. By contrast, in the product which merely apes the character of a work of art, purpose and rule lie on the surface, and seem so restricted and circumscribed, that the product is no more than a faithful replica of the artist's conscious activity, and is in every respect not for intuition, which loves to sink itself in what it contemplates, and finds no resting place short of the infinite.

b) Every aesthetic production proceeds from the feeling of an infinite contradiction, and hence also the feeling which accompanies completion of the art-product must be one of an infinite tranquility; and this latter, in turn, must also pass over into the work of art itself. Hence the outward expression of the work of art is one of calm and silent grandeur, even where the aim is to give expression to the utmost intensity of pain and joy.

c) Every aesthetic production proceeds from an intrinsically infinite separation of the two activities, which in every free act of producing are divided. But now since these two activities are to be depicted in the product as united, what this latter presents is an infinite finitely displayed. But the infinite finitely displayed is beauty. The basic feature of every work of art, in which both the preceding are comprehended, is therefore *beauty*, and without beauty there is no work of art. There are, admittedly, sublime works of art, and beauty and sublimity in a certain respect are opposed to each other, in that a landscape, for example, can be beautiful without therefore being sublime, and *vice versa*. However, the opposition between beauty and sublimity is one which occurs only in regard to the object, not in regard to the subject of intuition. For the difference between the beautiful and the sublime work of art consists simply in this, that where beauty is present, the infinite contradiction is eliminated in the object itself, whereas when sublimity is present, the conflict is not reconciled in the object itself, but merely uplifted to a point at which it is involuntarily eliminated in the intuition: and this, then, is much as if it were to be eliminated in the object. It can also be shown very easily that sublimity rests upon the same contradiction as that on which beauty rests. For whenever an object is spoken of as sublime, a magnitude is admitted by the unconscious activity which it is impossible to accept into the conscious one: whereupon the self is thrown into a conflict with itself which can end only in an aesthetic intuition, whereby both activities are brought into unexpected harmony; save only that the intuition, which here lies not in the artist, but in the intuiting subject himself, is a wholly involuntary one, in that the sublime (quite unlike the merely strange, which similarly confronts the imagination with a contradiction, though one that is not worth the trouble of resolving) sets all the forces of the mind in motion, in order to resolve a contradiction which threatens our whole intellectual existence.

[...]

§ 3. Corollaries: Relation of Art to Philosophy

Now that we have deduced the nature and character of the art-product as completely as was necessary for purposes of the present enquiry, there is nothing more we need do except to set forth the relation which the philosophy of art bears to the whole system of philosophy.

[...]

If aesthetic intuition is merely transcendental[1] intuition become objective, it is self-evident that art is at once the only true and eternal organ and document of philosophy, which ever and again continues to speak to us of what philosophy cannot depict in external form, namely the unconscious element in acting and producing, and its original identity with the conscious. Art is paramount to the philosopher, precisely because it opens to him, as it were, the holy of holies, where burns in eternal and original unity, as if in a single flame, that which in nature and history is rent asunder, and in life and action, no less than in thought, must forever fly apart. The view of nature, which the philosopher frames artificially, is for art the original and natural one. What we speak of as nature is a poem lying pent in a mysterious and wonderful script. Yet the riddle could reveal itself, were we to recognize in it the odyssey of the spirit, which, marvelously deluded, seeks itself, and in seeking flies from itself; for through the world of sense there glimmers, as if through words the meaning, as if through dissolving mists the land of fantasy, of which we are in search. Each splendid painting owes, as it were, its genesis to a removal of the invisible barrier dividing the real from the ideal world, and is no more than the gateway, through which come forth completely the shapes and scenes of that world of fantasy, which gleams but imperfectly through the real. Nature, to the artist, is nothing more than it is to the philosopher, being simply the ideal world appearing under permanent restrictions, or merely the imperfect reflection of a world existing, not outside him, but within.

But now what may be the source of this kinship of philosophy and art, despite the opposition between them, is a question already sufficiently answered in what has gone before.

We therefore close with the following observation. – A system is completed when it is led back to its starting point. But this is precisely the case with our own. The ultimate ground of all harmony between subjective and objective could be exhibited in its original identity only through intellectual intuition; and it is precisely this ground which, by means of the work of art, has been brought forth entirely from the subjective, and rendered wholly objective, in such wise, that we have gradually led our object, the self itself, up to the very point where we ourselves were standing when we began to philosophize.

But now if it is art alone which can succeed in objectifying with universal validity what the philosopher is able to present in a merely subjective fashion, there is one more conclusion yet to be drawn. Philosophy was born and nourished by poetry in the infancy of knowledge, and with it all those sciences it has guided toward perfection; we may thus expect them, on completion, to flow back like so many individual streams into the universal ocean of poetry from which they took their source. Nor is it in general difficult to say what the medium for this return of science to poetry will be. For in mythology such a medium existed, before the occurrence of a breach now seemingly beyond repair. But how a new mythology is itself to arise, which shall be the creation, not of some individual author, but of a new race, personifying, as it were, one single poet – that is a problem whose solution can be looked for only in the future destinies of the world, and in the course of history to come.

Note

1   intellectual.

Lectures on the Philosophy of Art (1802–4)*

§ 27. *Particular things, to the extent they are absolute in that particularity, and thus to the extent they as particulars are simultaneously universes, are called ideas.* […]

Elucidation. Every idea is = universe in the form of the particular. For just this reason, however, it is not real as this particular. The real is always only the universe itself. Every idea has two unities: the one through which it exists *within itself and* is *absolute* – hence the one through which the absolute is formed into the particularity of the idea – and the one through which it is taken up as a particular into the absolute as into its own centre. This double unity of every idea is actually the mystery by which the particular can be comprehended both within the absolute and, in spite of this, also as a particular.

§ 28. *These same syntheses of the universal and particular that viewed in themselves are ideas, that is, images of the divine, are, if viewed on the plane of the real, the gods,* for their essence, their essential nature, = *god.* They are ideas only to the extent that they are god in a particular form. Every idea, therefore, = god, but a particular god.

Annotation. This proposition needs no explanation, particularly since what follows will serve to illuminate it further. The idea of the gods is necessary for art. Our systematic construction of art leads us back precisely to the point to which instinct first led poesy at its inception. What ideas are for philosophy, the gods are for art, and vice versa.

[…]

§ 30. *The determining law of all gods is pure limitation on the one hand, and undivided absoluteness on the other,* for they are the ideas intuited in actuality. Particular things, however, cannot be within the ideas unless, for precisely that reason, they are simultaneously truly or absolutely separated and truly one, namely, essentially absolute (according to § 26). Hence, the determining law of the world of the gods is strict separation or limitation on the one hand, and equal absoluteness on the other.

Annotation. We must pay particular attention to this relationship if we wish to comprehend the enormous significance of the gods both as regards

---

*Translated by Douglas W. Stott from F.W.J. Schelling, *Sämmtliche Werke* (Stuttgart and Augsberg: Cotta, 1856–1861), Division One, Volume Five.

them individually and as a whole. The mystery of their charm and of their suitability for artistic portrayal actually lies, *first of all,* in the fact that they are strictly limited; hence, mutually limiting characteristics exclude one another within the same deity and are absolutely separated from one another. Nonetheless, within this limitation every form receives into itself the entire divinity.

This is the means by which art acquires separate, self-enclosed figures for portrayal, and yet within each figure simultaneously the totality, the entire divinity. In order to make this comprehensible by means of examples, I must here take such examples from the world of the Greek gods themselves, even though we will be able to construct that world in its completeness only in the entire following discussion. In the meantime, if you see that all the characteristics of the Greek gods fit our deduction of the law of all the figures of the gods, then right from the beginning it must be admitted that Greek mythology is the highest archetype of the poetic world.

Now, let us offer a few examples to support the proposition that pure limitation on the one hand, and undivided absoluteness on the other are the essence of the figures of the gods. Minerva is the archetype of wisdom and strength in unity; feminine tenderness, however, has been eliminated from her, since both characteristics together would reduce this figure to indifference and accordingly more or less to nullity. Juno is strength without wisdom and gentle charm, the latter of which she borrows from Venus in the form of a girdle. If, on the other hand, Venus were invested with the cold wisdom of Minerva, her influence would doubtlessly not be as destructive as it is in the Trojan War, which she causes in order to satisfy the desires of her favourite. Yet then she would no longer be the goddess of love and hence no longer the object of fantasy, for which the universal and absolute within the particular – in limitation – is the highest artistic virtue.

[…]

§ 38. *Mythology is the necessary condition and first content of all art.*

The entire preceding discussion serves as proof. The *nervus probandi* [crux of the argument] lies in the idea of art as representation, by means of particular beautiful things, of what is absolutely beautiful in itself, and hence as representation of the absolute within limitation without suspension of the absolute. This contradiction is resolved only in the ideas of the gods, who themselves can have no independent, truly objective existence except in the complete development of their own world and of a poetic totality that we call mythology.

Further elucidation. Mythology is nothing other than the universe in its higher manifestation, in its absolute form, the true universe in itself, image or symbol of life and of wondrous chaos in the divine imagination, itself already poesy and yet in and for itself the content and element of poesy. It (mythology) is the world and as it were the ground in which alone the exotic plants of art are able to bloom and grow. Only within such a world are abiding and definite forms possible through which alone the eternal concepts can be expressed. The creations of art must have the same reality as, indeed an even higher reality than, those of nature. The figures of the gods that endure so necessarily and so eternally must have a higher reality than those of human beings or of plants, yet must simultaneously possess the characteristics both of individuals and of types, including the immortality of the latter.

Insofar as poesy is the formative element of the material or content, just as art in the narrower sense is the formative element of form, so also is mythology the absolute poesy, as it were the poesy *en masse*. It is eternal matter from which all forms issue so wondrously and variously.

§ 39. *Representation of the absolute with absolute indifference of the universal and the particular* **within the particular** *is possible only symbolically.*

Elucidation. Representation of the absolute with absolute indifference of the universal and the particular *within the universal* = philosophy – idea –. Representation of the absolute with absolute indifference of the universal and the particular *in the particular* – art. The universal content of this representation = mythology. In mythology we thus find the second synthesis already accomplished, that of the indifference of the universal and the particular with the *particular.* This proposition is thus the principle of construction of mythology as such.

On the Relationship of the Plastic Arts to Nature (1807)*

[...]

For a long time how much has been felt, thought, and judged about art! How can this address therefore hope, in such a dignified gathering of the most enlightened connoisseurs and insightful judges, to bring new excitement

---

*Translated by Jason M. Wirth from F.W.J. Schelling, *Sämmtliche Werke* (Stuttgart and Augsberg: Cotta, 1856–1861), Division One, Volume Seven.

to the object unless it scorned foreign embellishment and offered an account of part of the universal favour and receptivity that it enjoys? For other objects have to be elevated by eloquence, or, if there is something effusive about them, they have to be made credible by exposition. Art already has the advantage from the outset that it is given as visible and that doubts regarding claims about sublime perfection, because they exceed the common level of understanding, can be met with an exposition in which the idea that was not intellectually grasped can in this region emerge incarnate before the eyes. Moreover, this lecture can avail itself of the consideration that the many doctrines formed around this object still went back far too little to the originary source of art. For most artists, even though they should imitate all of nature, nonetheless seldom obtain a concept about what the being [*Wesen*] of nature is. Connoisseurs and thinkers, however, because of the greater inaccessibility of nature, for the most part find it easier to derive their theories more from the contemplation of the soul than from a science of nature. Such doctrines are usually far too shallow. They may in general say many a good and true thing about art, but they are nonetheless ineffective for plastic artists themselves and utterly fruitless for their practice.

For plastic art, in accordance with the most ancient expression, should be a mute poetry. The inventor of this declaration doubtless meant this: they should express, just like those spiritual thoughts, concepts whose origin is the soul, but not through language, but rather, like silent nature, through figure, through form, through sensuous works that are independent from the soul. Plastic art therefore manifestly stands as an active copula between the soul and nature, and can only be grasped in the living intermediary between both. Indeed, because it has the relationship to the soul in common with every other art, including poetry, what remains peculiar to it alone is that which connects it to nature and that by which it has a productive force similar to nature. Only with reference to this can a theory be satisfactory to the intellect and productive and helpful to art itself.

We therefore hope, in contemplating plastic art in relationship to its veritable paragon and originary source, namely, nature, to be able to contribute something not yet known to its theory and provide some more precise determinations and clarifications of its concepts. But above all we hope to let the coherence of the whole edifice of art appear in the light of a higher necessity.

But has not science always recognized this relationship? Does not all modern theory even derive from the definite principle that art should be the imitator of nature? This was probably so. But how does the artist practise this broadly general principle when the concept of nature is ambiguous and when there are almost as many representations of nature as there are lifestyles? Some think nature is nothing more than the dead aggregate of an indeterminate amount of objects, or space into which objects are put as in a container. For others it is just the land from which they draw their food and sustenance. Only to the inspired researcher is it the holy and eternally creative primordial force of the world, which generates and actively produces all things out of itself. This principle would be highly meaningful if it taught art to emulate this productive force. One can hardly doubt what sense this intends if one reflects on the general state of the sciences at the time of their initial creation. How strange it would be for those who denied all life to nature to put it forward in art for imitation! The words of the profound man would apply to them: Your mendacious philosophy has done away with nature, so why do you demand that we imitate it? So that you could renew your enjoyment by committing the same act of violence against the students of nature?[1]

Nature for them was not just silent but a fully dead image with no inwardly native living word. It was a hollow framework of forms from which an equally hollow image should be transferred to canvas or hewn in stone. This was the right doctrine for those ancient and crude peoples who, because they saw nothing divine in nature, produced idols from out of nature. Meanwhile, for the sensuously gifted Hellenes, who felt the trace of the living and acting being [*Wesen*] everywhere, veritable gods arose out of nature.

And should the students of nature imitate everything of everything in nature without distinction? The student should only reproduce beautiful objects and within these only what is beautiful and consummate. This would seem to more precisely determine the principle but at the price of maintaining that in nature the perfect is mixed with the imperfect and the beautiful with the non-beautiful. How would the student who attributes no other relationship to nature than servile imitation distinguish one from the other? This type of imitator more likely and easily appropriates the defects of the original image than its merits because the defects present themselves as more comprehensible features to manage. And so we also see that with the imitators of nature in this sense the ugly is imitated more often and with more love than the beautiful. If we do not look at things with respect to the being [*Wesen*] within them, but rather with respect to their empty and abstract form, then they also say nothing to our interior. We must put our own minds, our own spirits, at stake before they answer us. But what is the consummation of each thing? It is nothing other than the creative life in it, its power to be there and exist. Hence one who regards nature overall as something dead will never achieve that deep process, similar to the chemical one, through which, as if purified by fire, the pure gold of beauty and truth emerges.

Nothing changed regarding the main view of this relationship even when one began more generally to feel the insufficiency of this principle. Nothing even changed with Johann Winckelmann's magnificent foundation of a new doctrine and insight. Indeed, he re-established the entire efficacy of the soul in art, and elevated it from its undignified dependency to the realm of spiritual freedom. Animated by the beauty of the forms in the plastic images of antiquity, he taught that the bringing forth of an ideal nature that is elevated above actuality, along with the expression of its spiritual concepts, is the highest aim of art.

But if we examine what was for the most part understood by art's exceeding of actuality, we find, even with this doctrine, the endurance of the view that nature is a mere product and things are lifeless existents. The idea of a living, creative nature was in no way awoken by it. For these ideal forms could not be animated through a positive insight into their being [*Wesen*]. And if the forms of actuality were dead for the dead contemplators, then they were no less dead for art. If spontaneous bringing forth was not possible for the former, then it was also not possible for the latter. Although the object of imitation was altered, imitation remained. Into the stead of nature entered the elevated works of antiquity, whose external forms the students endeavoured to copy, albeit bereft of the spirit that filled them. These works are just as unapproachable, nay, even more unapproachable, than the works of nature. They leave you even colder than the latter if you do not bring the spiritual eye to them in order to penetrate their husk and feel the active force within them.

On the other hand, since then, artists inherited a certain idealist verve and represented the sublimity of beauty above matter. But these representations were like beautiful words, which do not correspond to deeds. If earlier customs of art produced bodies without soul, then this view merely taught the mystery of the soul, but not that of the body. Theory, as it customarily does, rapidly took to the other side, but without finding the living intermediary.

[...]

Nature everywhere at first opposes us in more or less hard form and taciturnity. It is like the sincere and quiet beauty that does not excite attention through screaming signs and does not attract the common eye. How can we spiritually melt, so to speak, that seemingly hard form so that the pure force of things flows together with the force of our spirit in a single stream? We must go through and beyond form in order to win it back as comprehensible, living, and truly felt. If we contemplate the most beautiful forms, what is left over once we have excised in thought the acting principle within it? Nothing but purely inessential qualities such as extension and spatial relationships. If a part of the matter is near and external to another, does it contribute to its inner quiddity [Wesenheit] or does it make no difference whatsoever? Obviously the latter. The proximity of the parts does not make the form but rather the manner in which they are so. Only a positive force determines the latter, a force, which is apart from, and even counteracts, the being in proximity of the parts. It subjugates the variegation of the parts into the unity of a concept, from the force acting in the crystal to that which in human cultivation, like a mild magnetic current, endows the material parts with such a reciprocal position and location that their essential unity and beauty can become visible in the concept.

But just the acting principle in general, as spirit and active science, is insufficient to make the being [Wesen] appear in the form so that we can grasp it as living. Indeed, all unity can only be spiritual in kind and origin. And toward what does any investigation of nature strive if not toward finding science itself in this? For that in which there would be nothing to understand could also not be subject to the understanding; that which is without knowledge cannot itself be known. The science through which nature acts is certainly not the same as the human one, which would be tied to itself through reflection. In the former the concept is not distinguished from the deed or the design from its execution. Hence raw matter blindly strives, so to speak, toward orderly form, and unknowingly adapts purely stereometric forms, which nonetheless certainly belong to the realm of concepts and are something spiritual in the material. The most sublime art of number and measure is native to the stars and is performed in their movements without the stars having any concept of it. This more clearly appears in the living knowledge of animals, although they themselves cannot grasp this knowledge. We therefore see them perform countless acts as they unconsciously wander along, acts that are far more magnificent than the animals themselves: the bird, intoxicated by music, which surpasses itself with soulful tones or the tiny artistic creature that executes simple works of architecture without either practice or instruction. But an overpowering spirit leads all of them. It shines forth in individual flashes of insight, but it does not emerge anywhere as the full sun as it does with humans.

In nature and art, this active science is the copula between concept and form and between body and soul. An eternal concept, devised in an infinite intellect, manages each thing. But through what means does this concept transition to actuality and embodiment? Solely through the creative science, which is just as necessarily bound to the infinite intellect as the being [*Wesen*], which grasps non-sensuous beauty, is connected in the artist to sensual presentation. If the artist is to be called propitious and praiseworthy above all others, and upon whom the gods have bestowed this creative spirit, then the work of art appears splendid to the degree to which it displays to us this unfalsified force of nature's creation and efficacy in a design.

It has long been appreciated that in art not everything is accomplished consciously, and that an unconscious force must be bound up with conscious activity, and that the consummate concord and reciprocal interpenetration of both of these produce the highest art. Works, which are missing this seal of unconscious science, are recognizable by a palpable lack of the life that is self-sufficient and independent of the one who brought it forth. To the contrary, where this life is in effect, art simultaneously grants to its work, with the highest clarity of the intellect, that inscrutable reality through which it appears similar to a work of nature.

The position of artists with regard to nature is often clarified by the dictum that art, in order to be art, would have to first distance itself from nature and only in its ultimate consummation turn back to it. It seems to us that the true meaning of this dictum can be no other than the following. In all natural beings [*Naturwesen*], the living concept only displays itself by acting blindly. But were it the same way in artists, they would be altogether indistinguishable from nature. If artists consciously wanted to subordinate themselves entirely to the actual, and reproduce present existence with obsequious fidelity, they would bring forth masks, but not artworks. Artists must therefore distance themselves from the product or from the creature, but only to elevate themselves to the creative force and grasp it spiritually. Through this they are carried up to the realm of pure concepts. They abandon the creaturely, only to win it back with a thousand-fold profit, and at least in this sense they turn back to nature. Artists should at least emulate the spirit of nature, which acts within things, and which only speaks through form and figure as if they were symbols. Only insofar as they grasp this in living imitation have they created something true. For works that originated in an assemblage of residually beautiful forms would nonetheless be bereft of any beauty because that which actually makes the work or the whole beautiful can no longer be form. What makes it beautiful is beyond form. It is being [*Wesen*], the universal, the look and expression of the spirit of nature dwelling within.

There can be no doubt as to how to regard the general demand for a so-called idealization of nature in art. This demand seems to originate in a manner of thinking according to which the actual is not truth, beauty and the Good, but rather the opposite of all of these. If the actual were indeed opposed to truth and beauty, artists would not have to uplift or idealize it. They would rather have to sublate or annihilate it in order to create something true and beautiful. Yet how could anything except the true be actual, and what is beauty if it is not being [*Sein*] wholly without lack? What higher aim could art have than to present a being [*Seiende*] that is indeed in nature? Or how would art undertake an exceeding of so-called actual nature if it would always have to remain behind it? For does art endow its works with sensuous and actual life? This statue does not breathe, has no pulse, and is not warmed by blood. As soon as we merely posit that the aim of art is the presentation of a true being, than both of these, the former alleged exceeding of the actual and the latter apparent lagging behind the actual, turn out to be consequences of one and the same principle. Their works only seem to be superficially animated. In nature life seems to penetrate deeper and wholly to marry itself to matter. But do not the constant alterations of matter and the dissolution, which is the fate of all finite beings, teach us the inessentiality of this connection, and that this could not be an intimate fusion? Therefore art, in the merely superficial animation of its works, indeed only presents what does not have being as not having being [*das Nichtseiende als nichtseiend*]. How is it that to anyone with a somewhat cultivated sensibility, the imitation of so-called actual nature, driven to the point of illusion, appears untrue to the highest degree, even giving off the impression of ghosts, whereas in a work where the concept prevails, it grips them with the full force of the truth and even first transplants them into the genuinely actual world? From where does this originate if not out of the more or less dark feeling, which tells them that the concept is solely what is living in things and that everything else is but vain shadows without being [*wesenlos*]? The same principle explains all of the opposed cases, which are cited as examples of art exceeding nature. If art arrests the rapid course of human years, if it combines the force of developed masculinity with the mild charm of earlier youth, or shows a mother of grown sons and daughters in full possession of her forceful beauty: what else is it doing other than sublating what is inessential, namely, time? If, according to the remark of the splendid connoisseur, each wine of nature has only a single moment of truly consummate beauty, then we may say that it also only has a single moment in which it is fully present. In this moment it is what it is for the whole of eternity: beyond this only becoming and perishing are in store for it. When art presents the being [Wesen] in that moment, it lifts it out of time. Art lets it appear in its pure being [Sein], in the eternity of its life.

Once everything positive and essential is thought away from form, it would have to appear restrictive and, so to speak, inimical to the being [Wesen]. The same theory, which had conjured this false and impotent ideal, necessarily and simultaneously works towards the formless in art. Of course, if the form had to be restrictive for the being [Wesen], it would exist independently from it. But if form is with and through the being [Wesen], how could the being [Wesen] feel restricted by what it itself created? Violence would certainly occur if form were forced on it, but never when form flows out of the being [Wesen] itself. Rather it must rest satisfied in the latter and feel its existence as self-sustained and self-secluded. The determination of form in nature is never a negation, but rather always an affirmation. Admittedly, you usually think of the figure of a body as a restriction that it bears. But if you looked at the creative force, it would be evident to you that the figure is a measure that the creative force imposes on itself within which it appears as a veritably ingenious force. For the capacity to set one's own bounds is everywhere regarded as a virtue, even as one of the highest. In a similar fashion, most people consider the particular as negating, namely, as what is not the whole or the all. But no particular exists by virtue of its limitation, but rather by virtue of its indwelling force with which it asserts itself as its own whole in the face of the whole itself.

Since this force of particularity, and hence also of individuality, presents itself as living character, the concept of particularity as negating has, as a necessary consequence, an insufficient and false view of the characteristic in art. Art that wanted to present the empty shell or limitation of the individual would be dead and unbearably severe. We clearly do not demand the individual. We demand to see more, namely, the living concept of the individual. But if artists realize the look and being [Wesen] of the creative idea within themselves and lift it out, they form the individual into a world of their own, into a genus and an eternal archetype or primordial image. And whoever has grasped the being [Wesen] need not fear severity and strictness, for these are the conditions of life. We see nature, which appears in its consummation as the highest mildness, in all particulars as determination, even first and foremost as working toward the severity and taciturnity of life. Just as all of creation is a work of the highest renunciation, artists must first disown themselves and descend into the particular, not shying away from detachment or from the pain, indeed the agony, of form. From its first works onwards, nature is thoroughly characteristic. Nature seals up the force of fire and the flash of light in hard stone and the sweet soul of sound in harsh metal. Even at the threshold of life, and already tending toward organic figure, nature, overwhelmed by the force of form, relapses into petrification. The life of plants exists in silent receptivity, but in what precise and severe contours is this patient life restrained? The conflict between life and form really seems to begin in the realm of animals: it conceals its first works in hard shells, and where these were eliminated, the animate world, through the art drive, rejoined the realm of crystallization. It finally emerged bolder and freer with the appearance of active and living characters, whose genera were the same throughout. Indeed, art cannot begin as profoundly as nature. If beauty is dispersed equally everywhere, there are still different degrees of the appearance and explication of the being [*Wesen*] and thereby with beauty. But art demands a certain fullness of beauty. It does not want to play a particular sound or tone or even an isolated chord, but rather right away the full-toned melody of beauty. Hence art most prefers to reach immediately for the highest and most evolved, namely, the human figure. Since it is not granted to art to embrace the immeasurable whole and since only particular fulgurations appear in all other creatures, the whole and complete being [*Sein*] without division only appears in the human. Hence art is not only permitted, but also summoned, to see the whole of nature only in the human. Because nature collects everything into a single point, it also repeats its entire diversity, and takes the same path that it had run through in its broad scope a second time in a narrower scope. Here the demand originates that the artist first be faithful and true with regard to the limited in order to appear consummate and beautiful in the whole. What matters here is to struggle, not in slack and weak, but in strong and courageous, battle with the creative spirit of nature, which also distributes character and peculiarity in unfathomable diversity to the human world. Before artists may dare want to attain, through ever-higher combinations and the finite fusion of manifold forms, the extreme beauty in sculpture of the highest simplicity and with infinite content, they must first exercise restraint in the realization of that through which the peculiarity of things is something positive. This will preserve them from vacuity, softness and inner nullity.

Only through the consummation of form can form be annihilated and this in the characteristic is indeed the ultimate goal of art. But just as apparent accord is more easily achieved in shallow souls than in others but is inwardly hollow, so it is in art with rapidly attained external harmony without the fullness of content. And if doctrine and instruction have to counteract the spiritless imitation of beautiful forms, then they must first of all counteract the inclination toward a mollycoddled and characterless art whose fancy names just cover over its incapacity to fulfil the basic conditions of art.

Sublime beauty, where the fullness of form sublates form itself, was accepted by the modern doctrine of art after Winckelmann as not only the highest, but also the only, measure. But because one overlooks the deep ground upon which it rests, it so happened that, with regard to the paragon of everything affirmative, a negative concept was grasped instead. Winckelmann compares beauty to the water that was scooped out of the womb of the source. The less taste that it has, the more it is esteemed as healthy. It is true that the highest beauty is characterless. But it is characterless in the way that we say that the universe has no determinate dimensions. It has neither length nor breadth nor depth because everything is contained in the same infinity. Or that the art of creative nature is formless because it itself is not subjugated by any form. In this and in no other understanding can we say that Hellenic art in its supreme sculpture ascended to the characterless. But it did not strive after this immediately. They first turned upward toward divine freedom from out of the bonds of nature. It could not have been lightly seeded grain, only a deeply dormant seed, out of which this heroic formation sprouted. Only powerful movements of feeling, only profound tremors of fantasy through the imprint of omni-animating and ubiquitously working nature, could impress art with insuperable force. With this, from the stiffly reserved solemnity of the sculpture of earlier times until the works of overflowing sensuous charm, it always remained faithful to the truth and spiritually engendered the highest reality that mortals are granted to behold. Just as their tragedy commences with the greatest ethical character, their sculpture began with the solemnity of nature and the severe goddess Athena is the first and only muse of plastic art. This epoch is characterized by the style that Winckelmann described as abidingly austere and severe. The next or higher style, solely through the intensification of these characteristics to the point of sublimity and simplicity, was able to develop out of this. In images of the most consummate and divine natures, it is not only necessary to unite the fullness of forms, of which the human nature is eminently capable. The union must also be of the type that we can commemorate in the universe itself, namely, that the lower qualities, or the ones that relate to more modest qualities, were taken up by higher qualities, and finally by the single highest quality, in which they are reciprocally extinguished as particulars but still exist as being [*Wesen*] and force. If we cannot call this elevated and self-sufficient beauty 'characteristic' in the sense of the limitation or conditionality of appearance, it nonetheless continues to be indistinguishably in effect, just like in the crystal, which is utterly transparent even though its texture endures. Every characteristic element carries its weight, however gently, and helps bring about the sublime indifference of beauty.

The external face or basis of all beauty is the beauty of form. But since there can be no form without being [*Wesen*], it follows that wherever there is form, there is also character in visible, or at least in sensible, presence. Characteristic beauty is therefore beauty at its root, out of which beauty can then first emerge as fruit. Of course, the being [*Wesen*] outgrows form, but the characteristic nonetheless still remains the always-acting foundation of the beautiful.

The most dignified connoisseur,[2] upon whose kingdom the gods bestowed nature as well as art, compared the characteristic in its relationship to beauty with the skeleton in its relationship to the living form. If we interpret this splendid simile in our sense, then we would say that in nature the skeleton is not, as we customarily think, cut off from the living whole. The firm and the soft, the determining and the determined, reciprocally presuppose each other and can only be because of each other. For that very reason, the vital characteristic is already the whole figure, which originated out of the reciprocal effect of bones and flesh and of the active and the passive. But if art, like nature, at higher levels represses inwardly the initially visible skeletal structure, then it can never be opposed to the figure and beauty because it does not cease to cooperatively determine the latter as well as the former.

Given that high and indifferent beauty counts as the supreme measure of art, the question remains if it should also count as the only measure of art. This must seemingly depend on the degree of extension and fullness with which a specific art can operate. Yet nature in its broad range always presents the higher simultaneously with the lower. Creating the divine in the human, it acts upon the mere matter and ground of all of the remaining products, which must be so that the being [*Wesen*] as such can appear in contrast to them. Indeed, in the higher world of humans, the great masses again become the basis upon which the divine, purely embraced by the few, becomes manifest through legislation, dominion and the founding of faiths. Where art therefore operates more with the manifold of nature, it may and must also indicate again, along with the highest measure of beauty, its foundation and, so to speak, the matter of the foundation, in its own formations. It is significant that here the nature of the various art forms originally unfolds. Sculpture, in the more precise meaning of the word, refuses to give space to its object externally. It bears the space internally. But it is precisely this that prohibits its greater extension. Indeed, sculpture is necessitated to indicate the beauty of the universe almost in a single point. It must therefore immediately strive toward the highest, and it can only reach diversity separately and through the most severe segregation of what is reciprocally opposed. By separating the purely animal from the human nature, sculpture also succeeds in fashioning vulgar creations as agreeable, even beautiful, as the beauty of the many satyrs preserved from antiquity teaches us. Indeed, like the cheerful spirit of nature parodying itself, sculpture can reverse its own ideal, and by treating it with play and jest, as exemplified by the excess found in the statues of Silenus, it appears liberated anew from the duress of matter. But it is always necessary utterly to segregate its work in order to make it concur with itself and to make it into a world unto itself, because there is no higher unity into which it can resolve the dissonance of the particulars. In contrast, the scope of painting is better able to match the world and poeticize in epic proportions. In a work like the *Iliad* there is even space for a Thersites. Does not everything find a place in the great epic poem of nature and history? Here the particular hardly counts for itself. The whole takes up its stead and what would not be beautiful for itself becomes so through the harmony of the whole. If, in an expansive work of painting, which connects its figures through the assignment of space and through light, shading and reflection, the highest measure of beauty was ubiquitously applied, the most unnatural monotony would emerge because, as Winckelmann says, the highest concept of beauty is here everywhere one and the same, permitting few deviations. To avoid this, the particular must be favoured over the whole instead of subjugating it to the whole wherever the whole emerges out of a multiplicity. Consequently, in such a work, gradations of beauty must be respected whereby the full beauty, concentrated in the centre, first becomes visible, and equilibrium in the whole emerges out of an overweighing of the particular. Here the restricted characteristic also finds its place, and theory should at least not so much point painters toward that tight space that concentrically gathers everything beautiful, but rather more toward the characteristic diversity of nature, through which they alone can grant the full weight of living contents to a great work. This is what the splendid Leonardo, among the founders of the new art, thought. So too Raphael, the master of high beauty, who did not shy away from presenting beauty in its inferior measure so it did not appear monotonous and without life and actuality. He understood not only how to bring forth beauty, but also how to interrupt its uniformity through the variability of expression.

Character can certainly also be expressed in rest and equilibrium, but it is only in activity that it is first actually alive. We mean by character a unity of plural forces, which constantly works toward a kind of equilibrium and determinate measure and which, if undisturbed, corresponds to a similar equilibrium in the regularity of forms. But this living unity can indicate itself in action and activity, only when the forces are aroused into insurrection by some kind of cause and step out of their equilibrium. Everyone recognizes that this is the case with the passions.

Here that well-known theoretical prescription presents itself to us, namely, the demand that the passions in their actual outbreak be moderated as much as possible so as not to injure the beauty of form. On the contrary, we believe in inverting this prescription so that we would have to say that it is precisely through beauty itself that we should moderate the passions. We are right to fear that this requisite moderation will be understood negatively. The true demand is rather that a positive force counters passion. Just as virtue does not consist of the absence of the passions but rather of the dominion of the spirit over them, so too is beauty proved not through the expulsion or diminution of the passions, but rather through the dominion of beauty over them. The forces of the passions must actually be indicated. The possibility of their complete insurrection must be visible, but also that they were suppressed through the dominion of character. The passions break against the forms of fortified beauty just as waves of a torrent, which, although filled to the banks, cannot overflow them. Otherwise this undertaking of moderation would just be the same as vapid moralists, who, exhausted by humanity, prefer to mutilate the nature in them and have so utterly taken away anything positive from action, that these folks revel in the spectacle of great crimes in order to reinvigorate themselves with the sight of at least something positive.

In nature and art, the being [*Wesen*] first of all strives toward the actualization and presentation of itself in the particular. The greatest severity of form therefore indicates itself in the beginnings of both. For without limitations, the unlimited could not appear. If there were no harshness, there could be no softness, and making the unity tangible can only happen through ipseity, segregation and antagonism. Hence, in the beginning, the creative spirit appears utterly lost in form, inaccessible, taciturn and austere, even writ large. But the more it succeeds in uniting its entire fullness in a single creature, the more its severity gradually subsides. Where it fully develops form so that it rests satisfied in it and grasps itself, it cheers up, so to speak, and starts to move in soft lines. This is the state of the most beautiful ripeness and flowering, where the pure receptacle stands there consummated, and the spirit of nature is freed from its ties and feels its affinity with the soul. As through a mild dawn ascending over the whole figure, it heralds the advent of the soul. It is not yet there, but everything readies for its reception with the mild play of delicate movements. The stiff contours melt, becoming soft and gentle. A lovely being [*Wesen*], that is neither sensuous nor spiritual, but rather ungraspable, diffuses itself over the figure, and nestles into all of the figures and to each oscillation of the extremities. This being [*Wesen*], which, as we said, is ungraspable yet perceptible to everyone, is what the Greek language calls *kharis* and we call grace.

Where grace appears in fully effected form, it is from the side of nature consummate. It is not lacking anything and every requirement is satisfied. Here the soul and the body are also already in consummate consonance. The body is form, and grace is the soul, albeit not the soul in itself, but rather the soul of form, or the soul of nature.

Art can tarry and remain at this point, since its entire task has been completed, at least from one side. The pure image of beauty brought to rest at this stage is the goddess of love. But the beauty of the soul in itself, fused with sensuous grace, is the supreme apotheosis of nature.

The spirit of nature only seems opposed to the soul. But in itself, it is the implement of the soul's revelation. It certainly acts as the contradiction of things, but only to be able thereby to bring forth the singular being [*Wesen*] as the supreme leniency and reconciliation of all of the forces. All other creatures are driven by the mere spirit of nature and through it assert their individuality. Only in humans, as in the central point, does the soul arise, without which the world, like nature, would be without the sun.

The soul in humans is therefore not the principle of individuality, but rather that through which they elevate themselves above all ipseity and thereby become capable of sacrificing themselves. It is non-egoistic love, and, what is supreme, the contemplation and realization of the being [*Wesen*] of things and, precisely thereby, of art. The soul is no longer occupied with matter nor does it immediately associate with it, but rather only with the spirit as the life of things. Also appearing in the body, the soul is nonetheless free from it. The consciousness of the body is in the soul, and, in the most beautiful formations, it floats like a light dream that does not disturb the soul. The soul is not a quality, or a faculty, or any such thing of the kind. It does not know, but rather is science. It is not good, but rather the Good. It is not beautiful, as bodies can be, but rather beauty itself.

Of course, at first or proximately, the soul of the artist is indicated in the artwork by invention in the particular and in the whole when the soul as unity hovers above the particular in peaceful silence. But the soul should become visible in what is presented. It becomes visible as the primordial force of thought when human beings, utterly consumed with a concept, are lost in worthy contemplation. Or it becomes visible as the indwelling and essential Good. Both are also clearly expressed in the most peaceful state, but notwithstanding, they are more alive when the soul can reveal itself actively and by way of contrast. And because it is principally the passions, which interrupt the peace of life, it is generally accepted that the beauty of the soul first and foremost indicates itself through peaceful dominion in the storm of the passions.

However, there is an important distinction to make here. The soul must not be summoned to moderate those passions, which are only an insurrection of the base spirits of nature. Nor can the soul be indicated as in opposition to them. For if presence of mind is still struggling with the passions, then the soul is not yet at all arisen. They must be moderated through the nature of humans and through the power of spirit. However, there are higher cases in which it is not a particular force but rather the levelheaded spirit itself that breaks through all dams. There are indeed also cases where the soul, through the copula that combines it with sensuous existence, is subjugated by the pain that should have otherwise been foreign to its divine nature. These are cases where humans feel strafed and at the root of their lives attacked, not by mere forces of nature, but rather by ethical powers, and where inculpable error[3] dislodges them into crime and thereby into misfortune, and where deepfelt injustice summons the holiest feelings of humanity to insurrection. This is the case with all of the veritable and in the sublime sense, tragic, conditions that we witness in the tragedies of antiquity. When the blind forces of the passions are aroused, the levelheaded spirit is present as the guardian of beauty. But when the spirit itself is ripped away as if by an irresistible violence, what vigilant power protects holy beauty? Or when even the soul suffers with it, how does it rescue itself from pain and sacrilege?

It would sin against the meaning and aim of art arbitrarily to repress the force of both pain and factious emotion, and it would divulge a lack of feeling and soul in artists themselves. That beauty, grounded in great and solid forms, has become character, alone demonstrates how art has prepared the means to indicate the whole magnitude of feeling without violating regularity. Where beauty rests on powerful forms as if upon unshakeable pillars, we can infer the great violence that was necessary to bring about even a slight and hardly tangential modification of its relationships. Grace sanctifies pain even more. Its being [*Wesen*] consists of not knowing itself. Just as it was not arbitrarily acquired, it cannot be arbitrarily lost. When unbearable pain, even when insanity, fated by punitive gods, robs one of consciousness and self-control, grace still stands by the suffering figure as if it were a protective *daimon*, who lets nothing untoward and nothing that opposes humanity come about, and when it falls, at least it falls as a pure and immaculate sacrifice. Not yet the soul, but rather its premonition, grace brings forth in a natural operation what the soul does through a divine force, namely, the metamorphosis of pain, ossification, even death itself, into beauty.

However, grace, proven in the most extreme repulsion, would be dead without its transfiguration by the soul. But what expression befits it in this situation? The soul rescues itself from pain and emerges vanquishing, not vanquished, by renouncing its copula with sensuous existence. Although the spirit of nature may muster its forces for the preservation of the soul, the soul does not enter into this struggle. Yet its presence pacifies the storm of painfully struggling life. Each external dominion can only steal external goods. It cannot reach the soul. It can rend a temporal bond, but it cannot dissolve the eternal bond of a veritable divine love. Not hard and without feeling or renouncing love itself, the soul, however, indicates grace in pain as the feeling that outlasts sensuous existence and so elevates itself over the debris of external life and fortune and into divine glory.

This is the expression of the soul that the creator of the image of Niobe indicates. Every artistic means by which horror is moderated is in operation. The mightiness of forms, sensuous grace, even the nature of the object itself, assuage the expression through which pain, surpassing all expression, sublates itself again, and beauty, which seemed impossible to rescue alive, is preserved from violation by the entrance of ossification. However, what would all of this be without the soul, and how does the latter reveal itself? In the mother's visage, we do not just see the pain over the felled blossoms of her children, nor just the fear of death as she tries to rescue the remaining ones as well as her youngest daughter taking refuge at her coattails, nor just indignation at the cruel deities, nor, least of all, as has been claimed, just cold spite. We saw all of this, but not for itself; rather, through all the pain, fear and indignation, eternal love radiates, like a divine light, as all that endures. The mother is proven not as what she was, but as what she now *is*, namely, one who remains connected with her beloveds through an eternal copula.

Everyone acknowledges that the greatness, purity and goodness of the soul also have their sensuous expression. How could we think this, were not the active principle in matter also a being [*Wesen*] with an affinity for and homologous to the soul? In the presentation of the soul, there are in turn stages of art, depending on whether the soul is bound together with the merely characteristic or whether it visibly flows together with favour and grace.[4] Who lacks the insight that in the tragedies of Aeschylus a high ethicality holds sway that is native to the works of Sophocles? But in Aeschylus it is still sealed in an austere husk, and participates little in the whole, because it still lacks the copula of sensuous grace. The Sophoclean grace could nonetheless emerge out of the gravity and still terrible graces of this first art, and with the consummate fusion of both elements. It leaves us wondering whether it is more the ethical or the sensuous grace that enraptures us in the works of this poet. This is also exactly the case for the plastic productions that are still in the stark style as compared to those in the later gentle style.

If grace, beyond being the transfiguration of the spirit of nature, is also the binding intermediary between ethical goodness and sensuous appearance, then it is self-evident that art in all of its directions most operate in the direction of its midpoint. This beauty, which emerges out of the consummate pervasion of ethical goodness and sensuous grace, grips and enraptures us, wherever we find it, with the power of a miracle. Because the spirit of nature everywhere else indicates itself as independent from the soul, even to a certain degree striving against it, it seems here, as if through a voluntary concurrence and as if through the inner fire of divine love, to fuse with the soul. With sudden clarity, the remembrance of the original unity of the being [*Wesen*] of nature with the being [*Wesen*] of the soul comes over the beholder: the certainty that all opposition is only apparent, and that love is the copula of all beings [*Wesen*], and that pure goodness is the ground and content of the whole of creation.

Here art, so to speak, goes through and beyond itself, and again makes itself a medium. From this peak, sensuous grace again becomes the mere husk and body of a higher life. What was earlier whole is treated as part, and the supreme relationship of art to nature is thereby reached. Nature is made the medium within which the soul becomes visible.

But if in this blossom of art, like in the blossoms in the plant kingdom, all earlier stages repeat themselves, then we are also granted insight, on the contrary, into the divergent directions that art takes as it emerges out of that middle point. The natural diversity of both forms of plastic art especially show themselves here in their supreme efficacy. For sculpture, since it presents its ideas through corporeal things, the supreme seems to have to be in the consummate equilibrium between soul and matter. If matter is given too much weight, sculpture falls below its own idea. But it seems utterly impossible for sculpture to elevate the soul at the expense of matter. To do so, it would have to transcend itself. Indeed, consummate sculptors will not, as Winckelmann says of the Belvedere Apollo, apply more matter to their work than the attainment of its spiritual intention requires. Conversely, they will not place more force in the soul than is simultaneously expressed in the matter. For their art is based on an utterly corporeal expression of the spiritual. Sculpture can therefore attain its true peak only in natures, which bring along their concept, that is, in natures that are at all times in actuality everything that is in accordance with their idea or soul. As such, they are consequently divine natures. Had no mythology preceded sculpture, it would have arrived at the gods through its own means. If they did not find any gods, they would have invented them.[5] Moreover, since the spirit has at a deeper stage the same relationship to matter that we ascribed to the soul, namely, that it is a principle of activity and movement, while matter is the principle of rest and inactivity, the law of the moderation of expression and of passion is a basic law that flows out of its nature. But this law is valid not merely for the baser passions, but also likewise for, if we are permitted to put it like this, the loftier and divine passions, of which the soul is capable in rapture, devotion and adoration. Consequently, given that only the gods are liberated from these passions, the soul is also drawn from their side to the sculpture of divine natures.

Painting seems to be in a completely different situation than sculpture. For painting does not present [its content], as does sculpture, with corporeal things, but rather through light and colour and hence through incorporeal and, to a certain degree, spiritual media. Painting in no way produces its images as the objects themselves, but rather expressly wants them to be regarded as images. Painting inherently does not place the same weight on matter that sculpture does, and seems for this reason, in fact, to elevate matter over spirit and to sink deeper under itself than sculpture can in the same case. In opposition to sculpture, it may, with all the greater warrant, place a clear preponderance upon the soul. Where it strives for the supreme, it will, of course, ennoble the passions through character or moderate them through grace, or indicate the power of the soul in them. In contrast to this, however, these higher passions, which are grounded in the affinity of the soul with the Supreme Being [*Wesen*], consummately befit painting. Indeed, if sculpture consummately balances the force, through which a being [*Wesen*] exists external to itself and operates in nature, with the force, through which it lives inwardly as soul, and if it excludes mere passivity from matter, on the contrary, painting may diminish the character of the force and activity of sculpture to the advantage of the soul. Painting thereby metamorphoses them into adoration and forbearance, through which it seems that humans become more sensitive to the inspirations of the soul and to higher influences more generally.

From this opposition alone, we explain the necessary predominance of sculpture in antiquity as well as painting in the modern world. Antiquity was utterly disposed to sculpture while the modern world makes the soul into the passive organ of higher revelations. This shows that it does not suffice to strive after the sculptural in form and presentation. Rather, it is preeminently requisite to think and feel in a sculptural manner, that is, in an ancient manner. But if the debauchery of sculpture into the painterly is a depravation of art, then the contraction of painting into sculptural conditions and forms imposes an arbitrary restriction upon it. If sculpture, just like gravity, works toward a single point, then painting, like light, creatively fills the whole universe.

The proof of this unrestricted universality of painting is history itself and the example of the greatest masters who, without violating the being [*Wesen*] of their art, cultivated each particular stage of art for itself to the point of consummation. Hence we are able to find again in the history of art the same consequences that we were able to prove in art itself.
[…]

Notes

1   These are the words of J. G. Hamann from the *Kleeblatt hellenistischer Briefe* [*Cloverleaf of Hellenistic Letters*]. […]

2   *Translator's Note.* King Maximilian I Joseph, to whom the speech is dedicated.

3   *Translator's Note.* Schelling alludes to Aristotle's account of *hamartia*, the tragic flaw or error.

4   There are in the presentation of the soul two stages of art: the first, where the soul is still present as an indistinguishable element, more in itself than in consummate actualization; in the other, where the soul flows together with favour and grace.

5   *Translator's Note.* Schelling is playing on the relationship between finding [*finden*] and inventing [*erfinden*]. The prefix intensifies the verb, almost as if to say that had sculptors not found gods, then they would more intensely find them, i.e. imagine them.

Historical-Critical Introduction to the Philosophy of Mythology (1845)*

The question of *how* the mythological ideas were meant shows the difficulty or impossibility in which we find ourselves when assuming that they were meant as truth. For this reason then the first attempt is to interpret them figuratively; that is, to assume in them a truth, but a different one than they express immediately – the second attempt is to see in them an original truth, but one that has been *distorted*. But, rather, after the result just obtained one can open up the question of whether the mythological ideas were *meant* at all, namely, if they were object of an intent – that is, of a free holding for true. So here also the question was incorrectly posed; it was posed under a presupposition that was itself incorrect. The mythological ideas are neither invented nor voluntarily taken on. – Products of a process independent of thinking and willing, they were of unambiguous and urgent reality for the consciousness subjected to this process. Peoples as well as individuals are only tools of this process, which they do not survey, which they serve without understanding it. It is not up to them to elude these representations, to take them up or not to take them up; for they do not *come* to them externally, but rather they *are* in them without them being conscious of how; for they come from out of the inner part of consciousness itself, to which they present themselves with a necessity that permits no doubt about their truth.

Once one has hit upon the idea of such a manner of emergence, then it is understood completely that the mythology considered merely materially seemed so puzzling, in that it is a known fact that also other things resting on a spiritual process, on a particular and internal experience, appear as alien and incomprehensible to those who do not have this experience, while it has an entirely comprehensible and reasonable meaning for him to whom the internal process is not hidden. The central question with respect to mythology is the question of meaning. But the meaning of *mythology* can only be the meaning of the *process* by which it emerges into being.

Were the personalities and the events that are the content of mythology of the type that, according to the assumed concepts, we could consider them

---

*Translated by Mason Richey and Markus Zisselsberger from F.W.J. Schelling, *Sämmtliche Werke* (Stuttgart and Augsberg: Cotta, 1856–1861), Division Two, Volume One.

possible objects of an immediate experience, and were gods beings that could appear, then no one would ever have thought to take them in a sense other than an *actual* one. One would have explained the belief in the truth and objectivity of these representations – the belief that we absolutely must ascribe to heathendom, should it not, in a different way, itself become a fable for us – simply out of an *actual experience* of that earlier mankind. One would simply have assumed that these personalities, these occurrences, have in reality happened and appeared to that earlier mankind in such a way, and thus were also true for it in its proper and actual understanding – just like the analogous appearances and encounters that are recounted by the Abrahamites, and which to us in the current state are likewise impossible, were true for them. Now, just precisely that which was not thought previously is made possible by the presently justified explanation; this explanation is the first that has an answer to the question: how was it possible that the peoples of antiquity were not only able to bestow faith in those religious ideas – which appear to us thoroughly nonsensical and contrary to reason – but were able to bring them the most serious, in part painful, sacrifices. Because mythology is not something that emerged artificially, but is rather something that emerged naturally – indeed, under the given presupposition, with necessity – *form* and *content*, *matter* and *outer appearance*, cannot be differentiated in it. The ideas are not first present in another form, but rather they emerge only in, and thus also at the same time with, this form. Earlier in these lectures such an organic becoming was already demanded by us, but the principle of the process, by which alone it becomes explicable, was not found.

Because consciousness chooses or invents neither the ideas themselves nor their expression, mythology emerges immediately *as such* and in no other sense than in which it articulates itself. In consequence of the necessity with which the *content* of the ideas generates itself, mythology has from the beginning a *real* and thus also *doctrinal* meaning. In consequence of the necessity with which also the *form* emerges, mythology is thoroughly actual – that is, everything in it is thus to be understood as mythology expresses it, not as if something else were thought, something else said. Mythology is not *allegorical*; it is *tautegorical*. To mythology the gods are actually existing essences, gods that are not something *else*, do not *mean* something else, but rather *mean* only what they are. Earlier, authenticity and doctrinal meaning were opposed to one another. But according to our explanation both authenticity and doctrinal meaning cannot be separated, and instead of relinquishing the authenticity to the benefit of a doctrinal meaning, or saving the authenticity, but at the cost of the doctrinal meaning, like the poetic view, we are rather, conversely, obliged through our explanation to assert and maintain the consistent unity and indivisibility of the meaning.

In order to show immediately in practice the foundational principle of the *unconditioned* authenticity, let us recall that in mythology two moments were differentiated: 1) the polytheistic; in relation to this moment we will thus, after the repudiation of every inauthentic meaning, maintain that the talk is *actually* of gods; after the earlier explanations, what this means to say requires no repeated discussion. Only in the meantime the discovery has come to light that the process producing mythology already has its ground and beginning in the *first actual consciousness* of mankind. From this it follows that the representations of the gods could at *no* possible or presumable time have been left to that contingent emergence that is assumed in the usual hypotheses, and that, in particular, there remains for a presumably *pre*-mythological polytheism – as is in part presupposed by those explanations – so little time as for the reflections on natural phenomena, from which – according to Heyne, Hermann, or Hume[1] – mythology is supposed to have emerged, for the first actual consciousness was, according to the matter, already a mythological one. That merely so-called polytheism is supposed to rest on contingent representations of invisible, supernatural beings; but there was never originally a part of the human race that was in the position to come to representations of the gods in such a way. This polytheism prior to mythology is therefore a mere figment of the schools. It is, we can say, *historically* proven that there could not be another polytheism prior to the mythological one, that there was never another polytheism besides a mythological one – that is, that one that is posited with the process proven by us, thus none in which there would not have been actual gods, that is, in which *God* would not have been the ultimate content. But mythology is not merely polytheism in general, but rather 2) historical polytheism, so much so that that which would not (*potentia* [potentially] or *actu* [actually]) be polytheism historically could also not be called mythological. But in spite of this moment, the succession is to be understood as an actual one and the unconditional authenticity to be held on to firmly. It is a movement that *truly occurs*, to which consciousness is *in reality* subjugated. Even in the specifics of the succession, it is not arbitrariness, but rather necessity, that a particular god and no other precedes or follows some other god, and even in view of the special circumstances of those events, which happen in the history of the gods, no matter how odd they may appear to us, in the consciousness the conditions out of which the representations of the same naturally arise will constantly be proven. In order to take on a comprehensible and graspable meaning, the emasculation of Uranus, the regicide of Kronos, and the other countless acts and events of the history of the gods require nothing other than to be understood literally.

One also cannot, as has often been attempted with revelation, differentiate *doctrine* and *history* and consider the latter as mere wording of the former. The doctrine is not *external to* history, but rather precisely history itself is also the doctrine, and conversely the doctrinal of mythology is contained precisely in the historical.

Considered objectively, mythology is as what it presents itself: *actual theogony*, the history of the gods. Because, however, actual gods are only those for which God lies as the ground, the final content of the history of the gods is the production of an actual becoming *of God* in consciousness, to which *the gods* are related only as the individual, productive moments.

Considered *subjectively*, or as according to its emergence into being, mythology is a *theogonic process*. It is 1) a process in general, which consciousness actually completes, namely, in such a way that it is obliged to tarry in the individual moments, and in the one following constantly hangs on to the preceding one, and thus *experiences* that movement in the proper sense. It is 2) an *actually* theogonic process; that is, one that stems from an essential relation of human consciousness to God, from a relation in which it, according to its substance, is what is God-positing, thus in virtue of which it is in general that which posits God naturally (*natura sua* [by its own nature]). Because the original relation is a natural one, consciousness cannot emerge from this relation without being led back into it *through a process*. Hereby it cannot (I plead that this be noted) help but to appear as that which again *posits* God only *mediately* (indeed, precisely through a process) – that is, it cannot help but to appear as just the consciousness that produces God and thus as the theogonic one.

Note

1   *Editors' Note.* C.G. Heyne's, Gottfried Hermann's and David Hume's allegorical interpretations of mythology are critiqued earlier in the lecture course.

Further reading

The above reproduces only brief extracts from Schelling's 1802–4 lecture course on the philosophy of art and his 1840s lecture courses on the philosophy of mythology. We therefore recommend that the interested reader turn initially to these texts, as well as the middle period discussions of mythology, particularly *The Deities of Samothrace* (translated by Robert F. Brown [Scholars Press for American Academy of Religion, 1977]). For secondary literature, the following should be consulted:

Edward Allen Beach, *The Potencies of God(s): Schelling's Philosophy of Mythology* (SUNY Press, 1994).

James Dodd, 'Philosophy and Art in Schelling's *System des transzendentalen Idealismus*,' *Review of Metaphysics* 52.1 (1998): 51–85.

Markus Gabriel, 'The Mythological Being of Reflection: An Essay on Schelling, Hegel and the Necessity of Contingency,' in Gabriel and Žižek (eds), *Mythology, Madness and Laughter: Subjectivity in German Idealism* (Continuum, 2009), 15–94.

Mildred Galland-Szymkowiak, 'Philosophy and the History of Art: Reconsidering Schelling's Philosophy of Art from the Perspective of Works of Art.' *Critical Horizons* 3 (2015): 296–320.

Devin Zane Shaw, *Freedom and Nature in Schelling's Philosophy of Art* (Bloomsbury, 2010).

Daniel Whistler, *Schelling's Theory of Symbolic Language: Forming the System of Identity* (Oxford University Press, 2013).

Jason M. Wirth, *Schelling's Practice of the Wild: Time, Art, Imagination* (SUNY Press, 2015), Part III.

11

Religion

Introduction

The references to God, the Trinity, mythological theogonies and revelation scattered through the preceding chapters indicate quite clearly Schelling's interest in various religious themes and conceptual apparatuses – and this is indeed a constant in his thinking. At Tübingen in the early 1790s, Schelling received a theological education, submitting theses on original sin and Marcion, as well as taking a final oral examination on the Letter to the Philippians. When he moved to Bavaria in 1803, he collaborated with thinkers such as Franz Baader, who were seeking to breathe new life into the Neoplatonic and mystical writings of Meister Eckhart and Jakob Böhme. And Schelling's engagement with theological issues was finally put to the test on another, and very different, stage: in post-Hegelian Berlin, where he lectured on the philosophy of revelation.

Three features of Schellingian philosophy of religion are emphasized in the following: its naturalization of religious value, its introduction of difference into God as a means of avoiding pantheism and its emphasis on the irreducibly historical character of revealed truths.

In his earlier work, Schelling insists with Hegel that 'the orthodox concepts of God are no more'.[1] The early Schelling is committed to naturalistic explanations that refuse appeals to transcendent powers or persons, and he argues that those who have an orthodox conception of God fail to see the world for what it is: configurations of natural forces. The poem, *Heinz Widerporst's Epicurean Confession of Faith*, reproduced as the first extract below, is Schelling's scabrous satire on those like Novalis and Friedrich Schleiermacher who were intent on reintroducing religious transcendence back into the romantic philosophical project. Schelling lives up to his early reputation as a 'Jacobin' by parodying such accommodations to piety in the name of a sensual hedonism and an immanentist philosophy of nature that interprets all post-Christian dualisms as nature's self-misrecognition of its own underlying unity.

By 1809, however, Schelling's project had changed slightly: instead of refusing the reality of divine personality in the name of natural immanence, he attempts to incorporate it into an immanentist system. The *Freedom* essay puts forward this view of God, and it does so – as can be seen in the third extract below – by echoing the Kabbalistic doctrine of *tsimtsum*: According to Schelling God is *implicitly* (i.e. as ground, or nature) the immanent cause of all that is, whereas *explicitly* God exists as distinct from the finite creatures that are nevertheless 'in' him. Thus, during the 1810s, God's self-differentiation proves to be central to Schelling's philosophy of religion.

Finally, a connection between narration, history and religion is frequent in Schelling's work. The *Lectures on the Method of Academic Study*, published in 1803 and extracted below, call, for instance, for theology to become speculative history, and *Philosophy and Religion* of the following year includes, among other things, an oft-cited consideration of the 'fall' of finite beings from God. History is central to Schelling's philosophy of religion, in part, because – unlike the other major Idealists – he tends to understand the essence of religion as having something to do with creation. The final chapter in Schelling's engagement with religion is represented below in the passages from his famous 1841/2 *Lectures on the Philosophy of Revelation*, which he delivered upon first arriving in Berlin. In the excerpted passages, Schelling argues that God, in some important respect, transcends his creation as *pure act* and source of all that is (a view that also has consequences for how Schelling thinks about the relationship between mythology and revelation).

Taken together, the following five extracts demonstrate that, while Schelling's conception of God undergoes significant changes from one period of thought to another, he never ceases to understand philosophy to be intimately bound up with theological concerns.

Note

1   F.W.J. Schelling, *Historisch-Kritische Ausgabe*, ed. the Schelling Commission of the Bavarian Academy of Sciences (Stuttgart: Frommann-Holzboog, 2001), Series Three, Volume One, p. 22.

Heinz Widerporst's Epicurean Confession of Faith (1799)*

I cannot bear it any longer,
But must rise again to lash out stronger;
Once more stir up all my senses
Which've gradually lost their defences
To all those high, otherworldly screechings
Through which they force me to accept their teachings;
I must again become one of our own—
Made up of just blood, flesh, marrow, bone.
I just don't know how they can compose
All these endless pieces of religious prose;
I don't like to brood on it for an age,
Instead I will attack them in a rage.
So, to stop these spirits of high-standing
From blocking my words and my understanding,
In response, at this very moment I insist
That the only real and true things to exist
Are what one can feel with one's hand,
Not things you can only understand
Through mortification, suffering and fasts
'Till you wish for release from your body at last.
When they spoke so defiantly of it, it's true,
I was taken aback and had to think things through;
I read, as if I really knew,
The Speeches and the Fragment too.[1]
I'd have readily given such things the nod,
Renouncing work and life without God;
I hoped to mock evil, so thereby
Make myself a god up high,
And I had already immersed my soul
In the intuition of the universal whole,[2]
When my native wit reminded me
That I was as good as lost at sea,
That down the old tracks should I crawl

---

*Translated by Judith Kahl and Daniel Whistler from *Schellingiana Rariora*, ed. Luigi Pareyson (Turin: d'Erasmo, 1977).

And be nobody's fool.
I was not idle about following this call;
But did not become straight like old Saul,
I had to dispel whims of the kind
That had once upset my mind,
And reteach my body how to walk
By sending for as much wine as pork—
All of which proved very worthwhile.
When I had regained my old style,
Out of women I could get a rise,
See brightly out of both eyes;
And having had my fill of things to taste and bite,
At once I sat down to write.
I gave myself this brief:
Do not falter in that belief
Which helped you through fair and foul weather
And held your body and soul together,
Even though it's not susceptible of proof
Nor reducible to conceptual truth.
How they speak of the inner light!
They talk a lot and prove nothing outright,
They fill your ears with great speeches
About something that just falls to pieces,
That looks like poetry or hallucination,
But is, in fact, all poesy's negation.
They say nothing of themselves besides
What they feel within and bear inside.
Thus I intend to further confess
My creed to which all may acquiesce,
As I feel it burn within my frame,
As it swells in every vein:
In evil hours and in good, I have been
Happy with myself and contented within,
For it has slowly dawned on me
That matter is the only certainty,
It protects and guides everything, large or small,
Is righteous father to all,
It is the element to which all thinking does tend;
For all knowledge, the beginning and end.
I don't worry about the invisible too much,
Instead I remain with what I can see and touch:
What I can smell, taste and feel,

So all my senses grasp what's real.
Let my one religion be
To love a pretty knee
And breasts so full and hips so slim,
Flowers from which sweet smells overbrim,
All pleasures full of nourishment,
All loves sweet with encouragement.
This is why, should one religion still exist
(Though from it all I personally could desist),
Out of all that are around
Only Catholicism could break me down:
As it was in the good old days,
Without all the quarrels, without all the frays;
When in hard times and in good all were One,
Catholics didn't look to distant climes for fun,
Nor did they at heaven gape,
But still for God they all went ape,
Believed the earth was at the centre of a universal dome
And at the centre of the earth was Rome,
Where the chief resided
And the holiest scepter presided,
And there lived the parsons with all and sundry
Together, as in milk-and-honey country.
And in the house high up in the sky
The same people lived such luxury, whereby
They held a daily wedding fete
Between the virgins and their wizened old mates;
And at home the wife would scream and shout
And reign supreme, as happens hereabout.
I'd have laughed at this 'till my sides split,
While also getting much use out of it.
But events have now moved on apace;
It is a scandal, it is a disgrace
That now it is seasonable
For everything to be so very reasonable,
It is comme il faut to strut around with right and wrong,
And make a parade of fine speeches at the throng;
At every turn, even the youths
Are clipped with virtue's truths,
And one Catholic brother
Is as good as any other.
So all religion have I renounced and quit;

To none of them will I commit.
I go neither to church nor to hear the priest talk sweetly,
Have finished with all faith completely,
Except that one religion which rules within,
Leads me to sense and the poetic word,
Daily my heart is stirred
At its eternal instigation,
Its perpetual transformation
Without peace or delay.
It is a secret all can survey,
A poem that never dies,
Which speaks to my nose, ears, eyes,
So that I can no longer believe nor attest
But what this religion plants in my breast,
Nor is anything just or secure
But what its revelations make sure;
For in its features so deeply wrought
What is true must needs be sought;
The false ought never to seep its way in
And certainly never emerge from within;
Through forms and images my faith is revealed
And does not stay inside and concealed.
So that from the ciphers that lie to hand
We might solve the mystery and thereby understand
Without recourse to anything real
Except what our fingers are able to feel.
This is why if there's one religion I mustn't mock,
It would be found in mosses, rock,
Flowers and all things that are there
And which press forth into light and air;
It reveals itself in depths and heights,
These are the hieroglyphs it writes.
Before the cross I'd happily bend down prone,
If there were a mountain I could be shown
On which, for Christians' edification,
A temple emerged—purely of nature's creation—
On top of which shining towers rise
With magnetized bells of a great size,
And on the altars, in the great halls
Crystal crucifixes grace the walls,
Capuchins stand still as stone
Parading with everything vergers might own,

In chasubles fringed with gold
With silver chalices and ostensories to hold.
However, up until the present time
No one has heard such bells chime,
And so I will not lose my thread
But will persist in godlessness instead,
Until someone is sent my way
Who makes faith as plain as day—
Although I doubt he would.
Therefore, I intend to hold good
Until the Last Judgement is upon me,
Which no one else will live to see.
I believe the world exists eternally
And will never decompose internally;
For I'd like to know when it would
Burn all its shrubbery and wood,
And how they'd try to get hell hot
So as to cook up sinners in a pot.
I am delivered from fear's control,
I can now heal body and soul;
Instead of throwing about my arms
Losing myself in the universe's charms,
I immerse myself in the bright, deep hue
Of my beloved's eyes so blue.
I don't know why the world should make me frown,
Since I know it all the way down:
It's an animal who is docile and meek
Who never shows us a threatening streak;
There are laws with which it has to agree
And so it lies before me peacefully.
Within it, a giant-spirit has grown,
But all its senses have been turned to stone;
It cannot escape from its tight shell
Nor break out of its iron cell,
Although it is often stirred to flight:
To extend and move onwards with might.
In what is living and even what has died
It struggles towards consciousness with active strides.
This explains how all things appear,
For it swells up and makes them persevere;
This force, through which metals sprout,
Which forces trees in spring to fill out,

Which searches in all depths and heights
For what turns out towards the light,
Which struggles on and spares no pains
But now shoots up to higher domains
Stretching out its limbs yet further,
Before now shortening them together,
Twisting and turning it desperately tries
To find the right shape, form and size.
And struggling thus with its fingers and toes
Against that resistant element to which it's opposed,
It learns to live in a small space
In which its senses are first put in place;
It's but a dwarf: enclosed tight,
Finely formed and upright,
Named the son of man in the past,
The giant-spirit finds itself at last.
From a deep sleep and a long dream
He awakes to scarcely recognise how he seems,
He looks at himself with marvel and pleasure,
Eyes wide open, he examines and takes measure;
He would like to quickly with all his senses
Melt back into nature's expanses,
But he has now fallen away
And cannot flow back as he did yesterday;
Instead, small and enclosed must he stand
Alone in his own vast land.
Fearful that frightening dreams might foretell
The giant plucking up its courage to rebel,
And like the first god of the golden age
Devouring its own children in a rage.
He fails to realise that he and the giant are the same,
For he has forgotten his previous names,
And torments himself with ghosts of the dead.
And yet he could say to himself instead:
I am the deity who nourishes within
The spirit which moves what is and what's been.
From the early struggles the dark force induces
Past the gush of primordial life-juices,
Through which matter and force swell out,
And the first blossoms and buds sprout,
Up until the first beam of a newly-born light

That, like a second creation, breaks through the night,
And that for the world's thousand eyes,
Like day does night, illuminates the skies;
And at last dwelling within the youthful power of thought,
Through which nature recreates itself from naught,
As one power, one pulse, one life,
Restriction and expansion's one continual strife.
For this reason there is nothing that I do detest
More than a foreign, if distinguished guest,
Who struts about from North to South
With evil speeches in his mouth
About the essence of the natural sphere;
Who esteems himself so very dear.
These men derive from a distinct new race
With a special sense and spiritual grace;
They consign all others to a damned fate
And have sworn an eternal oath of hate
Against matter's works and existence;
Pictures strengthen their resistance
And they speak on religion as on a female
Whom one ought only to gaze at through a veil[3]
So as to prevent any sensuous allusion.
They produce verbal confusion,
Feel themselves all-mighty and a cut above,
And believe their members to have grown large from love,
Carrying the new Messiah still unborn
Who—elected by their decree—is sworn
To lead all the poor men
Great and small into a pen
Where they stop teasing and having fun,
But in a nice and Christian manner appear as One,
And they do anything else which is dubbed prophetic.
They are, indeed, by nature non-magnetic,
Although if they happen to touch a spirit who is true
And feel his power within them accrue,
They believe that they have brought about this existence
To now point North without assistance.
But their spirits are so very slack
That they can only speak of others' acts;
They understand how to shake and befuddle,
To leave all our thoughts in a muddle,

And think thereby they make spirits rich,
But all that happens is that noses itch,
Stomachs are polemically upset
And appetites are never whet.
I advise anyone who has read it,
So as to heal their corrupted spirit,
To take a beautiful girl aside
And in her the meaning of *Lucinde*[4] confide.
However, to all of them and their kind,
I will make known, and not stay resigned,
That against their sanctity and piety,
Their superior sense and otherworldly society,
I will scandalise intently all life long
As long as I can still hold on
To the worship of matter and light
And to German poetry's fundamental might.
So long as I cling to those two sweet eyes upon her face,
So long as I feel myself in the embrace
Of arms that promise admiration,
And by her lips am given consolation,
Her melody resonating in key,
Her life penetrating into me,
Then I can only strive for what's true,
All smoke and shimmer I will pierce through,
Then no thoughts in my head
Could flicker here and there like ghosts of the dead.
They would instead have nerves, blood, marrow and flesh,
And would be born free, strong and fresh.
But to the others I am still polite
And add, so as to conclude aright:
Let the devil and saltpetre fall
On Russians[5] and Jesuits all.
This text was written in Frau Venus' nest
Where I, Heinz Widerporst, have confessed;
The second called by such a name,
God give us still many seeds the same.[6]

Notes

1   *Translators' Note*. 'Speeches' refers to Schleiermacher's *Speeches on Religion to Its Cultural Despisers* and 'Fragment' to Novalis' *Christianity or Europa: A Fragment*.

2   *Translators' Note*. 'Intuition of the universe' is the central concept in Schleiermacher's *Speeches*.

3   *Translators' Note*. 'durch Schleier schauen': a pun on 'Schleiermacher'.

4   *Translators' Note*. Friedrich Schlegel's scandalous novel published in 1799.

5   *Translators' Note*. The attack on Russians here is seemingly a reference to the Russophile playwright, August von Kotzebue, whose burlesque, 'The Tower of Babel', satirizing the Jena and Weimar intellectual scene, was performed at Weimar on New Year's Eve 1799.

6   *Translators' Note*. These last lines reference the opening of Novalis's collection of fragments, *Pollen* (otherwise known as *Miscellaneous Observations*).

Lectures on the Method of Academic Study (1803)*

The Historical Construction of Christianity

The real sciences can be distinguished from the absolute or ideal science only because they contain a historical element. Theology, however, apart from this element, stands in a special relation to history.

It is primarily in theology, which deals with speculative Ideas, that philosophy becomes objective. For this reason, theology is the highest synthesis of philosophical and historical knowledge. To demonstrate this is the chief purpose of the following remarks.

My assertion that theology stands in a special relation to history is not based solely on the fact that religion, like every other type of knowledge, like civilization itself, could only have originated in the teachings of superior beings – in other words, that from the very outset religion was tradition. The current explanations – according to which the idea of God or gods was produced by fear, gratitude or some other feeling or was a crafty invention on the part of early lawgivers are unsatisfactory; in the former hypothesis the idea of God is reduced to a purely psychological phenomenon, while the latter fails to explain how it ever occurred to anyone to make himself a lawgiver in the first place, or how anyone could have used religion as a threat to enforce obedience unless religion had already existed. Among the falsest and shallowest writings in recent times are the so-called histories of

---

*Translated by E.S. Morgan from F.W.J. Schelling, *Sämmtliche Werke* (Stuttgart and Augsberg: Cotta, 1856–1861), Division One, Volume Five.

mankind. Their views of the primitive conditions of our species are inspired by travelers' accounts stressing the rudeness of savage peoples. Actually there is no condition of barbarism that is not a degenerated form of vanished civilization. The history of the earth will eventually prove that the savage tribes of today are the remnants of nations which were separated from the rest of the world as a result of revolutions. Unable to communicate with each other, robbed of their earlier cultural possessions, they have regressed to their present state. I firmly believe that the earliest condition of the human race was a civilized one and that the first states, sciences, arts and religions were founded simultaneously – or, more accurately, that they were not separated but were perfectly fused, as they will again be one day in their final form.

Nor does my assertion that theology has a special relation to history refer merely to the fact that the particular forms of Christianity in which religion exists among us can be known only historically. What makes this relation special is that in Christianity the universe is viewed as history, as a moral kingdom, and that this view constitutes its fundamental character. We can fully understand this only by comparing Christianity with the religion of ancient Greece. If I do not mention still older religions, notably that of India, it is because in this respect they provide no contrast (this is not to imply, however, that they are closer to Christianity). The limits of the present lecture do not permit a complete exposition of this view; hence, I shall only outline it briefly. The mythology of the Greeks was a self-contained world of symbols for the Ideas, which could be visualized as real only in the form of gods. Each particular divinity and the world of the gods as a whole were conceived of as clearly delimited on the one hand and as absolute on the other. The infinite was perceived only in the finite and, in this way, even subordinated to the finite. The gods were beings of a higher nature, abiding, immutable figures. Very different is a religion which is concerned directly with the infinite, in which the finite is not conceived of as a symbol of the infinite – nor as existing at the same time for its own sake – but only as an allegory of the infinite, wholly subordinated to it. The system in which the ideas of such a religion become objective is necessarily infinite itself, not a world completed and bounded on all sides; the figures which represent the godhead are not abiding but transitory – not eternal beings of nature but historical figures in which the divine is revealed transitorily, its fleeting appearance held fast by faith, yet never transformed into an absolute presence.

Where the infinite itself can become one finite thing, there it can also become many, there polytheism is possible. Where the infinite is only *represented* by the finite, it remains necessarily one, and no polytheism is possible except as a coexistence of divine figures. Polytheism arises from a synthesis between absoluteness and limitation, a synthesis in which neither formal absoluteness nor limitation is abolished. In this respect, a religion like Christianity cannot be rooted in nature, for it does not conceive the finite as symbol of the infinite, nor as existing for its own sake. Consequently, Christianity can be rooted only in what falls within time – that is, in history; and hence Christianity is, in the highest sense and in its innermost spirit, historical. Every moment of time is a revelation of a particular aspect of God, in each of which He is absolute. That which the Greek religion had as simultaneity, Christianity has as succession in time, although it has not yet achieved its definitive form.

It has already been pointed out that nature is to history what the real is to the ideal; the same is true of the relation between the Greek religion and the Christian religion. In Christianity the divine principle no longer reveals itself in nature and is recognizable only in history. Nature as such is the sphere in which things are in themselves, i.e. in which things have a life independent of the Ideas (though they symbolize the Ideas in virtue of the fact that their finitude embodies the infinite). This is why God becomes, so to speak, exoteric in nature; the ideal manifests itself in something different from the ideal – in an existent. Yet the divine is truly exoteric only insofar as this existent is taken for the essence, and the symbol is viewed as independent of the Idea; in terms of the Idea it is esoteric. The divine unveils itself in the ideal world – above all, in history; here the mystery of the divine kingdom is disclosed.

In nature the intelligible world is present only symbolically. In Greek poetry it was as though wrapped in a cocoon, still veiled objectively and unexpressed subjectively. By contrast, Christianity is the revealed mystery, and whereas paganism is inherently exoteric, Christianity is inherently esoteric.

With the advent of Christianity the relation between nature and the ideal world was thus inevitably reversed. In paganism nature was made manifest while the ideal world was veiled in mystery. In Christianity the ideal world was progressively revealed while nature inevitably receded into the background as mystery. To the Greeks, nature as such was divine; their gods were not supernatural or extra-natural. To the modern world nature was a closed book, for she was not conceived of in herself, but only as a metaphor of the invisible spiritual world. The most active phenomena of nature, such as electricity and chemical change, were scarcely known to the ancients – at least they failed to arouse the widespread enthusiasm they arouse in the modern world. The highest religious feeling, as expressed in

Christian mysticism, holds the mystery of nature and the mystery of the Incarnation to be one and the same.

[...]

Christianity represented a great turning point in human history, and this is why the science of religion in the Christian world is inseparable from history – indeed, why it must be identical with it. But the synthesis of religion with history, without which theology would be inconceivable, presupposes in turn the validity of the Christian view of history.

History is commonly opposed to philosophy, but this opposition holds good only so long as history is conceived of as a sequence of accidental occurrences – the vulgar theory – or as merely empirical necessity – a supposedly superior conception, but actually as narrow as the other. History, too, springs from an eternal unity and has roots in the absolute, just like nature or any other object of cognition. To the common understanding the contingency of events and actions seems to be founded on the contingent nature of individuals. But I ask: What is this or that individual but the very man who carried out this or that particular action? There can be no other definition of the individual. Consequently, if the action was necessary, so was the individual who performed it. Even from a subordinate point of view, what may appear as a free act and hence objective 'by accident' seems so merely by the circumstance that the individual supposes to be of his own choice what is predetermined and necessary. At the same time, however, so far as the consequences are concerned and whether for good or for evil, the act was an instrument of absolute necessity.

Empirical necessity is nothing but a device for extending the scope of contingency by making necessity regress indefinitely. If we allow this kind of necessity in nature only on the phenomenal plane, must we not a fortiori do the same where human history is concerned? What intelligent person will persuade himself that events like the development of Christianity, the migrations of peoples, the Crusades and other great events originated in the empirical causes assigned to them? Even were these in fact the controlling causes, still they have to be regarded as instruments of an eternal order of things.

What is true of history in general is especially true of the history of religion, namely, it is founded upon an eternal necessity, and consequently it is possible to construct it. By means of such a construction history becomes closely bound up with the science of religion.

The historical construction of Christianity can have only one point of departure, namely, the view that the world as a whole, and hence also its history, necessarily shows two different aspects and that the opposition between them, which is that between the modern world and the ancient world, is sufficient to account for Christianity's nature and special characteristics. The ancient world represents the 'nature' side of history in the sense that its dominant idea – what gives it unity – is that the infinite exists only in the finite. The end of the ancient world and the beginning of modern times, whose dominant principle is the infinite, could come about only when the true infinite was embodied in the finite – the purpose was not to deify the finite, but to offer it up as a sacrifice to God in His own person and thus to reconcile the two. Hence Christianity's leading idea is God become incarnate, Christ as culmination, the closing out of the ancient world of gods. In Him, as in the ancient gods, the divine principle becomes finite, but the humanity he assumes is not humanity in its highest estate but in its lowest. He stands as the boundary between the two worlds, decreed from all eternity yet a transitory phenomenon in time. He Himself returns to the invisible realm and promises the coming of the Spirit – not the principle which becomes finite to stay finite but the ideal principle which leads the finite back to the infinite and, as such, is the light of the modern world.

[...]

The all-pervasive antinomy between the divine and the natural is transcended within the subject only when both are – in an incomprehensible way – conceived as one. Such a subjective unity is expressed in the term 'miracle'. In this sense, every idea is a miracle, since it is produced in time without having any relation to time. No idea can come into being in a temporal manner; it is an expression of the absolute – that is, God himself reveals the idea, and this is why the concept of Revelation is absolutely necessary in Christianity.

[...]

The reconciliation of the finite which had seceded from God, a reconciliation effected by God's birth in the finite world, is the basic idea of Christianity; the idea of the Trinity, which expresses the whole Christian view of the world and of its history, is a necessary part of it. Lessing, in his *Education of Mankind*, attempted to develop the philosophical implications of this doctrine, and his observations on this subject are perhaps more profoundly speculative than anything else he wrote. But his interpretation fails to connect this idea closely enough with the history of the world. The true relation is as follows: the eternal Son of God, born of the essence of the Father of all things, is the finite itself, as it exists in God's eternal intuition;

this finite manifests itself as a suffering God, subject to the vicissitudes of time, who at the culmination of His career, in the person of Christ, closes the world of the finite and opens the world of the infinite, i.e. the reign of the Spirit.

[...]

On the Study of Theology

I find it difficult to speak of the study of theology because I am convinced that the method of that science and the proper perspective in which its truths must be viewed are today lost and forgotten. Its doctrines are interpreted in an empirical sense both by proponents and opponents. Removed from their native soil and planted in the soil of empiricism, they lose all meaning.

According to the theologians, Christianity is a divine revelation, which they represent as an act that God performed in time. Thereby, they themselves take the position that the origin of Christianity can be accounted for in terms of natural causation. You really do not have to know much about the history and culture of the early centuries to arrive at a satisfactory explanation of this type. It is sufficient to read the scholarly books that trace the 'germ' of Christianity not just to Judaism but to a single religious community which existed before Christianity. In fact, you do not even have to read those books; Josephus and the surviving fragments of early Christian historians (which have not yet been put to proper use) will supply ample evidence in favour of this theory. In short, Christ as an individual is perfectly intelligible, and it was absolutely inevitable that he would be conceived of as a symbolic person in a higher sense.

As for those who look upon the spread of Christianity as the work of divine Providence, let them study the period of its first conquests; then they will recognize that Christianity was merely a particular manifestation of the spirit of the age. Christianity did not create this spirit; it was only an anticipatory stirring of that spirit, its earliest expression. The Roman empire was ripe for Christianity centuries before Constantine chose to put the Cross on its banner. Widespread dissatisfaction with material things was producing a longing for the spiritual and the invisible; an empire in its decadence, whose power was purely temporal, failure of nerve in the face of the situation, a feeling of unhappiness – these necessarily brought about a collective readiness to embrace a religion which guides men to the ideal world, teaching happiness through renunciation.

Christian religious teachers cannot justify any of their historical assertions without first making their own the higher view of history which is prescribed by both philosophy and Christianity. They have fought unbelief long enough on its own terms, instead of attacking its intellectual foundations. They ought to have said to the Naturalists, 'You are perfectly right from the point of view you take, and we believe that in terms of it your conclusions are correct. What we deny is the point of view itself, or at best allow it to be of purely secondary importance. Your position is the same as that of empiricists who prove irrefutably to the philosopher that all knowledge involves external impressions.'

The same observations may be made concerning current interpretations of theological dogmas. Clearly, the idea of the Trinity, unless understood speculatively, has no meaning whatever. The dogma of the Incarnation is interpreted in the same empirical manner, namely, that God took on human nature at a given moment of time. This view simply makes no sense for God is eternally outside of time. Consequently, the process of God's becoming man has been going on from all eternity. The culmination of this process is Christ's assuming visible human form, and for this reason it is also its beginning; starting with Christ, it has been going on ever since – all His successors are members of one and the same body of which He is the head. History bears witness that in Christ God first became truly objective, for who before Christ revealed the infinite in this way?

[...]

The fact that Christianity existed before and apart from its appearance in the world proves the necessity of its idea, and also that here as elsewhere no oppositions are absolute. The Christian missionaries who went to India thought they were bringing unheard-of tidings to the inhabitants when they taught that the God of the Christians had become man. But the Hindus were not surprised; they did not in the least contest the incarnation of God in Christ, and only thought it strange that an event that occurs frequently among them should have occurred only once among the Christians. It is not to be denied that they had a better understanding of their own religion than the Christian missionaries had of theirs.

On account of the universality of its idea, the historical construction of Christianity presupposes the religious construction of history as a whole. Consequently, such a construction has as little in common with the so-called history of religion (which, incidentally, deals with anything rather than religion) as with the special history of the Christian religion and the Christian Church.

By its very nature, such a construction is possible only on the basis of a higher knowledge, one which rises above empirical causality; in other words, it requires philosophy, which is the true organ of theology as science, wherein the highest ideas of the Divine Being, of nature as its instrument and of history as the revelation of God become objective. Needless to say, no one will confuse the thesis that the principal theological doctrines are speculative in character with the Kantian thesis. Kant sought to eliminate all positive and historical elements from Christianity and to transform it into a pure religion of reason. The true religion of reason recognizes the existence of only two forms of religion – the religion of nature, which is necessarily polytheistic in the Greek sense, and the wholly ethical religion which apprehends God in history. Kant does not aim at a speculative but a moral interpretation of these forms of religion. He is not interested in their inherent truth but only in their possible subjective effects on morality, and he does not actually go beyond the empirical point of view.

Like dogmatism in philosophy, dogmatism in theology deals with objects of absolute cognition from the empirical standpoint of the understanding. Kant does not attack the one or the other dogmatism at its root, since he was unable to put anything positive in its place. In particular, to explain the Bible morally in schools, as he proposed, would be merely to use empirical Christianity for purposes which cannot be achieved without misinterpretation and which do not lead to the idea of Christianity.

The earliest books on the history and doctrines of Christianity are merely a particular – and, moreover, imperfect – manifestation of it; its idea is not to be sought in these books whose value is to be measured by the extent to which they express this idea and are in consonance with it. Already for St. Paul, the proselytizer of the Gentiles, Christianity had become something different from what it was for its founder. We must not stop at any arbitrarily chosen point of time; we must have the whole of history and the world that has produced Christianity before our eyes.

One of the operations of the modern pseudo-enlightenment – which, with respect to Christianity, might rather be called a dis-enlightenment – is the attempt to 'restore' it, as the saying goes, to its 'original' meaning, to its early simplicity, in which form it is sometimes referred to as 'primitive' Christianity. One might have thought that Christian teachers would have been grateful to later ages for having extracted so much speculative matter from the meager contents of the earliest religious books and for having drawn it up in a system. To be sure, it may be easier to talk about the scholastic chaos of the old dogmatism, to write popular treatises and to indulge in hairsplitting and playing with etymologies than to grasp the universal import of Christianity and its teachings. One cannot help thinking that full understanding of it has been hampered by the so-called Biblical literature, which in terms of genuine religious ideas is not even remotely comparable to many other works, old and new, especially the Hindu books.

[...]

[Modern] theology, totally divorced from speculative thought, finally spread to public instruction. Teaching, we are told, is supposed to be purely moral in intent, devoid of references to the Idea. And yet morality is not the distinguishing characteristic of Christianity; surely, it is not just for the sake of a few moral maxims, such as 'Love thy neighbor,' that it became such a turning point in world history? It is not the fault of vulgar rationalism that moral preaching has not sunk still lower and taken up economics. There is no reason why, as the occasion may require, preachers should not provide advice to farmers, physicians and what not. Why stop at recommending vaccination from the pulpit – why not instruct the faithful on the best method of raising potatoes?

I have had to speak of the present state of theology because I could not hope to say what seems needful concerning the true nature of this science without distinguishing it clearly from the kind prevalent today.

The divine character of Christianity cannot be recognized by any indirect method; it can only be recognized directly in the context of the absolute view of history. This is why the notion (among others) of an indirect revelation, quite apart from its intentional ambiguity, is inadmissible: it is wholly empirical.

Merely empirical matters, such as the critical and philological investigation of the early Christian books, have to be kept entirely distinct from the study of theology proper. The higher ideas can have no influence on exegesis, which – as also in treating secular texts – does not ask whether the things said by an author are rational, historically true or religious, but only whether or not he actually said them. Whether these books are genuine or not, whether the stories they contain refer to things that actually happened as described or not, whether their content is or is not an adequate expression of the idea of Christianity – such questions have no bearing upon the reality of this idea, for it does not depend on such details, but is universal and absolute. Indeed, if Christianity had not been viewed so exclusively as a mere phenomenon in time, exegesis would have advanced much farther in historical evaluation of these documents, and our knowledge of essentially simple matters would not have got lost along so many learned detours.

The essential thing in the study of theology is to combine the speculative with the historical construction of Christianity and its principal doctrines.

[...]

The lineaments of Christianity, not confined to the past but extending over an immeasurable time, can be clearly recognized in poetry and philosophy. The former requires religion as the supreme, indeed the only, possibility of renewal; the latter, with its truly speculative standpoint, has restored the true meaning of religion, has done away with empiricism and the latter's ally, naturalism, and thereby has paved the way for a rebirth of esoteric Christianity and the Gospel of the absolute.

Philosophy and Religion (1804)[*]

Introduction

There was a time when religion was kept separate from popular belief within mystery cults like a holy fire, sharing a common sanctuary with philosophy. The legends of antiquity name the earliest philosophers as the originators of these mystery cults, from which the most enlightened among the later philosophers, notably Plato, liked to educe their divine teachings. At that time philosophers still had the courage and the right to discuss the singly great themes, the only ones worthy of philosophizing and rising above common knowledge.

Later the once-secret mystery cults became public and contaminated with foreign elements from popular belief. In order to keep itself pure, philosophy retreated from religion and became, in contrast to it, esoteric. Religion, which against its originary nature had intermingled with the real, sought to become an outward power, and since it lost any momentum to reach the well of truth, it also sought to stifle any truth outside of itself.

Thus religion gradually dispossessed philosophy of those themes it had dealt with since antiquity, and philosophy found itself confined to that which had no value for reason.

On the other hand, the sublime teachings, claimed one-sidedly by religion for itself from the shared property of philosophy, lost their significance

---

*Translated by Klaus Ottmann from F.W.J. Schelling, *Philosophie und Religion* (Tübingen: Cotta, 1804).

and, having been replanted to a completely different soil than the one they sprouted from, became altogether transformed.

This opposition resulted in a false accordance of philosophy with religion, one that arose from philosophers having lowered themselves to treat the origins of reason and ideas as concepts. This is exemplified by the dogmatism with which philosophy gained broad and considerable recognition while completely sacrificing its true character.

As this dogmatic knowledge was questioned more precisely and subjected to critique, it became evident that while it was applicable to objects of perception and finite things, it was only a bystander or, in fact, outright blind toward matters of reason. Because philosophy was acknowledged and accredited now more than ever as the only possible knowledge, the increasingly thorough self-awareness of its invalidity ran parallel to the rising value of its opposite, i.e. faith, so that ultimately all that is essentially philosophical in philosophy was completely given over to religion.

It would not be hard to cite evidence: I simply call to mind that this period in general was sufficiently defined by *Kant*.

The last echoes of the old, true philosophy were heard from Spinoza. He led philosophy back to its proper subjects although he did not steer clear of the pretense and tawdriness of another, albeit different, kind of dogmatism.

Aside from the teachings on the Absolute, the true mysteries of philosophy have as their most noble and indeed their sole content the eternal birth of all things and their relationship to God. All of ethics, as a directive for a beatific life, is built upon this and is a consequence of it, as it is found in the ambit of sacred teachings.

Those teachings, detached from the whole of philosophy, are called, not without reason, Philosophy of Nature.

That such teachings, which by definition are nothing if not speculative, are met with the most contradictory and abrogating judgements is to be expected; just as every partial view can be opposed by another partial view, so a comprehensive view, which encompasses the entire universe, can be opposed by all possible partial views. But it is quite impossible, on the one hand, to accredit a doctrine with being a philosophy, and a complete one at that, and on the other, to declare it in need of being complemented by faith; this contradicts and nullifies its concept because its essence consists in possessing clear knowledge and intuitive cognition of that which nonphilosophy means to grasp in faith.

[...]

[T]he particular, that which premonition or religious intuition is said to have the advantage over rational cognition is, according to most accounts, nothing other than a leftover from the difference that remains in the former but has completely disappeared in the latter. Each of us is compelled by nature to seek an Absolute, even those still wrapped up in finite things, but if we want to fix our thoughts on it, it eludes us. It hovers around us eternally, but, as Fichte has said, it is only there if one does not have it; as soon as one possesses it, it vanishes. It appears before the soul only at the moment when subjective activity joins the objective in unexpected harmony, which because it is unexpected has an advantage over free, desireless rational cognition to manifest itself as happiness, as illumination or as revelation. But as soon as this harmony is brought about, reasoning sets in, and the apparition takes flight. In this fleeting form, religion – inasmuch as it is also still in the domain of reflective cognition and dividedness – is a mere apparition of God within the soul. In contrast, philosophy is necessarily a higher and, as it were, a more tranquil perfection of the spirit; it is always within the Absolute, with no danger of the Absolute running away from it because philosophy itself has withdrawn into a territory above reason.

I will therefore leave faith, the premonition of beatitude, etc. – which are described by Eschenmayer[1] and which I regard as beneath philosophy rather than above it – in its realm. I will return, as per my original intention, to reclaiming those topics that have been appropriated by the dogmatism of religion and nonphilosophy on behalf of reason and philosophy.

What these are will unfold in the following.

The Idea of the Absolute

It would be entirely in accordance with the objective of maintaining an empty space outside of philosophy – one that the soul can fill up through faith and devotion – to place *God* above the Absolute and eternal as the infinitely higher potency of the latter. However, it is quite self-evident that there can be nothing above the Absolute and that this idea excludes any kind of limitation – and not accidentally but rather by its very nature. Because God would again be absolute and eternal; but the Absolute cannot be different from absoluteness, and the eternal cannot be different from eternalness, since these are not generic concepts. It necessarily follows that whoever places anything above the rational Absolute as *God* does not truly perceive it as such and that it is therefore only an illusion.

How is it that this view recognizes the Absolute as an absolute but does not regard it as God?

This error is almost inevitably made by those who arrive at the idea of the Absolute through the description that philosophy provides, as they never achieve more than a conditional knowledge of it; but it is not possible to gain an unconditional knowledge from a conditional one. All descriptions of the Absolute come about as an antithesis of the nonabsolute; namely, the complete opposite of all that constitutes the nature of the latter is ascribed to the former. In short, the description is merely negative and never puts the *Absolute itself* before the soul.

Thus the nonabsolute, e.g. is recognized as something of which the concept is not adequate to being, since here being, i.e. reality, does not result from thought; rather, the concept needs something added for it to become being. It is thus conditional, nonabsolute.

Furthermore, nonabsoluteness is perceived by that in which the particular is determined, not by the general but rather by an external entity, and thus has an irrational relationship to it. The same opposition can be found in other concepts of reflective cognition. Now, if the philosopher describes the idea of the Absolute so that all difference contained in the nonabsolute has to be negated, then those who want to arrive at the idea of the Absolute from the outside understand it in the above manner – namely, by taking the opposite of reflective cognition and all possible differences of the world of appearances for the point of departure of philosophy – and regard the Absolute as the *product* that brings about the unification of opposites, whereby the Absolute is defined by them in no way in and by itself but through identification or indifferentiation. Or even more crudely, they think of the philosopher as holding the ideal or subjective in one hand and the real or objective in the other and then have him strike the palms of his hands together so that one abrades the other. The product of this abrasion is the Absolute. One may tell them hundreds of times that there is no subjective or objective for us and that the Absolute is the absolute identity of both only as a *negation* of those opposites; yet they still do not understand and instead stick with the only idea they do understand, namely that which is constructed into a *composite*. Little do they realize that the description of the Absolute as identity of opposites is merely negative and that the philosopher demands something *entirely different* for the cognition of the Absolute, thus declaring said description as altogether insufficient. Even intellectual intuition is according to their psychological concepts a mere intuition of this self-created identity by way of the inner sense and therefore entirely empirical since it is in fact a cognition that perceives the in-itself of the soul. It is called intuition only because the essence of the soul, which is one and the same with the Absolute, can have no other than an unmediated relation to the latter.

[...]

The essence *itself* of the Absolute, which as the ideal is also immediately real, cannot be known through explanations, only through intuition. Only a composite can be known through description. That which is simple demands to be intuited. [...]

The only instrument befitting a subject such as the Absolute is a kind of cognition that is not added to the soul through instruction, teaching, etc. but is its true and eternal substance. For as the essence of God consists of absolute, solely unmediated reality, so the nature of the soul consists in cognition that is one with the real, ergo with God; hence it is also the intention of philosophy in relation to man not to add anything but to remove from him, as thoroughly as possible, the accidentals that the body, the world of appearances, and the sensate life have added and to lead him back to the originary state. Furthermore, all instruction in philosophy that precedes this cognition can only be negative; it shows the nullity of all finite opposites and leads the soul indirectly to the perception of the infinite. Once there, it is no longer in need of those makeshift devices of negative descriptions of absoluteness and sets itself free from them.

In all dogmatic systems, as well as in the criticism and idealism of the theory of scientific knowledge [*Wissenschaftslehre*], there is talk of a reality of the Absolute that would be *outside of and independent from ideality*. In all these, unmediated cognition is therefore impossible because the in-itself, by way of the process of cognizance, becomes a product of the soul, a *mere* noumenon, and ceases to be in-itself.

In presupposing a merely mediated knowledge of the Absolute (irrespective of how the mediation occurs), the Absolute in philosophy can only appear as something that is presumed in order that it can be philosophized about; in fact, the opposite takes place, and all philosophizing begins, and has always begun, with the idea of the Absolute come alive. That which is true can only be recognized in truth; that which is evident, in evidence. But truth and evidence are clear in themselves and must therefore be absolute and of the essence of God. Until this was recognized, it was not even possible to conceive of the idea of that higher evidence, which is sought in philosophy. When, by way of tradition, the word and the name of philosophy reached those who lacked the inner impetus for such recognition – a recognition whose first beginnings were identical to those of philosophy itself – they attempted to philosophize without it.

Those who have experienced that evidence – which lies in and only in the idea of the Absolute and which any human language is too weak to describe – will regard as entirely incommensurate any attempts to reduce and confine it to the individuality of the individual by way of faith, premonition, sentiment or whatever one may call it. Not only will it not reach this evidence, but it will negate its very nature in the process.

The Origin of the Finite Things from the Absolute and Their Relationship to It

[…] Since the unmediated real, in the Absolute, is also ideal and therefore *idea*, it necessarily, being purely *as such* within itself, can produce nothing but negations of absoluteness or negations of the idea once it is separated from the Absolute. Since an unmediated reality it is also ideality, what is produced is a reality that, separated from ideality, is not directly determined by it. It is a reality that does not have the complete possibility of its being in itself but rather *outside of itself*; thus it is a sensate, conditional actuality.

[…]

To the extent that the sensate world is the self-objectification of the Absolute in the form – whereby the counter-image [*Gegenbild*] can exist in itself and remove itself from the originary image [*Urbild*] – it has a relation to the Absolute, albeit an indirect one. Thus the origin of the finite world cannot be traced directly to the infinite world but must be understood within the principle of causation, which itself is infinite and therefore has only a negative significance: *no finite thing can directly originate from the Absolute or be traced back to it*, whereby the cause of the finite world is expressed as an absolute breaking-away from the infinite world.

This falling-away is as eternal (outside of time) as the Absolute and the world of ideas. The latter, as ideality, is eternally being borne into another absolute as reality, and as this other absolute, as originary idea, it is necessarily double-sided (whereby it is both in itself [*in sich selbst*] and in the in-itself [*im An-sich*]). Likewise, the originary idea, and all of its innate ideas, is given a double life: one is in itself yet bound to finitude and is, insofar as it is separated from the other life, a pseudo-life; the other is in the Absolute, which is its true life. Irrespective of this eternal character of the falling-away and the sensate universe that follows from it, both are merely accidental with regards to the Absolute, for the cause of the falling-away lies neither in the one nor the other but rather in the idea seen under the aspect of its selfhood. The falling-away is extra-essential for the Absolute as well as for the originary image because it does not affect either one since the fallen world is thereby immediately brought into nothingness. In view of the Absolute and the originary image, it is the true *Nothing* and is only *for itself*.

Neither can the falling-away be *explained* (so to speak) because it is absolute and descends from absoluteness, even though its consequence and its necessarily entrained predicament is nonabsoluteness. For the self-dependence, which the *other absolute* gains in the self-intuition of the first, the form, only goes as far as the *possibility* of the real being-within-itself but no further; beyond that boundary lies the penalty, which consists in becoming entangled with finitude.

Note

1   *Editors' Note.* This text is, in part, a critical response to A.C.A. Eschenmayer's 1803 *Philosophy and Its Transition to Non-Philosophy*, which argues that faith transcends reason.

Philosophical Investigations into the Essence of Human Freedom and Related Matters (1809)*

Nothing can be achieved at all by such attenuated conceptions of God as *actus purissimus* and similar notions which earlier philosophy set forth, or by such concepts as the newer thought constantly produces in its concern to separate God as far as possible from all of nature. God is more of a reality than is a mere moral world-order, and he has in him quite other and more vital activating powers than the abstract idealists, with their lack of subtlety, ascribe to him.

---

*Translated by James Guttmann from F.W.J. Schelling, *Sämmtliche Werke* (Stuttgart and Augsberg: Cotta, 1856–1861), Division One, Volume Seven.

We have already explained that a view such as would be fully adequate to the problem with which we are here concerned, could only be developed from the fundamental principles of a genuine philosophy of nature. We do not however deny that this correct view was long since present in individual minds. But it was these very individuals who sought out the vital basis of nature, without fear of those terms of reproach – materialism, pantheism, etc. – which have ever been current against all genuine philosophy, and who were natural philosophers (in both senses of the word) in distinction to those dogmatists and abstract idealists who banished them as mystics.

The Philosophy of Nature of our time first established the distinction in science between Being insofar as it exists, and Being insofar as it is the mere basis of existence. This distinction is as old as its first scientific presentation.[1] As this very point at which the Philosophy of Nature departs from the path of Spinoza most decisively has been disregarded, it could be maintained in Germany up to the present time that the metaphysical principles of this philosophy were identical with those of Spinoza. And although it is this distinction which at the same time brings about the most definite distinction between nature and God, this did not prevent the accusation that it constituted the confusion of God with nature. As the present investigation is based on the same distinction, the following may be remarked for its explication.

As there is nothing before or outside of God he must contain within himself the ground of his existence. All philosophies say this, but they speak of this ground as a mere concept without making it something real and actual. This ground of his existence, which God contains [within himself], is not God viewed as absolute, that is insofar as he exists. For it is only the basis of his existence, it is *nature* – in God, inseparable from him, to be sure, but nevertheless distinguishable from him. By analogy, this relationship can be explicated through reference to the relation of gravitation and light in nature. Gravitation precedes light as its eternally dark basis which is itself not *actual* and flees into the night when light (which truly exists) appears. Even light does not completely break the seal by which gravity is held. For this very reason gravity is neither the pure essence nor even the actual being of absolute identity, but it is only a consequence of its nature; or else it is this identity when regarded in a specific degree. For that which appears as existing with respect to gravitation, itself belongs to the basis. And nature in general is therefore everything that lies beyond the absolute being of absolute identity. With regard to the precedence [of gravity over light], moreover, this is to be thought of neither as precedence in time nor as priority of essence. In the cycle whence all things come, it is no contradiction to say that that which gives birth to the one is, in its turn, produced by it. There is here no first and no last, since everything mutually implies everything else, nothing being the 'other' and yet no being being without the other. God contains himself in an inner basis of his existence, which, to this extent, precedes him as to his existence, but similarly God is prior to the basis as this basis, as such, could not be if God did not exist in actuality.

A consideration which proceeds from things leads to the same distinction. First, the concept of immanence is completely to be set aside insofar as it is meant to express a dead conceptual inclusion of things in God. We recognize, rather, that the concept of becoming is the only one adequate to the nature of things. But the process of their becoming cannot be in God, viewed absolutely, since they are distinct from him *toto genere* [in kind] or – more accurately – in eternity. To be separate from God they would have to carry on this becoming on a basis different from him. But since there can be nothing outside God, this contradiction can only be solved by things having their basis in that within God which is not *God himself*,[2] i.e. in that which is the basis of his existence. If we wish to bring this Being nearer to us from a human standpoint, we may say: It is the longing which the eternal One feels to give birth to itself. This is not the One itself, but is co-eternal with it. This longing seeks to give birth to God, i.e. the unfathomable unity, but to this extent it has not yet the unity in its own self. Therefore, regarded in itself, it is also will: but a will within which there is no understanding, and thus not an independent and complete will, since understanding is actually the will in willing. Nevertheless it is a will of the understanding, namely the longing and desire thereof; not a conscious but a prescient will, whose prescience is understanding. We are speaking of the essence of longing regarded in and for itself, which we must view clearly although it was long ago submerged by the higher principle which had risen from it, and although we cannot grasp it perceptively but only spiritually, i.e. with our thoughts. Following the eternal act of self-revelation, the world as we now behold it, is all rule, order and form; but the unruly lies ever in the depths as though it might again break through, and order and form nowhere appear to have been original, but it seems as though what had initially been unruly had been brought to order. This is the incomprehensible basis of reality in things, the irreducible remainder which cannot be resolved into reason by the greatest exertion but always remains in the depths. Out of this which is unreasonable, reason in the true sense is born. Without this preceding gloom, creation would have no reality; darkness is its necessary heritage. Only God – the Existent himself – dwells in pure light; for he alone is self-born. Man's conceit opposes this origin from the depths and even seeks out moral reasons against it. Nevertheless we can think of nothing better fitted to drive man to strive towards the light with all energy, than the consciousness of the deep night out of which he was raised into existence. The faint-hearted complaints that the unreasonable is in this way made into the root of reason, night into the beginning of light, are indeed partly based on a misunderstanding of the matter (since they do not grasp how the logical priority of reason and of essential being can be reconciled with the foregoing view), but these complaints express the actual system of contemporary philosophers who would like to make *fumum ex fulgere* [smoke from the flame], though even the most violent Fichtean precipitation is insufficient for this purpose. All birth is a birth out of darkness into light: the seed must be buried in the earth and die in darkness in order that the lovelier creature of light should rise and unfold itself in the rays of the sun. Man is formed in his mother's womb; and only out of the darkness of unreason (out of feeling, out of longing, the sublime mother of understanding) grow clear thoughts. We must imagine the primal longing in this way – turning towards reason, indeed, though not yet recognizing it, just as we longingly desire unknown, nameless excellence. This primal longing moves in anticipation like a surging, billowing sea, similar to the 'matter' of Plato, following some dark, uncertain law, incapable in itself of forming anything that can endure. But there is born in God himself an inward, imaginative response, corresponding to this longing, which is the first stirring of divine Being in its still dark depths. Through this response, God sees himself in his own image, since his imagination can have no other object than himself. This image is the first in which God, viewed absolutely, is realized, though only in himself; it is in the beginning in God, and is the God-begotten God himself. This image is at one and the same time, reason – the logic of that longing,[3] and the eternal Spirit which feels within it the Logos and the everlasting longing. This Spirit, moved by that Love which it itself is, utters the Word which then becomes creative and omnipotent Will combining reason and longing, and which informs nature, at first unruly, as its own element or instrument. The first effect of reason in nature is the separation of forces, which is the only way in which reason can unfold and develop the unity which had necessarily but unconsciously existed within nature, as in a seed. Just as in man there comes to light, when in the dark longing to create something, thoughts separate out of the chaotic confusion of thinking in which all are connected, but each prevents the other from coming forth – so the unity appears which contains all within it and which had lain hidden in the depths. Or it is as in the case of the plant which escapes the dark fetters of gravity only as it unfolds and spreads its powers, developing its hidden unity as its substance becomes differentiated. For since this Being [of primal nature] is nothing else than the eternal basis of God's existence, it must contain within itself, though locked away, God's essence, as a light of life shining in the dark depths. But longing, roused by reason, now strives to preserve this light shining within it, and returns unto itself so that a basis of being might ever remain. In this way there is first formed something comprehensible and individuated; since reason, in the light which has appeared in the beginnings of nature, rouses longing (which is yearning to return into itself) to divide the forces (to surrender darkness) and in this very division brings out the unity enclosed in what was divided, the hidden light. And this [forming of something comprehensible] does not occur by external discovery but though a genuine in-vention [*Ein-bildung*], since what arises in nature is conceived in it, or, still better, through revival, reason reviving the unity or idea concealed in the sundered depths.

Notes

1   *Editors' Note.* Schelling cites his *Presentation of My System of Philosophy.* The relevant passages can be found in the *Philosophical Rupture between Fichte and Schelling* (Albany: SUNY Press, 2012), Remark to § 54 and the First Remark to § 93, pp. 164–5, 174.

2   This is the only correct dualism which at the same time admits a unity. Above was mentioned a modified dualism according to which the principle of evil does not stand alongside goodness but is subordinated to it. It is hardly to be feared that anyone will confuse the relationship here established with that dualism in which the subordinate is always an essentially evil principle and for this very reason remains incomprehensible with respect to its origin in God.

3   In the sense in which one finds a Logos in Logogriphs. [*Translator's Note. 'Logogriph,'* a kind of anagram puzzle.]

Lectures on the Philosophy of Revelation (1841/2)*

How God Posits a Being Different from Himself through a Process

Only as Lord of a [kind of] being different from him is God wholly independent, absolutely free and eternal.

This assertion should startle those who acknowledge God only as the final concept of negative philosophy, the eternal absolute subject-object, or, according to Aristotle, *the eternally self-thinking [thought].*

But [were it this] there would be a tremendous limitation in this necessity to eternally think just himself; it could touch on nothing mortal. For a healthy constitution, to forever think just of oneself would be the greatest embarrassment. A human being does not cling to itself. *Johannes Müller* writes: I am only happy when I produce. *Goethe*: In producing, one is occupied not with oneself, but with *something beyond oneself,* and for that very reason is God the great blessed one (Pindar).

The process which in God is mediated by the potencies appearing within him, is in fact a process of suspending and reactivating the *actu* necessary being, but between these two moments lies the world. *The world* is the suspension of the *actu* existing [element] in the godhead, *it is the suspended* actus *of divine being.* Through the sublation [*Aufhebung*] of the *actus,* the essence is only enriched.

God does not reveal himself in the world but elevates himself in his divinity; he is revealed in an unprethinkable [*unvordenklich*] way; insofar as he suspends the *actus,* he turns inward. But all the same, *God suspends the* actus *of his necessary existence in order to put a being different than his in the place of this first existence.* God contains this immediate bare possibility for being [*Seinkönnen*] that eternally presents itself in him and that is something only if he *wills* it. As its real principle, God has the same indifference between

---

*Translated by Joseph Carew and Michael Vater from *Die endlich offenbar gewordene positive Philosophie der Offenbarung oder Entstehungsgeschichte, wörtlicher Text, Beurtheilung und Berichtigung der v. Schellingischen Entdeckungen über Philosophie überhaupt, Mythologie und Offenbarung des dogmatischen Christenthums im Berliner Wintercursus von 1841–42,* ed. H.E.G. Paulus (Darmstadt: Carl Wilhelm Leske, 1842).

the capacity-to-be and the capacity-not-to-be [*Sein- und Nichtseinkönnen*] that we viewed as *prima materia* [prime matter] in the purely rational philosophical science. *In the ability-to-be and not-to-be God has the real ground for what the negative rational science viewed as his passing from a state of mere possibility to actuality.* The same potencies that present themselves as *a priori* in negative philosophy do so again here, but not as items that precede being, but as ones that have being *before* them; through being – now posited as essential nature – they are contained in a hyper-material spiritual unity. They are held together through this unity even when they have become actual and placed in tension and differentiation through this unity.

This unity is not material but spiritual, indissoluble, and holds them together *uno eodemque loco* [in one and the same place], which is possible *only through process.* The unequal potencies are held together by the cause of the process through this hyper-material unity. If we abstractly consider how this process occurs, it will be an actuality that embraces and comprehends all possibilities *a priori,* even those possibilities derived from the primordial potencies; it will be a *pan* [totality], a *world from which the contingent is not excluded, but subordinated to the necessary* – so that from one side this world appears as real (and not logical), from another as logical, since the contingent is subordinated here to the necessary, to what-must-be [*das Seinmüssende*].

This unification of the real and the logical has always ranked among the thorniest issues, so that Kant assigned the contingent to the unknown 'thing in itself', but the necessary to the logical domain of cognition. Instead, the contingent pertains to what we have called the capacity-to-be and not-to-be, the necessary to what can be sublated in nothing and through nothing, ever and again realizing itself in the suspended *actus* of divine existence which is compelled to put itself *in actum* [in act]. (What must be.)

But it is yet to be seen whether through the *process* we have called 'possible' a being different from God can be established. The *entire process* is tied to a single point, another sort of being that previously was not, that emerged *ex improviso* [unexpectedly] as it were. Necessary being seems like the kind of being that no potency precedes. This being cannot be posited through overcoming an opposite potency. An opposite potency has no time to manifest. But precisely because this [original] potency was *not overcome* by the *actus,* it can present itself; a possibility cannot be excluded, only an actuality. Unprethinkable being, which we designated the *potentia potentiae* [potency of the potencies], first gives it the possibility to arise. It could not arise prior to this being, so that it is as if it has found a place within unprethinkable being that it did not have before. It cannot pertain to the existent itself, but only to the necessary element within it, which leaves the existent free to sublate primordial being, not in essence but in *actus*, by adopting the opposite potency. This possibility can be lodged only in that essence whose being falls outside the existent's *actus* [act] – or be *adopted* (after one's own children). The potency we are discussing is by itself an objective possibility, first made possible by unprethinkable being. By itself it cannot cross over *ad actum*, rather *it is only at hand for God. It can only attain actuality if God wills it:* but just because of its inability to pass *a potentia ad actum* [from potency to act], *there must be a will in God* whereby it is *the material potency of a divine will.* God can direct his will to it or not. Only as a means can it be incorporated in this plan of God's, for this plan must also include unprethinkable being, whereby God has the power to transform what stands opposite him into something that he can will *finaliter* [as an end].

Thus, God turns his being and essence into mere potencies for a future being that is distinct from him. He is without need of what is by nature necessary being, *natura necessaria.* Elevated beyond it, *God is the one who has posited his own essence and being outside himself,* invincible because he is no longer a material but a *hyper-substantial unity* in which the contrary being and the unprethinkable being negated by it are held together, so that *a process* between them is necessary. For the unprethinkable being is placed *ex actu* [out of actuality] by the contrary being, though it cannot be absolutely sublated because it has its root in eternity, yet its being *actu* [actually] can be sublated. Unprethinkable being is instead established through inhibition, negation, as the infinite potency of *actus* so that it *must* work to establish itself in its *actus purus* [pure act] through overcoming the opposed being.[1]

But how is the *overcoming of opposed being* to be conceived? What genuinely has being in this opposed being is a will that, as originally engendered and posited in this first-to-appear potency by God, is contingent (blind).

In this first sort of being – only effective in the divine will, something that has being merely by divine willing – we have what is also considered in the general doctrine of creation as the *proton hypokeimenon* [first substrate]. It is said that this is formed *from nothing*, i.e. *it has being merely in the divine will.* – But nothing [other than will] can be overcome and nothing except a will can resist. Will is primordial being, the stuff of everything.

A willing can certainly be overcome. When a chance desire arises in our calm interior (= *actus purus*) we feel our will displaced from its rest, confined, inhibited. Where it was before is now [occupied by] something else; the original calm will is made peripheral, but since it is negated by an external will, it acquires the power to negate and overcome the opposite willing, whereupon the calm will shines forth again. So too the other being that has been advanced to actuality can be overcome, since it has come to be through willing.

The overcoming could occur suddenly, but since the contrary potency has a share in being, it can be displaced only gradually. Referring to the contrary principle, the gentle Plato uses the locution: *it must be convinced*. The will that is the real energy of the opposed contingent being is its own independent willing; it is gradually vanquished by the self-producing *actus purus*.

But there still will have to be a principle that determines the levels, a principle that must be independent both from contrary being and of the principle that gradually conjures it. For the one has by its nature only the will to stay undetermined, the other the will to overcome. This determining principle is given to us in the third potency, *spirit*, the entity free of being that is unconcerned about being, but which arrives at being without disturbance or worry. Precisely because it is unmixed with being, it can command being. This third is therefore the regulative principle whereby different moments and levels really stay distinct.

In the process [of creation], therefore, we have *three potencies* (they are *very important for everything that follows*, although they appear *in different forms*).

1. The initiating cause of the whole movement is B, the other being opposed to primordial being; we have found its energy to be a contingent will posited outside the confines of mere possibility – limitless, blind and senseless. But this being acts to exclude primordial being so that what we once viewed as pure *actus* we must now think is simply sublated.

2. A [second] potency we call *reflective* reaches the depths of negation, although it was foreseen and accepted into the divine will. For reflection does not have its seat in will; excluded from being by the opposed potency, through its primordial being it attains the power to bring limitless will back inside its bounds. When this starts to happen, by the work of the second potency a capacity is crafted in limitless being whereby something that is not just the work of the *first* will but also of *the other* is posited; when actualized, it is a third potency derived from both.

Creation divides into two moments: a) Positing limitless being, so that it can be subsequently brought back to inwardness, potency and limit. b) Internalizing it, so that a potency is produced in being.

Creation is not something simply positive like an externalization. Rather, the original existent is put within limits so that it is something self-subsistent or self-contained in which a capacity can be produced. Through this, what comes into being is something self-empowered, a true third distinct from both potencies, a thing, indeed as the product of the two potencies, a concrete thing.

The second potency (A²) is the one originally negated, or put *ex actu*, which realizes itself only insofar as it negates the other. As originally real, it cannot actualize itself; this requires negation as a condition. And that is why the ability to actualize itself, the potential and power of the second principle, is something lent to it. The second potency is not the immediate, but the *secundo loco* [second place] capacity for being. *The first possibility* (B) must precede it. After B has ceased to be a potency, its role is to be the capacity-for-being within the *actus purus. Elevated to potency, it is* A² and through it the limitless will is conquered.

When this is accomplished, A² no longer has an object, so at the end of the process nothing genuinely active remains. Not until this point does ...

3. *the third potency,* A³, *attain actuality.* The final intent of the process is that the being that is the object of conquest be brought to *expiration, to breathing out the third entity, spirit,*[2] *the sole item to which being belongs.* But to some extent B is still subjected to A². (I use this notation to connect back to my earliest presentation.) B *is related* to A² as its *hypokeimenon* [substrate], *as the matter in which the latter is actualized.* Insofar as A² finishes its work in B, space is given to A³, which orders and determines the levels [of being], to govern the process. *Spirit is what establishes measure and boundary, and sets a limit to the ascendant potency's overcoming* [of the indeterminate].

Each of the three potencies acts to exclude the other, they coalesce only in their product which is therefore independent. Each of the potencies is still *potentia pura et ab omni concretione libera* [purely potential and free from all concreteness], a pure cause. We can show that there is something like a *triad of causes here:* B is the *causa materialis* [material cause], A² is the *causa efficens, per quam* [efficient cause, whereby], and A³ the *causa in quam* or *secundum quam omnia fiunt* [cause in which or according to which everything is made]. Yet in producing or creating, the two other potencies align themselves with the third; the third hovers before them as what genuinely ought-to-be [*das Seinsollende*]. The potencies look to it as a pattern, they obey its will, which decides between them. B obeys its will only if it casts off the measure (power) the second produced in it; the other potency obeys only if it drops the partially overcome B. The third is the potency that by its mere willing holds each of the evolving factors to its determined level.

Referring to this, it is said of God in the Old Testament: he commands and it comes to pass, i.e. it endures. The ultimate intent of the process is the overcoming of B, which in its *expiration* posits the highest all-encompassing power that rules the world of manifold being. [...]

On the Distinction between Revelation and Mythology and the Comprehensibility of Revelation

The principles of mythology are necessarily the principles of the revealed religion if only for the very reason that both – are religions. Nevertheless, their substantial difference is that the representations of mythology are products of a necessary process, or of a natural consciousness left to its own devices, upon which no free cause exerted an influence; in contrast, *revelation is conceived of as something that presupposes an* actus *outside of consciousness and a relationship to man that the freest of all causes, God, voluntarily took upon himself.* As a consequence, science here passes over into a completely new domain.

If you understand by 'philosophy,' as most people do, a science that reason produces purely by its own resources, then the philosophy of revelation would be the attempt to reduce the truths of the revealed religion to truths like those that reason can produce by its own resources. But the believers in revelation see in its subject matter truths the likes of which reason cannot reach. And if we want to be sincere, the only thing to do is to agree to the requirement that through revelation truths *must* be given that, in its absence, not only would not have been known, but more strongly could not have been known. For *why else would there be a revelation*[?]

Those who trace the truths of revelation back to the mere truths of reason – admittedly only violently, similar to many explanations of mythology – would, [even] if they single out for special honour the founder of Christianity as being, at very least, a highly gifted teacher, only be able to respond to the question, 'Why, then, did these events take place?' [with something to this effect]: so that, by such a means, humankind would come to a cognition of these truths simply *earlier*. On the other hand, however, they also renounce the strength [of such explanations] by claiming that the passage of hundreds of years was needed to cast off the mantel obscuring them; we would even have to see this event as the cause for why humankind's development has been so held up. Either the concept of revelation, therefore, has no meaning at all, or we must concede that the content of revelation cannot be known in the absence of revelation. Here, therefore, revelation turns into its own source of cognition.

But is there not a more general or universal concept under which revelation is to be subsumed? Everyone who strives after the highest possible unity of cognition confesses that there is not just one single source of cognition; experience is to be added to pure reason. But revelation is a knowledge that we are only granted through experience. There are as well other things that we only know through experience, *a posteriori*.

By what manner philosophy finds God, how it discovers the possibility within him to be he who brings forth being – we know that such a philosophical path exists. But that God actually wanted to be the creator – we can only know this as a result of him having actually created. Reasons do exist for why God made what is possible into something actual, which we found at [an earlier] point [in the lectures], but these reasons are partially taken from qualities that we ourselves only became acquainted with *a posteriori*. [...]

From this point on we find ourselves once again formally on the path of a necessary progression. As soon as *the tension of the potencies* is *posited* through the resolve for creation, we are situated within the domain of a necessity that is admittedly only hypothetical, but which is still a domain of necessary progression. Once posited as a process, it could not develop any other moments; our knowledge is, from the standpoint of the universal concept of the process, an *a priori*, foreseeing knowledge. But when its end was reached, at which point it was in man's control to eternally unite being with the divine or to take it for himself and alienate it from the divine, something yet again occurred that stands *a priori* unknowable.

The mythological process proceeds again according to objective laws, but only under the presupposition that the mediating potency holds out and remains within it. In its absence human consciousness would have been consumed. That it did stick around is something that we have only clearly seen from its movement itself. However, by posing the question, '*Why* does the mediating potency remain within this movement?', mythology refers to a higher order. To be sure, *mythology* is, with respect to its content, to be comprehended on its own terms. But *with respect to its own existence it is not to be comprehended on its own terms*. The philosophy of mythology is included within the philosophy of revelation like a concentric circle. There is no (*a priori*) necessity dictating that human consciousness would take a stand in separation [from God]; this can only be the resolve of a free will, and this free will can only be sought in him who, even at the risk of [it] being overthrown, still willed the world. Mythology can only be an accidental consequence of this will, never its purpose. God overlooked the times of ignorance, that is, he never willed them as having purpose; on the contrary, by not precluding them as something that would happen along the way, he permitted them.

Mythology is thus a consequence, not a revelation, of a divine will. It is only subsequent to mythology, beyond it, that the latter becomes manifest. While we may infer the divine will from mythology, it is not the effect of this will. *So how is this will cognizable?*

[...]

Paul speaks of a plan of God that has been kept secret ever since time immemorial,[3] but which has now been made manifest in Christ.[4] The mystery of God and Christ has been made manifest to the whole world through the appearance of Christ. Here we have reached the point at which the very possibility of a philosophy of revelation can be explained. It is not to be comprehended, like mythology, as a necessary process; on the contrary, [as something] completely freely posited, it can only be grasped by the resolve and deed of the freest will. Through revelation, a new, second creation is introduced. It itself is a completely free act.

But even if revelation is by no means equal to a necessary process, the philosophy of revelation will nevertheless not leave it standing as something incomprehensible. Even though we recognize that creation can only be a free act, we can nevertheless conceive of a philosophy that regards it as possible, once the will has revealed itself, to be able to partially comprehend it, to partially explain it. That resolve for revelation indeed surpasses human concepts, but it is still comprehensible insofar as the magnitude of the resolve is equal to the magnitude of God; all that we human beings can do in this respect is to expand the narrow scope of our concepts to accommodate for the magnitude of the divine ones.

If *the affect of philosophers* is *wonder*, then philosophy will have the drive to progress from what is to be seen merely *a priori* with necessity to that which lies outside of and beyond all necessary insight. It has no rest before it arrives at that which is absolutely worthy of wonder, at that which sublates thinking itself. Vain is everything that is without a determinate goal. Thinking must reach something whereby it is put to rest. *Doubt* takes place in movement. What is only a moment has doubt in itself, and progresses forward, but not into infinity; doubt will be conquered in an ultimate thought or event.

If you wanted to call this state in which thinking would be at rest *'faith,'* then you may do so; but then you do *not* have to view faith *as an ungrounded cognition.* The ultimate term in which all knowledge comes to rest cannot be *without ground,* only it cannot itself again become ground for an advance. Every point in the line of progression is an ultimate one, but you hardly have cast your eyes on what has been found before the *dialectic* discovers a negation that can only be sublated through the following position, and the latter itself contains a new possibility that cannot conceal itself. *Everything possible has to become actual, so that everything may be made manifest.*

After the *overthrowing* [of creation], reason would instantly feel the inclination to let the creator *intervene;* but God is greater than our thinking. He knows how to counteract the most extreme thing that can happen through something else just as extreme from his side. *Since the world was not to be produced through a creaturely will, it is to be produced through the indubitable deed of a supra-creaturely and still human will.* The certainty that sublates all doubt is *faith,* and the latter is therefore *the end of knowledge.* First the Law and then the Gospel! Thus, the strict discipline of science must lead the way to faith.

All the treasures of cognition are concealed in Christ, that is, they are comprehended in him. They must be comprehended with him; otherwise, we have not comprehended him. Faith, as the end of seeking, does not preclude seeking. Any science still in the process of seeking sees that everything that it finds once more sublates itself. *Ubi finis quaerendi, ubi statio inveniendi? Nihil ultra.* Christum scire *est omnia scire* [What end will there be to seeking, what point of rest for finding? Nothing further. *To know Christ* is to know everything] (Tertullian). *He is the end of knowledge; they who truly have and fully cognize him, have with him and within him all knowledge!* Faith is therefore not the beginning of knowledge, except in the sense that every beginning is faith in its end, but this faith drives itself toward knowledge and proves itself in actual knowledge.

When we say that the ultimate term would no longer contain any doubt, we do not mean that, subjectively, no doubt could remain at all. For it requires *a heart to grasp what is exalted.* Here doubt emerges from the magnitude of the matter and the *narrow scope of the soul.* 'Believe what your tiny heart permits you to comprehend!' Scripture calls out: Believe! If only to believe! Hence science call to us: Believe only if you see something really extraordinary present itself to you.

Here shall be shown how this faith is brought into connection with our science of other things, whether they be divine, natural or human.

Anyone can easily see that this connection is not to be found in just any old philosophy. A mediation between nature and grace is not possible for a philosophy that prevents all actuality from being examined. During *Fichte's* time, philosophy was in its true aphelion from revelation; he himself even had to reintroduce the not-I (the retired Kantian thing-in-itself) in the practical part [of his *Science of Knowledge*]. Another era arrived when one began to recognize that philosophy could really only develop itself while in contact with *actuality*. At that moment, *nature was for the first time incorporated* [into philosophy]. Even then a number of contemporaries instinctively foresaw that *history too,* where previously one saw only arbitrary concoction, would have to be involved. At that point philosophy had to *turn its attention to even the earliest origins of history, mythology.*

A philosophy that has no sensitivity for what actually is, makes up a story about how history ought to be. Strictly speaking, Christianity should not be. But now it exists, and demands explanation, like every natural formation is entitled to. If, however, *paganism* is an intentional deception, then Christianity must also be treated as so. But if a real principle is in paganism, then such a principle must also be *in Christianity.* I will not speak of those for whom God only is through existing reason. If reason is in every being [and] all being, where, then, do we get *the unreason* that is mixed into all being? Reason, however, is never capable of making itself into the Other of itself; it is just that which is immutably self-identical.

Others want at least a reasonable God, *a God who does nothing beyond reason,* though it is conceded that a human being can do things beyond reason. To be a reasonable person does not amount to much. Reason is everybody's 'thing'. But *to love one's enemies is beyond reason.* The will of God in matters of the human race, a race alienated from him, is a mystery and surpasses reason! One could well say this *without unreason.* But that is why this resolve [to overcome the alienation] is not incomprehensible; it is completely proportional to the extraordinary event to which it refers and to the magnitude of God.

Nothing is more dismal than *the business of all those rationalists who want to make what presents itself as beyond all reason into something reasonable. Paul* speaks[5] of the weakness and folly of God that is capable of more than the strength of man. Only the strong may be weak. *Hamann* asks: Do they not yet know that God is *a genius who is little concerned with the question of whether one considers him rational or irrational*? In fact, not everyone has it in them to comprehend *the profound irony of God in the creation of the world,* on display in every single one of his acts. *It is one who posits B, and another who overcomes it, but not another God. The freedom of God consists in holding together this absurdity.*

It's even so in humans! The sensitive connoisseur sees in every work of art whether it has sprung from a balance of productive force and wealth [of content with form], [or has instead] an infinite content that resists all form; to grasp [infinite content] in finite form is *poesy*. To be drunk and sober at the same time is the secret of enthusiasm.

God shows his *artistic* character in that that he seeks the infinite and brings everything into the most intelligible, most finite form. What is limited in Christianity is, for him, a purpose. You can see the divine folly in the following consideration: that God was not satisfied with merely contemplating a world that was, for him, possible. You can see the weakness of God in his weakness towards man. *'In creation God shows his spirit, in redemption his heart.'* The more powerful the spirit is, the more impersonal. God's most personal deed is revelation. At that moment, God became, in the highest sense, the most personal for us men. [...]

[...] *The major presupposition for this philosophy* is not a merely ideal relationship to God, mediated through reason or free cognition, but rather a real one; for there is a relationship of human beings to God that can be traced back into being itself, a relationship more ancient than cognition. Otherwise revelation could only be instruction; but instruction only concerns something that already exists. It could not change anything in humans' relationship to God himself; if it had the intention of introducing a new relationship [between them], then this would have to happen through an explicit, solemn act, before instruction would be possible. In general, then, this act is the intention of revelation.

Revelation has a real purpose. This [purpose] presupposes an originally real relationship of man to God. If human beings were not connected with God in a way other than through reason and cognition, then the real relationship that is in revelation would be simply unthinkable. [...]

The science of an earlier era could posit no relation to revelation other than [the one] it did to nature and actuality. Here it manipulated outer forms, and also sought the means to make revelation intelligible to itself [not in the content of revelation, but] outside of revelation in the particular philosophy of the time. *The true scholastics* completely ripped Christian theology from its natural soil. With the *Reformation*, the historical spirit awoke, but it could not immediately distance itself from scholastic forms. As the historical spirit awoke, unleashed itself, theology was taken to the extreme of a procedure that was merely outwardly historical.

Apart from these two interpretations, there is another one, *the mystical*, which dealt with the inner aspects of the matter itself, but for the most part did not seek these inner aspects by following the path of scientific cognition, instead taking that of contingent inspiration, unclear feeling. Its utterances, rather than objectively explaining or elucidating anything, were unclear, perplexing and not generally convincing. Mystical theology neglected outer historical investigation.

But *Christianity* is in the first instance and in an immediate sense *a fact*; it is only after an examination of [the material given by] critique, without ruling out any pointers, but rather by integrating everything, that one arrives at the true system that underlines even the Scriptures *as their presupposition*. *Christianity should not be proven. Rather it comes into consideration for us as a fact, as an appearance, that I want to explain, as much as possible, from its own premises.*

Notes

1   *Translators' Note.* God's unforeseeable nature, simultaneously both necessary being and capacity-to-be or not-to-be, once suspended, gives way to will. The first potency asserts itself as primordial being (B), blind being; it is suspended or (as Schelling also puts it) sublated by another sort of being that opposes it or is 'contrary' (A^2). As a contest or process between the two unfolds, B re-actualizes itself as *actus purus,* A^3 or spirit. Schelling introduces the notation in what follows.

2   *Translators' Note.* A play on the two meanings of *pneuma*, breath and spirit.

3   Romans 11: 33–36, 14: 24–27, 16: 25–27; Ephesians 3:5 [original editorial note].

4   *Translators' Note.* Schelling's translation of *apo ton aionon*, Ephesians 3:9.

5   1 Corinthians 1:18–25 [original editorial note].

Further reading

The reader interested in learning more about Schelling's late conception of Christianity – and his understanding of God as 'Lord of being' – ought to begin with the *Lectures on the Philosophy of Revelation*, a complete translation of which can be found in *Philosophy of Revelation (1841–42)* and Related Texts (translated by Klaus Ottmann [Thompson, CT: Spring, 2020]). One of Schelling's clearest discussions of his earlier, pantheistic conception of God can be found in the 1805 Aphorisms as an Introduction to the Philosophy of Nature, partially translated by Fritz Marti as 'Aphorisms as Introduction to Naturphilosophie' in Idealistic Studies, 14.3 (1984): 344–58. And Schelling's most compelling early account of the historicity of Christianity is to be found in his Philosophy of Art lectures.

The philosophy of religion has been the subject of some of the most significant studies of Schelling's thought. Any of the following would be a good place to begin reading about Schelling and religion:

Robert F. Brown, The Later Philosophy of Schelling: The Influence of Boehme on the Works of 1809–1815 (Bucknell University Press, 1977).

Emil Fackenheim, The God Within: Kant, Schelling, and Historicity, ed. John Burbidge (University of Toronto Press, 1996), Chapter VI.

Sebastian Gardner, 'Sartre, Schelling, and onto-theology.' Religious Studies 42.3 (2006): 247–71.

John Laughland, Schelling versus Hegel: From German Idealism to Christian Metaphysics (Ashgate Publishing, 2007).

S.J. McGrath, The Dark Ground of Spirit: Schelling and the Unconscious (Routledge, 2012).

S.J. McGrath, 'Is the Late Schelling Still Doing Nature-Philosophy?' Angelaki: The Journal of the Theoretical Humanities 21.4 (2016): 121–41.

Paul Tillich, The Construction of the History of Religion in Schelling's Positive Philosophy: Its Presuppositions and Principles, trans. Victor Nuovo (Bucknell University Press, 1974).

Paul Tillich, Mysticism and Guilt-Consciousness in Schelling's Philosophical Development, trans. Victor Nuovo (Bucknell University Press, 1974).

Daniel Whistler and Johannes Zachhuber (eds), Schelling's Afterlives: The Theological and Religious Impact of His Thought, Special issue of International Journal of Philosophy and Theology 80.1–2 (2019).

12

Politics

Introduction

A few months before Fichte began lecturing on the *Foundations of Natural Right* in Winter 1796 and Kant published his 'Doctrine of Right' in the 1797 *Metaphysics of Morals*, it was Schelling who was the first of the major German Idealists to employ the framework of transcendental idealism to try to make sense of the sphere of law and the state. Moreover, long after Hegel's *Philosophy of Right*, Schelling was still, at the very end of his career in the late 1840s, lecturing on political philosophy as part of his courses on 'purely rational philosophy'. Explorations of the political sphere thus occupy the beginning and, in fact, stand as one of the last words of Schellingian philosophy. And yet this is an area of his work that has been ignored like no other: it has consistently suffered from the false narrative that – in comparison to Hegel, in particular – Schelling takes flight from the social world of concrete institutions and intersubjective relations.

This chapter attempts to remedy somewhat the skewed impression of Schelling as an apolitical thinker. Schelling may have only ever published one treatise devoted to the doctrine of right: the 1796 *New Deduction of Natural Right,* which forms the opening extract in this chapter; nevertheless, explicit engagement with political philosophy can be found throughout his oeuvre. He frequently returned to questions about the nature of political life, the relationship between church and state, and the possibility for human individuals to organize themselves in a manner that would make fully manifest their inner freedom. This chapter therefore includes Schelling's reflections on these issues in his 1804 *System* and his 1810 *Stuttgart Private Lectures,* and it culminates in the first English-language translation of the political portion of his *Lectures on the Purely Rational Philosophy,* which some scholars have recently argued contains his most compelling political-philosophical vision.

New Deduction of Natural Right (1796)*

§ 27. Every moral being must assert his freedom *as such*. And that is possible only insofar as every moral being renounces unlimited *empirical* freedom. For unlimited *empirical* freedom leads to endless antagonism in the moral world (§ 26).

§ 28. Therefore, every moral being must yield his unlimited *empirical* freedom in order to save his freedom *as such*. Inasmuch as his striving is empirical, he must cease to assert himself as an individual in order to maintain himself through his striving *as such*.

§ 29. We must think that all moral beings are striving to maintain their individuality. Therefore this universal striving of moral beings for individuality *as such* must restrict the striving of each for *empirical* individuality in such a way that the empirical striving of all others can coexist with the striving of each.

§ 30. Since we must think that all moral beings as such have a will, this generic *will of all* must limit the *empirical* will of each individual in such a way that the will of all others can coexist with the will of each.

§ 31. Here we step over from the domain of morality into that of *ethics*. Morality as such lays down a law addressed only to the individual, a law that demands nothing but the absolute selfhood of the individual. Ethics sets up a commandment which presupposes a realm of moral beings and which safeguards the selfhood of *all* individuals by means of the demand addressed to the individual.

§ 32. Therefore the commandment of ethics must express not the will of the individual but the general will.

§ 33. Still, this commandment of ethics (§ 32) depends on the higher commandment of morality (§ 3).[1] Ethics sets up the *general* will as a law only in order to safeguard the individual will by means of the general. I do

---

*Translated by Fritz Marti from F.W.J. Schelling, *Sämmtliche Werke* (Stuttgart and Augsberg: Cotta, 1856–1861), Division One, Volume One.

not lay claim to individuality because I submit to the general will, but only because I claim individuality do I submit to the general will. *The general will is conditioned by the individual, not the individual by the general.*

§ 34. What determines the general will is the form of the individual will as such (freedom), setting aside all content of willing. *Therefore the content of the general will is determined by the form of the individual will,* not vice versa.

§ 35. The form of the general will *is freedom,* its content *morality.* Therefore *freedom does not depend on morality but morality on freedom. I am not free because I am moral, nor insofar as I am moral, but because and insofar as I want to be free, I ought to be moral.*

§ 36. Consequently, the problem of all ethics is to maintain the freedom of the individual by means of the general freedom, to safeguard the individual will by means of the general, or – (since the will of the individual can oppose the will of all others only insofar as it becomes empirical, that is, material) – to harmonize the empirical will of all with the empirical will of the individual.

[…]

§ 109. But [we now arrive at] the more general problem: Does *an individual will have any right at all in opposition to another individual will?*

§ 110. My will submits to the general will in order not to be subject to any individual will (§ 50), that is, I assert my individuality *absolutely,* in opposition to every other individuality.

§ 111. The general will alone, not the individual will, ought to determine the matter of my will. Hence the firmly established principle: *I have a right to the matter of my will in opposition to every individual will.*

§ 112. In *opposition* to any individual will (§ 109), therefore, I can have any right only insofar as that will endeavours to negate my will. And the general formal principle which asserts a right in opposition to any individual will is the following: *An individual will which endeavours to negate another will, and insofar as it so endeavours, is absolutely negated by that other will.*

§ 113. Therefore if I assert my will by means of negating the will of another, the presupposition is that this other endeavoured to negate mine. Now, the law of the general will demands that we will whatever all moral beings can will (§ 45). Therefore two wills in opposition cannot *both* be lawful, but either both or at least one of them must necessarily be *unlawful.*

First Case: *Both* are unlawful as to their matter.

§ 114. From the principle established above, that the *matter* of the general will is conditioned by the *form* of the individual will (§ 34), there follow immediately the following principles:

    a. I can act *against* the matter of the general will *(morality)* without also acting against the *form of individual will* (freedom); I can negate the general will as to *matter,* without negating the will *as such* as to form.

    b. I cannot act *against* the *form* of the general will (individual freedom) without at the same time acting *against* the *matter* of general will (morality).

    c. I cannot act *in line* with the general will as to its *matter* without at the same time acting in line with its form (the freedom of will as such).

    d. I can act *in line* with the form of general will (freedom) without at the same time acting *in line* with the *matter* of general will (morality).

§ 115. Therefore, in the case of a collision of unlawful wills two cases in turn are possible:

    a. Both are unlawful also as to *form*, that is, both endeavour to annul each other mutually.

§ 116. I have the right to negate absolutely every individual will insofar as it endeavours to negate mine. Therefore opposite wills that endeavour to annul each other *mutually* have also the *right* to annul each other, that is, neither of them has the right to assert *itself absolutely* against the other.

§ 117. Therefore this principle results:

    a. *Formally, unlawful actions, insofar as they collide, have mutually a right against each other.* There, where their conflicting wills meet in the empirical endeavour, in the world of phenomena, they annul each other mutually if they are as equal in what they *can* do as they are in what they *may* do.

    b. *One* of the two is *unlawful* also in *form,* yet endeavours to annul the other.

§ 118. A will that is unlawful in form is on that account also unlawful in matter (§ 114, b). If it were annulled because it was unlawful in *matter,* then the *form* of its willing would be conditioned by the matter of willing, which is impossible (§ 90).

§ 119. A will, therefore, that is unlawful in *form* is absolutely negated, however, without any regard to its *material unlawfulness,* but only because it endeavoured to annul the will of another.

§ 120. It is absolutely negated by the will of the other, not because this other will is *unlawful* in *matter,* but because it is simply will, without any regard to the matter of its willing.

§ 121. Therefore the question raised above (§ 108)[2] must be answered simply in the negative. An individual lawful will can never annul a materially unlawful will, because it can never annul it without becoming itself unlawful *in form* and therefore also in matter. Therefore *an individual will can never execute the general will's right to the matter of the individual will.*

§ 122. From this follows the principle: *I have a right to my materially unlawful will in opposition to every other formally unlawful will;* or: I have a right in opposition to every unlawful will, insofar as thereby I (formally) assert *my* unlawful will.

Second Case: Only one of the two is unlawful in its matter.

§ 123. No will can be lawful in its matter without, at the same time, being lawful in its form (§ 114). Therefore the lawful will can never endeavour to annul the materially unlawful will.

§ 124. Thus, if there is an antagonism between an unlawful and a lawful will, the ground of it can never lie in the latter. Only an unlawful will can endeavour to annul the will of the other.

§ 125. Therefore, according to § 112, the unlawful will, owing to its opposition to the lawful, will be absolutely negated, though not because it is materially unlawful (being opposed to the general will) but because it is formally unlawful (as opposed to the individual will).

§ 126. On the other hand, the lawful will can assert itself in opposition to the unlawful, though not because it is lawful materially but only because it is *formally* lawful. Therefore, with regard to the antagonism of these two, I inquire into the material lawfulness of the one only in order to prove the *formal unlawfulness* of the other.

§ 127. Consequently, another principle results: *I have a right to my* (materially) *lawful will, against every* (formally) *unlawful will.*

§ 128. There can be a *right* to a lawful will only in opposition to an individual will. For *in opposition to the general will* there can be only a (formal) right to *unlawful* will, and *in relation to the general will* only a *duty* to will lawfully.

§ 129. In opposition to both the individual and the general will, I have a right only to *formally lawful* actions. However, where there is no longer any will at all, there is no longer any lawful or unlawful manner of acting; my will becomes an absolute unlimited *power.*

§ 130. In the domain of nature, *all* willing ceases. The domain of nature is the domain of heteronomy. Consequently, here no other will can oppose mine, and my right to nature must be a right which I assert *in contrast to any will as such.*

§ 131. I declare my freedom by ruling over everything heteronomous [§ 6]. Now, I have a right to everything by means of which I assert my freedom. This yields the principle:

In opposition to every will, I have a right to assert my will by unlimited mastery over nature.

[…]

§ 140. If we enumerate all single rights in line with the above analysis of the supreme principle of right, they are the following:

1. *In contrast to the general will, the right to moral freedom,* that is, the right to full freedom of the individual will with regard to materially lawful as well as to materially unlawful actions.
2. *Right in contrast to individual will,* right of formal *equality* – the right to assert my individuality in opposition to every other (as to both form and matter).
3. *Right, in contrast to will as such* – *the* right to the *world of phenomena,* to *things,* to *objects* as such, *natural right* in the narrower sense.

Notes

1 *Editors' Note.* § 3 reads: '*Be!* In the highest sense of the word: cease to be *yourself* as a phenomenon; endeavour to be a noumenon as such! This is the highest call of all practical philosophy.'

2 *Editors' Note.* That is, 'May an individual will be executor of the right which pertains to the general will regarding the matter of my will?'

System of Philosophy in General and the Philosophy of Nature in Particular (1804)*

§ 325: *That in which science, religion and art become one in a mutually penetrating and living manner and become objective in their unity is the state.*

This is to be explained rather than proven.

Just as what appears in gravity, in light and in organism is of one and the same nature and infinite substance, and just as it is nevertheless absolute for itself in each of them, so too it is one and the same divine [principle]

---

*Translated by Lydia Azadpour and Daniel Whistler from F.W.J. Schelling, *Sämmtliche Werke* (Stuttgart and Augsberg: Cotta, 1856–1861), Division One, Volume Six.

that lives in science, religion and art. There are only these three absolute expressions for the three potencies of the ideal world. However, just as, in nature, substance itself which bears all potencies and grasps them within itself becomes objective in the world-body as what lacks all potency, so too the divine, separated into science, religion and art, although living absolutely in each of them, [becomes objective] through the state. Moreover, just as gravity, light and organism are only attributes of the planet, and all things are and can be only upon it, so neither true science, nor true religion, nor true art has another form of objectivity than the state.

Here it is to be remarked that:

a. No image of the state [drawn] from actual experience is intended.

b. No merely formal state, oriented by an external end, is meant, e.g. merely for the external securing of rights (as all states have been constituted until now). These are merely forced, necessary states, like all previous ones. Particularly since Kant, scientifically-constructed states have contained nothing but the merely negative conditions of a state, by means of which nothing positive is posited, nothing of the living, free, organic state, the only one which exists in the idea of reason.

c. When we determine the state as lacking all potency, it is self-evident that it has no true opposite. Such an [opposite] could only refer to a state in which there was no free, beautiful, universal life – a mere forced institute which must suppress the element of life in order to contain its opposite. – It is immediately clear from this that the other must be only one-sided. In the free organic life of a state, science and religion are simultaneously included. The church is nothing but such a state and exists within it. Outside of it, [the church] would be only in a state of merely *worldly ends* and *institutes*; however, this would no longer be a state.

d. In regard to how each [of the potencies] is grasped in the state, they are [so] not only insofar as each of the three, science, religion and art, must be a particular affair of the state, but they are grasped in its essence; when they pass over into the state, they come alive objectively in it: science through legislation (this is itself the most sublime philosophy; as Plato shows, the living whole of science must be imprinted in it); religion through public ethics and the heroism of a nation, art through which the creative spirit, hovering above the whole and feeling artistically not mechanically, [gives] beauty to its appearance, through the living rhythmic movement of public life.

§ 326: *What the state is objectively is subjectively* – not the science of philosophy, but – *philosophy itself as harmonious enjoyment and participation in all the goods and beauties of public life.*

As the state objectively lacks all potency, so does philosophy subjectively. Reason: cosmos = philosophy: state. Philosophy in this sense is the goal of all *science* of philosophy, even if – so long as it lacks the public life in which it can be intuited – philosophy can live only within the limits of science and only as science, not in itself. Philosophy – which is no longer science, but becomes life – is what Plato calls *politeuein* [being a citizen], life with and within an ethical totality.

Stuttgart Private Lectures (1810)[*]

The most compelling proof for the relapse of man into nature and to the first potency lies in what follows:

Man does not exist alone in this world, but there is a multiplicity of men, a *human species*, humanity.

The manifold human world strives for unity, and only there it attains completeness and happiness in the same manner as does the manifold of nature.

The true natural unity would have consisted in man and, through him, the divine and eternal. Yet nature has lost this sensitive unity through the fault of man and therefore must now seek a unity of its own. However, because the true unity cannot lie in her but only in God, nature is exposed to a continual struggle precisely on account of this separation from God. Nature seeks unity and yet does not discover it. Should it ever reach the point of its unity and transfiguration, nature would become fully organic and immersed in the spirit that has been awakened in man. Yet as nature proved unable to attain this organic unity, the inorganic raised its head. It too belongs to the species of nonbeing that has been elevated to a form of existence. It is contradictory to speak of the domain of the inorganic, for a domain is a unity whereas the inorganic = nonunity. It is precisely nonbeing, however, that has come to exist and *inevitably* strives to exist.

---

*Translated by Thomas Pfau from F.W.J. Schelling, *Sämmtliche Werke* (Stuttgart and Augsberg: Cotta, 1856–1861), Division One, Volume Seven.

Nature has lost its true point of unity in the same manner in which *mankind* has lost it. For mankind, this [point] consisted of a threshold or point of indifference, a point where *God Himself* would have been this unity [of mankind], for only *God* can be the unity of free beings.

Now we still have free beings, although in separation from God. They, too, must search for their unity and cannot find it. God can no longer be their unity, and hence they must search for a natural unity that, because it cannot be the true unity of free Beings, remains but a temporal and finite bond, analogous to that bond of all entities and that which binds together inorganic nature.

The natural unity, this second nature superimposed on the first, to which man must necessarily take recourse, is the *state*; and, to put it bluntly, the state is thus a consequence of the curse that has been placed on humanity. Because man no longer has God for his unity, he must submit to a material unity.

The idea of the state is marked by an internal contradiction. It is a natural unity, i.e. a unity whose efficacy depends solely on material means. That is, the state, even if it is being governed in a rational manner, knows well that its material power alone cannot effect anything and that it must invoke higher and spiritual motives. These, however, lie beyond its domain and cannot be controlled by the state, even though the latter boasts with being able to create a moral setting, thereby arrogating to itself a *power* equal to nature. A free spirit, however, will never consider [such] a natural unity sufficient, and a higher talisman is required; consequently, any unity that originates in the state remains inevitably precarious and provisional.

We all know of efforts that have been made, especially since the advent of the French Revolution and the Kantian concepts, to demonstrate how unity could possibly be reconciled with the existence of free beings; that is, the possibility of a state that would, properly speaking, be but the condition for the highest possible freedom of the individuals. Quite simply, such a state is an impossibility. Either the state is deprived of the proper force or, where it is granted such [force], we have despotism. (England and Greece, at least in part, are island-states.) Hence it is quite natural that at the end of this period during which people have been talking of nothing but freedom, the most consequent minds, in their pursuit of the idea of a perfect state, would have arrived at the worst kind of despotism (e.g. Fichte's 'closed Trade-System').

It is my opinion that the state as such can never find a true and absolute unity and that all states are merely attempts at finding such a unity; that is, doomed attempts to become a whole and, as such, subject to the fate of all organic life, namely to bloom, to ripen, eventually to age and finally to die. Plato has shown what we are to think of the idea of a rational state, of the ideal state, although he did not pronounce it expressly. The true state presupposes a heaven on earth, and the true *politeia* [political entity] exists only in heaven. Freedom and innocence being the exclusive conditions for the absolute state, Plato's state categorically presupposes these two elements. Yet Plato does not say that you may try to implement such a state as I am describing, but rather, if such an absolutely perfect state were to exist, it would have to be of this kind, i.e. it would presuppose freedom and innocence, and you may decide for yourselves whether such a state is actually possible.

The most convoluted situation arises with the collision among various states, and the most blatant phenomenon of the unattained and unattainable unity is that of *war*, which is as necessary as the struggle among the elements of nature. It is here that human beings enter into a relation strictly as natural beings.

To put the finishing touches on the image of a humanity that has entirely succumbed to a material and, indeed, existential, struggle, we merely need to add all those evils that can only originate in the state, such as poverty or mass hysteria.

Having thus far studied the degradation of man, let us now turn to his *redemption*. His degradation consisted in the fact that the bond between A^2 and $A = B$ had been dissolved, and that man himself had altogether fallen prey to the external world. This gap must not remain, for otherwise it would affect God's very existence. Yet how is this gap to be bridged? Certainly not by man in his present condition. Hence only *God himself* can reestablish the bond between the spiritual and the corporeal world, namely, by means of a second *revelation*, similar to that in the original act of creation. It is here that the concept of a revelation becomes a philosophical necessity. This revelation involves several stages; the highest stage is that where the divine defines itself entirely, in short, where it becomes *man* and thus, as the second and divine man, comes to mediate between God and man in the same manner in which original man was meant to mediate between God and nature. It was not possible to establish an immediate rapport between God and the world of *beings* without destroying the latter as the *proper* world which it now had become. If God had wished for this to happen, no revelation would ever be necessary. Rather, any revelation already presupposes the depraved condition of the world. Notwithstanding his failure, man has been destined as the mediator for nature. Eventually, though, it was man himself who proved to be in need of mediation. Yet precisely by virtue of being restored to spiritual life, man was once again enabled to mediate between God and nature; and specifically in the appearance of Christ, it becomes apparent what man was originally intended to be in relation to nature. Christ was the lord of nature by virtue of His mere will, and He entered into that magic relation with nature that man was originally meant to assume.

The state, when viewed as an attempt to produce the merely external unity, is opposed by another institution, one based on revelation and aimed at producing an inner unity or unity of the mind; namely, the *Church*. The Church is the necessary consequence of revelation or, actually, the strict acknowledgement of a revelation. However, once the division between an internal and an external world has taken hold, the Church can no longer become an *external force*; instead, for as long as that division prevails, the Church will be increasingly restricted by external forces to the realm of inwardness.

The mistake made by the Church during its earlier, hierarchical period was not that it actively interfered with the state but, rather, that it permitted the state to enter the Church by opening up to the state and by assimilating the [institutional] forms of the state, rather than remaining pure. That which is true and divine may not be promoted by an external force, and as soon as the Church began to prosecute the heretics it had already lost sight of its true idea. It should have been magnanimous and sufficiently conscious of its own, divine import so as to permit heresy, rather than putting itself in a position where it had, and accepted, enemies.

In surveying more recent history, which with good reason is said to begin with the arrival of Christianity in Europe, we note that humanity had to pass through two stages in its attempt to discover or produce a unity; first that of producing an internal unity through the Church, which had to fail because the Church simultaneously sought to become the external unity and eventually attempted to produce *external* unity by means of the state. Only with the demise of hierarchical [systems] has the state attained this importance, and it is manifest that the pressure of political tyranny has increased ever since in exact proportion to the belief that an inner unity seemed dispensable; indeed it is bound to increase to a maximum intensity until, perhaps, upon the collapse of these one-dimensional attempts humanity will discover the right way.

Whatever the ultimate goal may turn out to be, this much is certain, namely, that true unity can be attained only *via* the path of religion; only the supreme and most diverse culture of religious knowledge will enable humanity, if not to abolish the state outright, then at least to ensure that the state will progressively divest itself of the blind force that governs it, and to transfigure this force into intelligence. It is not that the Church ought to dominate the state or vice versa, but that the state ought to cultivate the religious principles within itself and that the community of all peoples ought to be founded on religious convictions that, themselves, ought to become universal.

Whatever the fate of the human species on earth may turn out to be, it is possible for the individual to repeat what man originally did with respect to the entire earth, namely, to forge a passage and seize in advance the highest being for himself.

Presentation of the Purely Rational Philosophy (c. 1847)*

One can recognize as a human feeling the wish that all humans would stand at the same rank, but it is a futile effort to set aside differences that, instead of first deriving from the world of freedom, were already designated in the intelligible world and hypothetically predetermined by the Idea. It is futile to try to eradicate an inequality that, instead of being made by humans, comes from an order that reaches beyond this world and is the consequence of that great law of all being [alles Seyenden], according to which not only no state, as Aristotle says,[1] but also no community can consist of only pure equals. Community requires beings that are different from each other according to the Idea, and thus in accord with their inner worth. There can be no type of order of possible or real things, in which one does not stand apart from the other, from birth onwards, by virtue of the fact that the one rules while the other is ruled.[2] This law, that Aristotle declared as a *general*, as a natural law, is the power that each feels and also reveres without even wanting to, the power that allocates to each his own (*suum cuique*), allotting to each the position in the world that is his to fulfil by virtue of an *innate, natural* right. To overstep such a right would have pernicious consequences for him. It is not, moreover, left up to the whim of another to respect or not respect it. It is

*Translated by Kyla Bruff from Lectures 22 and 23 in F.W.J. Schelling, *Sämmtliche Werke* (Stuttgart and Augsberg: Cotta, 1856–1861), Division Two, Volume One. The translator would like to thank first and foremost Joseph Lawrence for his extensive editing and proofing of the final version of this translation; Christian Stadler, Benedikt Rottenecker, Petr Kocourek and Sean J. McGrath for kindly providing their assistance at various points in the translation process; Claire Garland for help with the Ancient Greek; and last but not least, Iain Grant for allowing access to his translations of these lectures.

imperative that one accept that the will by virtue of which one wills oneself be directed to the position for which one is determined. It is for the sake of that position that one can be regarded as an end and thus as carrying one's purpose in oneself. It is an imperative, for this law does not come from man. Nor does he escape the law by making himself independent from God. On the contrary, *it was by stepping to the side of the other* [of that which is] *that he has made himself subject to the law.* The law appears for those who know nothing of God as an independent, self-enthroned power. It is independent of God, elevated to his equal (actually taking his place). It appears as a power that towers above the human, and as the source of natural 'law, common to all', of law that 'precedes the real community and any agreement amongst men'. It was not developed or apprehended through the understanding, but is a system of laws which of itself makes itself felt by all:

> For their life is not of today or yesterday, but for all time, and no man knows when they were first put forth.[3]

These are the familiar words of Sophocles' Antigone, which Aristotle did not fail to mention at that juncture where he speaks of a general premonition of the human race, the premonition of a power which, before and independently of any human contract, determines right and injustice.[4] This same power, in so far as it actually manifests itself, was celebrated in Greek antiquity as *Dike*, which, according to the old saying that Plato always mentioned in the *Laws*, always appears in the entourage of Zeus. As the tragic chorus reminds us, the inviolability of *Dike* had been invoked by Antigone (pure, but now consecrated to death) when she had earlier called upon *eternal* justice. The sudden emergence of *Dike* in unusual human destinies was perceived with terror, also in the general opinion of the people.

It is here where even Kant exceeds the limits imposed to theoretical reason. As a *moral* being, humanity is not released from the intelligible world, and what would be outside of the domain of the former (theoretical reason), is not so for practical reason. This is *reason*; for it too has as its last content the purely intelligible, that which is [*das Seyende*]. It is *practical*, because precisely this intelligible imposes itself as a law to the will that has become self-acting or acting as its own, demanding its submission. In this sense the moral law is therefore also to be named the law of reason, because it is namely the law that originates from the intelligible order and by virtue of which the intelligible is also in the world. At one point in his *Critique of Practical Reason*, Kant states about conscience: 'by means of this we become aware of a nature [*Wesen*] that is distinct from ourselves, yet is most intimately present to us.' After 'nature' he adds the explanation: 'of moral, legislative reason'. Indeed we cannot oppose this addition, if the thought is to be fended off that this nature would be God (for, in Kant's scientific and moral character, the asserted autonomy of reason, i.e. the moral law's independence from God, is one of its deepest – and despite what shallow, superficial people may bring against it – one of its most admirable features).[5] In contrast, we must however protest against thinking that this nature refers to *human* reason, as the unfortunately chosen expression of autonomy seems to say. It is not the latter; *it is reason that lives in being itself* that subjects the will to itself. (This reason is certainly autonomous, i.e. it does not receive its law from God.) That which in theoretical reason is only as latent (as an object of pure contemplation) has become, in relation to the will that is a practical end for itself, active. This intelligible power does not address itself to human reason, but only to the will. The consciousness of this is not called reason, but conscience. It is called conscience to express the constant and ever-recurring nature of this knowledge, the unremitting and untiring power by which it acts.

The end result of our last considerations is that an intelligible order precedes the real or external community between people. The sheer content of this order, however, would lose all meaning in a world of factual Being, if, with that content, the law did not also pass over, i.e. if the latter did not also receive a factual existence, appearing as a power, not merely in a person, i.e. in his conscience, but also *outside* of him – if thus a constitution armed with actual force did not enter into this world, a constitution in which domination and submission occur. This external order of reason equipped with coercive power is the *state*, which, materially considered, is a sheer fact, and has only a factual existence. But it is sanctified by the law that lives in it. It is a law neither of this world nor of human invention. Instead, it directly originates and emerges from the intelligent world.[6] The law become actual power is the answer to that act by which human beings posited themselves outside of reason. This is reason in history.

*

The domain into which we are now entering is that of practical philosophy. This is the part of my presentation that could easily appear as the most questionable, if for no other reason than that it concerns what seems to be, quite apart from science, the closest and most important thing to everyone. As a result, no one hesitates to make their own judgement. Moreover, because it is a topic that so many regard as of such ultimate importance that it alone seems able to fill the whole scope of a human spirit, there are few who will understand why, in the context of the present lectures, it cannot appear for its own sake and be examined accordingly. Instead, it is much rather the case that for it in particular (or at least above all), what we find ourselves emphasizing is not what leads one to cling to it, but what impels one to hurry beyond it.

In fact now, however, we see the I – as previously noted, the only thing that remains to which a further development can attach itself – we see the I in consequence of the law, lost and having completely strayed from all that it wanted, from Being-for-itself, from Being which is only itself, from Being which is the real absolute, i.e. from Being free of everything, where it would have nothing in common with anything else, and would be a law only for itself. In contrast, the I is now restricted by the law, which imposes itself on its will as something unwanted. It is delimited by the universal, and no longer belongs to itself, but to a different and foreign power, whose effect on the I can only be displeasure and rebellion against the law as it strives to free itself and take possession of its own will. One craving against the other. The *archomenos* [ruled] wants to be the *archon* [ruler]. This is the necessary other side of the matter. It should be just as much considered and recognized as is, from the other side, the holiness of the law.

Liberation from the law could at first be purely factual, a simple stepping beyond. Given that according to the law the I remains the unconditioned lord of his own action, nothing could withstand this, if it were not the case that, in reference to this world of purely, factual existence, the law itself had become the factual power that guarantees its fulfilment independently of the will. The obligation that had been imposed from within appears thus as an external, compulsive force. This power of reason emerges from the purely factual rejection of the law (the law does not always inhibit reason, but avenges and thus restricts it). Existing as a factual force, this power of reason is, as we have already seen, the *state*.

I do not doubt at all that such a factual power will bring offence to most, because it oppresses individual freedom before it can express itself. For it is firmly established that for the majority, and this is also an opinion favoured by Kant, the law itself makes human beings free, for it can in fact only be directed at moral beings. But insofar as it renders *each* of them responsible for their part in the real achievement of the community (where *no one* can do anything for this unless they all want it, and specifically, not a single time, but always want it and thus cannot do anything else but want it) – to this extent, the individual has no freedom either to act for or against the law, unless it is made impossible for everyone to act against it. To act for the law would make a person the victim of his legal disposition. To act against it would be to know that all others would later do to him what he did to them, so that his action would be absurd. And just as I am prevented from observing the law if all do not observe it, likewise I also cannot exert what I am entitled to, for example, make myself the lord of something, if all do not recognize it. It is thus evident that by virtue of the law alone people would be much rather unfree than free. The individual is only free at all, when, independent of one's solitary will while yet making it possible, the community already exists. This factual presence of the community – factual, i.e. independent of reason and thus also of the law – is thus a practical postulate of reason itself. It is a presupposition without which the law would not have any relation to the individual as such, and by which a moral disposition is first made possible to the individual. As the saying goes, the state, or as Kant more precisely states, the juridical legislation, is indifferent to the moral disposition. It would be more correct to say that it regards itself as the presupposition, without which the moral disposition would be impossible, and that it *cannot* demand that which only becomes possible first through it. Herein, as well as in the fact that it considers crime a priori as *impossible,* conceding its existence only in accord to the obvious proof that a crime has been committed, the state shows the proper feeling for its meaning. It is the same for the individual, who, from the mere lawfulness of his actions, does not make an immediate conclusion about his moral disposition. Nor does he impute to anyone a particular virtue for not attacking either the person or the property of another. In this way an individual seems to have a good intuition of the proper order of things. It is the most important consequence of a factually existing rational order, and furthermore of the state, that it elevates the individual to personhood. Before and outside this order, there would be individuals, but no persons. The person is the subject to whom actions can be imputed. But outside of the factually-existing legal order, there would be no imputation of guilt and the individual would be responsible for nothing. *The war of all against all* is according to Hobbes the state of nature that preceded the state as such. That it did not precede the state in actuality was clear enough. It should be equally clear that in such a state of nature there can be neither moral freedom, nor blame or responsibility. That the individual is morally free and a person first through the state is also attested to by the fact that whoever goes against its law, and above all whoever revolts against it and so sets himself outside of the state, ceases to be a person for it and can therefore be completely deprived of the exercise of his freedom and the circumstances of his personal existence (for this world).

'The human who enters into the state sacrifices his natural freedom,' so one says; but it seems rather to be the opposite, only in the state does he find and acquire real freedom. At the same time here, another delusion vanishes; for how, without freedom, could individuals discuss together and conclude on a voluntary agreement, a contract, which would lead to the state? Admittedly, this theory of the original contract presents many additional inadequacies (which David Hume, among others, already pointed out) that would keep a reasonably perspicacious observer from trying to build an explanation of the state on such an operation. But one finds it nevertheless useful to consider the state *as if* it originated in this manner, so that, for example, one would not admit any right, unless it could be assumed that everyone would have completely consented to it. Nor could one allow any new law and new institution to arise, for which, as they say, the collectivity – here meaning really each individual – had not given its consent. As the latter is impossible, so this path leads directly to the institution that subjects the individual to the most oppressive tyranny, subordinating him to the will of a contingent majority and thus to a despotism. This is ill-concealed by the fact that the individual is understood not as bound by duties, as formerly, but as having rights. They call such a state a state of reason. They do not mean by reason, however, that objective reason, in which things themselves live. Such reason demands, for example, natural inequality. Instead, they have in mind the reason of the solitary individual, of someone who could accept and agree to such an arrangement. That they deduce the state from this human, subjective reason can be seen from the fact that they believe they are able to *make* states and constitutions, and, to this end, to convene constituent assemblies. The attempts turned out poorly enough, and the total futility of all that was organized in this direction for the last half a century or so had to finally bring the most determined actors to completely cast aside the appearance of universality and of reason, in order to proclaim pure, unconcealed individuality as carrying within itself its own unique and absolute justification. To this end, they had to reach beyond the merely historical even into the supra-historical, seeking to sweep aside all differences, including those that had the sanction of the world of ideas, such as property and ownership, by virtue of which people are able to rise above the merely material to achieve a state of grandeur that, because of the exclusivity that belongs to its nature, introduces inequality. Their goal was to sweep it all aside, especially 'all authority and power', in order to establish as quickly as possible heaven on earth, without awaiting the lord, with whose arrival Christianity consoles poor and clueless humanity.[7]

Reason determines the *content* of the state – but surely not the spurious reason of the individual, rather reason that is nature itself, the abiding totality of what truly is [*das Seyende*] which stands above merely phenomenal being [*Seyn*]. But *the state itself* is even more, it is the *act* of eternal reason that has become active in view of this factual world. It is reason become precisely *practical*, an act that is no doubt recognizable, but cannot be investigated, i.e. that does not allow itself to be drawn into the circle of experience as an object of research. The state itself has, in this sense, a factual existence. But from nothing of this sort is contingency to be excluded. Even in nature, contingency thwarts the eternal order, but is never able to break it. It can cast a seed of grain that requires a strong sun in order to fully develop into a sunless place, or it can expose to the sun that which would thrive better in the shade. Contingency, in a similar way, surely also possesses humans, so that, by overcoming contingency, a real, eternal (not simply imaginary) destiny can be actuated. Thus, as reason that has become factual power, reason cannot expel contingency. This contingency that belongs to it is the price by which the essential, i.e. reason itself, is obtained. In this sense, there seems to be little understanding of the issue in such truisms as that factual right should yield more and more to rational right, continuing as such until a pure realm of reason is established. It is as if the goal were to make all personalities superfluous, removing the thorn from the eye of envy, which, in certain moments, extends all the way to regions, where one should not suspect it. For only in the face of the factual is there space for human ambition. The time that brings it about that the factual could be completely dismissed and discarded might think itself able to do well without its great men. Just this is foretold for our own time by its so-called spokespeople. With the pure realm of reason, the paradise of all mediocrity would be opened. My concern is not to please whatever party of the day. In general, I walk here a lonely path, one that must become more and more lonely, the more it leads to such matters as the state and constitution, matters about which everyone nowadays can judge and about which everyone has an opinion. Only those who have followed this entire development will be able to accept, from the mere necessity of thought (from the trust and belief in thinking) the idea of an act of the intelligible world that anticipated all of human thought.

For the rest, the very factual side of the state raises the expectation that this act has a historical side through which it might become accessible to the less practised. The law of the community, as we have seen, is namely a law for the species. The individual is incapable of serving the community for himself alone. He must thus expect and insist that the law really become a law for the species, that it be a power independent from individuals through which it becomes possible for each individual to fulfil his part. For even the most favoured (someone who belongs to one of the *archousi* [the rulers], of which as Aristotle said[8] there are many types) is not therefore free from the subjugated. They must also be an end for him, and he is responsible for the realization of the community. The question is then how the law can be brought out and away from the individual, how it can be seen as imposed on the species and thus as a power independent of the individual. To this end the means lie precisely in the distinction between rulers and ruled that is already posed separate from the individual and derived from the world of ideas. Amongst these individuals, one will easily be found who is sufficiently equipped with the power to in fact subordinate the others to himself. This will not happen by deliberation or agreement, it will instinctively happen. The ruling of an individual only over the family, then over the whole tribe, then over several tribes, whereby a people is created, is the first and oldest, the natural monarchy. In this way, then, the act by which the order of reason is realized can be historically explained and proven. From this natural (unconscious) monarchy runs the path to self-conscious monarchy, proceeding, as it is the fortune of humanity, through its opposite (through republican ideas). Self-conscious monarchy has compulsion as its basis but freedom as its product, not the reverse, which is why it grows into the most developed society. That initial monarchy cannot be the self-understanding one. Because the state belongs to the things *that are from nature* and arises independently of human intelligence, we must assume that for all that it addresses and concerns (the rulers themselves not exempt) it begins in a blind, non-recognized way, as something purely factual. Understanding first comes afterward. The perfectly constituted and self-constituting state is achieved only in a progressive way, whereby earlier *aspects* of the idea of the state will be there before the state takes on its true meaning. In this succession, however, no contingency is exercised. The state becomes the idea that hovers above the successive forms and which it contains philosophically (a priori). For this reason, the forms of the state do not emerge haphazardly but in a predetermined succession. This can now be recognized philosophically, as the subject of philosophy, and in particular of the philosophy of history.[9]

The state is that which, we say, first makes a moral disposition possible for the individual. But it itself never *demands* it. Precisely because it does not demand it, but only makes it possible, satisfying itself with external justice and caring only for it, the state makes the individual free and leaves him a place for voluntary (and thus also for the first time for personal) virtues, e.g. that one is fair. Instead of asserting his own right to the detriment of others, he prefers to give up something himself, even if the law would be backing him. Or one is brave. (It is true that Aristotle specifically mentions bravery under the virtues demanded by the state, because the law forbids anyone to leave his post in the battle array, to flee and to throw away his weapons.[10] Even so, bravery is not merely a virtue of the battlefield. The bravery that is demanded of us – the one that, as for the ancient Romans, one has no choice but to endure or to be punished to death at home – is not necessarily a personal one.) Or one is truthful, faithful to his promise, even when he cannot be forced to keep it, or communicative, benevolent, caring. These are virtues that reason alone cannot prescribe or realize. They are virtues that are purely personal and can also be called social. With them, there arises above the involuntary community the voluntary and therefore higher community. This is what we will call *society*. In this respect, the state is the *bearer* of society. For regarding what Kant says – freedom must be the principle and condition of all constraint[11] – the opposite is rather true. One would also have to say that *purpose* might also be called the principle, and therefore be the condition under which something that Is not for its own sake nevertheless Is. Kant, however, did not mean this; this is evident from how he applies this principle. The state should be the bearer of society, but it can also hinder or cut off the development of society, just as inversely from society the attempt can arise to weaken or subdue the state. From this the following types ensue.

The ruler is a despot, who does not allow any space to the voluntary virtues or any development to society. To speak in Kant's way such a ruler does not understand that freedom is the purpose of constraint. If the beginning of history and the first great empires were supposed to be in the East, and if furthermore it is true what Aristotle says, that the Asian peoples are by nature more inclined to servitude than the Europeans,[12] then it was no accident that the first empires were monarchies of a despotic kind. It was just as little fortuitous that the most aware and intellectual of the Greeks only came after the first, still paternal reign of hereditary kings had passed through different intermediary stages (including self-declared rulers that governed for a short time) that led to – especially after a glorious end to the Persian wars, by which they defended themselves against the Persian yoke, but also liberated their kinsmen in Asia minor – that definitive form of popular rule or *democracy* in which, as one could say, the state is completely subdued by society and society makes itself the bearer (the fundament) of the state. Such a state has surrendered to the fluctuations of society, and fundamentally and rightly considered, is little more a state than the despotically governed realm can be called a state. This is the case because the state is neither an issue for the despotic ruler, who seeks only himself, nor for democracy, where the state is only the tool of personalities, the fate of all democracies. This is all the more unavoidable, the greater the appeal of a rule so acquired and disputed. If the appeal is minimal in peasant democracies, it increases according to the extent to which the power serves a mighty will and a great talent. In the same relationship as personality, talent also becomes free and, in all directions, a free course and path is opened to it. It asserts itself not only at the head of armies or popular assemblies, but extends also into art and science. For where despotism rules, truth and beauty are also subject to a fixed type. Where society has become free, both strive to find a canon whose law is not determined by command but instead by general and voluntary agreement. If, in Asia, the despotic rule of one and, in Athens, the unlimited rule of the people, did not give rise to the standing of the state, it is an impressive spectacle to see how Rome fulfils its destination by making the whole majesty of the state appear. The state was never wanted for its own sake more than in Rome, where, on the one side, everything was subordinated to it. Even the priesthood was a state title. The augurs and the *pontifex maximus* were magistrates, who, once bestowed these dignities, were members of the senate. Even after the expulsion of kings, a *rex sacrorum* remained in the place of some of these performed, sacred ceremonies. On the other side, the *person* – not the one who goes beyond the state, but who is *in* the state – has become the highest point of attention for a legislation which, from the first beginnings to the most exhaustive achievement, developed with a necessity in a form which remains valid as a model for all times. There is in the Roman essence something which disappears neither with the expulsion of the kings, nor with the later passage to individual rulers of a different kind. Those who call the constitution introduced by that change *republican* are wrong. The form of the state was a republic, but the spirit of the state was monarchic in the highest sense. […]

Let us return now, however, to where we began. It was our task to show that the state (certainly not just any state), instead of suppressing individual freedom, far more makes it first possible. The state is that which raises the individual to a person. From this it does not follow, however, that the state is not nevertheless felt by the I as compulsion. It cannot be otherwise. The striving to escape this compulsion is only natural, and there is nothing to object to this, if it is deployed in the right manner. Even more, among those to whom the topmost direction of the affairs of the state is entrusted, the ones who are always taken to be the wisest are the ones who have made it the law for themselves to leave individuals as free as possible, while retaining for the general population a sharp eye and, where necessary, a sharp sword. The wisdom of our ancestors knew, moreover, the importance of forming certain autonomous circles within the state, inside which the individual knew himself to be free from the state. The honour conferred to each by his social estate (even the peasant and artisan) raised him above the humiliation of complete submission to the state.

It is otherwise, when the striving to make oneself independent from the state becomes the attempt to abolish the state itself, i.e. the state in its basis – *practically*, by a *coup d'état*, which, if it is planned, is a crime equal to no other. Only a parricide (*parricidium*) is similarly regarded. *Theoretically*, this can be found in doctrines that seek to make the state as comparable and suitable to the I as much as possible – completely contrary to the truth. For indeed, the state is not established to cater to or reward the I, but rather for its punishment. What it demands, we owe it, i.e. it is a debt which we must repay or clear. One can say: the intelligible order of things, from which a person has detached himself, is transformed into a debt owed to the state. Even so, these doctrines have met with near universal approval and have spread irresistibly. (No one could have suspected the number of learned men of the state who shared this attitude in the time that has just passed us by.) This general approval compels us to acknowledge that these doctrines emerged from something that speaks for them in every human being. In the final instance, this can only be that principle that, after it has once willed *itself*, now also wants to be complete of its own self. Feeling itself to be more powerful than reason, it creates a reason *for itself*. It is this reason at the service of the I that the edifying orators of the most recent times hold to be *reason itself*. This in turn serves as a pretext to attribute all sorts of calamity, including the political, to reason, and to proclaim that, as a result, it is now all over with reason.

It is this reason, as I have said, that serves the I, and which here – where a *practical* interest, and not a purely theoretical one prevails – can only be sophistic, and can only consistently lead to the total self-aggrandizement of the people, i.e. the undifferentiated masses. As a result, because an appearance of constitutionality is nevertheless not to be avoided, the people must be both sovereign and subject: as Kant explains, the sovereign as the *people united*, the subject as the *scattered crowd*. With *reluctance* (as one clearly sees), but conforming to the once accepted principles, Kant has to recognize the republic as the only rational and even legitimate constitution. Such a republic can accordingly only be the democratic one, which he himself says is the most all-comprising, the most intricate, i.e. to speak without beating around the bush, the most contradictory of all constitutions.[13] In general, with regard to these questions, Kant differs from his descendants, Fichte and others, by his great practical understanding, and by the honesty of his deliberation, qualities of which the contradictions, which his doctrine of right could not always avoid, are only results and witnesses.

We have recognized as justified and necessary a striving of humanity to overcome the burden of the state. But this overcoming must be understood as *internal*. With the application of an old word, we could say: first seek this inner realm, then the inevitable oppressiveness of the lawful external order will no longer be present for you, and you will not be especially bothered by 'the insolence of office' that Hamlet mentions as one of the intolerabilities which could drive us out of this life. To exist beyond the state inwardly – not only may I, but I should. Each should himself be an example of an independent moral disposition, and, if this moral disposition becomes that of an entire people, it is more powerful against oppression than the praised idol of a constitution, which, even in the country of its origin, has in many respects become a *fable convenue* [accepted fiction].[14] Do not envy England a constitution that owes its origin to the addition of non-reason – not through contract, but through force and violence. Indeed, it is unreason (in the liberal sense) that has ensured up to now its continuance and permanence. Be as little envious of England for its constitution as you would be for its large, raw masses, or its insular position that permits many things for their constitution (like that of Crete at one time[15]) that other states are denied by geography. Even worse, it can mislead an unscrupulous government through devious machinations to stir up insurrections in foreign states, even while afterwards easily leaving their implements high and dry. They incite a state of war that cannot be responded to, or, at least cannot be responded to by weak governments.

Let yourselves in contrast be scolded as a non-political people, because most of you crave more *to be governed* (although this is often not granted them and if so, badly enough) than to govern, because you esteem the leisure that leaves the spirit and the mind free for other things, for a greater than an annually recurrent political bickering that leads only to the formation of political factions – factions, whose worst aspect is to permit even the most incapable to gain a name and importance. Let yourselves deny all political spirit, because, like Aristotle, you regard as the first duty of the state is to grant leisure. Neither the rulers nor those who live without participating in the state are in a dishonourable position.[16] Finally, as the teacher of Alexander the Great might tell you, it is possible that even those who do not command land and sea will accomplish beautiful and felicitous things.[17]

The state is the intelligible order itself become factual in the face of the factual world. The state thus has a root in eternity and is the enduring, never-to-be-abolished and no-more-to-be-investigated fundament of all human life and all further development. Because it is the *precondition*, true politics has to be prepared to mobilize all resources for its preservation, just as in war, where the state is the *goal*. Insofar as it is the *fundament* it is not itself the goal, but the eternal (and thus never to be abolished or put into question) starting point for the higher goal of all spiritual life. Because the state is not an object, but only the presupposition of all progress, it is to be treated accordingly. How much better would it be, if this view were universal – not to search for progress in the state.[18] With regard to the ground of the state, we want all the more to let preside the whole seriousness of reason and the necessity of things. It is important not to jeopardize the higher goods for which the state is a prerequisite by false malleability in regard to principles. The progressive development will also benefit it, for it participates in progress without being its principle.[19] The state itself is the stable (the thing of the past). It should rest in silence, allowing only reform (not revolution). Like nature, it can be embellished, but it cannot be made to be otherwise than it is. It must remain as long as this world exists. To make itself insensitive, as nature is insensitive, to grant the individual rest and leisure, to be the means and the impetus to the attainment of the higher goal: that is what the state should do. In this alone lies its perfectibility. The task is therefore: to provide the individual with the greatest possible freedom (autarchy), freedom, namely, that rises above and, as it were, beyond the state. But it should not react back on the state or in the state. For with this the exact opposite occurs from what should happen, as our constitutional arrangements show when they allow the state to absorb all. Instead of granting leisure to the individual, it pulls him rather into everything. It claims everyone for itself, making each bear the burden of the state. True monarchy sees in the active working participants in the state not those who have privileges, but instead those bound by duty. This is what allows others to enjoy the advantages alone.

As a purely external, factual community in the face of the factual world, the state cannot be an end. For precisely this reason therefore, the *most perfect* state is not the goal of history. There is just as little a perfect state as there is (in the same line) a completed human being. The most perfect state certainly has its place in the philosophy of history, but completely on the negative side.[20] There was a time in which it was natural and forgivable to think an ideal as the goal of history and to seek it in the perfect state, in the state of accomplished right. But it is in general a false presupposition that there could be an ideal state of affairs inside this world. If it were ideal, it would also necessarily have to be enduring and eternal. We see that this world, as simply a passing state of affairs, cannot endure. The present order is not an end, it is only to be wiped away. It is thus not this order itself that is the goal, but the goal is the order that is determined to take its place. Even the 'moderate' monarchy, in which the state knows itself only as a fundament, is not the ideal of a (state) constitution that perfectly corresponds to reason – even when it can be found in the best arrangement possible.[21] When one seeks a perfect state in this world, what comes in the end is (apocalyptic) fanaticism.

Notes

1 Aristotle, *Politics* II.2.
2 Aristotle, *Politics* I.5.
3 Sophocles, *Antigone* 456–7.
4 Aristotle, *Rhetoric* I.13.
5 *Translator's Note*. Kant discusses conscience at *Critique of Practical Reason*, *Kants gesammelte Schriften* (Akademieausgabe), ed. the Königlich Preußische Akademie der Wissenschaften (Berlin: De Gruyter, 1900–), V, 98–9.
6 Just as this intelligible order in the world is independent of the individual and without his will, it is also self-initiating from itself, in that its natural existence is given in the family (paternal power).
7 In possession, the human rises above the material, as that which cannot be for itself, and appears to be only in order to be part of another Being [*Seyn*]. [...]
8 Aristotle, *Politics* I.5.
9 The negative side of this is that it is not said or meant by it that the idea of the perfect state ever takes place in reality.
10 Aristotle, *Nicomachean Ethics* V.1.

11 *Translator's Note.* Kant, 'Metaphysical First Principles of the Doctrine of Right', Part 1 of *The Metaphysics of Morals*, Ak. 6, 232–3.

12 Aristotle, *Politics* III.14.

13 *Translator's Note.* Kant, 'Metaphysical First Principles of the Doctrine of Right', § 47.

14 Precisely in England the time is approaching in which public political struggles no longer revolve around rights of closed classes, but around the interests and ambitious plans of individuals.

15 Compare Aristotle, *Politics* II.10.

16 Aristotle, *Politics* II.10.

17 Aristotle, *Nicomachean Ethics* X.8.

18 The presupposition here cannot be once again put into question. It is something factual buried in an abysmal past, and, as Kant himself says (Ak. 6:318–19), is inexplicable in a practical regard. But to bring about ruin, it is not necessary to question this last fact. The intention to combat all that is factual in the state is already pernicious enough, especially when it cannot be foreseen where this aspiration will stop and be restrained; whereas at the moment in which it would have been possible to eliminate all that is empirical and irrational, the state would have to dissolve, because only in precisely this empirical does it have its stability and strength. In fact, all those who get onto this slope cannot stop until even that which is morally commanded – marriage, property, possession – would have been eliminated.

19 One finds oneself in error thus regarding the causes of the revolution when one believes that the state is guilty, whereas that depends in fact on that which is situated beyond it.

20 [...] Here – on the negative side – reason only asks: What does the idea of the state (the community) entail? What possibilities? What goal? The positive side is that which divine providence comprehends as the agent of history.

21 Monarchy is incidentally in any case already moderate in that there are still only partial states.

Further reading

In addition to the above texts, important contributions to Schelling's views on politics – particularly concerning the construction of the state – are to be found in his *System of Transcendental Idealism* and his *Lectures on the Method of Academic Study*. As mentioned in the Introduction to this chapter, this is a relatively under-analysed area of Schelling's philosophy; however, the following important contributions are available:

Saitya Das, *The Political Theology of Schelling* (Edinburgh University Press, 2016).

Saitya Das, 'Schelling and Politics.' In Kyla Bruff and Sean J. McGrath (eds), *The Palgrave Schelling Handbook* (Palgrave, 2021).

Jürgen Habermas, 'Dialectical Idealism in Transition to Materialism: Schelling's Idea of a Contraction of God and Its Consequences for the Philosophy of History.' In Judith Norman and Alistair Welchman (eds), *The New Schelling* (Continuum, 2004), 43–89.

Sean J. McGrath, *The Late Schelling and the End of Christianity* (Edinburgh University Press, 2021).

Sean J. McGrath, 'Populism and the Late Schelling on Mythology, Ideology, and Revelation.' *Analecta Hermeneutica* 9 (2017): 2–20.

Günther Zöller, 'Church and State: Schelling's Political Philosophy of Religion.' In Lara Ostaric (ed.), *Interpreting Schelling: Critical Essays* (Cambridge University Press, 2014), 200–15.

Index